AF478121

THE CITY OF TRANSLATION

The City of Translation

Poetry and Ideology in Nineteenth-Century Colombia

José María Rodríguez García

First published in 2010 by
PALGRAVE MACMILLAN®
in the United States—a division of St. Martin's Press LLC,
175 Fifth Avenue, New York, NY 10010.

Where this book is distributed in the UK, Europe and the rest of the world,
this is by Palgrave Macmillan, a division of Macmillan Publishers Limited,
registered in England, company number 785998, of Houndmills,
Basingstoke, Hampshire RG21 6XS.

Palgrave Macmillan is the global academic imprint of the above companies
and has companies and representatives throughout the world.

Palgrave® and Macmillan® are registered trademarks in the United States,
the United Kingdom, Europe and other countries.

ISBN: 978–0–230–61533–5

Library of Congress Cataloging-in-Publication Data

Rodríguez García, José María.
    The city of translation : poetry and ideology in nineteenth-century
  Colombia / José María Rodríguez García.
       p. cm.
    Includes bibliographical references and index.
    ISBN 978–0–230–61533–5 (alk. paper)
     1. Caro, Miguel Antonio, 1843–1909—Criticism and interpretation.
  2. Translating and interpreting—Columbia—History—19th century.
  3. Politics and literature—Columbia. 4. Colombia—Politics and
  government—1810– I. Title.

PQ8179.C24Z86 2010
868′.509—dc22   2009052408

A catalogue record of the book is available from the British Library.

Design by Newgen Imaging Systems (P) Ltd., Chennai, India.

First edition: August 2010

10 9 8 7 6 5 4 3 2 1

Printed in the United States of America.

The grammarians, who are just as odious as tyrants although more ridiculous, managed to invest their impertinent laws [férula impertinente] with the judicial authority's detestable power, so much so that some innocent books could not be printed because their sentence structure or their language usage did not conform to the narrow limits set by the grammarian's poor decisions.

—Manuel José Quintana, *Semanario Patriótico* [1810]; repr. in Durán López 94

Regime *in grammar and* government *in moral philosophy are at bottom one and the same idea* [Régimen *en gramática y* gobierno *en filosofía moral son en el fondo una misma idea*].

—Miguel Antonio Caro, *El Tradicionista* [1872]; repr. in *Obras, tomo I*: 598

Some may puzzle over our decision to approach this question in its canonical and theological aspects. Every great political question—as Donoso Cortés once said citing Proudhon—involves a theological question [Tal vez algunos extrañen que hayamos empezado por tratar esta cuestión en su aspecto canónico y teológico. Toda gran cuestión política, decía Donoso Cortés citando á Proudón, envuelve una cuestión teológica].

—Miguel Antonio Caro, *La Nación* [1888]; repr. in *Libertad de imprenta* 18–19

CONTENTS

Figures

All the caricatures reproduced from the pages of *El Zancudo: Periódico cándido, antipolítico, de caricaturas, costumbres y avisos* (Bogotá, March 22, 1790–October 11, 1791) are by printer, journalist, and artist Alfredo Greñas. The journal dated each issue one hundred years earlier than its publication date to make the obvious point that by 1890–1891 the Regeneración administrations had all but succeeded in sending Colombia back to the pre-Independence years (see Figure 4). Greñas's caricatures used in this book come from the unnumbered front pages of the issues listed below. I have supplied the missing numbers to facilitate their location by other researchers. From the periodical's first issue to its last, the pages of *El Zancudo* were numbered consecutively as if they composed a single volume.

Acknowledgments

My fellow expatriate Galician José del Valle knows that without the tedious philology classes that we both took at the University of Santiago de Compostela since 1983, neither his work in sociolinguistics nor mine in political-intellectual history would have followed on the paths they took. The formalistic methods then in place at Santiago de Compostela's Facultade de Filoloxía contrasted sharply with the exciting political debates that Spain's Transition to democracy brought into the university at large in the same years. The memory of this *décalage* may well be at the root of my interest in Colombia's reactionary lettered city and José's studies of Rufino José Cuervo's linguistic ideology. Rufino José's paternal great-grandfather's presumed place of birth—the northwestern Spanish seaport of Ferrol, where I too was born—may have also helped realize this trans-Atlantic transference in mysterious or mystical ways. I did not discover this otherwise trivial fact until after *The City of Translation* was completed.

At Cornell University, where this book was written between 2006 and 2009, I was privileged to befriend one of Spain's towering philologists and intellectual historians, Ciriaco Morón Arroyo, whose many-faceted talents and skills have been a source of inspiration as constant as his affection. My generous colleague, María Antonia Garcés, periodically brought me hard-to-find books and newspaper articles from her native Cali, including the complete collection of the lavishly produced *Papel Periódico Ilustrado* (1881–1887), from which I have copiously cited in this book. Although she knew from the start that my project did not look kindly upon the Colombian intelligentsia's reiterated use of high culture as an retrogressive state apparatus, she has remained a loyal friend and a sympathetic interlocutor throughout.

I have incurred other debts of a different kind. Without the fastidious attention to research minutiae shown by right-wing philologists Antonio Gómez Restrepo, Carlos Valderrama Andrade, and José Manuel Rivas Sacconi, I would have been unable to date or contextualize several important texts. At the opposite end of the ideological spectrum, my most enduring intellectual debt is to the sociologist of history and economic historian Marco Palacios. He read and commented upon very early drafts of chapters 1 and 4, providing other valuable advice along the way. Just as important, for more than three decades he has been writing the type of historiography that could best support and enable my interdisciplinary research.

The City of Translation is dedicated to the living memory of my father, Jaime Rodríguez Ardao (1936–2006), who at age fourteen left his village to work as an apprentice in the nearest city's main shipyard. In Ferrol he worked hard and met my mother. Putting always family first, my parents did their best to educate themselves and their four children: two lawyers, one physician, and one philologist. My father would have been happy to discover that this book's underlying thread is the unresolved tension between authoritarian and liberal-democratic politics. For a great many years I was fortunate always to find a caring and reassuring confabulator in him, whose life spanned the entire history of Francoism and the ensuing Transition period. Without his encouragement and support, I would not have pursued a scholar's career.

I have throughout used the name Bogotá instead of Santafé de Bogotá, Cali instead of Santiago de Cali, etc., both in the bibliography and in the main text. I have used "New Granadan" and "Neogranadine" as terms synonymous with Colombian for the sake of stylistic variation. Other onomastic complications of a different nature present themselves when dealing with the name Cundinamarca, which once named a small, short-lived independent state created in 1811 but came to designate the sovereign state of which Bogotá was the capital in the country's federal system amply discussed in this book.

I have favored the terms "Roman Curia" and "Vatican Curia" in naming the papacy's administrative apparatuses in awareness that in the period under study its apostolic mission remained entangled with its political intrusions in world politics. I alternate the two terms although only the first one was an official designation during much of the nineteenth century, when government of the city of Rome belonged to the popes. This alternation has spared me the additional difficulty of having to deal with the complicated issue of how the Holy See (the ecclesiastical community in which the pope serves as bishop) relates to the Vatican City (the sovereign city-state to which the pope is monarch). The popes are *ex officio* heads of state and heads of government of Vatican City. The two offices are attached to the pontiff's appointment as bishop of the diocese of Rome. In the time covered by the present study, Pope Pius IX went from ruling over all of central Italy (until these territories were annexed by the Kingdom of Italy in 1860) to being the monarch only of the city of Rome (until the capital was claimed by the Republic in 1870). The papacy's temporal dominion was confined to the Vatican City in 1870 although this designation did not really come into juridical existence until the State of the Vatican City was formally established in 1929.

Some readers may legitimately ask themselves why Church nomenclature should be central to a book about nineteenth-century Colombia. As both an ecclesiastical and sacerdotal-monarchical city-state, ruled by a particularly confrontational bishop of Rome—Pope Pius IX—the Vatican became a blueprint for the ideal reactionary city of translation envisioned by Miguel Antonio Caro. The Colombian statesman and author deliberately confused (as much as the Roman Curia has done historically) the papacy's claims to influence the temporal affairs of nations that are primarily Catholic with the pontiff's strictly apostolic mission. Caro too believed that he wrote *urbi et orbi*. He wrote from Bogotá's cloistered lettered city to please Rome and a worldwide Catholic audience that remained unknown to him, who never traveled away from the centrally located State (later Department) of Cundinamarca.

As I explain in a footnote in chapter 1, I have capitalized Liberal and Conservative when these epithets designate political parties but not when they designate a position in the spectrum of possible political positions defined in relation to an alternative position either further to the left or to the right. This is what allows me to call Bello strategically a "moderate liberal" by comparison with the conservative governments in which he served. Upper case is also consistently used in writing the word Church when it is short for the Church of Rome. I have only capitalized state—as in State of Bolívar or Bolívar State—when it designates one of the nine "sovereign states" into which the Republic of Colombia was administratively divided under the federal system in place through 1886. For the same reason, Republic is also capitalized when indicating implicitly a specific country whose head of state is chosen at an election despite the fact that "Republic of Colombia" has been Colombia's official appellation only since 1886.

I have capitalized Revolution of Independence because this historical process was seen by its protagonists as a transformative event. This should not take away from the reasonable suspicion that (as discussed in chapter 4) a true revolution may not have taken place and that independence from Spain did not dramatically induce social emancipation across the board. Congress and Constitution are also capitalized whenever they designate—only in the singular form—a specific legislative body and a specific document, respectively. By contrast, the phrase *unwritten constitution* is given in italics; it is employed to suggest Caro's privileging of *ius naturale* and *mos majorum* over positive legislation. For stylistic variation's sake, "constitution" alternates with "charter of rights," "fundamental law," and "*magna carta*" (always in italics rather than upper case) although strictly speaking they do not designate the same type of document. Needless to add, I have maintained the lower case when the above-mentioned terms are used in the plural or when they refer to a type of institution and genre of juristic writing. When the context makes it clear that I am referring to an individual head of state or pontiff who is mentioned by name in the same or an adjacent sentence, the terms President and Pope may also be capitalized. The term creole is favored over *criollo* to designate a descendant of Spaniards raised on American soil in an environment of relative social privilege. The terms *letrado* and *caudillo*, which are indigenous to Hispanic studies, have been left in Spanish and given in italics, but cacique appears throughout in roman type.

The political platform and period (approximately from 1884 to the 1900 Conservative coup) that serve as backdrop to this book's main protagonists are called "(La) Regeneración." I have kept the term in Spanish and roman type, but have used Regenerator (in English and uppercased) to refer to its members and acolytes vis-à-vis other reformers who could also justifiably call themselves regenerators.

The most problematic set of terms used in this book pertains to Colombia's idiosyncratic presidential system. The taxonomy of "presidencies" in use in the later nineteenth century was based on the candidate's way of access to the highest executive office or else the way in which he assumed the full prerogatives attached to a head of state without necessarily being one (or without being always perceived as such). Miguel Antonio Caro is consistently referred to as President of Colombia by most historians although officially—and by his own design—he was a vice president in charge of the executive branch due to the titular president's absentee condition. These various presidential offices will be explained in the footnotes as needed. To keep ambiguities to a minimum, whenever possible I have referred to Caro as "head of state" rather than having to choose between "executive vice president" and "president *ad interim*." I make the exception of alternately calling him a "grammarian-president" because this a social "type" in Colombia's history—the quintessential embodiment of the *letrado* or bureaucrat-literator figure, which has dominated Spanish-Americanist approaches to the nineteenth century in the last twenty-five years. Calling Caro a "grammarian-vice president" would have been rhetorically infelicitous.

Citations of nineteenth-century periodicals are normally given only in parentheses in the main text to avoid extending an already lengthy list of works cited. The vast majority of these items are cited only once.

I have translated all modern foreign-language prose quotations except for just a few two- or three-word phrases that are immediately intelligible in the original and for a longer quotation in chapter 3, in which the Spanish original is meant to show Caro's tendency to doctor ever so slightly his quotations from other authors. There are also many instances in which—in the midst of a prose passage quoted in my English translation—I highlight between brackets a word or short phrase in the source language to satisfy my readers' curiosity about the original phrasing. In a book about translation, this is certainly a reasonable concern. Latin quotations are not always fully translated because they have been kept to a minimum to avoid excessively subjective renderings in English. The Regeneración's strategic use of Latin phraseology (in Congress, at church, and in the periodical press) was designed specifically to separate the less competent reader from the original ancient text and its true contexts of composition and reception. My survey of numerous Latin commonplaces that enjoyed great popularity in Caro's Colombia is meant to show that ancient languages (and foreign languages generally) furnish a transparent case of how ideology works. Latin's conceptual workings are somewhat removed from any speaker's modern linguistic usage in his or her native tongue. Ancient languages in particular could make the meaning of seemingly plain words self-evidently objective or else capriciously subjective, not least because in the nineteenth century such languages were used almost exclusively in settings in which the authority of the speaker (the teacher, the priest, the grammarian-president, etc.) was well established.

All translations from foreign languages are mine unless otherwise indicated, either in the works cited list or between parentheses in the main text. I have often left untranslated the titles of foreign-language works when they are easily understood in the original French or Spanish. This decision eliminates citation conflicts with the bibliographical list, where such works are referenced in the original language of publication.

Since there is not a uniform edition of the collected works by the main author under study, Miguel Antonio Caro, I have cited from several multivolume collections. Many of the later editions feature a critical apparatus, in most cases made possible by Valderrama Andrade's lifelong devotion to preserving the work of Colombia's illustrious grammarian-president. At times I have quoted from popular anthologies of Caro's writings because it was important for my argument to show that Caro wanted for some of writings across different genres to appear together—in a single volume—and at a specific time in his political career. This is certainly the case with *Artículos y discursos* (1888) and with *Libertad de imprenta* (1890).

The modern critical edition of Andrés Bello's *Obras completas* sponsored by Venezuela's Ministry of Education began publication in 1951, but was left unfinished as such. The Fundación La Casa Bello undertook a facsimile second edition in 1981 that renumbered some of the original volumes without altering their contents while also adding the missing volumes in the first edition. The joint publication of both editions was completed in 1986. This publishing overlap has created much confusion among research university bibliographers and librarians.

Unless otherwise indicated, civil constitutions are cited from the authoritative Internet site maintained by the Biblioteca Virtual Miguel de Cervantes, which under the rubrics "Biblioteca Americana" and "Constituciones Hispanoamericanas" also showcases various other constitutional documents cited in this book, from the Acta de la Independencia de Venezuela (1811) to the Decreto Orgánico de la Dictadura de Bolívar (1828). They can all be accessed at: http://www.cervantesvirtual.com/portal/constituciones/.

For my discussion of Bello's *Poema del Cid* in chapter 1, I have consulted the paleographic edition of the *Cantar* available also at the Biblioteca Virtual Miguel de Cervantes: http://www.cervantesvirtual.com/bib_obra/Cid/.

INTRODUCTION

The City of Translation is a threefold study of poetry and literary translation; grammar and philology; and positive jurisprudence and political theologies. Due to space constraints, I had to leave out much material dealing with the political uses of grammar and religious literature in more substantive ways. The main author under study is the president-grammarian-poet Miguel Antonio Caro (1843–1909), a Catholic writer of authoritarian laws and an occasional theorist of dictatorship and states of exception. Widely considered one of the most influential figures in Colombia's history, Caro was quite literally "one of us"—a scholar and a teacher of formidable productivity and synthesizing powers. His vast pedagogical, literary, and legislative output eloquently yet sadly illustrates Walter Benjamin's dictum: "Every document of civilization is also a document of barbarism."

After taking a seat at the extraordinary Consejo Nacional de Delegatarios in 1885, Caro reentered the arena of elected public office in 1892, when he ran as candidate for the vice presidency on Rafael Núñez's ticket. He had by then authored the controversial constitution of 1886 and enjoyed some twenty-five years of success as poet, translator, publisher, college instructor, and fiery combatant against the forces of secularism, positivism, and liberalism. These and other vectors of social progress were conveniently listed and stigmatized in Pius IX's *Syllabus errorum* (1864), one of the most important shorter political documents written in the nineteenth century along with Leo XIII's encyclical letter *Rerum novarum* (1891) and Marx and Engels's *The Communist Manifesto* (1848). Caro began attending congressional debates in 1868 and by 1872 he had established himself as a very influential right-wing journalist who supported the return to the Old Regime's theopolitical order in a state formally established as a parliamentary republic. In a gesture reminiscent of Catholic doctrine, he and the enabler of his career in high office, the former *independent* Liberal Rafael Núñez (1825–1894), called their political platform "(La) Regeneración."

Núñez was a lawyer, former President of the Bolívar State, and translator-poet who used his command of rhetorical and lyric expression to produce highly stylized addresses to the nation in times of crisis. Colombia was a country temperamentally predisposed to distrust positive legislation—this was Caro's original contention—but it cherished poetry as a calling at least as high as the priesthood (if not more so). The literature written by conservative Catholic literati functioned as an allegedly disinterested way to direct public opinion and socialize the undereducated masses into the habits of obedience. Literature thus assumed extraordinary powers. The world of letters became an exception to the rule of positive jurisprudence implemented by the legislative branch in the sixteen years of radical Liberal administrations called Olimpo Radical (1863–1878) and its transition into the Regeneración (1878–1884). While lawyers and journalists often joined the ranks of the Liberal state bureaucracy (with the less frequent recruiting of grammarians and decorated army officers), grammarians, poets, and theologians were more likely to occupy the highest state offices in periods of Conservative hegemony.

In the 1870s Caro forged an implicit alliance with other right-wing literati turned politicians who were disenchanted with the Olimpo's radicalism in order to undertake a systematic assault on the legally established liberal institutions. Since they could not easily overturn the constitutional order in a country that had institutionalized representative government as part of the Revolution of Independence's legacy, their insurrectionist efforts took the form of a vehement right of resistance and often a call to civil war (a more questionable right of rebellion) made from the pulpit or the Catholic press. Along the way, they discovered the kernel of truth in Carl Schmitt's later dictum about failed parliamentary democracies, namely, that properly speaking "sovereign" is only he who decides on the exception to the existing constitutional set of rules, that is, who constitutes himself as a sovereign subject. Since I will elaborate on this decisionist concept of sovereignty later, suffice it to add here that Schmitt also wrote about sovereignty/*imperium* in the more conventional terms of constitutional theory. In a broad sense, also shared by Schmitt, we call a power sovereign when it succeeds in organizing itself—and making itself obeyed—without having to acknowledge the existence of a higher normative order from which it may derive either its legality or its legitimacy, or both (Bidart Campos, *El mito del pueblo* 41–42).

The principal question that I set out to answer about late-nineteenth-century Colombia is this: how did poetry, philology, catechesis, and literary translation legitimate a coterie of reactionary bureaucrat-literati's rise to power, enabling them to dismantle Colombia's liberal-democratic state in 1885–1888 without explicitly derogating some of its constitutional freedoms? Literature, Catholic doctrine, and Spain's chaotic legal tradition (the former Viceroyalty of New Granada did not have a civil code until 1886) provided some continuity between a colonial past that was socially and juridically outdated and a republican present which had not delivered on its promise of order, freedom, and justice to the satisfaction of all New Granadans. During the Regeneración years, political cartoonist Alfredo Greñas cast Caro in the figure of a crab: both the *letrado* and the crustacean creature used a series of lenses or vision devices (Caro's spectacles; the crab's compound eyes) that paradoxically made them almost blind to their immediate surroundings; both had a thick skin (Caro's exuberant bigotry; the crab's hard exoskeleton) that also made them immune to criticism or attacks by others; and both had their feet or legs either literally or figuratively bent backwards. Caro walked backwards on the path of history since the political goal he pursued—reinstating the Old Regime's theocratic and absolutist philosophy of government—had been left behind long ago.

Caro was a fourth-generation *letrado*—a man of letters who doubled as bureaucrat and legist. His ancestors, in-laws, and immediate circle of friends and collaborators provided him with the cultural capital and network of influences required to challenge every text and every bill that the Liberal Party enacted into law. One of my fundamental hypotheses is that without accounting first for the slow but steady shift of literary-legislative institutions from the fringes of public life to its center, it is difficult to understand the literati's quick transition into an ideological advance guard. The reactionary coterie's powers of interpretation were at their most effective when they were used to undermine the legal order's legitimacy. This was done by paradoxically invoking the priority of long-standing *unwritten constitutions* and the discourse on natural rights over positive legislation, as if *ius naturale* (a convenient code name for Caro's defense of religious doctrine) could preexist and make unnecessary the practice of politics and any other form of feuding.

The City of Translation is a book about the influence of literature on political life and vice versa. Specifically, it is the first comprehensive study

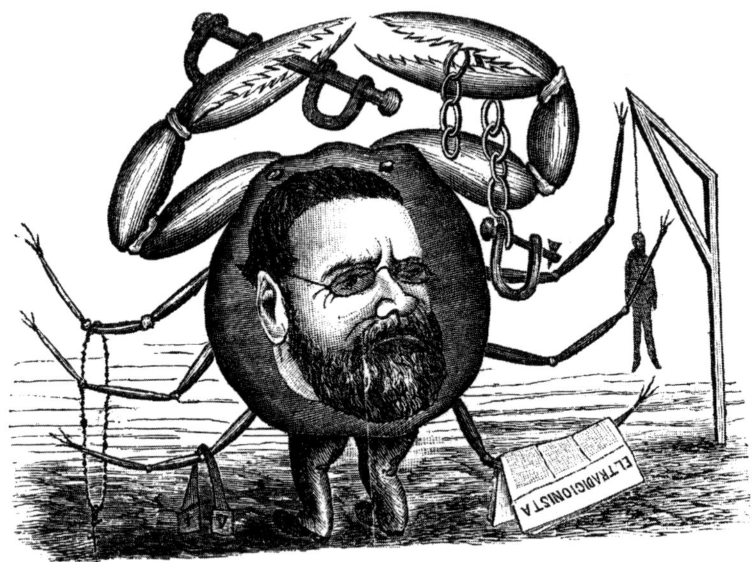

Figure 1 "Otro conspicuo cuasi-excelencia o la Regeneración-cangrejo," *El Zancudo*, vol. 2, no. 17 (April 1, 1791): p. 65.

of what I call "the reactionary city of translation" by analogy with an entire genre of literary-critical writing focused on Spanish America primarily in the nineteenth century. Since Ángel Rama devoted a book to this topic in 1984, the phrase "lettered city" has designated the textual creation, by organized circles of *letrados* variously connected to the apparatuses of the state, of a strongly hierarchized imaginary polity whose literary and juridical representations—the *legal city*—often conflicted with everyday reality's polymorphism—the *real city*.[1]

To my knowledge, the first mainstream work of nineteenth-century political sociology to posit the emergence of one such imaginary polity was Alexis de Tocqueville's *The Old Regime and the Revolution* [L'Ancien Régime et la Révolution] (1856), an interpretation of the French revolutionary process that lays great emphasis on the attendant linguistic revolution stretching from the middle of the eighteenth century through the time of the book's publication. Although Rama does not acknowledge Tocqueville's text, it seems obvious that this is where he found confirmation for a hypothesized lettered city which perhaps described Chile and Colombia more accurately than it did France:

> Above the real society [société réelle], whose constitution was still traditional, confused, and irregular, where laws remained varied and contradictory, ranks were separated, status was fixed, and burdens were unequal, there was slowly built an imaginary society [société imaginaire] in which everything seemed simple and coordinated, uniform, equitable, and in accord with reason. Gradually the imagination of the crowd deserted the former to concentrate on the latter. One lost interest in what was, in order to think about what could be, and finally one lived mentally in that ideal city the writers had built [cette cité idéale qu'avaient construite les écrivains]. (*The Old Regime* 1: 200–201)

The lettered city is eminently a city of the mind whose planning is always in the pipeline but whose realization as a beacon of progress—whether this be conceived in material or spiritual terms—is postponed just as frequently because the labor of writing never ends. As Tocqueville points out, in building the ideal polity in an ever expanding series of geographical, educational, juridical, and literary works, one runs the risk of not addressing the complications found in the empirical world, which may even disappear from one's horizon. This is what happened in Colombia, where the regime of grammarians implemented by insular Bogotá *letrados* was handicapped by a crucial *oversight*: two heads of state—Caro and José Manuel Marroquín—literally refused to see their *real* country. Not once in their lives did they leave behind the Andean plateaus of Cundinamarca and Boyacá on which the nation's capital lay isolated from most of the territory.

In the passage immediately preceding the quotation just given, Tocqueville praised the English commonsense approach to politics, in which "those who wrote about government" worked in constant contact with "those who governed." In contrast with the United Kingdom, in France sweeping "theories" of social progress were not balanced "with the help of facts." Rather, while the practical class "governed," the literati/*écrivains* "established the abstract principles on which all government ought to be founded" (*The Old Regime* 1: 200). Note also that one of Tocqueville's main insights is that the French Revolution was not a domino effect of the American Revolution's reception through the filter and the ferment of the same French rationalism that traveled to the American colonies in the first place. For Tocqueville, French institutions had undergone a slow yet steady process of symbolic relaxation. They paradoxically allowed the verbal expression of dissent from the absolute monarchy because the absoluteness of the king's prerogative made arbitrary repression legal through and through. The most influential early *American* revolutionary *letrado*, the Spaniard Manuel José Quintana, stated almost the same during the Cortes de Cádiz: under Carlos IV's absolutist rule, politically innocent acts were often punished and innocuous writings banned from publication while subversive ones might go unremarked as such. The situation that scandalized Juan Donoso Cortés in the mid-nineteenth century and Carl Schmitt in the years of the Weimar Republic, namely, the appearance of a feuding and restless class (the more radical ranks of the liberal bourgeoisie) capable of challenging what for these authors should be the undivided *potestas soluta* or sovereign executive power, already existed in Tocqueville's version of the Old Regime.

Because of its bookish and playfully abstract ideas (*l'esprit français*, in Tocqueville's formulation), French court society had long seemed ready to embrace men and women of letters who advocated heterodox ideas rather than settling for boring theologians. Despite the beauty of his prose, Bossuet could not really compete with Fénelon or Condillac. The disparity found between traditional justifications of the aristocracy's moral exemplarity and their actual behavior, which in Spain were also the subject of grave censorship (in the works of Goya, Jovellanos, and Cabarrús, among others), had prepared the way for the rise of the enlightened bourgeoisie as the principal maker of public opinion through the concomitant rise of the political press. From here to the bourgeoisie's consecration as the class of lawmakers par excellence there was a very short distance. This is Tocqueville again:

> An aristocracy in its vigor not only runs affairs, it still directs opinion, sets the tone for writers, and lends authority to ideas. In the eighteenth century, the French nobility had entirely lost this part of its empire; its moral authority followed the fortunes of its power: the place that it had occupied in the government of minds was empty [la place qu'elle avait occupée dans le

> gouvernement des esprits était vide], and writers [les écrivains] could occupy
> it at their leisure and fill it completely. (*The Old Regime* 1: 198)

With an admittedly differing emphasis and purpose, Tocqueville uses the concept of *place vide* in a manner vaguely reminiscent of Sieyès's *vuide de la chose* and Lefort's *lieu vide* (as I will explain in greater detail in chapter 1) to signify the deconsecration or *demiraculizing* of theo-political sovereignties that commanded assent among the ranks of Third Estate prior to the Revolution's outbreak. Tocqueville does not spare the monarchy and his own class any criticisms. First, it had proved very dangerous to allow antiaristocratic attitudes to flourish at courtly games, since what has validity in a courtly play situation may be extrapolated to real-world situations. And second, absolutist regimes were based on a vertical, one-directional chain of command, which was necessarily incompatible with the modern style of government administration in which accountability through polls and surveys of opinion undermined the absoluteness of royal and aristocratic authority.

The Old Regime and the Revolution devotes much attention to the work of *écrivains*—as Tocqueville calls publicists—who occupied the place left vacant by the collapse of the *habitus* and doctrines allegedly inculcated in the Third Estate through the aristocracy's exemplary moral conduct and use of theo-political symbols. This usurpation took place *before* the advent of the Revolution. In like manner, this book subscribes to the postulate that changes in economic and social relations often predate the circulation of ideas about those practices. I therefore also take the view that changes in political language do not necessarily coincide with changes in the conceptualization of existing fields of power, and, conversely, that the replacement of long-standing concepts or constructs may occur without significant changes in linguistic usage.[2] To put it differently, some practices and mental habits must have changed *first* for the appearance of new words or semantic acceptations to occur *next*, while some concepts in turn become more unstable and fluid to allow for the accommodation of those shifting discursive practices. Reinhart Koselleck has pointed out that the respective histories undergone by words and concepts commonly used in the political field are asymmetrical and asynchronous. Any given pair of antithetical concepts that we attempt to study reveals the traces of an anti-etymology, so to speak, in which concepts shift into counterconcepts independently of the words that convey them by convention: "The structure of the counterconcepts does not depend solely on the words from which the conceptual words are composed. The words are replaceable, whereas the asymmetric structure of the argument survives" (Koselleck, *Futures Past* 163). A good example of this conundrum is the generally derogatory connotation that "democracy" still had for the deputies gathered at the Cortes de Cádiz in 1812, even for those who were proto-liberals.

The City of Translation challenges extant presentations of the lettered city as an eminently liberal-democratic construct, arguing instead that one of its best examples—Colombia's extensive network of cultural and religious apparatuses that were implemented in the period of so-called "conservative hegemony" (1884–1930)—was also the most retrogressive.[3] My book also highlights the role of translational practices in the lettered city, which I understand in three interrelated ways. First, translation names etymologically the two possible juridical rationales for how a nation's sovereignty originates and circulates. I accordingly discuss the contractual *pactum translationis*, which was more amenable to liberal-leaning platforms, vis-à-vis the reactionary, providential *translatio imperii* that nineteenth-century counterrevolutionaries inherited from the Old Regime.[4] Second, *translatio* may also signify a conversion from a fallen or false subject position to a redeemed one. In yet another etymological extension, such a conversion became in Colombia's reactionary lettered city a form of political "translation." It enabled the systematic presentation of three republican luminaries of proto-liberal leanings (Bolívar, Bello, and Hugo) as *converts* to a Catholic conservative ideology.

And third, translation will also be discussed as a genre of writing across languages, which in nineteenth-century Colombia involved on a large scale the Christianizing of foreign texts in what is called—in patristic and exegetical writing—the practice of *translatio secundum* or rephrasing "in conformity with"—*secundum*—some preexisting orthodoxy.[5] It is a practice that I advisedly conflate with *translatio secunda* or rephrasing/recoding at a second remove, by which translators endow their renditions in the target language with certain metaphorical meanings normally—but not exclusively—found in Scripture. The purpose of the metaphorical elaboration is to override an uncomfortable or uninspiring literal meaning found in the pagan original being translated.[6] This network of semantic complexities is captured in the adage I would have used for an additional chapter of this book had I been able to pursue fully the theological sources that inspired nineteenth-century Catholic translators: "The translation of Scripture is twofold; the second translation—or translation on the second degree—is always more truthful" [Scripturae translatio duplex, veracior est secunda].[7] In other words, as one translates from one language into another—from Greek into Latin, for instance—not only does the denotative meaning need to be conveyed in the form of an equivalent word in the target language, but its connotative resonances—its metaphorical meaning—need to be accounted for too.

My reader will find numerous references to theological questions, doctrinal controversies, and ecclesiastical institutions whose influence on the minds of nineteenth-century *letrados* cannot be overemphasized. One of this book's secondary aims is to make the texts of religion and theology, as well as the jurisprudence that supported their production, more readily available to scholars of Spanish American lettered cities. José María Vergara y

Vergara (1831–1872), Colombia's first literary historian of note and a founding member of the Colombian Academy, took very seriously the existence of heavenly polities, of theological utopias that were best pursued in the career of letters. Although he served as Conservative congressman and undertook publishing ventures with opportunistic politicians, Vergara y Vergara was candid enough to go against party orthodoxies, as shown when he opposed capital punishment, criticized the Spanish Empire (in his view, it had been an abusive temporal power), and lamented the government's half-hearted efforts at schooling the poor. In his influential *Historia de la literatura en Nueva Granada desde la Conquista hasta la Independencia (1538–1820)*, first published in 1867, he declared at the outset his allegiance to Augustine's *civitas terrenal civitas Dei* binomial by which the faithful could live side by side with the pagans in the earthly city while they strove to be transported to heaven, if not specifically to the hypostatic *civitas Dei*, by means of a providential *translatio fidei*. Although it is a mirror image of the state, the *civitas terrena* does not correspond unilaterally to the state, nor does the *civitas Dei* correspond unilaterally to the Church. However, the elect are more likely to emerge from the Church than from pagan institutions.

The primary distinction for Augustine is between the body of the reprobate and the *communitas sanctorum*. These are mystical forms of society that coexist in a *corpus admixtum*—the *civitas permixta*—often working within the same state institutions although to differing ends. In early Christian theology, providential transportations to heaven were justified by the fact that the Church was not yet a large and complex community, and by the awareness that neither the *civitas Dei* nor the *civitas diaboli* could exist as such in this world. The prolonged limbo in which time and historicity manifest themselves corresponds to a fourth term—the *corpus admixtum* or *civitas permixta*, where Christians are forced to work side by side with non-Christians. Similarly, in the nineteenth-century real city, theocrats and radical liberals shared a common social space as they fantasized about the coming of their respective lettered cities, which ideally would be either monolithically ultramontane or monolithically ultraliberal. According to Augustine, the *corpora admixta* of civil polities may extend through an indefinitely long period, signified as "universum tempus sive saeculum," that witnesses the passing of endless generations (*The City of God* 4: 412–13). Aware that he was preparing himself for a celestial domain while still inhabiting its *permixta* incarnation on earth, Vergara y Vergara wrote: "I would want for my works to be at the service of the Catholic cause, and I would judge ill-spent the time that I do not devote to that enterprise…I do not wish to forget that I am also a citizen of eternity [ciudadano de la eternidad]" (1: 48).

This is a striking statement to make in the later nineteenth century, as the liberal Diógenes Arrieta pointed out in 1884 (21–23). An aggressive realpolitik variation on Vergara's profession of faith was Caro's defense of his newly created "Partido Católico," which did not exist as a registered organization, but was a designation used by Caro to drive the point that the only legitimate party possible was one which would partake in the universality of the eternal Church first established in the *urbs aeterna*. The difference with Vergara is that Caro used his partiality to the Church to spread winds of intolerance and fanaticism in an already agitated political field. He wanted to build not so much a theological city of the mind as an ecclesiastical one armed with repressive state apparatuses as powerful as those of the Weberian nation-state. In 1873, writing in his ultramontane periodical *El Tradicionista*, he stated that in the wake of Pope Pius IX's loss of the Papal States in 1861, he could not espouse the Count di Cavour's idea of "a free Church in the free State" [Libera Chiesa in libero Stato]: "For us the Church is greater than the motherland; we do not want to have *the Church within the State*, which would mean to enslave the Church although it may still be called free. We want the State within the Church, the only formula that respects freedom [única fórmula que consulta la libertad]" (*Obras, tomo I* 878; emphasis in the original).

To summarize: Vergara y Vergara's lettered city was completely removed from the world of *negotium*, that is, its vocation was to exist outside the realms of history and earthly concerns. By contrast, in Tocqueville's ideal polity able bureaucrats could pursue their statist designs with the fewest intrusions possible from ideologists although the Frenchman knew that this separation was impossible, and perhaps not even a desirable scenario after all. But his concern was with endowing secular civil governments with a much needed stability after the collapse of political theologies. Finally, Caro was committed to undermining Colombia's radical-Liberal Constitution of 1863, which (like its 1853 predecessor) barely acknowledged the rights of the Church within the free state. His heart was with the revival of Old Regime theo-political institutions.

The majority of Colombian bureaucrats who wrote literature turned their backs most of the time on the painful ethnic, social, and economic realities of their young country. Although they insisted on drawing analogies between New Granada and ancient Greece and Rome, the truth is that in 1884 Bogotá was, according to long-time resident Federico C. Aguilar and later commentators, a backward, isolated, and run-down provincial town (a "large village" [grande aldea] of 95,000 people, as Aguilar calls it), inconveniently located in the foothills of the Andes. Unlike Mexico City, Puebla, Buenos Aires, Lima, or Santiago, it had neither a sewer system nor gas lights or any kind of public transportation. Its unpaved streets, covered with "dirt" (*mugre* is the Spanish word Aguilar most often uses to describe the city), swarmed with uncouth Indians, barefoot beggars, starved children, derelicts, lepers, and self-serving politicians (Aguilar 70–74; Cané 156–57; Rivas 1: 92–99, 110–12). The Liberal *letrado* Medardo Rivas also pointed out the following contradiction: while many of his compatriots thought they were living heroically in one of Chateaubriand's or Lamartine's monumental epics, any foreigner who passed through Bogotá was more likely to think that the capital's streets had been taken out of a "socialist novel" à la Eugène Sue (1: 175). Colombia could boast in 1884, the year of Núñez's return to power, a virtual *ciudad letrada*, but the nation's capital had not yet become a *ciudad aseada*—a clean and comely city—to echo Francisco de Paula González Vigil's humane call in 1858 to transform Lima into a beacon of physical, moral, and patriotic hygiene (*Importancia* 119). This would require making practical education, steady employment, and full membership in the *res publica* accessible to the improvident masses.

Chapter 1 of *The City of Translation* surveys the triumph and protracted crisis of Colombia's federal model of the state. Federalism had been a contentious body of doctrines since the times of Antonio Nariño, Francisco de Paula Santander, and Simón Bolívar. On the one hand, the federal system became a perennial source of instability by allowing individual states within the federation to assert their self-differentiated identities and seek remedy for their individual grievances by violent means (whether these be symbolic or of a military nature). On the other hand, the system prevented the central state apparatuses from monopolizing the means of legitimate corrective violence, which in reality would have been impossible anyway given the inaccessibility and chronic underdevelopment of most of the territory. A threefold crisis in sovereignty emerged from the combined effect of multiple yet partial jurisdictions, the enforcement of *laïcité*, and the survival of local *caudillista* habits from colonial times through the Revolution and all the way to the present time. Liberalism and Conservatism vied to occupy sovereignty's empty space once the Old Regime's political theologies vacated the horizon of political self-legitimation. The fiction of a unified yet heterogeneous participatory nation thus became increasingly untenable in a country that was itself the fragment of the Greater Colombia ruled by the Libertador Simón Bolívar through the year 1830.

Chapter 2 is this book's cornerstone insofar as I do in it much of the groundwork in political-intellectual history on which my close readings are based. I discuss at some length the thinking of the counterrevolutionary ideologists who immediately preceded and succeeded Caro (Juan Donoso Cortés and Carl Schmitt, respectively) to convey to my reader the notion that the counterrevolution's discourse commanded in Spanish America important and significant support, and was brilliantly realized in Caro's antidemocratic interventions in legislation and executive decisions. In *The City of Translation* I have adopted a comparativist perspective: Spanish traditions of government receive as much attention as foreign doctrines. The subchapter titled "*Translatio imperii* and the *pactum translationis*: A

Short History of Sovereignty" illustrates the project's conceptual and historical ambitiousness. The chapter ends with a discussion of how Caro, as Colombia's quintessential textual editor and grammarian, arrogated to himself the task of interpreting the nation's past. He drafted in 1886 a Proyecto de Constitución full of sophistic traps that only he could elucidate due to the correctness of his writing and his existential proximity to the philological intentions encoded in the source text. These rhetorical ruses may not have furnished an instance of juristic philology or legal hermeneutics proper. Nevertheless, they were instrumental in allowing Caro to interpret, suspend, or otherwise supplement the 1886 Constitution with a wide array of literary propaganda, verbal orders, and emergency measures, which together amounted to declaring a literary-legislative state of exception. In terms of its argumentation, chapter 2 features the first historical approach to originally Hispanic theories of political sovereignty vis-à-vis their European counterparts from the late sixteenth to the late nineteenth centuries, taking the metaphor of *translatio* as the central trope in the debates around political legitimation.

Chapter 3 focuses on Spanish America's most versatile and able *letrado*, the Caracas-born Andrés Bello. I particularly look at the liberal Bello produced in Chile by Miguel Luis Amunátegui and the Catholic Conservative Bello produced in Colombia by Caro. Along the way, I also examine the Venezuelan *letrado*'s compromising of the moderate-liberal tenets that he generally upheld. I highlight his struggles with religious propriety and his determination not to alienate himself from the centers of power. The chapter also analyzes the reasons why (and the manner in which) Colombians by and large focused obsessively on Bello as an ultra-Catholic and philo-Spanish creole. His opinions on the unity of the Castilian language as well as the continuity of American and Spanish institutions were repeatedly decontextualized to make him look closer to the religious right than he actually was. In both chapter 1 and chapter 3 I show that Bello was considerably more progressive (as literary critic, policy maker, and juristic philologist) than he has been credited by those who tend to assume that he had the power to bring about a civil society by himself, but refused to do so. Caro successfully *translated* or *converted* Bello (I am once again echoing the common semantic matrix shared by *conversio* and *translatio*) to the terms of Colombian Hispano-Catholicism. Space constraints have not allowed me to offer a detailed assessment of Bello's and the Argentine Domingo Faustino Sarmiento's respective views on language, history, and representative government, a project started by Julio Ramos in *Divergent Modernities*, but which still calls for additional work in the context of the reactionary lettered city. Although Caro wrote at length about Bello, and frequently engaged Sarmiento as an antagonist, I leave the analysis of these polemics for a future occasion.

Chapter 4 subjects Bolívar's image and writings to a similar treatment, showing that the debates conducted in Colombia about the Libertador between the 1870s and the 1930s—when the translator-poet and presidential runner-up Guillermo Valencia wrote his much-cited speeches—were immediately perceived as attempts to either modernize or antiquate Colombia's political life. Bolivarian symbols and doctored texts were most often used to defer indefinitely the realization of republicanism's notion that direct representation and decision making legitimated themselves by fostering the expansion of society's enfranchised base. The incremental growth of both literacy rates and the franchise (which at the time were inextricably connected) had to be postponed for reasons of state if not for convenience's sake. This chapter makes a strong case for treating Bolívar as the epitome of a *possibilist* republicanism, which deviated strategically from the Enlightenment's ideal of adherence to the letter of positive legislation without hiding its discontent at having to postpone the gradual inclusion of the masses in the political process. In explaining the centrality of Bolívar to Núñez and Caro's Regeneración, I offer a close reading of one of Colombia's national poems: Caro's "To the Statue of the Libertador" [A la estatua del Libertador] (1883), which was written to commemorate Bolívar's centennial. I treat this ode as a literary-legislative speech act in which the author ventriloquizes his right-wing ideas through the character of the sculptor Pietro Tenerani, who was an eyewitness to Bolívar's career in addition to immortalizing the General in his moving bronze and marble representations. In analyzing Caro's Bolívar I naturally need to deal with the Venezuelan founding father's doctrines and policies on their own terms. Since chapter 2 and especially chapter 4 are more theoretically inflected than the rest of the book, I also resort in them to what Reinhart Koselleck calls exercises in the history of concepts or in conceptual history.

In the conclusion I succinctly take up again the many strands of argument first introduced in chapter 1, perform a final close reading of an important exchange of poems in a political context, and offer my final thoughts on nineteenth-century Colombia's *longues durées* in their relationship to the rise and decline of the reactionary lettered city. As I bring my narrative of Colombia's history up to the present time, I try to anticipate some of my readers' questions concerning the roads not taken by both literature and politics in the period under study. A sequel to this book is already in the works. While *The City of Translation* treats Caro as the centripetal force around which numerous right-wing bureaucrat-literati gravitated in the years 1864–1900, in the projected sequel Guillermo Valencia (1873–1943)—the Conservative bureaucrat-poet who was twice defeated at a presidential election—becomes the focus of attention. Valencia's emergence as Colombia's future national poet was visible enough in the year 1900, which is the chronological limit set for the present book.

At the turn of the nineteenth century into the twentieth Caro's neoclassical poetics and theocratic doctrines slowly gave way to Valencia's *modernista* generation, a process that correlates with the *historic* faction of Conservatism's claiming back of political hegemony from the party's so-called nationalist wing (the reactionary side influenced by Caro).[8] In Bogotá's *modernista* circles, Conservatives still outnumbered Liberals, but the poets' use of Catholic iconography and Spain's ultramontane traditions were now mixed with their orientalist fondness for exotic motifs and decadent subject-positions. The Parnassian faction of *modernismo*, to which Valencia belonged, searched for an *art pour l'art* aesthetic that nevertheless remained a powerful instrument to dominate and exclude the uneducated masses. An increasingly autonomous literary field first emerged in France—and later in Spain and the Southern Cone—but could not develop as quickly or easily in Colombia's confessional state due to the inexistence of a large-enough urban bourgeoisie (or a large metropolis for that matter) as well as the low literacy rates and the chronic social and economic underdevelopment that afflicted the country.

In what I think is a fitting afterthought to Caro's career and the recapitulation of Colombia's history presented in the conclusion, I reflect upon the centennial commemorations held on the occasion of Caro's passing in 1909. As I write these lines, Colombians who were born in the late twentieth century have had the chance to behold various displays of the Regeneración's iconography and copious literary output at the philological institute named in part after this book's main author—Bogotá's Instituto Caro y Cuervo— and elsewhere. It is my contention that the Regeneración movement can shed light on Álvaro Uribe Vélez's two-term presidency, which comes to an end in 2010. Núñez's last three administrations (those which commenced in 1884, 1885–1886, and 1892), like Uribe's two-term presidency (2002–2006 and 2006–2010), were made possible by their leaders' respective desertions from liberalism (their deconversions), by multiple acts of political *betrayal* (both tradition and traitor derive from the Latin verb *tradere*), and by the combined effect of several constitutionally incorrect interpretations of legality put forth and enforced in the wake of a massive fragmentation of sovereignty. But just as few would say that Colombia's public life unfolds today in a climate of undisturbed "libertad y orden"—the motto written into the Republic's coat of arms since 1834—this book casts into doubt that Caro and Núñez's Regeneración succeeded in restoring either liberty or order in New Granada after nearly one century of inner divisions and strife.

CHAPTER ONE

THE COLOMBIAN LETTERED CITY— PHILOLOGY, IDEOLOGY, TRANSLATION

The Historical Significance of the Regeneración: War without End

This book foregrounds the role of cultural translation in the formation of Colombia's literary and political field. By translation, I mean primarily the semantic transfers that take place between the source and target languages involved in the related processes of semiotic decoding and recoding. Translated texts can be antiquated or modernized versions of the original, and they can also be *foreignized* or naturalized as they become part of the translator's national repertoire. The main author under study, Miguel Antonio Caro (1843–1909), admitted to preferring the production of *archaicizing/ antiquating* texts in the target language because they were etymologically more trustworthy and they revealed the unity of the Spanish language. In addition, they had a kinship with Latin and they illustrated Church doctrine. Andrés Bello and the Spaniard José Gómez Hermosilla, by contrast, favored (so they claimed) a more contemporary register, thereby encouraging more meaningful cultural transfers with their immediate surroundings.

Acts of translation in other forms could align themselves with either conservative or progressive cultural enterprises. Translation has historically been envisioned as a discursive panacea by those wishing to endow an epistemologically weak or as-yet unconsecrated discourse with the authority of a consecrated one. The very words that designate the act of interlinguistic translation attest to this. From antiquity to the Middle Ages, the terms *translatio* and *transferre* coexisted in close contact, in a veritable *contaminatio*, as they also overlapped with related concepts imported from other disciplines. Interlinguistic translation was less frequently designated as *metafora/metaphorein*, whose primary meaning is a figure of speech consisting in the substitution of one term or concept for another related to it only by a shared accident or a connotation. Undoubtedly, *translatio* was the term that spanned the most disciplines, if we take into consideration the term's two opposing meanings in political theory, namely, *translatio imperii* or providential transfer of sovereignty from a declining to a rising empire, and the *pactum translationis* or renunciation of individual freedom to a representative body. In addition, *translatio* could be synonymous with *metaphora* (in rhetoric) and *conversio* (in theology) besides naming a movement of troops (in warfare) or populations (such as religious communities going into exile), a transmission of property (in contract law), and an interlinguistic transfer proper.

Understood in the manner that I have just outlined, the translational potential of a discourse depends on its convertibility into the terms of another.[1] In the 1960s, the limits of discursive translatability were seriously tested (notably in Michel Foucault's influential presentation of analogical discourse in *Les mots et les choses* [1966]) while simultaneously analogy and metaphor were held as the conceptual matrix of both surrealist and mystical poetics (notably in Octavio Paz's poetical and political essays written around 1970).[2] While several of the main acceptations found in the matrix *translatio*-translation are given their due in this study, I privilege the term *translatio* above all others because it embodies the ongoing, unresolved tension between the divine right of rulers (*translatio imperii*) and the immanent social contract (an inspiration of the *pactum translationis*). The allegiance that nineteenth-century publicists showed to either doctrine influenced their literary tastes as well as their translational practices, as this book shows. The authors I discuss in this chapter were all active in politics, literature, and (in many cases) religious proselytizing. The more reactionary ones in particular aimed at catechizing and re-Christianizing society in the wake of secular liberalism's series of triumphs and defeats. They aimed to convert and translate an incrementally secular nation by means of the word, producing the literary-legislative discourse continuum that would deliver them from sin and metaphorically effect the transportation or translation into heaven (*translatio fidei*) that was promised to them.

The City of Translation accordingly takes as its historical point of departure the failed experience of establishing a durable liberal republic in mid-nineteenth-century Colombia and the related resurgence of such disciplinary technologies as religious liturgy, the reduction of primary education to catechesis, and the centennial commemoration of founding figures such as Simón Bolívar and Andrés Bello in a form reminiscent of Catholic canonization.[3] At the risk of simplifying, I contend advisedly that religious fundamentalists aimed at burying the *pactum translationis* alive and resurrecting the Old Regime's defunct *translatio imperii*. The instituting and repeated performance of these rites created a public space, as well as a legitimating intellectual platform, for the return of political theologies to Bogotá in the 1870s.[4] After 1849, when the two-party system came into being, Conservatives began moving in great numbers to the far right—which then meant the religious right—while a core of Liberals moved to the radical left—which at the time meant supporting laissez-faire, educational reform, and the complete separation of Church and state. This book takes the view that the hegemonic sector within the polymorphous Liberal Party radicalized its position because it feared the far right's insurrectionist and theocratic impulses. In turn, the religious right defined its program as a holy crusade because it could not withstand the accelerated transformation to which Liberals subjected the state administration.[5] In the second half of the nineteenth century, the two parties became entangled in a spiral of constant feuding, second-guessing, and local uprisings that was often fueled by bitter literary polemics, but which was intermittently suspended at regular intervals by the literary friendships established between Conservative and Liberal *letrados*.

The strong men behind President Rafael Núñez's national-front administrations, the most virulent of whom was Miguel Antonio Caro, reclaimed the nation's sovereignty for an authoritarian executive branch that was at odds with Colombia's ultraliberal constitutional history. They called themselves "Regenerators" [Regeneradores], which was the same term used by countless reformist groups—progressive and otherwise—since the Enlightenment, although such designations also often took on theological overtones. They betrayed the spirit of *laïcité* under which the Revolution of Independence broke out and achieved completion, and which integrated the Church within the state. Under Liberal administrations, Colombians had the right to practice their Catholic faith as they wished —at home, in their parishes, and at school—with very few exceptions noted below. Under the Regeneración, on the contrary, the Vatican Curia's theo-political claims were forced upon them.

Caro and Núñez declared their allegiance—at times even the subordination of their state offices—to Pius IX's antimodernist agenda on the argument that the country's religious, linguistic, and political unity had long been under siege, but could be restored providentially in the form of a peaceful counterrevolution. Attempts at subverting the increasingly secular state go as far back as the threats of excommunication made repeatedly against Bolívar in the 1820s. They became more focused with the founding of the first Sociedad Católica in 1838 and Archbishop Manuel José Mosquera's refusal to accept the terms of the *ius patronatus* in 1851, which resulted in his banishment from Colombia in 1852.[6] It was only after Caro came into his own—as the devoted and fiery defender of Pius IX's ultramontane *Syllabus errorum* (1864) and the dogma of infallibility (defined at the First Vatican Council in 1870)—that the collapse of the secular state seemed a real and imminent possibility to many reactionary militants.[7]

The reactionaries' restoration of Catholic institutions, expressed most succinctly in the theo-political ancient concept of *regeneratio*, which Caro and Núñez adapted as "La Regeneración," was to legitimate itself by turning four state administrators and inspired writers into the country's four Mosaic figures: the foreign-born Bello and Bolívar—both were Venezuelan—as well as the native-born Núñez and Caro.[8] Like Moses's, each man's work was presented as that of a poet and a legislator who had to endure exile and vituperation in order to point out the way to the new Canaan in which his people would acquire their true freedom.

The Regenerators seized control first of the Colombian Academy, which had been established in 1871, under the sponsorship of Spain's Language Academy, to make up for the lack of diplomatic relations between the two nations. However, after Carlos Martínez Silva (1847–1903)—the founder in 1878 of the Academy's highbrow periodical, *El Repertorio Colombiano*—became disenchanted with the Regeneración, this cultural institution was to prove instrumental in fostering Caro's public discredit and accelerating his exit from active politics.[9] The Regenerators also founded a series of very successful Catholic periodicals, the main venue at the time for the newly instituted concept of public opinion. They used the school system—where priests and Catholic laypersons could still do considerable proselytizing—and especially the pulpit to gather support among the faithful. They particularly coveted the allegiance of a fifth column within the Liberal Party—the so-called independents or moderates, from whose ranks Núñez had come to save the nation.

The systematic undermining of republican freedoms by theocratically minded bureaucrat-literati [*letrados*] was not without its contradictions: reactionaries such as Caro and José Manuel Groot took advantage of the unlimited freedom of the press allowed by the same federalist Constitution of 1863 that they sought to derogate.[10] Moreover, they adopted federalist positions when they strategically endorsed the transfer of the nation's seemingly undivided sovereignty [*imperium/potestas*] to regional parliaments (the Legislative Assemblies of the nine sovereign states).[11] They did this in cases in which insurrectionist local *caudillos* who controlled their assembly could challenge the secular policies of Bogotá's central administration. They also literally demonized Catholic politicians and scholars who professed Liberal tenets, calling them, in a tone reminiscent of Joseph de Maistre's demagoguery, satanic denizens of the *civitas diaboli*.

As literati, the Regenerators flaunted their command of Latin, grammar, Spanish and Roman jurisprudence, colonial history, and Catholic doctrine, the last of which they held to be the basis of *ius naturale* on the first degree, and of civil codes on the second degree.[12] The *letrados'* bookishness allowed them to advance the idea that men should participate in government only according to their intellectual merits. They were not pleased by the fact that in 1870, Liberals made primary instruction secular, compulsory, and free for all Colombians until the age of fifteen. By contrast, Caro introduced an article in the Constitution of 1886 that made primary instruction voluntary and in conformity with Catholic doctrines. Although he explained in his defense of this article that he did not want to force Catholicism on the children of Protestants (note that Colombia had not received at that time significant numbers of immigrants from northern or central Europe), in reality, he sought to delay the general population's access to literacy and citizenship rights on a large scale (*Artículos y discursos* 371–77).[13] The abysmal gap between the highly literate and the unlettered in Caro's Colombia legitimated and naturalized social and economic differences in a Christian polity that otherwise claimed to be an *egalitarian* community.

Caro's subversion of rational-positivist science and jurisprudence, the people's sovereignty, and the separation of Church and state amounted to a "theological insurrection." I am here borrowing Max Stirner's apt phrase for the reiterated struggle in post-Napoleonic France between heavenly *auctoritas* (the claims of Old Regime politics on the present) and temporal *potestas* (the fallible legal realities following the deconsecration of theo-political sovereignty). This symbolic *coup d'état* by consent, so to speak, started with Núñez's slightly more moderate call for in-depth reforms in the Liberal state in 1878: "Complete administrative reform or catastrophe" [Regeneración administrativa fundamental o catástrofe].[14] Núñez's prediction came shortly after the Conservative rebellions in Antioquia (in 1876 and 1879) and the Cauca (in 1876–1877). Though the rebels once called their efforts also "Regeneración," the rebellion in the Cauca escalated into a full-scale two-year civil war. These rebellions triggered various other uprisings and attempted coups in almost every other sovereign state in the course of 1879, leaving the radical sector of Liberalism then in power fatally wounded.

Colombian parties were already at this time mostly interclass entities.[15] For example, under Caro's regime, Bogotá's *letrados* and artisans, like the country's landowners and their small tenants, could feel somehow united in the same cause, because Catholic bureaucrat-literati had convinced the artisans that laissez-faire in economics was as pernicious as laissez-faire in morality, and that the Liberals wanted to force both on the more vulnerable sectors of society instead of protecting agriculture and the handicrafts. Likewise, the penalties that the victorious central government imposed on the rebel landowners in Antioquia or the Cauca following their capitulation typically entailed enforced loans and expropriations, and were also often applied to the rest of the population, whether they had supported the rebel forces or not.[16] These abusive policies contributed to strengthening regional identities across party lines to the detriment of specific philosophies of government, each of which was identified with a particular party or class. To be among the defeated generally meant exclusion from government employment although Liberals also often used the tactic of boycotting elections during the Regeneración years to expose the lack of electoral guarantees under Caro's regime.

The Cauca's radical-Liberal president during the war of 1876–1877 was a grammarian-translator-poet, César Conto (1836–1891), one of the few

Liberal literati who could challenge Caro on his intellectual turf. Not only was he an illustrious alumnus of Bogotá's Colegio de Nuestra Señora del Rosario, where Caro did not complete his advanced degree, but he also produced original poetry and translations as well as philological studies. Conto appointed as secretary of education and minister of government Jorge Isaacs (1837–1895), who was a poet, ethnographer, and novelist. Isaacs, the acclaimed author of Spanish America's greatest work of regional fiction, *María* (1867), was, more so than Conto, an uncomfortable enemy for Caro and Núñez because he had started out as a Conservative only to become a radical later. In addition, he had the charisma of a beloved romantic novelist *and* poet. His life challenged the overarching pattern of conversion put forth by ultramontanists across Europe and the Americas. In this biographical framework, ideologically mature authors and politicians came back into the fold of the Church after their youthful embrace of revolutionary politics; their relapse from religion and the principle of authority was just an instance of *felix culpa* that made their restored faith stronger.

Isaacs found himself in the sovereign state of Antioquia in 1879, denouncing from the pages of *La Nueva Era* the alliance of independent Liberals and Conservatives to drive radicals out of public office and off the political field. In other words, the celebrated author of *María* seemed to fear the advent of a local mini-Regeneración in Antioquia.[17] Feeling increasingly alienated from the governments of both Medellín and Bogotá, Isaacs declared himself Antioquia's supreme civil and military authority (with the rank of general) and vowed to die on the battlefield if necessary. His declaration appeared in a series of widely circulated newspaper articles that attracted international attention and earned him the expulsion from his seat in Congress. In February of 1880, as the outbreak of war seemed almost certain, the Conservative Martínez Silva wrote in *El Repertorio Colombiano*, with his accustomed flair for revealing the unadulterated truth in such pathetic gestures, that he could not think of a greater shock to Colombians than their discovery that the nation's greatest writer had died heroically by the shot of "a cartridge made with a page torn from a copy of *María*" (1: 245–46).[18] Interestingly, because *María* was written during the last years of Isaacs's Conservative militancy, its young protagonists—the eponymous character and Efraín—read avidly the works of Tocqueville, Ségur, and especially Chateaubriand, whose imagery of martyrdom and ruination suited Colombian reactionaries' culture of defeat and restitution (39–42, 104–5).

After Conto and national president Aquileo Parra snuffed out the Conservative rebellion of 1877 in the Cauca, thanks to a local *caudillo* who would soon be president—General Julián Trujillo—nonradicals left and right began to orbit around Núñez. The Cartagena-born grammarian-poet nevertheless had to wait until 1884 to capture the presidency for the second time. Shortly afterward, in August of 1885, he uttered another of his oft-quoted pronouncements—"The Constitution of 1863 no longer exists" [La Constitución de 1863 ya no existe]—in an address to the nation in which he announced from the presidential palace the defeat of the Liberals in that year's war. Núñez's momentous triumph was achieved "not through human intervention, but with the assistance of Divine Providence" [no por la obra de ningún hombre, sino por la ayuda de la Divina Providencia].[19] The reenergizing of God's Providence—the resurgence of *translatio imperii*, to use the classical formulation pertaining to the Holy Roman Empire—happened concurrently with Colombia's canonization of Bolívar. The Libertador was known to be hostile to the concept of Providence, which belittled him and his self-sacrificing patriots. This did not preclude his characterization as "God's instrument" by Groot, Caro, José María Samper, and other Catholic publicists. The notoriously agnostic Núñez, who conveniently hailed from the State of Bolívar, would soon be called the new Bolívar by *providential* and *presidential* decree. More so than the Libertador, the accommodating Núñez went into Colombia's history books as a "providential man" [hombre providencial], as Bogotá's Jesuit Archbishop, José Telésforo Paúl, called him on account of his sponsorship of the confessional Constitution and the ensuing Concordat.

It has been said that the metaphysical jargon repeatedly used by the Regeneración's ideologues was primarily a ploy to achieve and secure the new authoritarian state's monopolistic control of the nation's resources. In this reading, Caro's invocation of theo-political struggles between "good" and "evil," or "salvation" and "damnation" would be in tune with the juridico-political arguments for administrative reform put forward by Núñez, Holguín, and others. This was the time when potential foreign investors had lost interest in Colombia because of the nation's chronic civil wars and inability to build infrastructures such as a much-needed railroad network, and when the price of coffee and tobacco fell dramatically during the worldwide recession of the early 1880s. According to the economicist hypothesis, the Regenerators would have made these concentrated resources available to the landowning elites while creating additional government jobs and protecting the artisans to delay large-scale industrialization, which would have required the participation of foreign investors anyway. Independent Liberals and ultra-Catholic Conservatives would have come together in an *étatiste* project (or perhaps an electoral national front) for the reasons just expounded and not because of the ideological and legislative fatigue of the Liberals coupled with the return to theo-politics championed by Caro.[20]

One important problem with the economicist thesis is that it places excessive emphasis on fiscal and administrative planning, neglecting the long historical perspective afforded by the slow yet steady growth of ideological extremism (left and right), the wars of religion fought at regular intervals since the 1850s, and the delegitimation of a law-and-order state. Colombia has long been regarded as an important prototype of the Spanish American failed state because until recently it lacked an effective standing army and police force and its nineteenth-century constitutions tended to last only a few years. Furthermore, these *leyes fundamentales* were frequently suspended by state-of-exception measures or were in conflict with the sovereign states' individual constitutions and bodies of legislation. It is fair to say that the economic crisis made the Regeneración's administrative reforms possible despite the many instances of corruption and government abuse perpetrated between 1880 and 1905. But the overarching ideological platform that legitimated those institutional reforms, including the issuing and immediate suspension of the 1886 Constitution, preceded the financial crisis by nearly two decades. As shown in the present book, already in the mid-1860s increasing numbers of influential bureaucrat-literati clearly took the side of reactionary politics despite the fact that Liberalism was then hegemonic, or precisely because radicalism's hegemony brought too many legal changes into the country and not enough real social and economic progress. The Glorious Revolution of 1868 and the proclamation of the ephemeral First Republic's federal regime in Spain in 1873 were two distant echoes that resonated potently with Colombian counterrevolutionary writers given their allegiance to philo-Spanish traditionalism.

It is not entirely irrelevant that Núñez, a former Liberal, allowed the ultramontanist José Joaquín Ortiz (like Caro, a holy crusader against Liberalism, which both called "satanic") to serve as one of the Regeneración's presidents of the Senate, very likely at Caro's request. This was a revealing gesture, given that one of the ostensible goals of the Regeneración was to induce an authentic national reconciliation by avoiding extremist positions.[21] The future regime's theological justification was first enunciated in full in Caro's tract against the teaching of Jeremy Bentham (1748–1832) at New Granadan schools and universities, *Estudio sobre el utilitarismo* (1869): "When the innocent man serves the Lord, the wills of all creatures are reconciled. In ushering in the *age of regeneration*, Jesus Christ gave us the example and offered us the formula of this *miraculous reconciliation*" (*Obras, tomo I* 239; emphasis added).[22]

As Marco Palacios has contended, economic history often neglects to take into account the superstructural process that unfolds simultaneously with economic production and innovation as well as shifting consumption patterns. In Colombia's case, Palacios adds, a particularly urgent task confronting today's historians is to investigate the unstudied "connections that must have existed between a considerable group of career politicians who were secondarily literati (and whose biographies unfold in the government bureaucracy or in elected state offices), and the formulation of an authoritarian, eminently bureaucratic, political system" (*La clase más ruidosa* 48–49). This book constitutes the first attempt to date at answering Palacios's call for such a study.

Philology and Jurisprudence: From *mores* to *leges* and Back

The Regeneración was an emergency solution for a country whose bleeding had not stopped since the days of the failed Declaration of Independence in 1810. Although well-meaning Conservatives such as Carlos Martínez Silva and Liberals such as Diógenes Arrieta welcomed at first Núñez's shift to the center-right, their expectations were soon belied. Left in Caro's hands, the Regeneración became synonymous with the right-wing reaction that since Joseph de Maistre's *Considérations sur la France* (1797) went by the name of Catholic "counterrevolution." In de Maistre's memorably repugnant formulation, what France needed most was not "a contrary revolution, but the contrary of revolution." This meant the return to a *natural constitution* in which ancient traditions of government were restored (186, 185). De Maistre realized, like his constitutional nemesis—Emmanuel Sieyès—that the revolution had left a void in the transfer of sovereignty, that democratic representation existed in the shifting space that radical democracy has more recently called an "empty place" [*lieu vide*].[23] This realization, which registered for a long time with several generations of Spanish American authors, plays an important part in this book's arguments. According to de Maistre, no sooner is the *natural and unwritten constitution* restored to its place than theo-political regimes become viable again and "a universal well-being will announce the presence of sovereignty" (*Considérations* 185).

Domingo Faustino Sarmiento (1811–1888) acutely observed in 1845 that for the executive and legislative branches of government to make their sovereign claims on the social body without breaking the constitutional consensus, a national consciousness that made everyone identify with the institutions of the state had to arise first. Sarmiento was remarkably modern in his early distrust of *pactist* theories of sovereignty, which in his opinion opened the door to the instituting of aggressive negotiation and rhetorical feuding as democratic life's everyday reality:[24]

> When authority is removed from its center and planted elsewhere, it will be long before it takes root. *El Republicano* said a few days ago that "authority is nothing but a covenant between the rulers and the ruled"…Authority is founded upon the indeliberate assent that a nation gives to a permanent fact. Where there is deliberation and individual will, authority cannot exist. That transitional state is called *federalism*; and [after] all revolutions effect the ensuing change in authority, all nations have their days in—and attempts at—*federation*. (*Facundo* 178)[25]

Sarmiento's concept of "indeliberate assent" is meant as a way out of the impasse created by the arbitrariness of social contracts. It involves the notion that the longevity of republican institutions and representative government will one day make the question of legitimacy redundant. In the meantime, the challenge was to make a temporary, historically contingent fracture—the republican debunking of Old Regime forms of representation—look permanent. The now-deliberating and feuding citizens of early republicanism would one day stop arguing about the democratic protocols in place because they will have internalized them as a political second nature.[26] In other words, because within the liberal-parliamentary system one can always have the chance (if not exactly the expectation) to win following the rules of democratic participation, one should get used to losing as well without questioning the rules of the game. As it turned out, this obstinate questioning continually happened in Argentina, Colombia, and other Hispanic countries in their early experiments with representative government.

Elsewhere in *Facundo*, Sarmiento shrewdly advances a contrast between enlightened and revolutionary Buenos Aires—a site of "deliberation and individual will"—and the theocentric and philo-Spanish Córdoba—a site of Old Regime "authority."[27] One could experience the nostalgia for colonial rule everywhere in Córdoba (Miguel Cané also wrote that Bogotá was, like Córdoba, a colonial theocratic cloister), mostly because one would like Buenos Aires to be ideally as politically cohesive as Córdoba without relinquishing its liberal-democratic polymorphism or its chorus of dissonant voices. Since taming these instincts by peaceful means remained a theoretical impossibility, the nineteenth-century subject of rights lived in a perpetual longing for a past that he or she simultaneously did and did not want. Sarmiento harbored mixed feelings about a future that was uncertain by definition, given the nature of modern politics. The related notion that Colombian ultramontanists were not willing to entertain was that human liberty could be envisioned in the modern world without the possibility of disorder becoming a threat to the new subject of political rights. This liberty could now exist only outside the Church and within a liberal-democratic state that should be flexible enough to allow its citizens to push regularly the state's extant legal limits for political action and participation.

As a mid-century liberal, Sarmiento had the requisite long view to accept as inevitable the centrifugal dispersion of theo-political sovereignty's fragments. The Old Regime's *imperium* was obliterated with the Third Estate's access to full political representation after the short experiments with universal suffrage were under way in France in 1849. The shifting group alliances and factionalist realignments that constituted parliamentary politics' everyday reality were made visible to all in what Claude Lefort theorized (possibly inspired by the differently inflected concepts of *vuide de la chose* by Sieyès and of *place vide* by Tocqueville, but without crediting either) as the "empty place" (*lieu vide*) left at the "center" of the nation's transcendent body of old. This body could be temporarily taken over by any participant in the debate over political legitimacy—a debate now envisioned as being "necessarily without any guarantor and without any end."[28] This void could only be filled again—and only partially—with republican institutions as long as discussions and deliberations did not attempt to undo the Republic's existing Constitution and its tripartite division of government.

For Sarmiento and nineteenth-century liberalism, the institutions that one day would be held as the new "center" of a changing yet revered authority needed to be made visible—as visible, if not more, as theo-politics' empty place. They also had to be made ubiquitous and above all durable at all times. This is what the lettered city attempted to do through its emphasis on the production of constitutions, civil codes, educational tracts, geographical surveys, and national poems. In contrast with Sarmiento and Bello, those who joined Núñez's Regeneración longed for an alternative, *natural constitution*, whose latent existence they situated in Colombia's literature, Church doctrine, and folklore imported from Spain during the three centuries of colonial rule. It was therefore imperative that the Regenerators also restored diplomatic relations with Spain, as Carlos Holguín Mallarino (1832–1894), a former congressman and long-time magistrate to the Supreme Court, was instructed to do in 1881.[29] Numerous right-wingers who played major roles in this retrogressive movement, whether they were Liberals turned Catholic Conservatives (like José María Samper) or lifelong ultramontanists (like Marco Fidel Suárez), were elected to the Colombian Academy. Their literary qualifications were still less important than their proximity to the centers of power and their ability to deliver a good speech because the Academy served primarily as the institution that accredited oratorical prowess as the main attribute needed to rule the nation, along with the almost indispensable family pedigree. The selection criteria that made admission into the Academy possible, namely, possession of demonstrable skills in the regular production of articulate cultural discourse, turned this institution into an alternative parliament in which Colombia's alleged *natural* and *unwritten* laws could be discussed, particularly because the Conservative and ultramontane literati greatly outnumbered their Liberal counterparts.

Justinian's sixth-century *Instituta* had long been a very influential body of legislation in the Spanish-speaking world. In this work the emperor's discrete *lex regia* coexisted with the great Roman jurisprudents' answers (e.g., Gaius's and Ulpian's compilations), the *senatus-consulta*, the *plebiscita*, the magistrates' edicts, and various strands of consuetudinary norms and *ius gentium* or the laws of nations. *Ius gentium* coexisted in Rome with the originally Greek concept of *ius naturale* (also *lex naturae*) or what right reason was supposed to command to all men and women. Since the basis for natural law was that human morality was enjoined by the same laws that directed the universe, and in the Judeo-Christian tradition the natural and cosmic worlds were of divine creation, some Doctors of the Church seized upon *ius naturale*'s authority. The latter was conflated with the authority of revealed religion; it thus became an invaluable tool to influence positive legislation.

Ancient Rome's standardizing legislative policies were already fundamentally concerned (and confronted) with the customs or traditions of heterogeneous peoples who came under Roman rule. Gaius could thus theorize the notion of an "unwritten law" [non scripto jus] that is nevertheless daily sanctioned by "usage" [usus]. Justinian's *Digesta* collected the adage "laws imitate customs and tradition" [mores legem imitantur], adding that "custom is the best interpreter of the law" [optima legum interpres consuetudo] (*Digesta* 1.3.37).[30] When Caro began to seek reelection to the presidency in 1897 despite his party's opposition and the Constitution's interdiction against serving a second consecutive term, he evoked the idea that the Colombian people could show their spontaneous support for an exception to this rule.

Similarly, in chapter 4, I explain how Bolívar became persuaded that a spontaneously gathered assembly of deputies at the Convención de Ocaña, who allegedly represented a widespread popular sentiment—perhaps in imitation of an *assemblée constituante* proper—demanded *extra legem* that he declare the Dictatorship in 1828. It should be emphasized here that Roman and canon law, Spanish legislation, and the fluid and easily distorted continuum of heterogeneous archival materials called *traditio* exerted enormous pressure on nineteenth-century constitutional scholars. These texts, customs, and ritual practices continued to inhabit the Neogranadine citizens' legislative horizon for as long as the nation lacked both a civil code and a long-lasting *magna carta*—that is, for as long as the concept of "state" did not take priority over those of "nation" and "people." Acts of legislation had yet to prove that they could survive the alternation in power between Conservatives and Liberals. As Colombia's religious right constantly exerted this pressure by any means within its reach, radical Liberals reacted all the more energetically in their defense of *laïcité*, fighting intolerance with intolerance.[31]

Andrés Bello in Chile and Salvador Camacho Roldán in Colombia were among those moderate Liberals who noted that Spanish jurisprudence amounted to a chaos of contradictory and convoluted opinions slowly gathered across centuries of territorial expansion.[32] Napoléon Bonaparte's *Code civil des Français* (1804) and Bello's *Código civil de la República de Chile* (1855) managed to do away with the ingrained practice of accumulating sources without letting later laws supersede and derogate earlier ones.[33] Under the federal system, Colombia could not easily enforce a civil code for reasons similar to those of Spain although the State of Santander adopted almost verbatim Chile's code in 1858 (Cundinamarca did the same in 1859). Peninsular Spaniards did not find a way to articulate the *derechos forales* or local statutory laws particular to Spain's self-differentiated nations-without-a-state. These kingdoms had been annexed by Castile, but the Bourbons, who otherwise pursued a centralizing legislation, did not entirely derogate their common-law repertoires. Colombians had to wait until the Regeneración abolished the federal system in the Constitution of 1886 to implement—with important changes that will be discussed shortly—an adaptation of Chile's code nationwide. This code took lawmaking prerogatives away from the province.[34] Ecuador had done this in 1858 while Bolivia promulgated in 1830 its own code—the "Código de Santa Cruz," sponsored by the liberal President Andrés de Santa Cruz —based on the French model. Interestingly, Rufino José and Ángel Cuervo wrote that in 1829 that Bolívar instructed Miguel Tobar (Caro's maternal grandfather) and Rufino Cuervo (Rufino José's father) to translate into Spanish France's 1804 *Code*, adapting it to Colombia's customs and institutions. The manuscript-in-progress disappeared mysteriously and its paper was later found to have been used to pack commercial seeds; as the Libertador renounced the presidency soon afterward, this project was abandoned (R. J. Cuervo, *Obras, tomo II* 983–84).

The coexistence of multiple constitutions and jurisdictions under federalism meant that conflicts of interpretation concerning every issue under the bar were bound to occur. This situation demanded that the jurist have philological training, or that he show at least some philological sensibility. To declare oneself in favor of pre-nineteenth-century Spanish jurisprudence, and to exaggerate the Spanish and *ius naturale* contents of Bello's *Código civil* to the detriment of its French sources, was to argue implicitly for the rephilologizing of the law. This is what Manuel Montt did in Chile (under whose authoritarian presidency Bello's code was finally promulgated in 1857) and Monsignor Rafael María Carrasquilla did in Colombia.[35] Although attempts were made by individual sovereign states to implement the Napoleonic code, alternative efforts were also made at collecting extant legislation, such as Lino de Pombo's *Recopilación de leyes de la Nueva Granada* (1845).[36] The *Recopilación* contains the type of overlaps, contradictions, and format inconsistencies characteristic of this genre. Such shortcomings are seen most clearly in Spain's antiquating and linguistically unstandardized *Novísima Recopilación* (approved by Carlos IV in 1805; pub. 1806). Once again, the civil code's cross-reference system, uniform writing, and critical apparatus tried to minimize those inconsistencies.[37]

In Bello's time, philology and jurisprudence shared many interpretive protocols. Literary and legal hermeneutics were confronted with the same challenge of ascertaining the primary meaning of words whose appearance in the linguist's library or the justice's court entailed an instance of "witnessing." Even the elucidation of that meaning had its unavoidable pitfalls. As Bello stated in his notes to the *Código civil*'s Preliminary Title (arts. 19–29), words could be interpreted in three ways: first, in their immediate acceptation in language usage; second, in their immediate acceptation in legal discourse; and third, in the sense that the legislator gave them and whose intention is the subject of hermeneutical exegesis. Civil codes should try to stay within the limits of the first two ranges of meaning since access to the law by the majority of the people with the least ambiguity possible is positive legislation's programmatic goal. In fact, one should not use the law's *"obscure…*intention or spirit" as an excuse to neglect the law's "literal tenor" (Bello, *Obras completas* 12: 41–42). This is what philologists call the text's *lectio difficilior*; it is also one of Caro's chief strategies to deviate systematically from enacted positive law.

Nevertheless, jurists tend to feel challenged by, and drawn to, the legislator's intended meaning. In a note published in *El Araucano* in 1842, Bello called this attraction the "hermeneutical sublime" of jurisprudence: "lo sublime de la hermenéutica legal es adentrarse en la inteligencia del legislador y asistir a sus consejos" (*Obras completas* 12: 42). Bello hastens to add, like a good republican, that of course, the interpreter will always substitute his personal opinion for that of the legislator.[38] In other words, because language is inherently unstable—Bello, a scholar of language usage and language variation was very aware of this—multiple meanings could be assigned to a single legal term at any given time. A similar practice in theology was already theorized in full in Augustine's *On Christian Doctrine* [De doctrina Christiana], where the symbolic words of Scripture are said to have at least three meanings. It is tempting to see Bello's devotion to prescriptive grammars as the easiest point of entry into his legislative efforts. The codification and standardization of languages can certainly be correlated with analogous endeavors in the promulgation of new laws of universal applicability. However, the traces of irregularity that grammars want to erase appear most visibly in historical philology.

Textual criticism could in principle provide the tools not just to understand shifts in morphology and semantics, but also to neutralize the discrepancies seen in two *lectiones* of the same text once a *recensio* or critically established and agreed-upon edition could be published. Yet, the establishment of a more authorial—and thus more "difficult"—text seems to have been the common thread between literary philology and the neutralization of inconsistencies in the legislative text. Of course, once an edition was published, the discrepancies were resolved and made somewhat "invisible" unless they remained present in an apparatus.

Bello's "Prólogo" to the *Poema del Cid* (last drafted in 1862; pub. 1881) explains both the challenges that editors of vernacular ballads and epics had to face in his time, and the reasons why Bello committed himself to this project in textual criticism. My critique of the prologue does not concern Bello's errors in judgment (this is not important for this book's argument), but the relationship of his philological ideas to the textual hermeneutics implicit in his understanding of jurisprudence.

For Bello, the great Castilian epic could be studied as a series of vernacular *traditiones* transmitted orally through troubadour recitation; these were analogous to the paralegal customs (common law/*usos y costumbres*/*derecho consuetudinario*) observed by medieval communities despite their potential conflict with legislation enacted in the form of a standardized royal code and in a constitutionally correct setting.[39] The second section of Bello's prologue begins with a diatribe against *jongleurs* and vernacular copyists who had removed their defaced text from the historical Cid (itself an ideal image) through an endless series of "interpolations," "transpositions," and "mutilations," that is to say, through almost every instance of *contaminatio*, which Bello refers to as "degradación" (*Poema del Cid* 3–4).

Before I move to my explanation of why Bello reacted so defensively against the *traditio* informing an ancient manuscript's *recensio*, let me make the following clarification: in addition to its legal and philological meanings, *traditio* has an eminently theological acceptation. A bit like the Muslim *hadith* or chain of authorities, the *traditio* in patristics collides in some ways with the meaning of *recensio* in textual criticism, namely, the value-laden organization of the extant witnesses into a genealogical tree or stemma. *Traditio* designates, as José Manuel Groot (1800–1878) explained in his essay "Autoridad de la tradición" (Caro numbers it as the fifth installment in the series "Misioneros de la herejía" [1853]), the "doctrines," "discipline," and "historical facts" set forth in Scripture. Specifically, the *traditio*

> is God's unwritten word [palabra de Dios no escrita] that the Apostles received from Jesus Christ's mouth and which they transmitted through their disciples and successors. It has been handed over to us through the Pastors' teachings. Put differently, *traditio* is the universal Church's constant, perpetual, and uniform teaching recognizable in its Pastors' unanimous voice [voz uniforme]—these are called Fathers—in the Episcopal Councils' decisions, in the practice of public worship, in liturgical prayers and ceremonies, and even in the testimonies of pagan authors as well as heretics. (Groot, *Obras escogidas* 177–78)[40]

Note the synecdoche in Groot's formulation: every unwritten word and every teaching, however minute and fragmentary, become a sign of Jesus Christ's universal triumph on earth. How do we know that we have run into one such holy textual relic? Any fragment or legend becomes an authentic piece of the *traditio* when it has been authenticated by its uninterrupted transmission and by the sanctioning of bishops gathered in an assembly. To be sure, this core of authenticity does not reside in the fragment's teachings per se, but in the accrediting bodies that sanction those teachings in a given form, which were often not the Episcopal Councils themselves, but the Vatican Curia. Although the bits and pieces that form the *traditio* are supposedly fragmentary and discrete, they are also paradoxically uniform and universal. This contradictory status allowed the papacy for many centuries to hold almost exclusive control over doctrinal interpretation on the primary argument that the pope was the highest deciding authority within the Church, although in reality, no authority could have lawfully overruled a council of bishops.

As a jurisprudent and a grammarian, Bello wished to produce texts that would show internal cohesiveness, that is, texts in which the *traditiones* would be homogenized in a core narrative. His *Poema del Cid*, which seems to have been left unfinished, is composed of a "Prólogo"; a heavily annotated "Relación de los hechos del Cid anteriores a su destierro, sacada de la Crónica del Cid"; the poem proper, "Gesta de Mío Cid," also generously annotated and which Bello was the first scholar to divide into three cantos [*cantares*]; the "Apuntes sobre el estado de la lengua castellana en el siglo XIII (Apéndice I)";[41] the shorter note "Origen de la epopeya romancesca (Apéndice II)"; and a "Glosario." Bello's text, which deviates substantially from his base text (edited in 1779 by Tomás Antonio Sánchez), presents itself as the outcome of applying modern phonetic and morphological rules to an existing critical text (Bello did not have access to the only manuscript copy known in his time and ours) riddled with anachronisms and other instances of uncorrected *contaminatio*.

The preexisting edition that Bello uses as his base text is itself a palimpsest of oral and written *traditiones* that span several centuries and various geographical regions (everywhere the legend of El Cid reached), for which reason morphological and orthographical consistency were not Sánchez's concern.[42] Unlike Sánchez, Bello struggled with the suspicion that overzealous literate copyists had regularized the metrical and rhythmic patterns of many passages in the poem, which should have been left untouched. He suspected that a carefully crafted metrical variation was one of the poem's defining features. Bello applied phonetic and morphological laws, as well as metrical patterns, to Sánchez's text to demonstrate the original hegemony of assonant rhyme in Spanish poetry. He also wished to illustrate the relatively regularized development of Castilian in the twelfth century. Bello conceived of the *Gesta* as a vehicle for reconstructing linguistic and metrical changes in the history of the Spanish language and publicizing centralist political regimes in which the citizens' trust in the continuity of the rule of law would never be lost. At the same time, he was frustrated at noticing how many errors less literate scribes had slipped into their manuscripts. In his opinion, the *traditio* had damaged the text both through hypercorrection and through contamination. Finally, since the poem had always existed as what the nineteenth century called a "legend," Bello took it upon himself to separate history from fiction.[43]

Bello's attraction to the *Gesta del Cid* was spurred by his conflicted biography as much as his work as constitutional *letrado* and his lifelong study of the Castilian vernacular's history. Like El Cid, Bello was the target of slanderous accusations in Venezuela and Chile because of his moderate political views; Sarmiento went so far as to request publicly Bello's banishment from

Chile, just as El Cid was banished from Castile.[44] The Campeador wants the king to abide by Castile's ancient laws, but he does not question royal authority because he understands that the kingdom's transcendent body will outlast King Alfonso VI's mortal body.

The fact that the unjust King Alfonso chose to banish El Cid instead of having him killed, and that El Cid chose to subject himself to that higher authority's decisions, illustrates the poem's faith in the possibility of ensuring the continuity of a legally administered justice in a constitutionally adequate setting. The pangs of exile and the obedience to the law are two of the poem's dominant themes. To be sure, the epic does not feature an anachronistic simulacrum of democratic participation. Nevertheless, the *Gesta* (Bello's name for Per Abbat's rendition of the epic) also implicitly supports the view that princes should not use excessive force; that they should show mercy and equanimity in administering their kingly prerogative of *iustitia*; and that they must themselves obey the law. Just as the political regime implemented in the *Gesta* keeps the jurisprudential exception at bay—El Cid does not rise up against an unjust king—so does Bello keep *contaminatio* from making its presence felt in the edited text. His regularizing positivism in philology matches his disciplinary positivism in jurisprudence.

In contrast with Bello, the Popayán-born theocrat Sergio Arboleda (1822–1888) wrote in 1869 that the *romancero* and the *refranero* were primarily repositories of Catholic doctrine; as such, they encapsulated Spanish America's *ius naturale*, which should be adopted as the "foundation of its legislation" (*La República en la América española* 61). Interestingly, the Spaniard Joaquín Costa (1846–1911) used the *Cid* cycle in exactly the contrary way; for him this cycle was the cipher of Spanish "constitutionalism" and "representative government," which, he insisted time and again, was separate from modern concepts of "parliamentary democracy" (63–76). Costa's account is in stark contrast with Arboleda's and the Regeneración's views on popular poetry and folklore. He believed that medieval municipalities and estates shared the nation's sovereignty with the king, who presided over the freely *federated* realms while respecting their local rights and privileges lest the people exercise their legitimate right to resistance. The *romancero* would thus give voice to the autonomy of civil and municipal government from ecclesiastical and magnate meddling, which is how Costa—an agrarian republican who moved closer to socialism in his last years—interprets the adage *vox populi vox Dei*, also in contradistinction to Arboleda.[45]

The stylistic and formal notes that Bello includes in his edition of the *Gesta* alert the reader to the textual corrections he had made to Sánchez's text despite the fact that Bello had no access to the poem's only surviving manuscript—a fourteenth-century fragmentary copy of an earlier one dating from roughly one century previously. He most often employs the criterion of regularization by bringing "witnesses" from other genres (the *coplas*, the *romancero*, Berceo, etc.) and by incorporating his own discoveries into the history of metrical patterns in the medieval epic.[46] As he will do in the *Código civil*, Bello privileges the *lectio facilior* or *lectio clarior* over the *lectio difficilior*. The question about the *difficilior* perhaps merits a little more argument and additional examples. In literary texts, it is quite common to choose the *difficilior* because it shows the author's genius over the copyists' bastardization. Since Bello distrusted copyists, in the *Gesta* he at times proposed hard readings that have not been accepted. One of his well-known (and generally rejected) emendations is that the "nine-year-old child" [nin*n*a ∂e nuef an*n*os] who greets El Cid in Burgos must have been a "sixty-year-old woman" [naña de sesenta años] (Bello, *Poema del Cid* 90). Since "nin*n*a/niña"would be the *facilior* here, Bello was choosing a *difficilior*. His alternation of easy and hard readings is an interesting tendency, given the fact that in legislation, he leaned decisively toward the *facilior*. To this extent, Bello's jurisprudence and philology seem to work not only in tandem but perhaps also in a more complex relationship of mutual implication whose analysis exceeds the scope of this book.

Bello's historical notes are of great interest to us because in them he seems bent upon separating the historical truth from the ornaments of fiction. Clearly, for him the *Gesta* is a literary-legislative act: while still a poem and a work of art, it conveys a comprehensive picture of king-vassal relations and of a hegemonic Iberian kingdom answering the call to fulfill the mission of political centralization.[47] In his jurisprudence work, Bello deviated from Arboleda and Monsignor Carrasquilla in not wanting the *Siete Partidas* and other royal codes to remain in force to the detriment of civil codes. At the same time, however, he wanted to present the *Gesta* as a document attesting to the emergence of a centralizing rule of law in the Peninsular kingdoms in the tenth and eleventh centuries. For this reason, his notes reference the *Partidas*, the *Fuero Juzgo*, and other medieval sources.

Similarly, Bello's *Código civil* makes use of a critical apparatus in which notes, glosses inserted in the main text, and a series of internal cross-references allow the reader to focus exclusively on the letter of the law without precluding the possibility of a historical investigation. Yet, just as his *Poema del Cid* attempts to separate the *traditio* from the *recensio*, subordinating the former to the latter, the *costumbres* briefly mentioned in the *Código civil* are forcefully severed from positive law, again subordinating the former to the latter.[48] The philologist's earlier commitment to literary and linguistic standardization (Bello's interest in the Spanish epic dates back to his arrival in London in 1810, resulting in his first substantive essay on the poem in 1827) informs and legitimates the *liberal* commitment to a homogeneous body of jurisprudence. Leaving aside questions of format, the outstanding ideological difference between Colombia's and Chile's civil codes—each having been sponsored by a grammarian-*letrado*—lies in Caro's insistence on including various provisions authorizing interpretations based on *ius naturale* and Catholic doctrine whereas Bello did away with those completely. This is an interesting difference for us to note because Caro also gave wide circulation to oral *traditiones* citing Bello's habit of attending mass daily. To conclude, Caro silenced Bello's philosophy of government, choosing instead to highlight his poetry's Catholic overtones and his defense of Spain's literary culture. In Caro's estimation, Bello's literary rescripts and churchgoing legend overruled his juristic writings.

In Niels Falck's *The Scientific Study of Jurisprudence* (drawn from his posthumously published *Juristische Encyclopädie* [1821; definitive ed., 1851]), the German theologian and legist used the phrases "juristic philology" and "general literary History of Jurisprudence" to designate, respectively, the study of historical and comparative grammar, and the multigenre *traditio* that lawmakers regularly draw upon (Hastie 203, 219). This historical tradition featured biographies of great personages and related genres such as patristics, historical chronicles, ballads, ancient epigraphs, marginal notes by *glossatores*, and so on.[49] Both the philologist and the jurist engaged in summoning "testimonies," as the metaphor of witnessing was a trope common to textual editing and the interpretation of the law. The scholar of textual criticism, like the scholar of historical jurisprudence, needed to be aware of copyists' errors and to gain access to incunabula and *editiones principes* of the texts under scrutiny in addition to knowing the "grammatical rules" and the "rules of general Philology" (Hastie 209).[50] Many of these complications, which somehow empowered clergymen and literati who wished to attain a high office in the modern nation-state's bureaucracy, were greatly attenuated by the advent of the compulsively legislating liberal-democratic state, one of whose principal goals was the promulgation of a civil code that was intelligible to the entire body of citizens. Francisco Martínez Marina's *Juicio crítico de la Novísima Recopilación* (1820) set the tone for Bello and later positive jurisprudents in the Spanish-speaking world. Martínez Marina, an early advocate for Spain's adoption of a civil code in the manner of the Napoleonic one and the most important theorist of Castile's Cortes as well as the Cortes de Cádiz, singled out "brevity and clarity" [brevedad y claridad] as the two main criteria for eloquent legal writing, as if he had in mind philology's emphasis on the *lectio brevior* and the *lectio clarior* as opposed to the convoluted *lectio difficilior* (*Obras escogidas* 1: 373).[51] In contrast with Martínez Marina's preferences, in the later eighteenth century, reactionary Protestant theologians across Europe began to privilege "difficult" or "hard" readings of Scripture over "easy" ones. They aimed to isolate the common reader—now the universal subject of newly acquired political rights—from the articulation of doctrinal meanings.

Martínez Marina's main objections to the heteroclite *Novísima Recopilación* were accordingly philological:

> Obscurity and confusion increase due to stylistic redundancies. The excess of words covers up the inexactitude and falsity of the ideas set forth while verbose locutions obfuscate the law's basic meaning…these laws are prolix, diffuse, and have seemingly no end; they are full of exotic clauses, heterogeneous digressions, anacoluthic propositions that do not follow upon the main one [proposiciones inconexas con la principal], useless parentheses and minutiae, ancillary phrases and paragraphs that do not pertain to the law proper. They are crowded with quotations, adventitious prologues, and historical dissertations, all of which makes the study of the law arid and disagreeable; the laws become impossible to memorize; in short, this legislation amounts to a fountain of obscure matters [manantial de oscuridades], which are good only to cover the legislator's will with a veil. (*Obras escogidas* 1: 373)

Bello certainly worked on the assumption that jurisprudence and philology shared a common textual matrix, and that modern civil codes could be somehow analogized to prescriptive grammars. Like Martínez Marina, he was inclined to separate the historical study of the law from the much-needed standardizing practices by privileging positive jurisprudence over *ius naturale* and the forms of *traditio* advocated by less progressive *letrados*. In his *Código civil de la República de Chile*, Bello voiced a few opinions about the nature of positive law to which centralist liberals across the Americas could readily adhere, but believers in the divine right of rulers (such as the main Colombian authors under study) could not: "Customs [*la costumbre*] do no constitute law [*derecho*] except in cases in which this jurisprudence [*la ley*] specifically refers to them" (Tít. Prelim., art. 2; *Obras completas* 12: 27).[52] As can be seen in Bello's passage, the views of Falck, Boeckh, and Bello on the relationship of oral traditions, philology, and hermeneutics to the law were to be applied not to the promulgation of a new legislation, but to the interpretation of existing ones. These authors' legal positivism was thus easily reconciled with a liberal politics. By contrast, the Regeneración's legists were careful to emphasize the ways in which not just "hermeneutics," but "*ius naturale*" and "Christian doctrine"—two sources of jurisprudence that Bello all but left out of his *Code*—could complement and even overrule positive legislation (*Código civil colombiano* 11–12).

If one is able to argue successfully that Christian doctrine could complement, perhaps even correct, positive codes, the next step forward in the debunking of the liberal-democratic state is to argue that poetry and historiography written by laypersons (but who have been anointed by the Church for that office) can also have the force of law. The Regenerators' literary-legislative acts tried to assume these extraordinary faculties when they put forth the notion that the Liberals' secular state had corrupted the sources of both morals and legislation by turning its back on *ius naturale*.

It is worth noting here that Giorgio Agamben reads Carl Schmitt's concept of the "state of exception" as a deregulated or *deconstitutionalized* space that acknowledges a "force-of-law" [forza-di-legge] in executive decisions that are not legal. This is a twofold process: first, defenders of the nonlegislative sources of jurisprudence try to invest their every utterance with a *vis coactiva* through their seizure of extraordinary executive faculties, as Caro certainly did; and second, the existing "norm remains in force but is not applied (it has no 'force')" [la norma vige, ma non si applica (non ha 'forza')] (Agamben, *Stato di eccezione* 50–54). This process is somewhat analogous to how literary-legislative acts can behave without doing violence to the legal order even as they call (explicitly or otherwise) for the disappearance of that order. As I show in chapter 4, when the Regenerators characterized Bolívar, the lawmaker, as a great poet, they were granting poetry—*their* poetry, not Bolívar's—the power to legislate or at least induce similar legitimating or deterring effects to those found in positive jurisprudence.

The Neogranadine civil code was promulgated the year before the signing of the Concordat with the Vatican Church, perhaps the world's only self-governed corporation whose various charters of rights, obligations, and privileges repeatedly call for the mediating use of philology, patristics, and hermeneutics.[53] Caro wrote that the colonial regime ushered in a golden age in the Americas because it forced the vast continent's scattered populations to live immersed in their "customs" and encircled by the town's "walls"—in Bogotá's case, by the Andes no less. Virgil had referred to the basis upon which Rome was built as the combination of consuetudinary conventions and architectonic walls: "*moresque viris et moenia*"(*Aeneid* 1.264). In Caro's estimation, present-day Colombia needed more "*mores ponere*"—the instituting or setting up of sacred customs and the preservation of natural law—and presumably less *leges facere*—the enacting or dictating of positive legislation in a political assembly (*Artículos y discursos* 186).

In general, nineteenth-century reactionary ideologues thought very highly of themselves as administrators of a linguistic regime in which they assumed the extraordinary faculty of finding *acceptable acceptations* for rapidly changing, overdetermined concepts. At times this practice involved something as simple as changing the form of a word to make it fit the proposed meaning. To give an extreme example, Sergio Arboleda requested that the word *igualdad*, which was consecrated in the French Revolution's republican slogan, be kept safely enshrined in the realm of catechesis, where it belonged, and away from Congress and government offices, where it did not. We are all equal before God's eyes, he reasons, but society does not—and should not—acknowledge equal rights of representation since nature did not make us equal. As a counterbalance to the ubiquitous *desigualdad* seen everywhere, positive legislation should recognize instead what he calls (fusing the words "equanimity" and "equality") *ecualidad* (*La República en la América española* 174–77).[54] In Arboleda's view, individuals should not participate in civil government according to the democratic criterion, but according to their merits, by which he meant knowledge of rhetoric, Latin, Church doctrine, and historical jurisprudence as well as the *unacquired* moral superiority that comes with several generations of uninterrupted good breeding. This is one general way in which translational transfers presented themselves in the nineteenth century, as just any form of transmissibility of texts or any textual manipulation that purports to make historical change intelligible and acceptable in a legitimate context of reception.

Although more could be said about how the Old Regime correlated theories about the origin of language (as *verbum Dei*), the origin of property (as absolute *dominium*) and the origin of sovereignty (as *imperium*), suffice it to add for now that all three were part of the same analogical matrix that pitted forms of transmission understood as a secular contract or pact (*pactum*) against forms of transmission understood as a providential concession (*translatio*).[55] With few exceptions, those who from the seventeenth century adhered to the providential creation not just of "Man," but of human language—a perfect organism crafted *ex nihilo*—also subscribed to the divine concession of ownership rights and to the divine right of rulers. By analogy with the genre of the religious "rescript" [*rescriptum*] (e.g., the pope's encyclical letter, the bishop's pastoral letter), Colombian publicists of the providential *translatio* crafted original poems for recitation at public events and dissemination in the periodical press, assuming that they had been asked for spiritual direction or that their readers were in need of moral and political admonition.

Among the daring local arguments presented in this book is the contention that the first American writer of secular rescripts was a Peninsular Spaniard, Manuel José Quintana (1772–1857). His speeches and institutional messages [*proclamas*] delivered on behalf of the Spanish Cortes were imitated by countless patriots such as Andrés Bello who rejected the French invasion of Spain. Quintana became the focus of important philological discussions among such luminaries as Bello and Caro, who saw in his body of writing (as legislator, poet, critic, and educational reformer) a foil to their more eventful and successful careers in public service. They also saw in him the first Hispanic *letrado* who sacrificed the integrity of his literary writing on the altar of a loftier political cause. If Quintana had not lived at a time when lyric genres had to be declamatory and literally *exaltados*—the mock-heroic epithet assigned to radical liberals—he would have developed into a better poet than he actually was.

The Regeneración was the culmination of insurrectionist efforts carried out across party lines by a coterie of grammarians and writers with no university degrees (in 1850, the Liberals waved most accreditation requirements for the exercise of high-skilled professions) and limited knowledge of jurisprudence, but who were endowed with portentous rhetorical skills. They used their literary capital to create a favorable climate of opinion for the promulgation of new law while trying to endow their Christianized translations of foreign poetry also with the force of law.[56] The various groups that produced a certain amount of writing in their respective pursuits of *sacerdocium* (theology), *studium* (letters), and *imperium* (the law) constituted what Ángel Rama called, in a broad Latin American context, "the lettered city" [*la ciudad letrada*] in 1984.

The main features of the lettered city, whether Liberal or Conservative, are these: first, the superimposition (Rama's words are *traslación* and *transculturación*) of a preexisting order of signs on an uncontrollable and unpredictable phenomenal reality that may go unacknowledged as such; second, the use of a highly cultured language, often disconnected from everyday usage and fully understood mainly by the minority in power; and third, the displacement of the community's immediate economic and social problems by ambitious cultural projects in keeping with the imperatives of nation building.[57] Colombia's lettered city achieved its climax in the last decades of the nineteenth century, in the *longue durée* that Néstor García Canclini has characterized as the discontinuous, sinuous, and heterogeneous modernization of Latin America, but which in Colombia followed the path of the Regeneración's counterrevolution.[58] The Colombian literati (*literatos*) who later became state apparatchiks (*letrados*) were for the most part Conservatives who often expressed no interest in scientific development, free trade, or the secularization of public life despite their humanistic background. Moreover, they attacked the freedom of the press and did surprisingly little to spread secondary instruction beyond the one hundred families from Bogotá and Popayán that for Marco Fidel Suárez and Sergio Arboleda still constituted the country's main elite group at the turn of the nineteenth century.

This may be the reason why Rama refrained from highlighting Colombia's regional and cultural idiosyncrasies vis-à-vis those of Chile and Argentina, where Andrés Bello, José Victorino Lastarria, Juan Bautista Alberdi, Bartolomé Mitre, and Domingo Faustino Sarmiento were good examples of the highly visible and influential bureaucrat-literati of mid-century liberalism. The same anxiety informs Julio Ramos's brilliant *Divergent Modernities* (2001; expanded English edition of *Desencuentros de la modernidad en América Latina* [1989]), which rivals Rama's book in perspicuity and scope. Ramos's four intellectual heroes are Bello, the Argentine Sarmiento, the Puerto Rican Eugenio María de Hostos, and the Cuban José Martí—four liberals if we take the view that Bello was a *double agent*: someone who worked from within the conservative Chilean institutions to advance liberal policies in education and civil rights.[59]

Sarmiento was in his Chilean years a radical liberal and an early critic of Bello's linguistic and literary conservatism. Although Sarmiento later moved to the right without renouncing his radical views on education, he would still attract Caro's attacks for his populist politics, his continual criticisms of Bello and Spain, and his appreciation for vernacular speech and cultural self-differentiation, notwithstanding the mounting racialist overtones of his later work. In the early 1840s, Sarmiento's radicalism meant primarily that he was profoundly antiecclesiastical; further it meant that he rejected the heritage of Counter-Reformation Spain (instead, he was a literary Francophile and Anglophile) and favored the universality of primary instruction as well as a decentralized federal system over a central government that put the executive power above the legislative in ways analogous to those of colonial administrations. It also meant that he wished to fight conservatives to the death in both culture and politics, particularly admirers of Spain and ultramontanists who nostalgically evoked the colonial rule's religious and political unity as the Americas' golden age.

In contrast with Sarmiento, Bello is best described as a moderate liberal, and an accommodating one at that, as shown by his collaboration with Portales and Mariano Egaña in editing the last draft of the 1833 Constitution and his writing of a civil code that consecrated the social elite's controversial ownership rights.[60] Although probably one should not dismiss Bello's modernizing efforts because of these blind spots, one cannot completely exonerate him either. In the last analysis, he endowed Chilean institutions with legal continuity while sponsoring the opening up of a public sphere through his lifelong fight against censorship and his launching of numerous publication ventures, literary contests, celebrations, and so on. He also ensured the intellectual continuity between Spain's Golden Age and Enlightenment literature, on the one hand, and its American mutations in the postindependence era, on the other.[61] In sum, he was largely responsible, through the compromises he made and the risks he took, for putting Chile on the map of polite and political Spanish American societies.[62]

The pervasiveness of lettered-city policies in Colombia can additionally be understood as the creole elite's self-empowering design to compensate for the perceived inferiority of their nation's material and social development vis-à-vis Europe, North America, and even the rest of South America,[63] or simply to conceal the bleak picture of a city that was considerably more destitute in 1883 than in 1859. Bogotá was now inhabited by an increasingly undifferentiated mass of proletarians: to adjust Klaus Kautsky's famous dictum, unemployment (rather than overwork) and underconsumption constituted a frequent condition of Colombia's underclass. The capital's isolation from the sea and other cities did not even make possible the export of the cattle raised in the savannah. In a city of beggars, there was no market for the artisans' handicrafts, while the elites only consumed goods manufactured abroad. This situation helps explain in part why bucolic poetry became the dominant highbrow lyric mode in the later nineteenth century: as the tobacco and farms scattered around the Bogotá savannah closed down in the 1860s, and the land was used just for raising cattle or left uncultivated while insecurity increased, throngs of desperate peasants flocked to the city, where they added to the numbers of destitute and homeless residents and where salaries were lower than the daily cost of proper food.

The sober Medardo Rivas vows that Bogotá's population of 80,000 in 1883—at the onset of the Regeneración—was composed in great numbers of naked and barefoot beggars and ill-nourished vagrants of all ages and races, whose lives often unfolded in poorly ventilated and humid spaces dangerously close to the unsewered city's gas and detritus miasma. A few hundred homes sheltered the civil and ecclesiastical elites from unwanted contacts while a slightly larger group of artisans and government bureaucrats struggled to keep above the poverty line (Rivas 1: 97). The elites naturally used their writing and oratorical skills to dominate the subaltern classes. Rivas is very critical of the populist agitations sanctioned by both the Liberal Sociedades Democráticas and the Conservative Sociedades Católicas.

The founder of Colombian sociology, the Liberal politician, entrepreneur, and jurist Miguel Samper (1825–1899), candidly admitted in his classic *La miseria en Bogotá* (1867) the following[64]: "[A]lthough there are many exceptions to this, the priest and the *letrado* normally completed their studies so that they could subject the common people" [el sacerdote y el letrado, naturalmente con muchas excepciones, estudiaban para dominar los pueblos] (*Selección de escritos* 43).[65] To put it bluntly, if Colombia still had a disheartening 80 percent illiteracy rate in 1870 (compared to only 20 percent in the United States), its tiny political elite may well have been the most superficially cultivated in the American continent, as Rivas also concedes. The Argentine writer Miguel Cané, who traveled extensively through Colombia and spent some time in Bogotá in the early 1880s, attested to the truthfulness of Rivas's account. If Rivas characterized the capital as an enclave of "politics" and "poverty," for Cané—who seems to have avoided as much as he could Bogotá's *other half*—the city was taken over rather by "poetry." When remembering the New Granadans' virtuosity at improvising well-crafted verses in place of dinner-table conversations, Cané recorded this hyperbole: "After a while they all speak in verse" [Al fin todos hablan en verso] (197). In a similar vein, the Cuervo brothers suggested that despite their lack of letters, creole women also had an "innate talent" for versification—this had been first noted by the Spanish Jesuit jurist and geographer Pedro Murillo Velarde in 1752—and so "could improvise a quatrain or a *décima*" [dejaban brotar una cuarteta o una décima] besides regularly engaging in lofty conversations with *letrados* (R.J. Cuervo, *Obras, tomo II* 895).

Was Bogotá the city of politics *and poetry* or the city of politics *and poverty*? The creole families "wanted to close their eyes to avoid seeing the country's social foibles" instead of correcting them (Rivas 1: 97). The representations of Bogotá in the *Papel Periódico Ilustrado* and *El Repertorio Colombiano* made no reference to the proverbial insecurity and abjection of the capital's street life in the immediate surroundings of the cathedral. The *letrados*' fixation with landmark monuments and cultural celebrations was geared toward the performance of a civil society that did not exist as such; thus, it also functioned as a compensatory fantasy for Bogotá's insularity and limited role in national politics. In 1907, the Liberal *caudillo* Rafael Uribe Uribe followed up on the images of Cané, Rivas, and the Cuervos. After his heroic resistance to Caro's Regeneración and his ill-advised rebellion of 1899, which triggered off the War of the Thousand Days, Uribe Uribe became, with future Republican president Carlos E. Restrepo, an impassioned advocate for scientific and practical education. He took offense whenever an Argentine or a Chilean asked him to recite his own poetry—which he did not write—upon learning that he was Colombian. For many foreigners, so it seemed to Uribe Uribe, "verses" were the only recognizably Neogranadine product, in the same fashion as Bolivia produced silver, Ecuador, cocoa, Chile, copper, and Brazil, rubber (2: 288). The argument can be easily made that Colombia could not have a strong literature because authors who showed some talent for versification or storytelling were quickly co-opted by one of the hegemonic parties. They could not conceivably find a large enough audience to ensure the continuity of an independent literary career in a country where (by Uribe Uribe's calculations) the illiteracy rate remained at 70 percent even at the dawn of the twentieth century.

Uribe Uribe was not preoccupied by the lack of good poets—although he realized that these were sparse—but by Colombia's inability to produce substantive jurisprudents, economists, or engineers. In his opinion, no sooner did these professionals obtain a lucrative employment than they devoted the better part of their time to writing verses or collaborating in various cultural enterprises. They did this because there were no real incentives (commercial or institutional) to grow intellectually in one's profession and because social prestige correlated with cultural self-expression as much as it did with money. Furthermore, cultural distinction legitimated the elites' sense of superiority in a country without a capitalist market and whose streets were full of beggars and hungry peasants. Uribe Uribe hinted that the country might well have as many beggars as it had citizens who could read. The conclusion is obvious enough: the amateur bureaucrat-poets' potential readers were primarily their own cronies in their *letrado* profession, while the audiences to whom they regularly recited those verses were attendees at social *tertulias* as well as literary-political ones (Ricardo Carrasquilla and Vergara y Vergara's *El Mosaico* or Caro's Librería Americana). Occasional verses were also recited at the political dinners described in Lorenzo Marroquín and Rivas Groot's novel *Pax* (1907), and at electoral meetings (as Guillermo Valencia did during his campaigns of 1918 and 1930) or in the midst of congressional speeches.

From *Idéologie* to Ideology:
On Legal Fictions, Paraphrasis, and Living in Latin

I have left for last, in this preliminary description of the field of letters, a brief discussion of Latin's place in Colombian society. This description will enable me to transition into a discussion of the ideology of grammar and rhetoric in Caro's time. In *Universidad y sociedad* (1992), the sociologist of education Renán Silva adduces a wealth of evidence to support his claim that instruction in Latin grammar subsided at schools and universities (at both Bogotá's religious *colegios mayores* and the University of Popayán) as early as the middle of the eighteenth century because grammar teachers in particular were very poorly paid (340–43). However, Silva neglects to mention that through the end of the nineteenth century and well into the twentieth, Latin remained a staple of private education at the homes of Catholic laypersons while domestic worship was also conducted in Latin. José María Cordovez Moure provides examples of genteel women who did not know ancient Rome's language but had memorized the prayers they heard at church, which they recited daily to their children in their "Macaronic Latin" accompanied by copious "solecisms" and "barbarisms" (339). He also remembers learning the rules of Latin grammar without ever knowing how or when to apply them. His confusion was made all the worse by his simultaneous realization that almost every classic writer violates the rules of composition in his native language. He probably found this learned opinion in Gómez Hermosilla, the best-selling author of handbooks of rhetoric who did not believe in strict rhetorical rules at all.

After a few decades of relative decay, Latin came back with a vengeance in mid-nineteenth-century Bogotá in the form of a second flowering of grammars and neo-Latin poetry as well as the translation of vernacular compositions into the language of ancient Rome. The quintessential primal scene of ideological concealment in Caro's Colombia was the instructional setting of the grammar class. The centuries-old status of Latin as the language of Church liturgy asserted the authority of a hypostatized, transcendent entity over and against that of individual readers of Scripture and participants in the liturgy. Latin was also the language of classic theo-political discourse. From a strictly political standpoint, Latin was the visible symbol of an enigmatic discursive machine that had not yet vacated the place where theo-political sovereignty was once thought to reside. However, pedagogically speaking, the Latin language has always been something else or something more. The use of spoken Latin in a classroom in which the students' first language is a vernacular provides an extreme example of the construction of a discursive identity whose legitimating source has been strategically placed outside language, specifically in the authority of the master and the teaching institution.[66]

The enigma and appeal of living languages (one is reminded here of Hegel's revealing passage in the *Phenomenology of Spirit*) is that they are both internal and external to the speaking subject; that is to say, one's native language is learned through a network of articulations with other subjects who temporarily escape the learning subject's instrumental control. This twofold articulation is eliminated in the teaching of Latin. In the classroom setting, learning is referred always to the external authority of the teacher, whose mastery of the rules does not admit any questioning. Two related fictions are used to reinforce this authority: first, that there is a place outside language where linguistic authority originates; and second, that this authority is nowhere better represented than in the Jesuit priest. Bogotá's Jesuits founded the colonial Colegio de San Bartolomé. They were the first educational religious order to prohibit the use of vernaculars in the Latin grammar classroom. The Jesuits were expelled from Colombia in 1850 and again in 1861, which allowed some of San Bartolomé's buildings to house temporarily part of the secular Universidad Nacional in 1867.[67] In foregrounding the banished order's authority-enhancing strategies, Caro settled several accounts with the Liberal governments that systematically challenged the principle of authority. This was the same principle that inspired, on one hand, the teacher in the Latin grammar class, and on the other, the providential ruler in divinely ordained absolutist regimes.[68]

Just as the Latin teacher's special charisma was dimmed by the growing use of vernaculars in the classroom, so did the Old Regime's *plenitudo potestatis* become dislodged by the spread of parliamentary democracy. The Enlightenment's theorization of the state as a unified universal will is predicated on the condition that it can never show itself as such. The generative distinction between the nation's constituent legislative power and the constituted (or properly constitutional) legislative branch is all-important. In the former, minority opinions are de facto obliterated since the sovereign power can speak with only one voice—the voice of universal reason in Kant and the voice of the numerical majorities in Sieyès. In the constituted branch, however, dissenting voices are always heard and often overpowered by the majority's commanding presence, but minority opinions never cease their bickering in Congress. The feuding inherent in modern democratic politics can remain visible and audible at all times because the arbitrary violence of *pouvoir constituant* remains invisible.[69] In classic constitutional theory, *pouvoir constituant* comes into being as the fiction of unanimous and universal assent to the rules governing disputes over future legislation; that is to say, all delegates must approve the fundamental law or *nomos* that will allow them to fight mercilessly over all other decisions. It thus implicitly recognizes the right of the individual to veto the first constitutive decision that has already been made, but not any of the contingent decisions that remain to be made. *Pouvoir constitué* is the power wielded by legal majorities in constitutionally correct settings, majorities that can impose their discrete decisions on the defeated minorities because the latter cannot veto majoritarian ballots lest democratic representation would collapse.

But what if *pouvoir constituant*'s invisible violence is rehearsed time and again, at the enactment of each new Constitution, as happened in Colombia, with the intervening years between charters filled with civil wars and local uprisings, not to mention the federal state's conflicting jurisdictions? In this scenario, politics ceases to have as its primary goal the conquest of hegemony by symbolically violent yet ultimately peaceful means when a polyphonous and polymorphous social body is forced to speak with one voice. And what would happen if there were no consensus regarding who can enter (and under what conditions) the daily parliamentary debates—as happened repeatedly in late nineteenth-century Colombia—once the long-sustained fiction of unanimity ceases to be upheld completely? In other words, when *pouvoir constituant* is desacralized, the factions represented in Congress will cease to recognize themselves and each other as part of the same *natural* community and state defined in the Constitution of the day. Instead, they take their respective places in a symbolically violent confrontation that may end with the *extra legem* obliteration of one party by another.

According to Marco Palacios, Colombia has historically been a "*país de ciudades.*"[70] The chronic weakness of the central state's coercive force and economic policies has made the rural population flock to the cities in perhaps greater numbers than in some of the neighboring republics. Paradoxically, the city's hypertrophied production of legal and paralegal discourses only increased widespread skepticism about the enforcement of specific laws and the general guarantees announced in each constitutional charter of rights. Colombia provides a good example of what Marx and Engels called the "juridical illusion" of contracts that cannot be enforced because the law is too weak and the parties involved do not believe that a free will is revealed in their signing (*The German Ideology* 58–61). The legal city was repeatedly challenged and most often overcome by the real city. The convergence of ideal and real polities in Colombia was probably not helped by the incorporation of Jeremy Bentham's and Antoine Destutt de Tracy's writings into the official school curriculum at different moments in the nineteenth century, whenever Liberal governments felt the need to undermine the theocentric mind-set still entrenched in civil society.

One of Bentham's key concepts, the "legal fiction," was more devastating to the building of the modern, Weberian state than Marx's juridical illusion because it was taught at schools as the *doxa* of emancipated republics wishing to *form* free-willed citizens. Bentham also equates legitimate discourse with translatability, which he discusses especially in connection with his concept of "legal fiction." In its simplest formulation, his "theory of fictions" contends that any abstract idea that cannot be translated into a concrete one is false. It thus challenges the institutions and protocols of philology and legal hermeneutics, reducing the culture of textual transmission to what Locke called dismissively "the copy of a copy" and "the hearsay of a hearsay" (*An Essay*

Concerning Human Understanding 2: 377–78). Both Destutt and Bentham set out to demystify the great abstract categories whose study did not stand the test of experience yet were legitimated by recourse to scholastic theology's *causa prima* or else were hypostatized in the sovereign people's universal will.[71]

To be sure, their purpose in doing this was not solely or mainly to unmask the Catholic Church's moral hypocrisy or expose the false consciousness that simultaneously conceals and unveils structures of domination in society. The Catholic imbued anti-Benthamite polemics in Colombia were as virulent under Bolívar as they were in the middle years of the Olimpo Radical, when Caro made his name as a ferocious controversialist following the reinstatement of Bentham's textbooks in the university curriculum in 1868. Bentham drew a problematic contrast between the devious fictions produced by lawyers and clergymen, on the one hand—these would be the "legal fictions" par excellence—and the poet's fictions, on the other:

> The Fictions of the poet, whether in his character of historic fabulist or dramatic fabulist, putting or not putting the words of his discourse in metrical form, are pure of insincerity, and, neither for their object nor for their effect have anything but to amuse, unless it be in some cases to excite to action—to action in this or that particular direction for this or that particular purpose. By the priest and the lawyer, in whatsoever shape fiction has been employed, it has had for its object or effect, or both, to deceive, and, by deception, to govern, and, by governing, to promote the interest, real or supposed, of the party addressing, at the expense of the party addressed. In the mind of all, Fiction, in the logical sense, has been the coin of necessity—in that of poets, of amusement—in that of the priest and the lawyer, of mischievous immorality in the shape of mischievous ambition; and too often both priest and lawyer have framed or made in part this instrument. (*Theory of Fictions* 18)

Contrary to the way in which he was misrepresented in Colombia, Bentham acknowledges here literary fictions' power to spur readers to action without necessarily making them confuse the truth of fiction—the excitement of the passions, as in satire, the dominant genre of poetry in Bentham's time—with factual truth. In the treatises on legislation, he also acknowledged that religious beliefs were a worthy source of morality, and that those who lost their faith could still live in conformity with those principles. The strong fictional component of religious belief could make a suffering people very brave, sustaining it in times of persecution, as any other strong set of civil principles and beliefs, or like even hope does. Leaving aside the fabulistic nature of the Bible and the saints' lives, Bentham and Miguel Samper found fault with the priest's and the lawyer's reiterated recourse to fictive discourses analogous to poetry, that is to say, with their excessive use of metaphors. The metaphorical nature of the Old Regime's religious and legal discourses prevented their audience's rational engagement with the *moral* basis implicit in religious belief and the subject's deliberate assent to the law. These audiences thus became an easy prey to the publicists' rhetorical manipulations, rhetoric being the main discipline privately taught by Colombia's Catholic Conservative teachers in their homes or in their small elite schools.

Priests and legists bestowed upon their fables of good and evil a theological or juridical authority (in some cases, the authority of theo-politics) that precluded any further discussion of the principles expounded therein. This conflation of genres enabled the reactionary lettered city's assumption of extraordinary faculties: the "literary-legislative mode"—as I like to call it—that became widespread in Colombia's public life (in the newspapers as well as Congress) encompassed, first, poems and speeches that transcended the scholastic rhetorical exercise in order to become repositories of political or religious doctrine, and second, political speeches and government messages [*proclamas*] that sought to elicit an emotional rather than a rational response from the targeted audience.

Bentham admitted that the pressures of organized coexistence had long made societies speak about fictitious entities—abstractions—as if they were real ones. His three most frequently used examples are "rights," "duties," and "contracts."[72] All three are fictions of a first remove because they can be paraphrased by turning a single word into a more descriptive term or phrase. This term will, in its turn, be entered into a dialogue with a second paraphrase of the sensory perceptions awakened by the fictitious entity even if it is supposed to be a rational construct. Thus, the fiction of "rights" induces the real experience of "pleasure" whereas the performance of "duties" induces "pain" (*Theory of Fictions* 138).[73] Because of Bentham's choice of terms, Caro accused him of being a godless sensualist and an Epicureanist. He did the same to Destutt de Tracy.[74] It may be argued that, although Donoso and Caro devalued the rational-empiricist discourse on which the rising bourgeoisie had founded its idealist notion of analytical reason, their writings are crowded with images of martyrdom, apocalypse, and holy crusades. Starting from the opposite direction, Bentham and Destutt contributed to this ongoing undermining of philosophical discourse by constantly subjecting words to translations between conceptual matrices and epistemes. It seemed as if their translating machine had a primarily autotelic purpose, namely, to produce a cornucopia of empty or fictive signifiers whose quantitative abundance matches the lyrical and declamatory excesses found in the reactionaries' essays and pamphlets.

A fundamental linguistic problem lies at the heart of "ideology," whether we take this concept in the eighteenth-century rational-empiricist sense of creating a new anthropology of culture that is beyond idealism and metaphysics (the meaning of Antoine Destutt de Tracy's *Idéologie*), or in the Marxist sense of a system of illusory beliefs that mask relations of domination, making them alternately visible and invisible in the realms of social and economic organization.[75] Bentham's treatises on legislation became the most influential body of juristic thought taught intermittently at Colombian universities through much of the nineteenth century. Bentham was concerned with key aspects of both concepts of ideology, and repeatedly complained about the lack of reliable definitions for the primary motives behind accepted and unaccepted human actions. He was confident, however, about his interpretation of the signifying process, which he characterized as a chain leading from the empirical, subjective perception of raw data to the codification of universal laws, as a "species" gives way to a "genus" (note his eighteenth-century passion for the jargon of classification), a tenor to a vehicle, and real entities to fictitious ones. More so than Destutt, Bentham intersperses his discussions of lexicalized misnomers with occasional attacks on Old Regime institutions, referring to "Tyranny" and "Intolerance" as "the first-degree of the second degree Religion" (*Deontology* 76). Religions ask of their faithful that they accept authority at face value—dogmatically—renouncing arguments based on deductive reasoning or empirical demonstration. To this extent, they are conducive to tyrannical attitudes when they become politically organized and meddle in the institutions of representative government.

Bentham's most reiterated example of a legal fiction is the word "right," the second-degree fictitious entity that the Old Regime passed on to the liberal state. For him, even the discourse of universal rights conceals the existence of a complex system of "privileges" and "exemptions." Both terms are the species of a "superior genus 'right,' the word 'right,'" that is to say, "rights" is the mystifying translation of a privilege although normally the translative maneuver remains hidden from sight (*Deontology* 78). When it is not possible to produce demystifying countertranslations from the genus written in the law—"right"—back to the species left out of the law—"privilege"—the Benthamite or objectivist mode of exposition will shift from "translation" to "paraphrasis," which Bentham characterizes in the following manner: "By the word *paraphrasis* may be designated that sort of exposition which may be afforded by transmutation into a proposition, having for its subject some real entity, a proposition which has not for its subject any other than a fictitious entity" (*Theory of Fictions* 86).[76] Destutt adopted a more constructivist perspective than the Englishman. He contended that in reducing "complex" ideas to "sensations," language produced new knowledge in the manner of algebraic equations (108–9, 114–15).

In Bentham's system, one can exercise a right only because an existing positive law guarantees it. Likewise, the phrase "natural rights," which James Lorimer and Caro would like to see reinstated in modern codes, makes sense only by reference to a code of a different kind. Natural rights presuppose the existence of a "natural law," which means that they are twice removed from the institutional reality of positive legislation. Although natural law was discovered after positive laws came into existence, the latter are but imperfect realizations of a universal norm answerable only to human reason as directed by God, "the one Primary Source of natural law" (Lorimer 5, 15). As I will argue shortly, in positing the existence of a natural law, one moves from visible to invisible realities in the same ideological way in which medieval theologians moved from everyday meanings to sacred ones by means of the metaphorizing instrument called *translatio secunda*. Caro regularly uses both second-degree metaphors (in his writings about society and politics) and the *translatio secunda* (in his literary criticism and verse translations). In the remainder of this study, I will accordingly be centrally concerned with their convergence across Caro's broad range of writings and in nineteenth-century Colombia's cultural plurisystem generally.

"Religionists," as Bentham calls the enemies of the secular state, may wish to argue that "natural rights" can exist independently of civil jurisprudence and that they can be demonstrated and implemented each on their own, without the mediation of the law-and-order state. In this hypothetical case, positive jurisprudence as well as human institutions and corporations—including the Church, which for the ultramontanists succeeded Rome's earthly empire—would provide no inputs in regulating human engagements and affairs. If such "rights" as the social expectation that children be supported by their parents existed already in nature, the institution of marriage (whether civil or ecclesiastical) would not have had to be enforced by any positive law (Bentham, *Tratados* 93). The same applies to private property and numerous other institutions.[77]

The chief objection that Caro expressed to Bentham's critique in his accustomed incensed way, and that James Lorimer voiced in a more subdued manner, was that Bentham did not accept the juristic condition of *ius naturale*. This is certainly true, but just as important for Bentham is the blurring of distinctions between civil codes and penal codes. In his exposure of civil societies, one citizen's right to be free is implicitly and invisibly predicated only on the basis of another citizen's ability to deprive the former of his freedom, or to impose a penalty on him: "To understand the relation between these codes, is to be able to translate the one set of terms into the other" (*Theory of Fictions* cxxxi). Lorimer also complained about the objectivists' unwillingness to offer a transcendental theology with which to explain—in a century so anxious about the waning of political sovereignty's theological foundation— the sufferings, feuding, and schisms that continued to afflict society despite its many triumphs and social conquests in the recent past. By contrast, for Bentham, only positive laws may be said to exist, and even these may have a fictive existence most of the time. Citizen rights are just a metaphor enabled by civil law's already conflicted existence as a hypostasis of arbitrary penalties legitimated only by reference to the state's monopoly of coercive power. What Caro and theo-political proponents of *ius naturale* called theological punishments was translated by Bentham into human punishments enforced by the stronger members of society upon the weaker ones in a manner not entirely unlike that in which Hobbes realistically conceived of the social contract. Utilitarianism's simultaneous *demiraculizing* of both "rights" and "sins" entailed their downgrading to humanly inflicted penalties besides reversing the priority formerly accorded to *translatio secunda/translatio secundum*. The spiritual amelioration—by means of *translatio* qua *metafora*—of the literal meaning found in a text other than Scripture and religious doctrine finally met its match in Bentham's philological downgrading of the metaphorizing process that enabled the consecration of theological fictions in a code of law.

Caro approached the question of *translatio secunda*'s eschatological symbolism in "La religión y la poesía" (1882). In this work, he correlates experimental science with divine inspiration at the same time as he condemns "positivism" (an important element in *liberal* philology and jurisprudence) for its focus on the prosaic and for turning away from the world of the ideal, away from "fictions" in Bentham's derogatory sense (*Artículos y discursos* 307–8). This is how Caro arrives at the nucleus of his defense of *translatio secunda*—the *regimen duplex* of translation—in modern poetry, which I am here presenting as the antithesis of Bentham's *demiraculizing* paraphrasis:

> Ideality posits the existence of a supernatural world; invisible types to which must conform our acquired notions of truth and the forms of beauty that we know. Visible creatures are signs of divine thoughts [Las criaturas visibles son signos de pensamientos divinos]: Creation is a book of symbols, God's poem. And the greater the poet will be who is capable of translating the symbolism of the universe into human speech. For this reason, the language of poetry is eminently metaphorical. The arts in general engage in images and fictions filled with a deeper meaning: its purpose is not to photograph, but to represent, to approach divine revelation by means of the symbols that are found in the forms of creation. (*Artículos y discursos* 309–10)

For Caro, true poetry involves more than literature per se; it addresses the "literary-theological question" [la cuestión teológico-literaria]. Virgil is already a "theologian-poet" (in Gaston Boissier's formulation) while all later pagan authors can be converted *a lo divino* so long as their "negative side" [lado malo] is balanced out by "the energy of a burning feeling susceptible of being rectified and sent on the right path" (*Artículos y discursos* 321).

Caro's position was remarkably close to the *claustralis* tradition's understanding of *translatio* qua *metafora* as a symbolic transposition of meanings from the visible to the invisible world. As the Neothomistic intellectual historian Marie-Dominique Chenu showed in his survey of twelfth-century sacred philosophy, the mental operation proper to symbolism was "*translatio*," which he defines as "a transference or elevation from the visible sphere to the invisible through the mediating agency of an image borrowed from sense-perceptible reality. This is what we mean by 'metaphor,' except that here the term had a particular orientation; metaphor was obedient to the necessities imposed by transcendent realities, above all in pseudo-Dyonisian theology" (138).

Having thus outlined a historical framework for the resurgence of a theology of the word in nineteenth-century Colombian politics, I can now reassess Bentham's objectivist critique of symbolism (whether eschatological or political) in the context of Claude Lefort's Marxist critique of nineteenth-century liberal ideologies. Ideology is for Lefort "materialized invisibility" because it plays out a structure of oppositions as if it denoted an irrevocable division in nature while simultaneously concealing the social divisions kept in place by those oppositions (*The Political Forms* 198). To be sure, oppositions also have a social history, even if it is possible to treat concepts as more or less stable ideas attached to words whose etymological history projects a deceitful continuity. A recurrent justification for the Conservative lettered city's indifference to the need to improve public education was that moral and intellectual talents were distributed unevenly at birth by divine Providence.[78] Those who favored *practical* education vis-à-vis Christian catechesis for strictly *practical* purposes could thus be stereotyped as atheists even when they were God-fearing Catholics. We can then concur with Lefort's assertion that ideology is "the sequence of representations which have the function of re-establishing the dimension of society 'without history' at the very heart of historical society" (*The Political Forms* 201).

For Lefort, ideology is also a discursive frame whose encyclopedic breadth may be used to make the bare facts of domination appear as facts of scientific knowledge circulated through cultural institutions (*The Political Forms* 185).[79] For instance, the social and intellectual elites in mid-nineteenth-century Colombia arrogated to themselves privileges that were at odds with the idea of an inclusive and participatory republican regime. To continue with the battles over the universality of primary instruction, many Neogranadine Liberals stopped supporting compulsory primary education sponsored by the state when they began to realize that the more educated laboring poor were not likely to become Liberals, but socialists or anarchists instead, as was already happening in Europe and the River Plate metropolis. These Liberal misgivings notwithstanding, Conservatives routinely abused progressive politicians and publicists—not necessarily radical ones—calling them communists, anarchists, socialists, heretics, atheists, freemasons, barbarians, and even terrorists.[80] They *positivized* and *objectified* their fear of a heterogeneous and politically marked community in a multisided series of threats that seemingly covered the entire spectrum of possible imperfections and deviations preventing their *communitas perfecta* from achieving perfection. This completion could not be predicated on the basis of an all-encompassing inclusiveness (Lefort's "democratic invention"), but rather on the moral exclusion of other groups seen as fringe elements that militated against the existing political system. Augustine's *De civitate Dei* provided the model for the insurrectionist politics of sacred communities.

Slavoj Žižek has written that the irrational projection of one's negative identity onto a heterogeneous, contingent *other* construed as a foil to one's seamless self-image is the quintessential ideological position of modern populist politics. For the Slovenian philosopher, "'[i]deology' is also the name for the guarantee that *the negativity which prevents Society from achieving its fullness does actually exist*, that it has a positive existence in the guise of a big Other who pulls the strings of social life" (Butler et al. 100–1; emphasis in the original). At the risk of simplifying an admittedly more complex set of tensions, I will add that nineteenth-century movements in favor of enforced *laïcité* legitimated themselves as the engine that propelled the advent of a "full society." In doing so, they represented the Church as *the Other* that prevented such a perfect community from coming into being. Conversely, the Church routinely represented the secular state as its satanic antagonist, for which endeavor it took Augustine's *civitas Dei/civitas terrena/civitas diaboli* triad as its primary model. Furthermore, the Church held on to the fiction that it had always been a sovereign corporation, the locus in which the machinery of the providential *translatio imperii* was set into motion, graciously making the concession of civil government to the state. This is why debates about the *ius patronatus* remained such an important event in Colombia's public life and why Núñez staged the Republic's national reconciliation with Rome through a much-publicized and declamatory Concordat.

The Regeneración staged a shift away from earthly pursuits that had nothing spiritual or uplifting in them. This ideological contradiction was eloquently echoed in Alfredo Greñas's caricatures, whose grotesque desecration of national icons rang truer than the solemn use of the original state symbols. Consider "El escudo de la Regeneración" [The Regeneración's Coat of Arms] (1890), which is nearly as famous as the "Escudo de Colombia." Where the official coat of arms— in 1886 it had acquired almost all its present features—parades a cornucopia of gold and tropical fruits symbolizing Colombia's substantial mining and agricultural resources, Greñas's macabre baroque parody features the vacuity and sterility of a skull and bones. And where the official coat of arms foregrounds—right at its center—the Frigian cap (also called "Liberty cap"), symbolizing the republican freedoms brought about by the Revolution, Greñas placed the biretta worn by the Roman Catholic clergy whom Holguín and Caro invited into their administrations. The ecclesiastical lettered city was thus back in power. In a Lefortian reading of Greñas, one would point out how soon the cartoonist perceived that the king's transcendent body had been legitimated by the rotating offices of democratic representation. This explains his interest in depicting Caro as an absolutist ruler. He understood that the Regeneración had capitalized—through the magical trick of *pouvoir constituant*—on the disincarnated or disembodied condition of modern parliamentary politics. In performing his own desecration, Greñas exposed the preexisting frauds of both Liberalism and the Regeneración, letting the traces of those mystifications remain alternately visible and invisible, and inviting his audience to recuperate them as *ideology*—not through identification with either the Church or the state, *ius naturale* or positive codes, but through the *critique* of both.

Figure 2 "Escudo de Colombia" (undated print). Courtesy of Spain's Biblioteca Nacional (Madrid).

As Žižek put it in an earlier statement, the "ideological misrecognition" that takes place in the process of being interpellated as a subject by cultural or political institutions may summon us to "accept a certain delusion as a condition of our historical activity, of assuming a role as agent of the historical process" (*The Sublime Object* 2). We may construe the transfers between *ius naturale* and positive legislation, and between philology and jurisprudence, as the strategic transformation of particulars into universals or as the politics of hegemony as usual (as Lefort still does to a degree). Whichever path we choose, it becomes apparent that the extent of ideological concealment in public discourse practiced under Caro's "regime of translation" had seemingly no end. Colombian ultramontanists defended the right of Catholics not to be offended by secular policies; they represented themselves as persecuted martyrs who had a monopoly on suffering; and they promoted the fiction that beggars and Indians lived lives of privilege, thanks to the elites' charity and paternalistic oversight of their rights and obligations. The creoles' flaunting of their "natural rights" and "inalienable freedoms," including their

EL ESCUDO DE LA REGENERACION.

Figure 3 "El escudo de la Regeneración," *El Zancudo*, vol. 2, no. 12 (July 20, 1790): p. 45.

patriotic *and* Catholic sacrifice for the unlettered masses who daily received their Christian love, was an instance of what Bentham calls "privileges." José Eusebio Caro (1817–1853), Sergio Arboleda, and Miguel Antonio Caro were the three master demagogues whose command of doctrinal commonplaces and populist rhetoric allowed them to deny the auspicious social transformations that were taking place outside Bogotá's and Popayán's colonial cloisters. Through an analysis of the Colombian lettered city's literary productions, this book seeks to expose its translational strategies for concealing social and economic privileges as natural rights. Taking my cue from Bentham, I will often proceed in the opposite direction, paraphrasing the reactionary *letrados'* defense of their rights as attempts at perpetuating creole privileges whose survival required the reactivation of a theologico-political horizon in public life.[81]

CHAPTER TWO

THE REGIME OF TRANSLATION IN CARO'S COLOMBIA

The Reactionary Lettered City and the Twilight of Parliamentary Democracy

This chapter sets out to interpret the relation of translational practices to the exercise of power in late nineteenth-century Colombia. To this end, it surveys a broad spectrum of writings by Caro, whose literary output is inextricably bound up with his career in politics. Along the way, I also explain how theorists of sovereignty whose ideas enjoyed wide currency in Caro's time—from Augustine to Juan de Mariana and on to Antonio Nariño— often resorted to the tropes of translation (notably the *translatio imperii* and the *pactum translationis*) to signify the transmission and legitimation of political authority. Although Caro does not mention such concepts by name, he engages them in ways that anticipate Carl Schmitt's powerful critique of parliamentary democracy. Caro is today best remembered by the legislative efforts he undertook between 1885 and 1898 (especially in the Regeneración's early years), when his term as omnipotent vice president ended. Concurrently with these seemingly *étatiste* pursuits, and stretching back to around 1870, he also produced a long series of pamphlets and tracts against positive jurisprudence and the legislative state. In his pamphlets, he argued, as he did in the notes to the *Código civil* (see chapter 1), for the need to use the *traditio* as well as canon law to cast light on ambiguous points of doctrine in civil jurisprudence and to legislate in conformity with the nation's delicate Catholic sentiments.

Under Caro, the executive branch directly appointed the Supreme Court judges and the attorney general [*procurador general*], who routinely validated his decisions, and used illegal means to prevent nonmembers of the National Party from being elected to Congress (Liberals also opted out of the elections for the most part). As a result, a hydra-headed single branch of government was de facto created to be in charge of proposing, implementing, and overseeing the exceptional daily decisions forced upon individuals and the nation as a whole. Caro, the juristic philologist and grammarian, became a historical-decisionist jurisprudent, or simply a *decider* with remarkably few limits on his office and no accountability to an autonomous branch of government. As Carlos Martínez Silva wrote in *El Repertorio Colombiano* in November of 1896, the sessions of Congress held during that year left no record of deliberations and issued only a handful of inconsequential dispositions. Caro did not allow a captive Congress or his ministers to introduce bills that would yield important legislation. He preferred to use instead the edict signed collectively by the cabinet, but he most often resorted to executive verbal orders that he communicated directly to any of the following: a high-ranking army officer, one of his cabinet members, a magistrate, or the police. The important decisions affecting the nation, including abusive and illegal ones, were made discretely by Caro behind the scenes and sanctioned after the fact by the government press through the publication of succinct telegrams and carefully written letters sent to these venues' respective directors. A simulacrum was constantly being created by which *the people* writing these letters to the newspapers spontaneously applauded every one of Caro's arbitrary acts (Martínez Silva 2: 339–43).

The various versions of the *translatio* that coexisted in the later nineteenth century have historically been attached to specific Spanish American models of the state. As was indicated in chapter 1, it is now a critical commonplace to refer to the proliferation of text-bound images of a modern bureaucratic state and its attendant cultural and educational institutions as the emergence of a "lettered city" [*ciudad letrada*]. The concept of *ciudad letrada* should be placed at the center of debates around uneven modernization in nineteenth-century Spanish America because the ideal polity it designates existed in contradistinction to the polymorphous and untamed *ciudad real* that it desperately tried to conceal through the work of ideology. The Colombian *letrados'* interest in high culture and its attendant institutions (the Colombian Academy, the Bogotá Atheneum, the literary prizes and honors that constantly separated the elite producers of discourse from its consumers, and so forth) did not necessarily carry over into a related interest in fostering public instruction. As a matter of fact, the reactionary *letrados* who favored a career in letters over the bureaucratic track as a means of social advancement often lacked the conventional academic accreditation of a university degree (Carlos Holguín was the Regeneración's only degree-holding head of the executive branch), and could even brag about being self-taught. Caro in particular went so far as to suggest that intellectual gifts were transmitted from one generation to the next, following a logic analogous to the transmission of original sin (*ex traduce peccatum est*) or the divine right of kings (*studia et potestas ex Deo sunt*).

The few families that constituted Bogotá's political elite tried to distance themselves from the masses by promoting a cosmopolitan culture that required expertise in history, classical philology, and the knowledge of colonial law. At the same time, between 1860 and 1930 numerous Colombian statesmen (including several presidents) expressed their concern with the less than satisfactory language proficiency shown by their notoriously underprivileged fellow citizens. This anxiety is borne out by the titles of the books written by these same presidents and their close associates and allies in a country where illiteracy rates reached over 80 percent of the total population in Caro's time and newspapers that were not government-sponsored normally did not reach a circulation of 1,000 copies. Among such language manuals were *Compendium of Castilian Grammar: A Neogranadine's Handbook for Teaching* [Compendio de gramática castellana...por un granadino dedicado a la enseñanza] (1853), by Santiago Pérez; *Basic Elements of Pronunciation* [Tratado primero de la pronunciación] and *Elements of English Pronunciation, Prosody, and Orthography* [Elementos de pronunciación, prosodia y ortografía de la lengua inglesa], both prepared sometime in the 1860s by Lorenzo María Lleras; the monumental *Critical Notes on the Language of Bogotá* [Apuntaciones críticas sobre el lenguaje bogotano] (1867), by Rufino José Cuervo, the only major grammarian who did not hold a high state office, but was the son of a vice president and presidential runner-up; the impressionistic *Treatises on the Orthoepy and Orthography of the Castilian Language* [Tratados de ortología y ortografía de la lengua castellana] (jointly pub. in 1859), by José Manuel Marroquín; *Notes on the English Language* [Apuntaciones sobre la lengua inglesa. Obra que contiene un tratado sobre las preposiciones...] (1883) and *A Complete Course in Italian for Spanish Speakers according to Robertson's Method* [Curso completo de lengua italiana, según el método de Robertson, para el estudio de los que hablan castellano] (1875), both by César Conto, which Cuervo praised highly; *Rudiments of Latin Prosody* [Nociones de prosodia latina] (1893), by Miguel Abadía Méndez; and Caro's *Latin Grammar for Spanish Speakers* [Gramática de la lengua latina para uso de los que hablan castellano] (1865; third ed., 1876)—coauthored with Cuervo—and the best-selling yet arid *Treatise on the Participle* [Tratado del participio] (1870).

Caro also encouraged the careers of two protégés who were first introduced to him as authors of grammatical works. One was Marco Fidel Suárez, the author of *Studies on Grammar: An Introduction to Mr. Andrés Bello's Philological Works* [Estudios gramaticales. Introducción a las obras filológicas de D. Andrés Bello] (1885), an earlier version of which won a prize from the Colombian Academy and was published with an introduction by Caro. The other was Enrique Álvarez Bonilla, whose *Treatise on Spanish Grammar* [Tratado de gramática castellana] (third ed., 1881) rescued him from provincial obscurity. In Bogotá, Álvarez Bonilla would later publish a *Treatise on Rhetoric and Poetics* [Tratado de retórica y poética] (1893) at a time when his career as Regeneración *letrado* was well under way. More than increasing the literacy rates among the citizenry, these books contributed to increasing their authors' intellectual and political capital as well as the authority of the administrations that gave them employment. The Regenerators aimed to impose an interpretive monopoly on Colombian culture and history.[1] Both Álvarez Bonilla and Suárez became directors of the Biblioteca Nacional and members of the Colombian Academy (like Caro), and served in Caro's cabinets. The two caught his attention because of their interest in grammatical studies and their willingness to supplement a very conservative perspective on language usage with an ultramontane political outlook. Álvarez Bonilla may have been a less eccentric character than the spiritually exuberant and tormented Suárez. Nevertheless, he was adept at turning his academic work (his textbooks in jurisprudence, history, and rhetoric written for their use at the universities) into opportunities for proselytizing. These pedagogical works repeatedly defend, in less than subtle ways, the divine right of rulers, the division of society into classes along hereditary lines, and the state's subordination to the Church.

Caro was aware of the political and pedagogical capital accorded to grammarians and scholars of rhetoric in the Hispanic world. Not only did he attempt to fashion his career after that of Bello—the paradigmatic republican grammarian, *letrado*, and legislator—but he was also well acquainted with the noted literati (many of them translators and grammarian-poets) who constituted Spain's first lettered city of grammar and translation. This network of literati emerged during the years of Bonapartist rule in France and Spain. It featured a number of prominent Frenchified authors who embraced radical politics to varying degrees only to be deconverted from liberalism to either absolutism or skeptically disenchanted positions. Because they all had a liberal past, as did Bello, but were not known (unlike Bello) for their Catholic piety, Caro was very ambivalent toward some of them including Manuel José Quintana, José María Blanco-White (a self-exile Catholic priest converted first to Anglicanism and later to Unitarianism), Leandro Fernández de Moratín, José Mamerto Gómez Hermosilla, Alberto Lista (the only strong Catholic), Antonio Capmany, and Vicente Salvá (perhaps the only one to remain a bona fide liberal to the end of his life).

Although Bello considered Salvá to be the author of the most important Spanish grammar book of the earlier nineteenth century, Caro predictably cites him very sparingly for political reasons. For his part, Gómez Hermosilla went from applauding the French Revolution's early achievements to becoming a proponent of absolutism. He embraced Hobbes and Mariana instead of Bossuet's Gallicanism or Bellarmino's proto-ultramontanism, thus breaking away from the orthodox line of counterrevolutionary discourse first laid out in de Maistre's and Bonald's writings. To Gómez Hermosilla's credit, he did not recant his early abandonment of theo-political arguments, which makes him a more reliable judge of human actions and institutions than those who at times felt compelled to feign the religious fervor demanded or expected by their ultramontane allies. To varying degrees, Colombian statesmen such as Núñez, Holguín, Marroquín, and Valencia had to flaunt a pious observance that was not entirely indigenous to their temperaments.

No other country in the modern history of the West has had so many men of letters and rhetoricians who occupied the highest political offices.[2] In fact, membership in the Colombian Academy (founded by Caro, Marroquín, and José María Vergara y Vergara in 1871), like starting a successful newspaper, often became a springboard for a presidential hopeful.[3] If a learned candidate belonged to the Conservative Party, he also needed the approval of Bogotá's Archbishop, on whom the Regeneración bestowed the rare privilege (not listed in the Concordat of 1887) of handpicking the Conservative candidate at the presidential election out of the group of contenders. Although he did not follow exactly on this path, Caro became the undisputed head of state in 1894, upon the death of Rafael Núñez, under whom he had served as vice president with full executive powers since 1892.

He was then the acclaimed translator of Virgil's entire body of poetry (1871–1876), numerous other ancient and modern poems (including several by Lamartine) collected in the volume *Poetry Translations* [Traducciones poéticas] (1889), and some of Leo XIII's encyclicals and poems. He was also the author of a potpourri of anti-Enlightenment essays called *Studies on Utilitarianism* [Estudio sobre el utilitarismo] (1869); the militant *Catholic Unity and the Multiplicity of Worships* [La unidad católica y la pluralidad de cultos] (1873); the short economic tract *Notes on Credit, Public Debt, and Paper Money* [Apuntes sobre crédito, deuda pública y papel moneda] (1892); the collection of articles *The Freedom of the Press* [Libertad de imprenta] (serialized in 1888; pub. in book form in 1890)—where he of course writes against such freedom, since it was one of liberalism's main tenets; an *Elocution Handbook* [Manual de elocución] (1888); and a critical edition of Bello's metrical studies (1882). Caro was also the intelligence behind the anthologies *Romancero colombiano* (1883), compiled by the Chilean diplomat José A. Soffia, and *Parnaso colombiano* (1886), compiled by Julio Áñez; he was the editor of *Poesías de Bello* (1882), *Obras escogidas de José Eusebio Caro* (1873), and *Poesías de Julio Arboleda* (1883), and the author of four volumes of original poetry and numerous articles and essays, some of them collected in his lifetime in *Artículos y discursos. Primera serie* (1888).

By the time he reached Colombia's highest executive office, Caro had long been advocating the Catholics' right of resistance to the secularizing policies of the parliamentary legislative state created by the Liberals, often calling his ultramontane supporters to a just war against Liberalism. On becoming head of state, however, he lapsed into the office to which he had analogized the Liberals' decentralizing policies, that of a *tyrannus ab exercitio*, defined by Carl Schmitt as he "who arrives at the seat of power in a legal manner, but then exercises and abuses power badly and tyrannically" (*Legality and Legitimacy* 29). It was ironic that a Liberal-dominated Congress unable to enforce its own legislation in the nation's dismembered territory should be called tyrannical, especially given the legal status of smaller administrative units as sovereign states, each with its own president and Legislative Assembly. The abusive concentration of power in just one body or branch of government was an impossible proposition until the Regeneración's centralist Constitution was approved in 1886. The new charter was soon called "monarchical"—not without apprehension and alarm—by some of Caro's fellow Regenerators" (Hernández Peñalosa 123). Like Schmitt, Caro also held that legitimacy and sovereignty are the privileges of the ruler who interprets the "community will," frees it from both the bondage of extremist parliamentary groups and arithmetical majorities without moral content, and enforces decisions that have the legal weight of a statute.[4] As Schmitt famously wrote, "Sovereign is he who decides on the exception" (*Political Theology* 5).[5] Despite reaching the state's highest elected office and writing in part a republican constitution for a country that was named República de Colombia in 1886, Caro was a monarchist. This already becomes apparent in his early poem "Maximiliano" (1867), in which the executed Emperor Maximilian I of Mexico is memorialized as a self-sacrificing Catholic "príncipe" while the secular patriots led by Benito Juárez are called "usurpador infame" (*Obras poéticas: Musa militante* 26–29). This poem was intertextualized in Alfredo Greñas's depiction of Caro as a bloody absolutist king in the caricature titled "A Candidate's Dream" [Sueño de un candidato], which presents Caro adorned with the symbols of kingship, but treats him also as a ruthless despot from whose wall hangs the picture of a firing squad performing its miserable duty. A slightly earlier, lighter treatment of Caro's unsuitability to govern casts him as Cervantes's unlettered Sancho Panza (left) being offered before titular President Núnez (Don Quixote, center) the imaginary realm of Barataria as a practical joke in the presence also of Holguín. Both cartoons date from the summer of 1891 (Caro succeeded him at the helm of the executive branch the following year).

Also like Schmitt, Caro longed for a return to a monarchical order in the broad sense of the rule of the Thomistic *unus*, on whom the *potestas* to make new law without parliamentary approval (and yet still within the formal bounds of a parliamentary democracy) could be conferred by promulgating a constitutional article regulating "extraordinary powers" [facultades extraordinarias]. In writing and enacting the Constitution of 1886, the Colombian polymath did just that.[6] His career illustrates the course of action that Schmitt advises for those who wish to transfer a nation's sovereignty from its legislative central parliament (which often mortgages it to the smaller states) back to an authoritarian ruler with the power to make independent decisions and act upon them expeditiously. Caro was encouraged

Figure 4 "Donde se ofrece a Sancho el gobierno de la ínsula Barataria," *El Zancudo*, vol. 3, no. 28 (June 14, 1791): p. 109. Repr. in final issue of *El Zancudo*: vol. 5, no. 49 (October 11, 1791).

by the fact that several committee members in charge of drafting the new antiliberal Constitution of 1886 were themselves former Liberals with large constituencies won over to Núñez's program for national regeneration.

In the making of the Regeneración's Constitution several protocols of legal theory were violated. There was neither a "Congreso Constituyente" proper [*assemblée constituante*] chosen by those who qualified for the franchise in a country that had for a brief spell already known universal suffrage with gender and age restrictions nor was the finished *carta magna* voted at a referendum.[7] Furthermore, numerous members of the extraordinary assembly went on to assume executive offices or serve as ordinary congressmen. This situation involved the same conflict of interest denounced by Quintana at the Cortes de Cádiz because it violated the principle that extraordinary delegates should always protect—according to Sieyès—"the national interest alone" (*Qu'est-ce que le tier état?* 130–32, 138–39). Caro was thus able

Figure 5   "Sueño de un candidato," *El Zancudo*, vol. 4, no. 31 (July 5, 1791): p. 121.

to convince Núñez's government of the need to promulgate a new constitutional charter that allowed the president to declare, by means of his extraordinary faculties, who the state's foreign and domestic enemies were. It also allowed him to establish the criteria for democratic citizenship.[8]

The Constitution of 1886 featured a polemical article (no. 121) authorizing the president to assume at will *facultades extraordinarias* and included an appendix containing a series of transitory dispositions (articles K and L) that allowed the *medidas de excepción* already in place to prevail over the new fundamental law. To paraphrase Sieyès's and Schmitt's useful juridical discussions, Caro devised a form of extended *pouvoir constituant* that he was always careful to present as existing contradictorily within the limits of republican institutions and constitutional guarantees. This mechanism de facto suspended the current legal order by treating government policy as a series of exceptions to the rule of law that could not be monitored, let alone challenged, by the legislative or the judiciary (both now controlled by the Regeneración's strong executive branch). When he assumed the executive vice presidency in 1892, following in the footsteps of his brother-in-law Carlos Holguín, Caro was already acting like a "sovereign" rather than a "commissarial" dictator, although legally he was neither. Six years earlier, he had framed the new Constitution with a series of transitory dispositions that broadened the gap between legality and legitimacy, while in his speeches and various other writings he continued to invoke God's Providence and the dogma of infallibility as a higher law.[9] His *pouvoir constituant* had therefore a theological foundation, which encompassed the Neogranadine *magna carta* but remained safely outside of it. In sum, the Regeneración's rule of Colombia between 1888 and 1900 by means of transitory and verbal orders that at times contradicted the text of the retrograde Constitution of 1886 amounted to declaring a permanent state of exception.[10]

González Vigil will help me flesh out a secondary aspect of my argument. The absoluteness of power, he writes, is nowhere better represented than in a ruler's ability to make his spoken words enacted ad hoc into law. The absolutist pope imitates the absolutist temporal ruler in displacing the authority from the uttered proposition's logical and rational plausibility to the person who utters it. In other words, the authority of reason (the Enlightenment's key to truth) is taken over by the reason of authority (the Old Regime's key): "If the Pope speaks with excommunicated people with the intention of giving them the absolution, the excommunicated person is absolved. This is so because the Prince grants freedom at will [con su solo querer], as the *Digesta* states. The Highest Pontiff grants gifts or proffers oracles aloud [de viva voz], like the Supreme Ruler" (González Vigil, *Compendio* 91). Still, for these speech acts to be felicitous, they need to take place in a constitutionally correct environment. According to the absolutist doctrine set down by Pope Innocent III (1161–1216), the first self-denominated "Vicar of Christ" and one of the chosen antagonists of González Vigil, the pope's chief prerogative is both spiritual and temporal since princes were men capable of great sins, and only the pontiff can judge when their sinfulness may put the principality at risk. The pope thinks and acts *ratione peccati*—he administers on earth the regime of sin.

The pope's superior *potestas* was based very loosely on the passage in Matthew 7:13–14, in which the gates of heaven are said to be opened with Peter's key. According to Innocent III, the pontiff could overrule the decision made by the German assembly or high council of princes (the Diet) to elect an emperor. Pope Innocent reversed the terms of the relationship between the ordinary rules and the exception. Although he arrogated to himself extraordinary powers of interpretation that only Christ could have as both prophet and Son of God, he represented those powers as coming directly from Peter to him, through his legitimate succession to the Roman chair. Nowhere in the Bible is it suggested that Peter had higher powers than the other apostles, or that the latter could not pass their extraordinary powers—if they indeed had them—on to their successors, whose modern counterparts gathered periodically at the councils of bishops. According to González Vigil, who was an excommunicated prelate (a "renegade prelate," as the phrase went), the equation of extraordinary faculties with the "writing of sacred books," in which such claims could be made, applied only to the early Church, which was truly a persecuted entity and long remained in need of proselytizing by any means possible. Once the evangelizing of the Roman world was completed, these miraculous and exceptional events became very sparse, rendering providentialist philosophies of history very problematic. All along, the sovereignty of the Church continued to reside in the national synods of bishops rather than in the pope's *ecclesiastical city of translation*—the Vatican Curia. In conclusion, for the Peruvian theologian, only Peter was truly the Vicar of Christ, and only he could have had "extraordinary faculties" with no term limit attached to them *along with* the rest of the apostles (*Compendio* 84–85).[11]

How a constitutional president's unconstitutional orders can become law is as much the concern of jurisprudence as it is of literary studies since rhetoric and the performance of legitimacy play a key part in that transformation. The compilers of Justinian's *Instituta* quote Gaius's contention that a verbal or written command from the emperor pronounced in due form can be construed and received as a *lex* to all purposes and effects: *legem esse constat* (10). No advocate for the executive branch's primacy over the legislative assemblies had ventured to say as much prior to Ulpian. Gaius added that it had never been doubted that an emperor's will, when expressed in a constitutionally adequate setting, should receive the attention owed to a *lex*: *legis habet vigorem* (Justinian 10).[12] Gaius's express words also state that any imperial edict, like any *senatus consultum*, should be assigned the status of a *lex*: *legis vicem optineat*. He gives one reason and one alone for his valorization of the power to decide over the power to deliberate, namely, that "the emperor himself receives his *imperium* by virtue of a *lex*" [*cum ipse imperator per legem imperium accipiat*] (Justinian 11). This is, to be sure, a fantastic instance of *petitio principii*, which appropriately captures the Regeneración's spirit: because the law authorizes my becoming king, as king I will make the very law that sanctions my assumption of kingly prerogatives.

The next step in this breach of legality will be to that the sequence of "deliberation" followed by "decision" characteristic of classic constitutionalism can be reversed. This is what Augustus (Octavius) did in his insurrectionist dealings with the Senate in the years 37–27 BC. The words that you act upon as if they carried the force of law without emanating from a legislative body, can retroactively—ex post facto—be granted the status and force of law. In other words, once you have been invested with the supreme magistracy by legal-constitutional means, the field is cleared for the assumption of exceptional powers. The more the breach of legitimacy (breaches of legality are a different matter) goes unperceived in the public sphere, the more frequent becomes the subversion of the legal order. Legitimacy's opacity made literature's opinion-making and paralegislative powers all the more important in a country that had long worshipped its *letrado*-literati. I take up this topic again in chapter 4 with reference to Bolívar and Augustus Octavius. Suffice it to say for now that as Regenerators, Caro and Holguín promoted the issuing of illegal, unconstitutional edicts and government dispositions from 1885, when the antepenultimate Liberal rebellion of the century broke out. These arbitrary acts of government would not be derogated by Caro's Constitution of 1886, while many articles of a republican bent in the same charter would not be developed for years to come. Still others would be suspended immediately on the excuse that the country was immersed in a prolonged state of internal commotion.

The expression of linguistic, religious, and political differences could thus be banned from public life even if they could not be completely outlawed. Moreover, one of the striking similarities between Caro and Schmitt is their restrictive notion of democracy, which they subordinate to the preexisting entelechies of nation and *Volksgeist*:

> The method of will formation through simple majority vote is sensible and acceptable when an essential similarity among the entire people can be assumed. For in this case, there is no voting down of the minority. Rather, the vote should only permit a latent and presupposed agreement and consensus to become evident. As noted, since every democracy rests on the presupposition of the indivisibly similar, entire, unified people, for them there is, then, in fact and in essence, no minority and still less a number of firm, permanent minorities. (Schmitt, *Legality and Legitimacy* 27–28)[13]

Caro articulates a definition just as narrow of Colombia as a nominally democratic nation, in which there is no longer room for the daily plebiscite fostered by the deconsecrated liberal state. On the contrary, identitary orthodoxies are enforced including the need for even the large indigenous population to identify with the Spanish language, the Catholic religion, and the institutions of paternalistic, semifeudal domination administered by the educated creole elite. Admittedly, the Liberals contributed their share to the vanishing of self-differentiated identities from Colombia's public sphere. However, under Caro's rule, Liberal *letrados* continued to be stigmatized as an unassimilable extremist minority and were often being equated with Indians. In "El darwinismo y las misiones" (1886–1887), Caro explicitly described Jorge Isaacs—the leader of a failed government-funded scientific expedition that Núñez approved in 1881—as a heretical lover of barbarian heathens and an unlettered philologist. What was all this fuss about? Although Isaacs was expected to produce a botanical or geographical study, he produced instead an "Estudio sobre las tribus indígeneas en el Estado del Magadalena" (1884), which lets the aboriginal Americans speak their own truth without the filter of Catholic doctrines. Caro found disgusting that the indigenes should have *evangelized* Isaacs in their customs in a naturalistic way while Isaacs would *not* attempt to bring the Gospel to *them*.

According to Caro, the Indians could not be directly approached by ethnographers or philologists, who had no business collecting data from heathens. There was no good reason either for these vernacular repositories to be preserved once an evangelizer had described them, as the missionary priest Rafael Celedón did in a well-known *Gramática, catecismo i vocabulario de la lengua goajira* (1878). As Isaacs corrected silently Celedón's transliterations without mentioning him, he was also questioning this Church representative's theo-political prerogative of translating everyday indigenous realities into an authoritative language that could only deal with the heathens in the dogmatically infallible context of evangelization. Once the missionaries succeeded in fixing the extant indigenous languages and cultures in their grammars and reports for later philologists to use them in comparative philology's "demonstration of linguistic laws," those languages could be destroyed through systematic acculturation (Caro, *Obras, tomo I* 1089–91). For the time being, however, any contact had to take place through the evangelizer's grammar book and by following a doctrinal approach; the indigenous peoples had to be quarantined until their *analogia fidei* was completed.

Isaacs had long attracted Caro's inquisitorial attacks after he turned away from the Conservative Party in which he started out in politics. In faithfully recording now the dignity and beauty of the unevangelized Indians' naïve vernacular speech, Isaacs also discoursed on the immanent value of primitive languages and Darwin's evolutionist hypothesis, which to Caro was the same as denying the divine origin of language and humankind.[14] The Colombian ultramontanists did not accept that there were such things as primitive peoples; these isolated tribes were *degenerate* creatures who had lapsed from God's way (as the Liberals did). Both groups could be instantly *regenerated* through the violence of conversion and their embrace of the Gospel.

For much of his adult life, Caro claimed to be *affiliated* only with the Catholic Party [Partido Católico], which had no legal existence (it was a kingdom not of this world, one might say) outside the pages of *El Tradicionista*, as Carlos Valderrama Andrade once remarked ("Estudio preliminar" xlvii). In an early issue of this periodical published in 1871, the grammarian turned jurist outlined this party's main tenets, including the problematic one of unconditional obedience to the temporal authority of preunification "Rome," which in his writings stands for the Vatican Curia, and more specifically for the popes' Latin encyclical letters. This program was to have two disastrous effects when Holguín and Caro became—in quick succession—chiefs of the executive in 1888 and 1892: the first was that the executive branch's accountability and the *pro tempore* enactment of the extraordinary faculties were fused to animate the *civitas Dei* into which Caro wished to transform the *ciudad letrada*. The second was that civil law was overshadowed by the writings that Rome produced throughout its history: the Latin Bible, the early commentaries, the hagiographic accounts of testimonies and saintly opinions (the *traditio*), the collection of encyclicals and related Vatican documents, and so forth, out of which evolved first a complex corpus of canon law and later the episcopal teachings conducted on the basis of the reason of authority (*magisterium*). As was mentioned in chapter 1, the highlighting of *traditio* in a civil code that did not do away with *ius naturale* and the signing of the Concordat attested to this development. These writings lent themselves better to interpretations performed through exegesis, hermeneutics, and philology than modern civil codes, which were usually written in a familiar register of the language; they were said to contain few (if any) ambiguous or polysemous meanings and generally omitted any reference to their history and transmission. Caro was aware of his privileged status as a prestigious grammarian (he was not a philologist proper although I occasionally treat him as one) and acclaimed poet (primarily a religious poet). In his hands, the interpretation of Colombian law and literature became an extension of patristics.

The momentum achieved by the Regeneración movement in the mid-1880s was a direct consequence of the Liberals' failure to articulate a cohesive national identity in the previous two decades, in which they exercised hegemony almost at will. The party was also gradually disintegrating into a series of factions more interested in advancing the particularist agendas of powerful families in increasingly autonomous regions than in serving the interests of the nation. This tendency of the party was best represented by the coercive institutions of the democratic state. To put it in Norberto Bobbio's apt terms, Colombian Liberalism proved unable to reconcile itself with the concept of an incrementally homogenizing, egalitarian, and inclusive set of democratic institutions. The integration of larger segments of the population in processes of decision making demanded the growth of the centralized coactive power, but this in turn restricted the sphere of action in which individuals could pursue their own self-interest outside the state's confines.[15]

There was also often little difference at the local level between the Liberal and Conservative elites in the way they violated the legal order. Colombian creoles from either side of the political spectrum had in general little need to change their thoroughgoing vertical understanding of social relations (women, minorities, the illiterate, and the poor remained almost politically invisible until the 1930s) since they were not challenged (unlike their Mexican and Venezuelan counterparts) by revolutionary movements.[16] For these reasons, divisions along party lines often masked long-standing family alliances and rivalries in local settings. To be sure, a series of more committed Liberal leaders (notably José Hilario López, Santiago Pérez, and Manuel Murillo Toro) tried to articulate a socially inclusive, stimulating participation from below (as the circles of artisans also did), but their efforts to enforce party discipline across the nation proved futile.[17] It can then be said that, in the nineteenth century, Colombia knew liberalism mainly by omission. It consisted in a loosely articulated policy of laissez-faire across the board and an ongoing derogation of recently approved laws and constitutional charters, each of which commanded very little respect and for a very short time. From a strictly economic standpoint, the fluidity of this ideology induced, on the one hand, an uneven process of social and economic development characterized by largely intuitive deregulation policies and habits, and, on the other, a preference for formulae of minimal government that did not allow the state to come fully into being as an interlocking network of participatory institutional apparatuses.[18] If one defining feature of Colombian Liberalism is to be found in the denigrating literature of the period, it is its programmatic adherence to the tenets of French *laïcité* and laissez-faire as well as federalism (and less often the extension of the suffrage). Such tenets contrasted sharply with the Spanish Empire's neofeudal and theocratic traditions that were still being nurtured by Conservative hardliners and the fringy ultramontanists whom only Caro was able to bring into mainstream Colombian politics.

The Regime of Translation in the City of Grammarians: Philology and Politics

As a working hypothesis, I will argue that Caro was a translator-poet who implemented a style of government in which his main assumptions about the transmission of culture (he was a historicist critic) informed his understanding of how the faculties of *imperium* and *dominium* (the main attributes of sovereignty) are legitimated and made into a tradition. Suffice it to say for now that *traducere* and *transferre* are the two Latin verbs most commonly used in the Latin literature on the legitimation of power from Thomas Aquinas and Otto von Freising to Francisco Súarez and Juan de Mariana. Caro's involvement in Colombia's political life in the last quarter of the nineteenth century was marked by his tendency to cast his concept of a decisionist regime of government (one which needed no external justification in a country used to abuses of power and a chronic fragmentation of sovereignty) in the guise of a philological fable about the transmission and authentication of quasi-sacred national texts.

The regime of translation sponsored by Caro is easily reconstructed by reference to the moments when his literary texts draw on powerful metaphors of government and when his juridical texts draw on metaphors of translation and textual production. It is not clear whether the Colombian reactionary was fully aware of this intratextual interpenetration of genres of editing and genres of legislating. Caro did accept and welcome the intertwining of hegemony's political and cultural forms, rehearsed most forcefully in the doctrine of *translatio imperii et studii*. Although he did not refer to this concept by its name, in his literary output he came close to giving it its classic formulation. As a translator, he rendered into Latin Rafael María Baralt's faux sonnet, which he—Caro—called "Greatness and Decay" [Grandeza y decadencia], producing a version titled "The Transfer of the Scepter" [Translatio sceptris]. "Grandeza y decadencia" was originally published as the opening of Baralt's lengthy historical ode inflected by neobaroque *desengaño* and titled "A España."[19] In fact, it is most likely that the longer poem evokes the topos of the consolatory glance backward made famous by Dante Alighieri: "And she to me: 'No sadness is greater than in misery to rehearse memories of joy'" [E quella a me: 'Nessun maggior dolore / che ricordarsi del tempo felice / ne la miseria'] (*Inferno*, Canto V, ll.121–23).[20] Caro's Latin version builds an argument for the Augustinian coming of the *civitas Dei* on what is—in Baralt's text—a conventional *translatio imperii* image in a larger poem concerned with Bourbon Spain's decline.

The two poems—the truncated Spanish original and the Latin version—begin with a rhetorical question: Is it possible for an empire to resurrect itself from its own ashes? Both use the image of the scepter that changes hands, and which Caro adopts as his title—*translatio sceptri*. However, Caro completely departs from the original's clichés by creating two parallel time schemes that unfold simultaneously as signified by the conjunction "dum" [whilst/until]: *dum gens alia exit adulta*. This "*other* nation," which in the original is the holder of sovereignty after the *translatio imperii* has been completed, becomes in the Latin text an underage nation that will grow into adulthood—*gens alia exit adulta*—under the *novum imperium*'s supervision. The nation growing into an "*other* adult" or "adult *other*" exists *in tempore suo* while the *novum imperium* exists, naturally, *ad aeternum*, another dimension inserted in line 6 of Caro's Latin, but which is absent from the original Spanish, as is the verb form in the future tense: "That nation which has been vanquished rests and will rest everlastingly" [Gens ea quae victa est, iacet aeternumque iacebit]. Baralt's succinct thought goes: "La que vencida fue, vencida yace." In sum, while Baralt's poem unfolds in civil history, Caro's does in ecclesiastical and civil history simultaneously, as do the chronicles of Augustine, Otto von Freising, Vergara y Vergara, and Groot. Caro's use of the Latin language, which at the time was for Colombians quickly becoming only the language of Catholic rescripts, suggests that his *novum imperium* (also absent from Baralt's poem) designates specifically the Vatican Church's contested sovereignty in the new paradigm of *laïcité* that had quickly spread across Europe and Latin America. The *novum imperium* will soon be realized at the onset of the Regeneración regime, with the signing of the Concordat—a *translatio* or *concessio* of sovereignty—that subjected the Colombian state to Rome, as Constantine was said to have subjected the Roman Empire to Pope Sylvester through his legendary Donation.

Caro also glossed the *translatio*'s defining features in the inaugural lecture delivered before the recently established Academia Colombiana and in the year of Bello's centenary (1881): "It is well known that Spain, in her age of greatest dominion, reproduces in relation to Italy the same features that characterized ancient Rome at the apex of her glory—the vanquisher of Greece in arms, but vanquished by her in letters" [Sabido es que España, en la época de su mayor poderío y en relación a Italia, repite los rasgos que caracterizaron a la antigua Roma, en los días de su grandeza, vencedora de Atenas en armas, por ésta vencida en letras] (*Obras, tomo III* 53). In the same essay, Caro states that the populace's shifting habits constitute a form of tyranny and despotism, which can only be accepted when purged of its imperfections through the philologist's benign intervention. Juristic philology has the exclusive power to elevate empirical data to the status of axioms and laws:

> I demand laws, be them as they be, because legality is a form of justice and justice is the realization of rights; and the older the law I discover, the more it satisfies me, since I see in its antiquity the loftiness of its origin and the beneficial effects of its institution. With the jurist I will acclaim the just legality, with the philosopher I will acknowledge it as enlightening, and with the theologian I will accept it as divine. (*Obras, tomo III* 44)

Here Caro emphasizes the mediating agency of the interpreter, who has the ability to go back to the "original" Latin roots of Western culture and so arrogates to himself the privilege of both interpreting the past and launching the future. In 1878, in a lecture that was part of a course given at Simón B. O'Leary's Academia Mercantil, he had dared to flesh out the connections between philology and law. The lecture was tellingly titled "The Question of Authority in Matters Pertaining to Language" [Cuestión de autoridad en materia de lenguaje]. The argument presented here is that lexicographers and grammarians cannot privilege the authority of "language usage" over that of distinguished writers. Doing this would be as disastrous as upholding the authority of "numerical majorities" vis-à-vis the authority of "the minority" [la minoría], which in this case are "writers."[21] New authors can probe into the traditional repository of words and ideas (preferably in older stages of the language), so that human progress is transformed into a long juridical and philological archaism: "when what has preceded us is more perfect than what exists in the present, we must look for progress in that which is gone by. In short: we must be very progressive and conservative, and even 'retrogressive' [retrógrados], looking for perfection in that which was more perfect than what we now have" (Caro, *Obras, tomo III* 1116).

Caro explains in his lecture, which followed an unusually nuanced discussion of competing philosophies of jurisprudence, how neologisms are created out of archaic words, and how new constitutions are written.out of antediluvian ones. He also makes the distinction between the "philosophical" and the "historical" schools. In Colombia, Bentham and Destutt de Tracy embodied the claims of the philosophical method; this was an optimistically rational-empiricist approach that shunned the historical record, while Bonald and de Maistre represented the historical method's demands on the present. In this pessimistic approach, the authority of human reason is rendered powerless before the historical record's overwhelming accumulation of past revolutions and cataclysmic events. The present and the future will inevitably repeat the past. Bello held the middle position, particularly in his writings about the Revolution of Independence, and was therefore criticized by both Liberals (they wrongly considered him too much of a historicist) and Conservatives (they rightly thought that there was too much of the impious rationalist in him).[22] Caro states that he also wishes to follow a middle path, which is neither radically historical nor radically philosophical. To say this in nineteenth-century Colombia was to declare allegiance to Wilhelm von Humboldt's moderate conservatism.[23] In reality, however, Caro finds Humboldt unsatisfactory because the German philologist did not embrace the worship of absolutist and archaic institutions, as they are represented in the literary and juristic language of the medieval and early modern periods. Caro fleshed out his position by adding that all innovations required by the urgency of the present's demands upon us can be devised through a revival of forgotten concepts and words found in the historical record.

This coining of new words is inseparable from the resuscitation of archaic usages, just as the promulgation of new constitutions resurrects archaic institutions. One important consequence of this argument is that—in Caro's scheme—philologists and grammarians are given an unprecedented power to deliberate and decide on points of legal doctrine. The historical jurisprudent Martínez Marina had encouraged fellow legal scholars, in the *Juicio crítico de la Novísima Recopilación* (1820), to do away with antiquities because they did not amount to a systematic or coherent treatment of the law and did not conform to the moral imperative of dispensing justice. Whereas Martínez Marina wanted a positive legislation whose only intelligibility requirement would be that of "knowing how to read," Caro, Arboleda, and Monsignor Carrasquilla insisted on preserving the historical specificity and unregularized literalness of archaic laws besides disauthorizing legal interpretations by those who did not know Latin and Roman law.

Martínez Marina's humane argument begins by pointing out that the chaos of Spanish legislation affects every citizen in very adverse ways: "hence the embarrassments and difficulties that we all experience in court and at the Cortes [en el foro], the arbitrary and specious interpretations, and the people's inability to learn the laws enacted for their own governance. The national code should not have been compiled only for scholars, for magistrates and jurisprudents, but for all the citizens. It must be accessible and familiar to all, understood by all: it is the people's catechism [el catecismo del pueblo]" (Martínez Marina, *Obras escogidas* 1: 372). The Colombian ultramontanists did not envision even one such reader-friendly positive code for as long the radical Liberals remained in power. They favored instead *ius naturale* and Christian doctrine. With the Regeneración's coming to power in 1884 and the ensuing enactment of its prohibitory legal instruments, the situation did not substantially change. The Regeneración's expeditious naturalization of the state of exception as its legal norm of choice continued to prevent the Republic of Colombia's citizens from the *normal* exercising of their rights. In contrast with Martínez Marina, Caro limited the range of the common people's reading to the exclusive teaching of saints' lives and the Catholic catechism.

Caro's worship of the archaism echoes Joseph de Maistre's argument against translating sacred texts.[24] In his chapter on translation in *Du Pape* (1819–1821), de Maistre makes an important digression on the topic of language variation and language immutability to argue that French is inadequate to conduct religious worship or convey the contents of sacred texts (I quote from the 1824 Spanish edition): "In short: any changing language is hardly suitable for an immutable religion" [En fin toda lengua mudable conviene muy poco á una religión inmutable] (1:249). De Maistre anticipated Caro in stating that Latin was the language not only of the Romans, who sought to "destroy the human race" [destruir el género humano], but also of the Spanish conquistadors, who came to America to "enlighten, heal, and save" the pagan Indian [á ilustrarle, á curarle, á salvarle] (*Del Papa* 1: 242); that like the Savior, Latin has shown the power to die and be resuscitated in order to live eternally (*Del Papa* 1: 246); and that the common people do not need to understand Latin to conform to their allotted role in the Catholic Church: "if they cannot understand the words, so much the better: the intelligence loses nothing while the respect increases. He who understands nothing, understands more than he who understands poorly" [si no entiende las palabras, tanto mejor: la inteligencia nada pierde, y el respeto gana. El que no comprende nada, comprende mejor que el que comprende mal] (*Del Papa* 1: 249).

In de Maistre as in Caro, language change is managed by a regime of law-making and law-applying policies that traces its authority back to a transcendent, ineffable source alternately hypostatized as "the language of the Roman Church" and "divine law." In turn, the interpretation of the law, that is, its application in the form of either exceptional measures or decrees by the state's administration, revolves around a linguistic regime of translation. This is very apparent in Caro's defense, before the Council of Delegates [Consejo Nacional de Delegatarios], of two documents he coauthored: the

Bases de reforma constitucional (1885) and the *Proyecto de Constitución* (1886), which are the source texts of the later Constitution of 1886, written single-handedly by him at least through article 45. Aware that many of the delegates were *letrados* with a hypertrophied flair for erudition and rhetoric, Caro made the following statements: (1) only he could interpret a draft written by him, since authorial intention did not admit of translations or interpretations by a proxy; (2) following a contrary argument, that the phrasing of specific points in the *Bases* and the *Proyecto* required a good deal of translation by an authorized deputy with legal expertise, since such points had not yet been cast in the form of law; (3) laws had to express universal interests rather than particular ones, and so all citizens had to abide by consecrated traditions even when these went against their conscience; and (4) he could not accept, as a philologist, the numerous emendations that other legislators (all more experienced and accredited jurists than Caro) suggested to the text of the *Proyecto*, since every single suggestion contained grammatical and semantic errors.

The last two points are eloquently illustrated by his later insistence on changing the following principle in the *Bases*: "The nation recognizes that the Catholic religion is that of the near totality of Colombians, principally for the following purposes" [La nación reconoce que la religión católica es la de *la casi totalidad* de los colombianos, *principalmente* para los siguientes efectos] (base 6ª; *Estudios constitucionales* 13; emphasis added). In the *Proyecto*, Caro phrased it thus: "The Roman-Catholic and apostolic religion is that of the nation: state powers will protect it and will make sure it is respected, as it is an essential element of the social order" [La religión católica, apostólica, romana es la de la nación: los poderes públicos la protegerán y harán que sea respetada, como esencial elemento del orden social] (art. 35; *Estudios constitucionales* 32). The Catholic majority, whether its members supported the establishment of a secular state or not, is here hypostatized in the universalist concept of a militantly Christian nation, while it is made explicit that religion will be used by the confessional state as a mechanism of control. This sentence would become verbatim article 38 of the promulgated charter. A Concordat was signed on the last day of 1887 by which complete control of the educational system at all levels (including the sanctioning of teachers) was handed over to the archbishop of Bogotá (arts. 12–14). At the same time, the Church recuperated its complete immunity in a civil court (arts. 2–4).[25] To put it in the idiom of canon law, the *judicium practicum* or freedom of conscience that the Church traditionally grants the faithful in modern liberal democracies was replaced by a *potestas indirecta in temporalibus*, that is to say, the Church instructed its members to follow their religious conscience irrespective of the demands of civil law.[26]

The figure of the lawmaker as translator of the doctrine contained in the Regeneración's jurisprudence draws attention to the mediating agency of the *letrado*. Translation becomes for Caro the space in which a text produced contingently in the present ceases to be contingent by projecting itself onto the past and receiving from this earlier moment a legitimating authority that it lacked until then. In other words, when writing is conceived in translational terms, one is driven to posit the existence of a source text that authorizes the production of a target text in the actual act of writing. It is in this same space that a secular continuity between time-bound texts (ideology) can be confirmed in spite of the evidence to the contrary. Caro repeatedly puts between brackets, so to speak, the historical interruptions and ruptures that constantly remind him of the fact that change may be both unavoidable and advisable. The *letrados'* monopoly on textual interpretation is legitimated by their technical expertise or at least by their public image as a class of highly literate experts. The translator-legislator writes his own texts while pretending that he is rendering foreign ones into his native language. He connects arbitrarily his literary-legislative acts in the present to a shifting signifier (the "Spanish Empire," "Bolívar," "tradition," "morality," and so forth) whose traces are alternately made visible and invisible as best befits the project at hand.[27]

Caro's understanding of the Colombian nation (and of the world of Latinity in general) is encapsulated in two revealing opinions. The first one is that the modern state's legitimacy continues to be based on the concept of a "Roman-Catholic communion and community" [comunión y colectividad católico-romana] ("La raza latina" [*Obras, tomo I* 734]). A corollary of this proposition is that the bishop of Rome becomes a higher authority than the Republic's head of state, and that the doctrines of the Catholic Church can overrule the laws written in the nation's *magna cart*a. As he put it in the fourth sonnet in the series "The Founding Fathers" [Los padres de la Patria] (1884): "You must all love Spain and worship Rome" [Amad a España, venerad a Roma] (l.11).[28] The second opinion is that "[o]ur democratic institutions are…something too cold, colorless, and altogether inappropriate for our kindled and magnanimous sensibilities" [Nuestras instituciones democráticas son…algo demasiado frío, deslustrado e impropio en suma, para nuestros vivos y magnánimos sentimientos] ("La independencia y la raza" [*Ideario hispánico* 110]).[29] This statement predates the Constitution of 1886, which incorporates many of those "sentiments," such as the need for confessional state, the concentration of powers in the executive branch, and the president's lack of penal responsibility for his decisions. In the ominous year of 1897, Caro was so desperate to find ways to justify his much-desired—yet perhaps unconstitutional—second term in office that he addressed a personal letter to the Director of *El Progreso* in which he covertly belittled democratic institutions as artificial forms that could not do justice to the people's intangible spiritual preferences.

Elections were for Caro just an accident in government. Like grammatical structures, they featured a hierarchical order in which the stronger, substantive parts rule the weaker, adjectival ones. Democratic elections were the contingent and fallible form taken by the only legitimate government of the people: that of a God-fearing spiritual majority. For that reason, Caro went on, if enough people wrote letters in support of his unconstitutional candidacy, if enough journalists echoed a seemingly national sentiment for his desired continuity in government, and if at small municipalities enough mayors reported that Colombian parishes declared en masse for Caro's candidacy, his confirmation at the polls might produce a "legitimacy" emanating directly from the people's "conscience" and "will," of which "there is no appeal whatsoever" (Caro's text qtd. in Martínez Silva 2: 422, 423). By contrast, abiding by the constitution and refusing to run for a second term would produce only the confirmation of "legality," something too cold, colorless, and inappropriate for the Latin race's kindled and magnanimous Catholic sensibilities.[30]

If the federal Constitution of 1863, promoted by the Liberal Party, was initially meant to counter the Church's overpowering influence, but had the disastrous effect of encouraging the country's territorial dismemberment, the Regeneración's 1886 replacement neutralized that threat. Caro drafted a *ley fundamental* that repressed any regional, ethnic, and individual identities that deviated from a set pattern of permitted identifications, making the temporal and religious powers one and the same with the signing of the Concordat. He thought he was solving the characteristic crisis of sovereignty experienced since the early nineteenth century by parliamentary-democratic regimes in which the legislative and the executive branches of power fought each other to make their respective decisions the last authority. With this purpose in mind, he devised for Colombia a happily unfulfilled quick transition from a regime in which the president's faculties are limited by Congress' legislative acts to one in which the president is also a legislator; that is to say, the chief of the executive exists simultaneously and contradictorily *infra et extra legem*.

Although Caro would continue to claim, for the benefit of the nominal democracy still in place, that he embodied the legal order as the holder of the nation's highest *officium*—the depositary of *merum imperium* to the detriment of a weak or submissive Congress—in reality he would have wanted to place himself outside of it. If reelected while violating the Constitution and enjoying immunity for his arbitrary verbal orders, he would have ceased to be bound by the law (he would no longer be *infra legem*). He would have become what sixteenth-century theorists called the holder of *plenitudo potestatis* or *potestas (ab)soluta* (the extraordinary faculties proper, fit only for times of internal commotion and temporarily assumed on the ground of their public utility) in contrast with those of *princeps legibus solutus* (the law-abiding legislative prince's ordinary faculties).[31]

Translatio imperii and the *pactum translationis*: A Short History of Sovereignty

In *European Literature and the Latin Middle Ages* (1948; English trans. 1953), Ernst Robert Curtius defines *translatio imperii* as the transfer of dominion from one people to another as the latter conquers the former. This doctrine, which originated in the Romania in the eighth century, implied that the prerogatives inscribed in the modern conceptual kernel of what we call sovereignty/hegemony are rightly transferred from those who use them unworthily. Soon *translatio imperii* would also encompass the transfer of learning (*studia*) from Athens and Rome to Paris (Curtius 27–30). The idea that a sinful misuse of power might result in loss of legitimacy was highlighted especially by later authors who were congenial to various strands of republicanism, such as the Florentine humanists or John Milton, who admired the Roman Republic but explicitly rejected the Roman Empire. Concurrently, beginning in the sixteenth century, when unconditional religious allegiance to Rome was dwindling, Emperor Charles V and Elizabeth Tudor appropriated the medieval doctrine of *translatio* for an imperial project of spiritual *and* political *renovatio*. The two monarchs were invested with the dignity of *defensor fidei*. As Virgil was to Augustus, so were the artists and writers at the courts of Charles V and Elizabeth I to both Renaissance monarchs. The works of Antonio de Nebrija, Fernando de Herrera, Edmund Spenser, Thomas North, and the later Shakespeare (e.g., *The Tempest*) attest to the centrality of these arguments.

Roberto Bellarmino (1542–1621), who is one of the striking absences in Caro's works, wrote at length about the Franks as the heirs to imperial Rome. In *Disputed Issues in the Christian Faith* [Disputationes de controversiis christianae religionis] (1586–1593)—under the epigraph "On Civil Government" [De laicis sive saecularibus]—he expounds on a passage in 1 Kings in the following manner: "I say that political power is transferred from nation to nation on account of injustice [dico transferri regna de gente in gentem propter injustitiam] because God, on account of the sins of kings, often gives the victory to their enemies, but the right to rule is not lost by the mere fact of their having sinned" (23). Besides stating the doctrine of *translatio imperii* in a terse formulation, here Bellarmino counters the notion, put forth at different times by Amarcanus, John Wycliff, and John Huss (and by Juan de Mariana in his defense of regicide's legality in cases of chronic tyrannical oppression), that God may authorize popular uprisings against an abusive and sinful king. Nevertheless, his main thesis is clear: "A kingdom is transferred from one people to another because of injustices" [Regnum a gente in gentem transfertur propter injustitias] (22).

Bellarmino championed *ius naturale*, particularly the tenet that all men were created equal in the eyes of God, and therefore were all, including the rulers, equally fallible. For this reason, temporal sovereignty had been conferred upon the totality of humankind (as in the case of Israel). For Bellarmino there are two powers, one civil, and the other religious, which are independent of each other. Both derive from God their right to rule, but while secular power, as embodied in civil institutions, requires the people's consent to be led by a prince or any other magistrate, the Church of Rome's *imperium* is a divinely anointed institution founded on the gift of grace, which can be legitimately carried *ad aeternum*. The pontifical powers' exceptionality, which Bellarmino compares to Moses's, leads the Italian Jesuit to defend the legitimacy of Rome's intrusions into the civil affairs of Catholic nations, including the Republic of Venice as well as England and Scotland.[32]

As if inspired directly by Bellarmino, Álvarez Bonilla could contend in 1904 that the Concordat was both a consequence of a *translatio imperii sine fine* (the Church's sovereignty extends providentially through the four corners of the earth with no restrictions or time limits) and a *pactum societatis* (the Church graciously allows the state to have temporal jurisdiction over the nation). In Álvarez Bonilla's tortured reasoning, "the state simply recognizes rights that the Church has in and of itself...Therefore, of the two *potestates* the one that makes concessions to the other is the Church" (*Elementos de derecho público* 59). Bellarmino's work as old-school controversialist provides us enough information to make a crucial point regarding the history of sovereignty, its ramifications in Colombia's politics, and the sources of Schmitt's thinking. Bellarmino places ecclesiastical power simultaneously *infra et extra legem*, under the law and outside its jurisdiction, by treating Scripture as the juridiclly original and natural basis of any modern state legislation, and by implication of sovereignty.

Bellarmino's support for papal absolutism is built on an act of repression as scandalous as Schmitt's, namely, the doubtful notion that medieval and early modern theories of the state, from Augustine to his great nemesis Jean Calvin, were Christianized versions of the engine that set the Roman Empire's law in motion: the *lex regia*. To state, as Schmitt did in 1922, that all modern concepts in state jurisprudence are secularized theological concepts (*Political Theology* 36) is to forget the claims of Roman philology and jurisprudence to historical priority.[33] Augustine, Bellarmino's main hero, was to *derogate* the civil authority's *potestas* in the aftermath of the Christian—yet Aryan—Visigoth Alaric's sack of Rome in AD 410 (an important context for the writing of *De civitate Dei*), substituting in its place an incommensurable *lex aeterna*.

At the opposite end of sovereignty's range of meanings, one finds the already mentioned Roman *lex regia*, which is not a theological concept; nor can it be downgraded to an adaptation of Israel's Covenant.[34] The *lex regia* is the legitimating source of the Spanish Jesuits' concept of the *pactum.* There were, to be sure, at least two main forms of the *pactum translationis* in the Renaissance: the *pactum societatis* (the forerunner of Rousseau's social contract) and the *pactum subjectionis* (the Renaissance avatar of the *lex regia* proper, as was understood by Mariana and Suárez). Marsiglio of Padua's thinking on papal prerogatives is the antithesis of Pope Innocent III's and Bellarmino's respective conceptualizations. He favored the *pactum* in his explanations *in abstracto* of the way in which sovereignty and legality presided over the relationship between a prince and his subjects, but resorted to the providential *translatio imperii* to assert the Holy Emperor's independence from Rome. Like González Vigil, he encouraged literalist readings of Scripture, accepting in addition the early Church Fathers' *traditio* but not the more recent exegesis performed by *clerici* or ecclesiastical *letrados* in the service of the Roman Curia.

In a series of works published under the German King Ludwig IV's patronage, Marsiglio advanced startlingly secular arguments, which are often more in tune with nineteenth-century theories of sovereignty than with medieval or early modern ones. In *Defensio minor*—a recapitulation of his larger *Defensio pacis* (1324)—he outlined four types of law: three coactive ones, which could be exercised only by the temporal ruler, and a communicative one representing the evangelical or pastoral efforts deployed by spiritual authorities (Padua 1–4). Although Marsiglio does not use this word, the communicative or evangelical type of law is the *rescriptum* proper, which I treat as the immediate antecedent of nineteenth-century Colombians' literary-legislative speech acts. Since not even Peter, who never visited Rome, "had coercive jurisdiction over the remaining apostles or other…ecclesiastical ministers," the "Roman bishop" and all other "ecclesiastical ministers" are subject to the "jurisdiction of the judges and government under the authority of the human legislator" (Padua 4). At best, the popes could retain effective dominion only over the Italian possessions directly placed under their jurisdiction as temporal rulers.

Again, like González Vigil, Marsiglio did not accept the myth of Emperor Constantine's Donation of the Empire to Pope Sylvester in the fourth century. As was already mentioned in an earlier footnote, this legend of a massive temporal *concessio*—a sort of voluntary and unnecessary capitulation—would have been conveniently reciprocated by the pontiff. Satisfied with the symbolic significance of this grant of lordship, the Church was said to have returned to the emperor the day-to-day administration of the multinational realm. This legal fiction was the origin of both the Holy Roman Empire and the institution of the Concordat, understood (as Colombian reactionaries insisted in the early twentieth century) more as a "concession" made by the Roman Catholic Church to secular governments than the other way around.

On the side of the secular realists, the absolutist Gómez Hermosilla stated that there was no historical record, prior to the appearance of the ad hoc practice of the *pactum subjectionis*, of any demonstrably originary *translatio imperii*, let alone a *pactum societatis* entered by free individuals in which they all alienate their freedom to place the entire nation's sovereignty in the strong hands of a corporation or a monarch. The counterrevolutionary de Maistre went farther in the denunciation of progressive fictions. In *Considérations sur la France*, he also flatly stated that the *pactum subjectionis* was recorded in history, but that it was allowed to exist legally as part of God's providential design: liberalism and socialism might subject and persecute true Catholics, but ultimately the divine right of absolutist rulers would prevail. What made de Maistre a more formidable rival for liberalism than Donoso Cortés could hope to be is that he was a historicist constitutionalist. His prose also exhibits the sensibility for nuances shown by historical-rationalist theologians, but which incensed reciters of catechesis like Donoso lacked. Echoing Gómez Hermosilla, de Maistre also invoked Minerva's authority, repeatedly asking to be shown the historical record. Thus, he writes:

> The rights of the *people*, properly so called, often enough proceed from the concessions of sovereigns and in this case can be verified historically; but the rights of the monarch and the aristocracy, at least their essential, constitutive, and *radical* rights [les droits essentiels, constitutifs et *radicaux*]…have neither date nor author. (*Considérations* 81–82; emphasis in the original)

In the end, de Maistre would meet his match in the tenacious historical scholar and resident of Lima who wrote in the Frenchman's favored language—Latin—against Pius IX's absolutist pretensions.[35] In *Cartas al Papa Pío IX* (1871), which he dedicated "To the American Youth," Gónzalez Vigil protested against the retrogressive attacks of bishops and the Vatican Curia on legally established secular governments in the Americas, arguing that these governments had been legitimated by a constitution and the civil laws emanating from it. Civil governments were entitled to denounce the Church's intrusion into civil affairs as acts of usurpation because nowhere in the early doctrinal literature was it documented (the Peruvian uses the words "documento" and "testimonio," which designate evidentiary instruments in both philology and jurisprudence) that the Curia had any jurisdiction outside the papal state: "Among us, miserable human creatures from all ranks, whether civil or ecclesiastical, any conflicted issue of authority [cuestion de autoridad] must be reduced to an issue of fact [cuestion de hecho]" (*Cartas al Papa Pío IX* 71).

As Colombia was a republic, the supranational entity that made concessions to the people qua homogeneous nation had to be sought outside the state. Since 1824, when Bolívar decreed the separation of Church and state in all of the Greater Colombia, the state had retained the right of patronage [*ius patronatus*]. In exchange for allowing the Church to exist inside the state and sponsoring within certain limits the priests' evangelical efforts, the civil government took upon itself the appointment of bishops who would be amenable to the protocols of *laïcité*. Nevertheless, the Constitution of 1863 explicitly prohibited any form of taxation that would directly support organized religion (art. 23). When in 1887 Carlos Holguín had the Concordat signed with the Vatican, the system of education was placed back in the hands of the Church, which also took possession again of its full ecclesiastical *immunitas* and assumed its own right of patronage—understood by the Regeneración as the moral oversight of civil institutions.[36]

In the Spanish-speaking world, the authoritarian concept of *translatio imperii* was often countered by recourse to the *pactum translationis*, enunciated by sixteenth-century Spanish theorists of empire as the contract by which the people willingly renounced their native freedoms, entrusting themselves to the monarch's undivided rule. The balanced combination of philosophies of government based on either the *translatio* or the *pactum* prolonged the perceived legitimacy of the Spanish rule over the American territories until the end of the eighteenth century. However, with the first occupation of Spanish cities by French troops in 1794–1795 and the banning of courses in *ius gentium* (the discipline to which the *translatio imperii* and the *pactum societatis* originally belong) at the universities in 1795, the institution of the monarchy underwent its most severe legitimation crisis yet. The situation was made all the worse by Carlos IV's abdication in March of 1808 and the ensuing surrender of the Bourbons' dynastic rights to the Spanish throne to Napoléon I's brother, José I, in June of the same year. It was then remembered that the *pactum* sealed an alliance between the people and the person of the king, which could be revoked, in what Roman law called a *translatio legati* or annulment of contract, if the king abused his power or if the throne was usurped or left vacant.

For constitutional thinkers writing in the French Revolution's aftermath, the *pactum* remained the central legal instrument of government. Francisco Martínez Marina made it clear in 1813, in the *Discurso sobre el origen de la monarquía* written during the Cortes de Cádiz, which were given *pouvoir constituant*. There he argued that the only legitimate "potestad regia" was the one emanating from a "covenant"; *convenio* and *contrato* are his two alternating terms. Like Rousseau, he could have taken this term from Thomas Aquinas's concept of "covenant" [*pactum*] by which a multitude willingly subjects itself to a king, or from any of the Jesuit thinkers who revisited Aquinas in the sixteenth and seventeenth centuries. Aquinas's pact was not only legal, but also legitimate insofar as all the prerogatives assumed by the king could be "revoked" by an assembly's decree: *omnibus juste et salubriter in irritum revocatis* (Aquinas, *On the Governance of Rulers* 59; Martínez Marina,

Discurso 141–42). The Spanish legist's third example of a covenant featured Moses and the Lord. It is called *contrato social, alianza,* and *pacto* (*Discurso* 142–43). In this account, Moses plays the part of a *primus-inter-pares* notary and convenor of the Israeli people's *assemblée constituante.* Although Martínez Marina seems aware of the difficulty in reconciling the people's two contrary positions as *both* sovereign and subject (the same conceptual problem beset Rousseau, Nariño, and Bilbao, among many others), and of the theoretical challenges created by the delegating or mediating agencies that enable the transformation from sovereign into subject, he falls silent on both issues.

Moses's thanksgiving prayer for the delivery of the Hebrew people from their Egyptian oppressors (Exodus 15:1–18) was translated in part by Caro as "Cántico de Moisés" (included in *Poesías,* published simultaneously with the Constitution of 1886). This inaugural text helped him advance the romantic idea that poets were indeed legislators of the world. It was not an original thought; the same idea was cast in transcendentalist terms by Shelley, Whitman, and Emerson, but adapted to the needs of a highly educated reading public by the more fantastically pantheistic Victor Hugo. Besides Hugo, Andrés Bello, José Eusebio Caro, his son Miguel Antonio, Rafael Núñez, and Guillermo Valencia fell under Moses's spell because he seemed to anticipate the *letrados'* polymathic talents and had undergone an experience of conversion. Another illustrious convert, Saint Paul, became understandably intrigued by Moses's double duty as legislator and prophet, as did two early modern theorists of sovereignty: Bellarmino and Jean Calvin. The Italian Jesuit cardinal realized that Moses posed a problem for Church history and for the assumption (or rather, the usurpation, as González Vigil reminds us) of temporal prerogatives by the Vatican Curia. Moses is said to have acted as a pre-Christian pontiff in that he assumed an interpretive monopoly of God's intentions for his entire people without the mediating agency of a council of high priests. However, he was also the temporal ruler of that people.

Bellarmino was an advocate for the papacy's *potestas indirecta* over temporal rulers, which at the time meant that the pontiff could interfere with kings and emperors only when the nation's spiritual well-being was at risk, but not when the subjects thought that their ruler was being tyrannical. God had given absolute power to the head of the Church because the latter needed undivided sovereignty. Moses was therefore an "exception" to the rule of Hebraic jurisprudence. In a moment of proto-Schmittian insight, Bellarmino proclaims in jubilation that Moses's assumption of extraordinary faculties constituted a "continuo miracolo" (232), a statement that predates by more than three centuries Schmitt's dictum: "The exception in jurisprudence is analogous to the miracle in theology" (*Political Theology* 36).[37]

The twofold status of Scripture as a source of both civil and ecclesiastical law was especially problematic because figurative meanings were often defended at the expense of literal ones, which is exactly what modern civil jurisprudence (Martínez Marina, Quintana, Bello—Bentham predates them all) wanted to avoid. In *Teoría de las Cortes* (1813; rev. 1820), Martínez Marina pointed out that the deputies at the Cortes de Castilla held in 1469 discussed the *fact* that the people of Israel did not simply receive their *constitution*; rather, they voted on it after it was proposed in the manner of a covenant, with Moses acting as their "deputy" [*procurador*]. For the Spanish jurist, the absolutist monarchy was a very recent invention, and an unconstitutional one. It consisted in the monarch's use of *dominium* (the treatment of the people more as property than subjects of rights guaranteed by both *ius naturale* and *ius gentium*) rather than *imperium*, which for him was the sovereignty only partially alienated by the people to their ruler. Despite his moderate liberal leanings, Martínez Marina, a Catholic faithful, transforms God into a medieval Iberian monarch who can propose new laws, but cannot promulgate them without the consent of the "people" duly gathered in the assemblary Cortes (*Teoría de las Cortes* [*Obras escogidas* 2: 373]).[38] Although this is an admittedly lax interpretation of the *pactum*, it falls within the framework outlined in Aquinas's *De regimine principum*, which is—along with Rousseau and the medieval Spanish chronicles— among the Spaniard's main theoretical inspirations (Martínez Marina, *Obras escogidas* 2: 14–15).

From 1793, when the Colombian founding father Antonio Nariño (1765–1823) had his Spanish translation of the French "Declaration of the Rights of Man" (the seventeen articles of 1789) published, the *pactum societatis* became a constant leitmotif in nineteenth-century Andean historiography dealing with the events that took place between 1795 (the year of Nariño's trial and imprisonment in Cádiz) and 1808 (the year of Carlos IV's abdication). The towering historiographic narrative in this tradition is the Bolivian Gabriel René-Moreno's *Últimos días coloniales en el Alto-Perú* (1896–1897).[39] In this and related works we find the idea that the covenant of obedience to the monarch could be revoked unilaterally by the sovereign people, who would have renounced their *imperium* (the attribute of sovereignty that specifically refers to the prerogative to create new law) but not their right of self-determination. The *translatio imperii*, with its emphasis on the providential transfer of sovereignty (understood here as full executive and legislative powers unrestricted by a higher authority) from a declining nation to a rising one, became a cornerstone of conservative doctrine as well as philo-Spanish platforms.[40] By contrast, the *pactum translationis* became a legitimating tool of the liberal discourse of rights that argued for the location of the nation's sovereignty in the congressional body—the Cortes—whose members were elected by the people residing in the nation's territory. Having still fresh in their memory the lesson taught by the demise of the Spanish Empire and the tradition of secessional politics begun with the revolution, the only option that Colombian ultramontanists had in the

1880s and 1890s—the years of the Regeneración's reactionary backlash—was to place themselves under the Church of Rome's political patronage.

The version of the *translatio imperii* upheld by Caro closely resembles the pioneering model put forth in Otto von Freising's *Chronica, sive historia de duabus civitatibus* in the middle of the twelfth century.[41] In Books III and IV of this work, Bishop Otto argued that Rome was destined to be the last of the great secular empires. As if to make good on Jove's announcement to Aeneas of an *imperium sine fine* (*Aeneid* 1.279), for Otto, the *civitas Dei* would be embodied by the Roman Empire in its centrifugal, evangelizing movement away from the center and toward an ever-expanding periphery that waited to be conquered. Bishop Otto's theory was of great help in countering Francisco Suárez's argument in Book 3 of *Defensio fidei catholicae et apostolicae* (1613), in which the *pactum translationis* that was to become a cornerstone in the ideology of independence acquires its most forceful formulation.

Drawing on Augustine and Thomas Aquinas, Suárez argues three very important points. The first one is that the greatest act of freedom is to give up one's liberty, but that such renunciation is never complete. In translational terms, we would say that the maximal mobility of individual signs/subjects that characterizes the prepolitical stage of human relations gives way to the rule of a transcendent signifier, that is, the undivided executive power invested with the prerogative of *dominium* or eminent domain. Second, Suárez states that smaller communities are established by analogy with the patriarchal family, in which the father holds the attribute of *potestas*, which itself derives directly from the condition of being a father. As the familial community expands, turning into a *communitas perfecta*, the ruler's power is also perfected, that is, it becomes absolute insofar as it reaches everything and everyone under his dominion (Suárez 2: 223).[42] The third and most important point (and a problematic one in relation to number two) is that God always makes peoples sovereign, but at the same time approves of a people's decision to delegate or transfer that sovereignty "by the voluntary consent of the people" [per voluntarium populi consensum] (Suárez 2: 223).

Another Jesuit theologian, Juan de Mariana (ca. 1536–1624), went farther than Suárez in many ways in *De rege et regis institutione* (1599), dedicated to Philip III. Relying on both Florentine republican thought and the parliamentary traditions of the medieval Iberian kingdoms, he declared that civil or temporal authority was transferred from the people (in the medieval period, through the Cortes) to their lawful ruler. Most crucially, it also originated in the people, whose desire to organize themselves in a commonwealth arose from the need to seek protection from anarchy and abuse.[43] For Mariana, Christendom cannot be organized in a single commonwealth (in this he differs from fellow Jesuits Luis de Molina and Roberto Bellarmino); nor is there such a thing as an unquestionable divine right of kings. Instead, sovereignty for him is already the people's inalienable right: "For the commonwealth did not transfer the rights to rule into the hands of a prince to such a degree that it has not reserved a greater power to itself" [neque ita in Principem iura potestatis transtulit, ut non sibi maiorem reservarit potestatem] (146). In the same work Mariana highlights the succession to the throne (a crucial issue in the year 1808) as one of the legal actions in which the people retained their sovereignty before the king, especially if they showed themselves wholly united in one resolution: "Assuredly, in…abrogating laws, and especially in the matters that concern the succession, if the multitude opposes, the authority of the Prince is not a match for it" [Certe…abrogandisve legibus, ac praesertim quae de successione in regno sunt, mutandis, resistente multitudine impar unius Principis auctoritas sit] (159).[44] In chapters V–VII of his work, Mariana also characterized the figure of the tyrant—understood by him in the modern sense of an abusive prince rather than the Greco-Roman one of a magistrate's uninterrupted continuity in office—and the conditions under which the people could overthrow him by either peaceful or violent means. Now with his emphasis on the interrelatedness of *consensus* and *imperium*, Suárez lucidly articulates a new variety of sovereignty, which authorizes the making of laws that apply to all rather than the prince's arbitrary management of property and subjects (as *dominium* does). He thus provides a strikingly modern conceptualization of "hegemony" as *domination by consent*.[45]

Suárez's concept of the *pactum translationis* was invoked by the earliest ideologues of Spanish American emancipation precisely when the first interruption in the transmission of *imperium* from one ruler to another took place in 1808, as the Bourbons left the throne vacant, or, in an alternative interpretation, as the throne was taken unlawfully from them. The series of concatenated events comprising the emancipation of the original thirteen Anglo-American colonies, the success of the Third Estate in France in staging a more violent bourgeois revolution, and the Haitian people's successful revolt against revolutionary France, had inspired the intellectuals of New Granada since the 1790s. The Bogotá creole *letrado*, Antonio Nariño, was prosecuted in 1795 for having published a translation of the revolutionary Declaration of the Rights of Man, which he took from volume 3 of Keverseau and Clavelin's *Histoire de la Révolution de 1789 et de l'établissement d'une Constitution en France* (1790). This document's impious contents were certainly incompatible with the early Bourbons' active role in the European alliance to fight the French Revolution. In September of that year, the contents of Nariño's opuscule were paraphrased by his prosecutors as follows: "That no man received from Nature the right to rule over the rest; that the king's authority originates in the people; that a prince receives his authority from his subjects; that without the consent of the Nation one cannot exercise that authority; that the

Crown, the Government, and related public institutions are the patrimony of the nation; that the nation is its owner and the monarchs only its usufructuaries" [Que ningun hombre recibió de la naturaleza el derecho de mandar á los otros; Que la autoridad de los Reyes dimana de los Pueblos; Que el Príncipe recibe de sus súbditos la autoridad; Que no se puede disponer de ella sin el consentimiento de la Nación; Que la Corona, el Gobierno, la pública autoridad son bienes de la nacion; Que esta es la propietaria y los Príncipes usufructuarios] (Pérez-Sarmiento 84).[46]

Manuel José Quintana was another forerunner of liberalism who was tried in Cádiz for his publication of subversive tracts. He had to face twice the questions of a state attorney [*fiscal*] who visited him in prison. The second of these interrogations, conducted in April of 1815, is an exceptional document because the accuser shows a remarkably accurate understanding of the *letrado*-poet's literary-legislative acts: first, he understood that Quintana's articles of opinion in the *Semanario Patriótico* predated, foreshadowed, and indeed influenced the writing of the 1812 Constitution (the patriotic writings of the accused would thus have become the first literary-legislative speech acts to be incorporated into a law); and second, he knew that Quintana was the main author of the anonymously published pieces in the journal because "the same thoughts, expressed almost with the same words as in the *Semanario*, are found in the *Poesías* published by the author in 1813" (Quintana, *Obras inéditas* 269).[47] The attorney also remarked that one particular ode, "España libre," was published in 1808 under French domination and pirated the following year in Mexico, where it came out padded with paraphilological notes that equated the institution of the monarchy with tyranny and presented Quintana as an enemy of the Bourbons (*Obras inéditas* 270–71).[48] In other words, Quintana first articulated his "love for democratism's ideas" [afectos á las ideas del democratismo] (this is the attorney's wording) in the genre of poetry, and later converted his poem into a newspaper article. The Madrid-based *Semanario* (1808), like its Seville (1809) and Cádiz (1810–1812) sequels, had therefore the power to influence the text of the 1812 Constitution.

Similarly, the unauthorized annotated edition of *España libre* must have influenced the American Declarations of Independence in 1810.[49] Yet, in the interrogation of 1815, when a reluctant Fernando VII was still bound by the Cádiz Constitution, Quintana endeavored to keep his discussion of representative government within the accepted limits of a *pactum societatis* that had been broken by the extraordinary event of Carlos IV's abdication and self-exile. Monarchs and dynasties come and go, Quintana reasoned, but the people's sovereignty remains unchanged through the uninterrupted sequence obtained from one generation's succession by the next. In sum, only the nation can *translate* itself into itself, "before any government has been constituted, or after any government has ceased to exist," and only the nation can translate power and dominion fully without loss of sovereignty (Quintana, *Obras inéditas* 262–63).

In Bogotá, don Rufino Cuervo taught the doctrines of Suárez and Aquinas at the Colegio del Rosario from 1822 to 1825. He had to step down from his professorship when Vice President Santander's executive Decree (November 8, 1825) instituted Bentham's *Tratados de legislación* as an official textbook at Colombian universities. His two sons, Rufino José and Ángel, summarized and extracted these teachings under the heading "Tratado de ética" in *Vida de Rufino Cuervo y noticias de su época*, first published in Paris in 1892. The sons strategically placed their father's production of his lesson summaries at a time when Bentham's influence had not yet been greatly felt in Bogotá:

> The proponents of tyranny and despotism have always contended that the authority of rulers is derived from God, and to prove this they have taken some passages from the Scripture: *Per me reges regnant, et legum conditores justa decernunt* (*Proverbs* 8.15); *Non est potestas nisi a Deo* (St. Paul, Romans 13.1).[50] These are the weapons with which the people's sovereignty is attacked. We hold that the authority of rulers derives indirectly [*inmediatamente*] from the people, and directly [*mediatamente*] from God, and in this way we respond to the passages just quoted. The people of Israel were ruled theocratically. As they longed for a king in the manner of other nations, God granted their wish by means of the prophet Samuel, and they chose Saul for their king. This is the best of our proposition. (Rufino José Cuervo, *Obras, tomo II* 1440)

As seen in chapter one, don Rufino's defense of the divine origin of sovereignty was countered not only by Bentham's theory of legal fictions (which also subjects Rousseau's social contract to a scathing critique), but also by contemporary publicists who were positioned further to the right than he was. Among authors whose work of the 1820s reached a wide audience in Spain and the Americas, Gómez Hermosilla stands out for the clarity of his formulations and the urgency with which his arguments are connected to immediate postrevolutionary contexts. Having internalized some of the teachings of Destutt de Tracy and Bentham, Gómez Hermosilla does not idealize human actions and finds no consolation in the existence of a *Dios derechurero* or litigating deity who may have (as he does in Cuervo) a *potestas mediata*. Gómez Hermosilla translated Hobbes and Mariana for a society that he thought of as already secularized, in which theo-political sovereignty's *lieu vide* could be filled only by the need that the weak have of the strong and vice versa. Order, peace, and unity of purpose were of utmost importance to Gómez Hermosilla, who had lost all faith in the benefits of early liberalism and its play of multiple and fragmented sovereignties always bickering with each other or going to war to continue their unfinished negotiation of contrary viewpoints by other means. Unhappy with the Spanish *letrado*'s secular outlook on civil government and human affairs, Colombian reactionaries delved deeper than ever before into the history of the Church and the revival of religious ideals.

This nineteenth-century revival of theology had been dialectically induced by the downgrading of positivism to an instrument of domination and the threat of Rome's disappearance as a temporal power. Caro was prone to take this debate into the disciplines of history, grammar, and philology. However, he did not feel equally confident defending the divine origin of sovereignty in a strictly juridical setting until President Núñez started the Partido Nacional, which placed in his hands the preparation of the new *magna carta*. He knew that, for as long as the radical Liberals remained in power, a theo-political jurisprudence could not get much traction in a Spanish American country that had gone far in the direction of federalism without successfully creating a homogeneous state, much less a civil society.

For many years, then, Caro fell in the habit of displacing his love for absolutist and archaic institutions onto the ideological apparatuses of the educational system, the Colombian Academy, and the Catholic publishing industry. *Artículos y discursos* (1888) was brought out by his publishing house (the Librería Americana) just months after the signing of the Concordat. The anthology is clearly meant as a justification of his reactionary legislative endeavors. It may be described as a multichapter rescript addressed to the nation because it adamantly states the superiority of Scripture and *ius naturale* over positive jurisprudence. The essays in *Artículos y discursos* are well attuned to the miscellaneous series of texts produced in the previous years: the ode "To the Statue of the Libertador" [A la estatua del Libertador] (1883), the Constitution of 1886, and the Concordat. The arguments laid out in the doctrines underlying the Concordat are easily keyed into one or more of the pieces gathered in Caro's volume of 1888. Their lasting influence is seen in such works as Álvarez Bonilla's university lectures, *Elements of Public Civil Law* [Elementos de derecho público interno] (1904), which were published at the end of Marroquín's presidency and still adhered to the notion of the divine right of rulers (4–5).

De Maistre, Donoso Cortés, Caro, and Álvarez Bonilla denied (as Schmitt would do in his monograph on Donoso) that it was possible to speak of sovereignty without making the people's obedience to what Donoso called an "inviolable authority" [autoridad inviolable] conveniently located in a theological realm beyond dispute and strife. Christian dogma provided the ideal ground for this project "by making obedience something sacred, and by making self-denial and sacrifice, or, to say it better, charity, something divine" [haciendo de la obediencia una cosa santa, haciendo de la abnegación y el sacrificio, o, por mejor decir, de la caridad, una cosa divina] (Donoso Cortés, *Obras completas* 2: 464–65).

Caro also often denied that a revolution broke out in Spanish America in 1810, claiming instead that the colonies' independence could be compared to a son's feud with his father. Notwithstanding the War-to-the-Death policy decreed by Bolívar during the Revolution of Independence, he insisted that the natural bond of affection between father and son could not be broken.[51] In other words, Caro reverted to Suárez's paternal, precontractual stage in the constitution of community, which was based on the family unit to avoid dealing politically with a confrontation between a declining colonial power and the emergent discourses of self-determination.[52] However, Bishop Otto's attempts at producing an overarching pattern for cataclysmic transfers of power provided Caro with a potent, if outdated, philosophy of history and government that seemed more suited to his diatribes against parliamentary democracy. The *Chronica* also suited the revival of Scholastic doctrine in the second half of the nineteenth century. Its two main champions were Pope Pius IX and Pope Leo XIII. Caro either translated into Spanish or commented at length on some of their encyclical letters. Just as these two pontiffs devoted much of their writing to anathematizing liberalism, socialism, freemasonry, the freedom of the press, and other collateral effects of the secularizing impulse ushered in by the Age of Revolution, so did Caro focus his energies on exposing the foundations of the modern liberal state as an illegitimate and impious human creation.

According to Bishop Otto, in the divine plan of salvation that informs theologically his entire scheme, the Roman Empire's primary function was to serve as protector of the expanding Christian Church. For him, the abstract entities of the *civitas mundi* (Augustine's *civitas terrena*) and the *civitas Dei* are embodied in concrete powers. This reconceptualization entails a significant departure from Augustine's open-ended historicism, whose main features were sketched out in this book's introduction. At the same time, Otto's chief contribution to the concept of *translatio imperii* (in his own phrasing, *imperium transferre*) was to posit the existence of the *civitas mundi* as a necessary step for the growth on earth of the *civitas Dei* or *civitas Christi*. There are two reasons for this. The first one is that the *civitas Dei* has two "swords," one temporal and one spiritual, that is to say, it brings together the priestly authority and the kingly *imperium* over the entire world for which *translatio* as transportation to heaven (i.e., conversion or salvation) and *translatio* as movement of troops (conquest) provide a neat conceptual synthesis. The second reason is that *translatio imperii* models have to confront the superimposition of a pattern of continuity on the perceived chaos of historical discontinuity. In the examination of past stages in world history, this is quickly averted by activating teleologically the preexisting patterns of continuity, which had hitherto lain hidden beneath the contradictory appearance of historical contingency.

To return to Caro, he clearly wished to appropriate the *translatio imperii* to legitimate an authoritarian regime whose two main sources of authority— the universality of Catholic teachings (particularly the doctrine expounding the relation of the Church to the state) and the infallibility of the pope's judgments in his apostolic literature when speaking *ex cathedra*—many found difficult to accept as a civil government alternative to positive legislation. Following Augustine, Bishop Otto suggested that the city of God's dual composition created some conceptual difficulties at the same time as it cleared others. He was not the first expositor of Church doctrine to imply that undivided authority/power (*monarchia*) was unthinkable outside or after the Roman Empire and that the *renovatio* of *imperium* of the Caesars and Charlemagne (an event antedating the millenarian Second Coming) would inevitably be *Roman*. This was one of the celebrated insights in Jerome's commentary on Daniel's prophetic book, and was given a more elaborate formulation in Dante's treatise *De monarchia* (ca. 1313), in many ways a distant precursor of Italian ultramontanism although it remained on the Index until 1881.[53]

What Bishop Otto seems to have worked out by himself is the paradoxically productive economy (the dialectic, one might say) of temporal power and divine *imperium*.[54] At the outset of Book IV, he asks his baffled reader to pay close attention to the new philosophy of history he is espousing: "Note that as the sovereign kingdom of Christ expands, the worldly kingdom is constantly diminishing" [Vide regno Christi crescente regnum mundi paulatim imminui] (191). On the one hand, the "weakening of Rome's sovereignty" [regnum debilitari] (189) was suggested by the abundance of sinners living within the temporal incarnation of the *civitas Dei*. But, on the other hand, God made it clear that "the sovereignty of Rome" was to "rule over the rest" [regnum Romanorum, quod ceteris dominaretur] (von Freising 189). In other words, the transformation of pagan Rome into a Christian empire did not do away with the *civitas mundi*; rather, the two cities fight a battle of the titans through the end of time. Indeed, no other empire was able to take the place of Rome from the moment the latter became the holder of two swords—one temporal, the other spiritual—through the legal fiction and forgery of Constantine's Donation.[55] According to this fiction, Catholic nations were invested with a religious mission because all popes were heirs not only to Peter, but to Constantine, who signified his desire to unite Church and state by investing Pope Sylvester with the authority that he had as Roman Emperor. Modern Concordats are to a certain extent an updated and much attenuated version of the Church of Rome's extravagant claims. Unlike Augustine, Bishop Otto literalized the Catholic Church's meaning as the visible *civitas Dei/civitas Christi* existing in medieval Europe's here and now. In addition to suggesting the pope's primacy over the emperor's (a position that Otto tries hard to avoid stating explicitly), the *Chronica* construes any threat to Rome as just one more challenge that is neither the first nor will be the last; rather, it is transitory relapse and interruption (a *felix culpa*) in the history of the Church's everlasting triumph. This is the philosophy of history that was to be recuperated by Vico, de Maistre, and Bonald. Such an idea was not incompatible with the Catholic evangelizers' *translatio* of Rome to New Granada, as the founder of Bogotá, Gonzalo Jiménez de Quesada, saw in the sixteenth century.[56] Furthermore, in late nineteenth-century Rome, Bogotá, and Popayán, the near annihilation of the visible symbols of the Church's earthly power appeared to many as the ultimate omen of its certain, imminent triumph and the multitudinous conversions resulting from it. Sergio Arboleda, for one, argued in 1880 that the unprecedented worldwide attacks on the Church were an unmistakable sign that the *translatio* and *regeneratio* of the unfaithful were indeed close at hand (*Las letras, las ciencias y las bellas artes* 55–56).

Caro must have found these interpretive tools germane to his theocratic project. Schemes like Bishop Otto's clearly attended to his need to rationalize Colombia's history of civil wars and present ruinous condition. The legitimate Spanish monarch whom Pope Clement VII anointed in Bologna as Emperor Charles V had presided over the early colonization of New Granada, which was then and forever placed under the spiritual aegis of the last empire and the eternal city. The Revolution's revocation of the *pactum translationis* in force since the Spanish conquest reinforced the idea that the growth of Rome elsewhere was made possible by its erosion in the Andean region. The internecine struggles between Liberals and Conservatives, and between federalists and centralists, which traversed Colombia's history through the end of the nineteenth century exemplified the *corpus admixtum*—the *civitas Dei*'s earthly counterpart. At the risk of oversimplifying, suffice it to say here that Caro's aggressive championing of the *état clérical* in the wake of the separation of Church and state decreed by the Constitution of 1863 reflects his attempts at situating the source of sovereignty in an authority larger than individual states (i.e., beyond strife and dissent).[57] For Pius IX as for Otto, the Church of Rome's *imperium* was not of this world and it became all the greater as the Kingdom of Rome's temporal power diminished. Interestingly enough, it was therefore possible for the ultramontanists to feel increasingly optimistic about the *renovatio* of Christian *imperium* as the temporal power of the papacy also dwindled under Pius IX (exiled from Rome from 1848 to 1850) and Leo XIII, as did the influence of the Church in Colombia in the years of the federal republic (1863–1886).

In 1877, the British publicist William Arthur wrote one the longest indictments of Pius IX's propagandistic efforts to use the Vatican's loss of power as a dialectical springboard for the launching of a crusade that would restore Rome's *imperium*. His work was flamboyantly titled *The Pope, the Kings, and the People: A History of the Movement to Make the Pope Governor of the World by a Universal Reconstruction of Society from the Issue of the Syllabus to the Close of the Vatican Council*. Arthur raised many of the issues that centrally concerned both Caro and González Vigil from their mutually opposing political positions. The *Syllabus errorum* mentioned in the title, which Pius IX attached to the encyclical letter *Quanta cura* (1864), was for the Colombian statesman a higher law than the impious Constitution of 1863—a present-day Ten Commandments supported by the dogma of papal infallibility issued at the First Vatican Council (1869–1870).[58] In one of his irrational tirades against Liberalism serialized in *El Tradicionista*, the article "The New Civilization" [La nueva civilización] (1875), Caro exaggerated the restrictions that Napoléon III imposed on Pius IX's freedom of movement. He called the pontiff "the Vatican captive" [el cautivo del Vaticano] and misrepresented the liberal-democratic state and the Christian *imperium* as "the right of force" [el derecho de la fuerza] vis-à-vis "the force of right" [la fuerza del derecho]:[59] "Behold now if Pius IX was right in condemning that modern civilization. The *Syllabus* is the banner of natural law: in it war is declared on pantheism, naturalism, rationalism, and the remaining abortions of Protestantism" [¡Ahora ved si Pío IX ha tenido razón en condenar esa civilización moderna! El *Syllabus* es la bandera del derecho: en él se declara la guerra al panteísmo, al naturalismo, al racionalismo, a todos esos abortos del protestantismo] (*Obras, tomo I* 629).[60]

Donoso Cortés denounced as a diabolic creation the liberal model of representative democracy in which no sovereignty exists prior to or beyond a people's free will as the people become organized in a parliamentary body. As a politician and historiographer who blamed liberalism for the feuding nature of nineteenth-century social life, Donoso Cortés tried to reconceive the history of humankind in negative terms, for which purpose he also resorted to the tropes of translation. The as-yet unredeemed nature of "man" could be explained on the basis of the uninterrupted series of events that lay at the heart of the "doctrine of the hereditary translation of penance and guilt" [doctrina de la transmisión hereditaria de la pena y de la culpa] (Donoso Cortés 2: 642).[61] The main teaching of Jesus's life and sacrifice had been to show how the stain of the original sin could be washed off only through an endless series of blood-shedding sacrifices. Donoso Cortés was thus echoing Augustine's belief that the so-called "generationist" hypothesis, according to which the soul of the offspring originated from the parental soul in a mysterious way, offers the best—if not also the only—explanation for the transmission of original sin insofar as sinfulness becomes the attribute of the person who acquires it by generation.[62] Caro would add to this in his essay "Fundación de la Academia Colombiana" (1874): "Yes, one inherits everything, and everything is transmitted through generation" [Sí, todo se hereda, todo se transmite por la generación] (*Obras, tomo III* 87). This meant that it was not possible to renounce Jesus, whose martyrdom pointed out the way for purging the original sin through self-immolation.

Just as sinfulness could not be disposed of, but can only be attenuated, so did transmission operations function according to a "law of reversion" [ley de la reversibilidad], by which it was not possible for humankind to forfeit its obligation to succeed to the institution of sacrifice (Donoso Cortés 2: 686). The individual's relative freedom to disobey God was not incompatible with the latter's absolute power, which simply *dilated* in time the fulfillment of his will. In this space of dilation, the uninterrupted work of blood-shedding sacrifices took place. This doctrine's veracity, as the Catholic thinker wrote, was demonstrated by the pervasiveness of violence and the sanctity of those who embraced the violence of self-immolation in Jesus Christ's name. Donoso Cortés went on to add in one of his fallacious syllogisms that Spanish liberalism had proven unable to do without the figure of the king. Since the king's sovereignty derives originally from God, and precludes the liberal threat of an endless "debate" or "dispute" [discusión] through which all concepts are confounded, he concluded that liberalism lacked the legitimacy that only God's constitutive sovereignty could provide (Donoso Cortés 2: 595–97).

The negation of the absolutist model of undivided power (*monarchia*), first by the republican revolutionaries and later by the hegemonic Liberal Party, created the conditions for the emergence of a militantly Catholic ethos that turned its temporary defeat into a badge of honor. Colombia's Liberal lettered city, with its emphasis on the freedom of the press, the state's sponsorship of secular, utilitarian education, and the substitution of a wholesomely disputing ethos for the Old Regime's authoritarianism, became the modern incarnation of Augustine's *civitas diaboli*. The *milites Christi* who mingled with godless Liberals in the *corpus admixtum* of profane institutions such as Congress, the Atheneum, and the Academy—in other words, those among the faithful inhabit a purgatorial *civitas terrena* to fight incredulity better—were also waiting for the Regeneración's reinstatement of the divine right of rulers. This restoration of sovereignty would fill the void left by the event of *vacatio regis* and the vanishing of theo-politics' mystical symbols. Caro thus felt entitled to treat the local uprisings of Liberal *caudillos* as if they were acts of insubordination that challenged not only the authority of Bogotá, but also that of Rome.

Caro against the State: The Constitution, the *Vice* Presidency, and the Institutions of Patristics

Caro was discontented with the legacy bequeathed by the first two presidents of New Granada: Bolívar and Santander. The legitimacy of this republic had been predicated on the basis and the strength of the *pactum translationis*, which opposes providentialist narratives, particularly the historicist construct of the *translatio imperii*. Although widely perceived as simply a legitimating fiction throughout Western history, the *translatio* found a counterbalance in another fiction, the *pactum*, appropriated by Colombia's liberals from the time Nariño led the fight for New Granadans' self-determination. The *pactum* and the *translatio* presupposed each other dialectically. Thus, the detractors of pactism were forced to acknowledge that the liberal-democratic state (the *civitas diaboli* within which the *civitas terrena* of ultramontane *letrados* existed) needed to come into being so that the widespread corruption it engendered could in turn spur the backlash of the monolithic *civitas Dei*—the forever postponed "future City" [Ciudad futura], as Caro calls it in the last line of his sonnet "Against Egoism" [Contra el egoísmo] (*Obras poéticas: Sonetos—Cantilenas* 94).

Toward the end of his life—in the late essays on "Dictatorships" [Las dictaduras] (1903)—Caro recanted, however partially and indirectly, his longtime use of what he now called "fictions of law/right" [ficciones de derecho] (*La oda* 262). Note, first of all, that his choice of phrasing faithfully translates Justinian's *fictio iuris*, the figure that creates the rhetorical effect of constitutional continuity in Rome's complex transition from the republican to the imperial regime. In any educated Colombian's mind, *ficción de derecho* must have conjured up immediately Bentham's much-maligned concept of "legal fiction"—an ideological mystification that should always be avoided for the sake of evidentiary logic and verification. Caro's *translatio legati* or legal revocation of Liberalism's hegemonic position, which was achieved by constitutionally unsound means, called for a number of *fictional* transvaluations of extant discourses on the law, rights, and sovereignty. On the level of juristic and philological rigor, in the surprisingly antistatist "The Right to Define" [El derecho de definir] (1884), Caro held that the Church Fathers' opinions were in fact "infallible" laws because they were divinely inspired, while positive codes—he had Liberal jurisprudence in mind—were no more than "opinions" that could not legitimately be imposed on the citizens. The latter professed some "necessary truths" [verdades necesarias] that already had their "definitions" outside the dictionary: these transcendent opinions "are simple, unreformable, and compulsory" (Caro, *Artículos y discursos* 347).

By contrast, positive laws functioned like the multiple acceptations of a word found in the dictionary. They could help writers give shape to their thoughts, but they do not bind an author to obey a doctrine's teachings (*Artículos y discursos* 347, 349–50). This fascinating antiliberal argument unsurprisingly builds on the liberal tenet, popularized in France in the 1790s, that constitutions could no longer be treated as the *données* of political organization promulgated by a hypostatic, exterior authority. Instead, they had to be the outcome of a concerted decision arrived at in the participatory milieu afforded by the nation's *asssemblée constituante* and the preexisting public opinion that the people's deputies should echo in their deliberations. Caro challenged this notion when he stated that a document resulting from fallible opinions and deliberations was not worthy of preservation.

Nevertheless, only two years after publishing "The Right to Define," Caro expressed the contrary view in "The Law's Empire" [Imperio de la legalidad] (1886), one of his many addresses to the Council of Delegates in defense of his *Bases* (*Artículos y discursos* 378–83; repr. in *Estudios constitucionales* 89–93). The time had finally come for him to produce constitutional text of his own preference and design. On the level of nation-building storytelling, Caro's various writings on Bolívar suggest that the Libertador did not favor a model of the state in which the people's elected representatives could be treated as the guardians and interpreters of the nation's sovereignty, or in which increasingly larger groups of the population would be granted the franchise. He resorted to the stereotyped phraseology of the "tyranny of the majority" to render liberal democracy illegitimate. For him, as for Donoso Cortés, only the elites who are morally superior should be entitled not just to govern, but also to vote. In his speech defending a very restrictive right to vote before the Council of Delegates, Caro argued that moral superiority originated in the elites' experience in government (the historicist argument) as well as their knowledge of Catholic doctrine and Church history (the elevation of evangelical opinions to the status of doctrinal truth).

In his address to the Council of Delegates on the topic of "Sufragio," Caro tellingly rejected the idea that wealth and instruction could be correlated in any way with moral worth, going so far as to claim that "the invention of writing was not included in the original plans of Providence regarding the human species" [la escritura no entró en los planes primitivos de la Providencia respecto de la especie humana] (*Estudios constitucionales* 172). In a revealing turn of phrase, he equated the silent majority's education in citizenship rights exclusively with catechesis: "good moral habits, which are a constitutive part of the idea of citizenship in a well-ordered republic, are not propagated by reading, but by oral traditions and good counsel" [las buenas costumbres, base esencial de la ciudadanía en una república bien ordenada, no se propagan por la lectura, sino por la tradición oral y los buenos consejos] (*Estudios constitucionales* 172).[63]

To be sure, allowing oneself to be counseled in the discipline of obedience to a higher authority was incompatible with the consolidated Enlightenment ethos of thinking critically, which fostered the debate among conflicting viewpoints held by opposing parties in a gradually inclusive political field. In the liberal mind-set, decisions are made and acts in government are carried out only after a laborious process of negotiation, which often results in the paralysis of government. This is exactly what Caro wished to avoid following the collapse of parliamentary democracy within the federal system instituted by the Constitution of Rionegro in 1863. To put it in Schmitt's jargon, Caro favored a "decisionist" model of government conceived within a limited democracy, in which the state of exception (the suspension of a parliamentary assembly's right to question the authority of the executive's decisions) would in fact constitute the executive branch's normal mode of operation.[64] In this reactionary model, legitimacy is created performatively through a series of uncontested acts in government and legislation regardless of their degree of arbitrariness. Caro's derogation of the laws guaranteeing the freedom of expression was a near-fatal blow to what Donoso Cortés and Schmitt called the liberal "feuding class."[65] This action allowed him to perpetuate the fiction that Colombia's political body was a monolithic totality, in which the best interests of what Aquinas called the *multitudo* were best served and given Catholic, universal expression by the autocratic *unus*.

Understandably, Caro's attempts at thwarting the expression of self-differentiated identities—ethnic, religious, and so forth—required that he place Colombia under both the Vatican's spiritual *imperium* and Spain's cultural tutelage, which he continued to identify with the sixteenth-century Habsburg Empire. This was a nonexistent Spain insofar as the former superpower could no longer pose a threat to the American nations' political sovereignty, nor could it be reconciled with the liberal state in place during the Federal Republic and the early Restoration period in the Peninsula (1870–1898). In such key texts as the essay "The Conquest" [La Conquista] (1881), the ballad "The Reconciliation" [La reconciliación] (1883), and the ode "To the Statue of the Libertador" [A la estatua del Libertador] (1883), Caro celebrated the notion of a traditionalist Spain in which the figure of the fatherly king ensured the uninterrupted transmission of Catholic teachings. In later texts, he also was to transform Bolívar into an advocate for the institution of the monarchy, an unwitting defender of the Catholic faith, and the proponent of rigidly hierarchized and centralized social and political structures.

What interested the ultramontane polymath from Bogotá was not that Colombia would become a hegemonic power in the theater of world politics (this was beyond his wildest dreams), but that the sovereignty snatched away by the federated states would be returned to the central government. To do this, he had to derogate the Constitution of 1863 and even suspend the application of its 1886 substitute. With this purpose, he resorted to his philologist's skills, which like jurisprudence placed great emphasis on the editing and interpretation of preexisting texts. Similarly, he was fond of interpreting the main texts of classical antiquity in the light of Christian doctrine. One of his most influential acts of literary translation was his Spanish rendition of the *Aeneid* in *octavas* (an eight-line stanza of rhymed verses ending in a couplet).[66] When Virgil's epic introduced the topic of the *translatio imperii*, Caro doctored the text to make it fit his idea that divine providence presides over the history of humankind. It will be remembered that in Book III, Aeneas meets Andromache in Buthrotus, a city built on the eastern shore of the Ionic Sea. In conversation with her, the Trojan hero recalls his speech to Dido in which he explained his plans for founding a new Troy on Italian soil that would be joined to its sister city on the eastern shore of the Ionic Sea by their mutual descent from Dardanus's lineage. But where Aeneas says "quipus idem Dardanus auctor / atque idem casus" (ll. 503–4)[67], which could be rendered as "Dardanus the common founder of both / and our trials the same," Caro substitutes a line of his own, which he utters as a Christian faithful rather than a faithful translator: "may heaven answer our prayers" [tales el cielo cumpla nuestros votos] (Book III, stanza xciii, l. 7).

It would not be an exaggeration to refer to Caro's patriotic and religious poems as acts of translation between genres of writing. He was, after all, making intelligible to a large audience the prosaic history of Colombia's self-inflicted defeat through a long series of civil wars and attempted secessions by analogy with the stories of Troy's and Rome's decline. With Bishop Otto's thoroughgoing interpretation of human history in light of Scripture and Church doctrine, the corrupt city's destruction became a clear sign announcing the imminence of Christianity's universal rule over the world (*monarchia universalis*). Just as Rome's paganism was redeemed by the *imperium Christi*, as de Maistre began to preach shortly after the Reign of Terror came to an end in France, so did the early Colombian republic lapse into satanic vices, which could only be corrected by leading the nation back to the Catholic Church's womb. For apologists for Christian violence such as Caro and Pope Pius IX, the greater the persecution of Catholicism in Colombia was, the greater the universal victory of the undivided Church would be.

Modern nation-building projects based on the medieval doctrine of *translatio imperii* involve a rationalization after the fact of cataclysmic changes in the balance of world power. They are also used to hide the combined effect of moments of agency and moments of inertia inherent in any historical process. Any power that succeeds in making decisions and carrying them into effect can extract from the nation's past certain experiences of fall and redemption, and arrange them in a paradoxical time frame that will speak to resonant contemporary events. He who decides on the exception (i.e., retains undivided sovereignty) may assume *imperium* not only in the sense of domination by physical coercion, but more importantly, in that of domination by consent. However, for this to happen, it seems that both the exception and the decisionist measures must be inscribed within what Schmitt will call a *theological* design. The competition between philosophies of the *translatio* and philosophies of the *pactum* or contract attests to each philosophy's inability to establish an uncontested foundation on which a discourse of rights can be instituted. The pact is thus demoted to the status of a consensus struck on a fiction—the people's representatives' willing suspension of disbelief in the sacredness and ineffability of their own source of sovereign power.

In late colonial New Granada, even Enlightenment enthusiasts feared that political authority would not survive the demise of theological interpretations of sovereignty. Already Antonio Nariño had become aware of this danger around the time when preparations were being made to draft the first charter of rights upon the proclamation of independence in 1810. Responding to leaders of several regions who had expressed their preference for a federal system, in which the authority of the central government would be smaller but in which conflicts over jurisdiction would multiply, Nariño wrote:

> In a sudden state of revolution the people is said to claim back its sovereignty [reasume la soberanía], but in practice, how can the people exercise it? Some will answer that through their representatives. And who appoints these representatives? The people itself. And who summons this people to a meeting? When? Where? Under what regulations?...The concerted mobilization of all the residents of a province, at the same time, in the same direction, and with the same purpose is a purely abstract concept, and ultimately an impossible one to carry into practice. This is the mobilization we have experienced ourselves because of the law that necessity imposed on us: a few enlightened and trustworthy men among *us* have had to appropriate part of the people's sovereignty so that *they* could take the first steps toward independence before *they* returned the sovereignty to the people [restituirla al pueblo].[68] (qtd. in Pombo and Guerra 1: 56; ellipses are mine)[69]

Although the phrase "reasume la soberaría" is an unequivocal reference to late sixteenth- and early seventeenth-century Jesuit theories of sovereignty, Nariño is in this passage mainly interested in finding an answer to Jean-Jacques Rousseau's own predicament concerning the relation of popular sovereignty to democratic representation. As we read in Book III of *The Social Contract*: "Sovereignty [*La souveraineté*] cannot be represented, for the same reason that it cannot be alienated; its essence is the general will, and will cannot be represented—either it is the general will or it is something else [*elle est la même, ou elle est autre*]; there is no intermediate possibility. Thus the people's deputies [*députés*] are not, and could not be, its representatives; they are merely its agents [*commissaires*]; and they cannot decide anything finally" (141).[70] Admittedly, neither Rousseau nor Nariño goes so far as to question representative democracy's legitimacy. However, implicit in Nariño's thinking is the idea that such a regime cannot be safeguarded from illegitimate appropriations and abuses of power unless the merely quantitative and expansive notion of "the people" coincides with the culturally selective one of "the nation"—a fiction whose existence must nevertheless be upheld to justify a revolution of independence. The existence of a culturally homogenous people (some would find this to be a sufficient definition of "nation") is, let us remember, Schmitt's main proviso for granting democracy a legitimate status vis-à-vis the undivided, uncontested notion of sovereignty: "democracy rests on the presupposition of the indivisibly similar, entire, unified people." In a regime of representation thus constituted, there would be no "voting down of the minority," no fracture in the necessarily indivisible nature of sovereignty, since that minority would not even exist as such (*Legality and Legitimacy* 27–28).

Reading Nariño with Caro and Schmitt, the concept of the "people's sovereignty" is reduced to little more than a rhetorical effect of the language of rights, used strategically by republican ideologues to offset earlier theories of *imperium*, when this protean institution of Roman *ius gentium* still designated a fluid domination/hegemony binomial. Although in practical terms the efficacy of such theories revolved around the ruler's monopoly over the means of physical coercion, formally speaking, it rested primarily on the subject's consent to be dominated, expressed through the Cortes or a related institution. Perhaps a sovereign power's legitimacy can only be substantiated when reexamined and renewed periodically in a daily plebiscite. Ideally, the "will" of the people would have to be consulted at all times, since the people cannot partially dispense with its sovereignty through agents of any kind, as Rousseau had warned as early as 1762. In nineteenth-century Colombia, Liberalism *did* push to its limits the praxis of the *pactum*, which since the pioneering writings of Nariño, Torres, and Zea in favor of the American colonies' independence from Spain had loomed large over the ideologues of both republicanism and Enlightenment progressivism.

If Nariño and his successors down to Bolívar and Santander reclaimed the sovereignty mortgaged to the monarch in the Old Regime, later generations used the local instruments of the state assembly and the governorship to challenge the sovereignty of a forever desacralized central executive power—they *willed* a thorough *translatio legati*. This questioning no doubt attests in many ways to the legitimacy and *catholicity* of the liberal-democratic state, which is predicated on the inclusiveness of the voices admitted into the debate. However, it also invests the criticisms that Donoso Cortés and Schmitt made of liberalism with a new sense of urgency. When partisan conflicts of authority become the rule rather than the exception, they may fatally destabilize the precarious balance among the three branches of government, placing legislative democracy under the permanent threat of dissolution.

Caro's answer to the challenge of how to translate the people's changing will into an uncontested concept of the state was as simple and as disturbing as Schmitt's. Instead of positing that Colombia's sovereignty could be represented as the sum total of every citizen's will, he argued that there was no such thing as "the people's sovereignty," since the people had to be organized first in a transcendent corporation, impermeable to feuding and dissent, in order to claim their rights of citizenship.[71] Not only is here the mutable will of the people replaced by a mystical authority in an exclusionary way, but the enforced homogeneity of the nation is itself subordinated to a larger body—the Church of Rome—that demands that the previously inalienable sovereignty be surrendered in the name of God. This is the import of the already cited article 38 in the Constitution of 1886. In writing the *Proyecto*, Caro succeeded in replacing the earlier statement in the preliminary *Bases*—"The nation recognizes that the Catholic religion is that of the near totality of Colombians"—with the phrasing that would eventually make it into the new *magna carta*'s final text—"The Roman-Catholic and apostolic religion is that of the nation."[72]

Caro's discourse of national redemption was to be realized through his fellow citizens' partial yet willing renunciation of their civil rights. This sacrifice would enact their long-awaited reconciliation (and *regression*) to the maternal bosom of Rome.[73] Nevertheless, the grammarian's discourse often slipped into an elegiac lament for a long-lost past, which could only be recuperated as a prolongation of the traumas of civil war in the form of a *revanchard* dialectics of loss and restitution. His lyric production conforms to the pattern of heightened narcissistic responses frequently adopted by the vanquished in the face of defeat. For late nineteenth-century Catholic intellectuals, victory was likely to become a curse while defeat remained a type of moral purification and salvation, which combined "the ancient idea of hubris with the Christian virtue of humility, catharsis with apocalypse" (Schivelbusch 20).[74]

Caro emerged as an important spokesperson for many Colombians' nostalgia for an authoritarian state at a time when his fellow citizens became utterly skeptical about the potential that the parliamentary state and the motherland had to act as a *transcendent* apparatus—the mechanism by which multiple contingencies are reduced to a necessary unanimity, if not of opinion, at least of feeling. Moreover, because he knew that Colombians had also come to distrust the systematic *de*-Christianization of values carried out relentlessly by the liberal state, he announced a movement similar to the waning of the Roman Empire to give way to a *regnum universalis* that was not subject to earthly contingencies. This event was construed also as the time when the restlessness always awake in the multitude was finally reduced to the perfect government of the *unus*: the papal Curia. Caro's proposed reduction of multiple meanings to one in the light of Scripture, Church doctrine, and ultramontane tracts also attests to his adherence to patristic exegesis, where meaning is generally given in advance of any direct rapport with the text. Everything is interpreted translationally and transcendentally, with the Catholic grammarian engaging at all times in the textual hermeneutics that we may call—adapting freely Tertullian's concept—*analogia fidei* (later on, *translatio fidei*) or conversion of non-Christian subjects *and* texts to the Christian faith.

Similarly, medieval interpreters of Aristotle regularly spoke of a *translatio secundum*/*translatio secunda* or privileging of a text's metaphorical connotations that are amenable to Christian doctrine over and against everyday, denotative meanings. Stories and poems should not just be morally edifying, thus fulfilling patristics' tropological imperative, but they are immersed in a multilayered network of allegorical and anagogical meanings. Biblical types foreshadow antitypes, just as Bolívar foreshadows Núñez, who in turn may for some (in an allegorical reading) foreshadow our contemporary Álvaro Uribe Vélez. Likewise, for Caro all significant stories worthy of that name speak to the promise of Christian salvation or to the nation's *regeneration* (this would be patristics' anagogical reading). These hermeneutical operations are incorporated into the reading of a text at the expense of the methodological self-consciousness and cautiousness posited by modern philology as a strategy for moving from the objective description of the text's parts to the understanding of the whole.[75]

For a *liberal* philology to have existed in Colombia in Caro's time, it would have had to free itself from the constraints imposed on it by the imperative to build a monolithic past and sacralize the motherland. The fact that in the realm of politics such emancipation was already taking place is indicated by Donoso Cortés's derogatory phrase, "feuding nations" [razas disputadoras]. It was the emergence of the liberal intellectual (whether radical or moderate) in Spain and Latin America, in a genealogy that goes from Manuel José Quintana and Sarmiento to Julián Sanz del Río and Manuel González Prada, that justified the ultramontane reaction to it. Influenced not just by Augustine, Dante, and Bishop Otto, but also by Vico, Hegel, and de Maistre, the main representatives of this reaction in the Spanish-speaking world (Donoso and Caro) cast the purpose behind it dialectically, as the perpetual struggle between the *civitas Dei* and the *civitas diaboli* through the shifting mediation of the *civitas terrena* or *civitas mundi*—the here and now of lettered city politics.

Caro's preference for the interpretive mode of patristics is seen, first, in his digressive use of Latin quotations and his tendency to rely on a priori truths and certainties that will not be altered ever so slightly by any argument or discussion. These strategies are reinforced by the proliferation, in his copious output, of translated texts as well as texts about translation and transfers of authority. And since his Latin versions of vernacular poets also have a primarily didactic purpose (they indeed belong to the genre or practice of catechesis), we may conclude that he specifically adhered to the medieval ethos of *translatio secundum*, producing the strategic anachronism of a Virgil, a Quevedo, a Bello, and even a Bolívar *a lo divino*.[76] In this enterprise, he was following in the footsteps of the first mover and translator of human and divine actions, the *auctor* of the transubstantiation. For who was this God whose writing had fallen implacably on the world since the first day of Creation, if not a translator of verbal chaos into verbal order—a maker of usable, if constraining, national fictions?

Chapter Three
Hugo, Bello, Caro

Hating Hugo's Politics, Loving Hugo's Prayers

Victor Hugo finished writing his poem "La prière pour tous" on June 15, 1830, published it the same year, and subsequently included it in the volume *Les Feuilles d'automne*, which came out in 1831.[1] The poem is one of several pieces in which an alter ego of Hugo confesses himself a sinner before a thinly disguised persona of his daughter Léopoldine, whom in the poem he asks to pray for forgiveness and atonement of his sins.[2] "La prière pour tous" runs to 420 lines divided into ten sections. Admittedly, it is not one of Hugo's most felicitous compositions. The alternation of stanzas featuring short, incantatory lines with others that are digressive and anecdotal results in an uneven structure. This imbalance is made all the more evident by the fact that the composition's second half reiterates the same images and statements employed in the first. In the course of the poem, Hugo's lyric "I" uses variations on the phrases "My daughter, go and pray!" or "Pray for this and that…" at least fifteen times. As a central element in the Catholic liturgy, prayers rehearse a predictable ritual; they constitute a performance of faith and show the faithful's *willing* submission to the Lord's higher power. Hugo's lyrical prayer for the most part conforms to these genre expectations, but it also contains, halfway through, an unforeseen disclosure. This revelation was difficult for many Catholic Spanish American readers to anticipate as they were still unfamiliar with his complex perspective on religious matters.

Since "La prière pour tous" is not Hugo at his best, it is not widely considered part of the massive Hugo canon, and, as far as I know, was first published in English translation by Henry Carrington in Britain in the later nineteenth century. This translation was reproduced in the 1909 Boston edition of *Poems*. Parts of a different version appeared earlier in the periodical press and were collected in volume 3 of *Selected Poems* (1897). The French poem's insufficiencies have fueled the desire of Bello's hagiographers to prove the superiority of the Venezuelan's abridged Spanish version over the original. In short, "La prière pour tous" lacks in France the status that "La oración por todos" was soon accorded in Spanish America, particularly in Chile, where Bello's version was first published in 1843, and Colombia, where Caro had it printed at least six times between 1860 and 1889. Suffice it to say, for now, that Bello's approach to Hugo's text can be said to illustrate Nietzsche's argument against letting a self-restrained moralist like Bello translate imaginatively adventurous works. For all their local infelicities, Hugo's works are animated by a free-spirited *tempo* that the classically minded translator would have trouble imitating successfully.[3]

Born in 1802, Hugo started out as a monarchist poet, in no small part because his mother, after a hard-fought legal separation from the General Joseph Hugo (a decorated hero of the Peninsular campaigns), taught him to hate the French Republic. Having received a pension from Louis XVIII for his precocious poetic accomplishments in 1822, Hugo gradually moved from his moderately conservative position to a more liberal persuasion between 1830, when he wrote in the preface to *Hernani* that "Le romantisme…n'est…que le *libéralisme* en littérature" (*Théâtre complet, tome I* 1147), and 1848, when he was elected first to the Assemblée Constituante (his candidacy being still center-right by the standards of the day) and immediately after to the Assemblée Legislative.[4] Bello echoes this distinction in his "Juicio crítico de don José Gómez Hermosilla" (pub. in *El Araucano* in 1841–1842), taking the side of romanticism and challenging the principle of "authority": "The classical school divides genres with the same care used by the legitimist sect to separate the various social hierarchies… The romantic school, on the contrary, flaunts the confusion and approximation of social classes" (*Obras completas* 9: 375–76). This is an unmistakable reference to the plot of Hugo's *Ruy Blas* (1838). Bello goes on to add that romanticism had to be born necessarily on English soil, since representative government and trial by jury had originated there too. By contrast with Hugo, Gómez Hermosilla would now be, after renouncing his youthful Jacobinism, an "ultra-monarquista en política, y ultra-clásico en literatura" (Bello, *Obras completas* 9: 376), a characterization that foreshadows T. S. Eliot's notorious self-presentation in the preface to *For Lancelot Andrewes* (1928).[5]

José Victorino Lastarria was just one among several Spanish-speaking authors who quoted admiringly from the preface to *Hernani*. In *Recuerdos literarios* (1878), he reproduced the page-long passage in which the definition of romanticism just cited is given. He added that Hugo had been embraced by the French Academy and *Hernani* was now considered to be a work as classic as Corneille's *Le Cid*. Lastarria and his Argentine collaborators (he was possibly thinking of Sarmiento) were quick to see that Hugo was no longer a threat to either the making of a national literature or a republic's social stability (117–18). Medardo Rivas expressed a similar idea when he devoted a *cuadro de costumbres* in the manner of Larra—"My Nephew" [Mi sobrino]—to the life of a young Parnassian poet *and* grammarian in 1880s, Bogotá, who had embraced French Hellenism without giving up the Colombian Conservatives' obsession with grammatical correctness. Recaredo is called a "classic poet," a "monarchist," and a "grammatical automaton" or "metro-grammarian" (Rivas 1: 217, 220). We know that he translated Virgil's complete works (although, unlike Caro, he did it "word-by-word"), had "bellicose instincts," and bears the name of a Visigothic king—Recaredo—at a time when extreme Conservatives were already being called "godos." The two main differences between Caro and Recaredo are that the latter lived in his library's ivory tower (rather than the political arena) and was no longer a Catholic.

Recaredo cannot accept Hugo's poetry because the Frenchman's works and high opinions are "mingled with the messy drama of life" (Rivas 1: 220); furthermore, his writing is directed by the heart's passions and the mind's fantasy in their respective correspondences with great social conflicts and causes (1: 219). Rivas's sketch treats Victor Hugo not only as a magician of words, but also as the prototype of the *engagé* poet. Although this poet has not sacrificed to politics his commitment to renewing the French language through its contact with the Third Estate (the "*turba-multa*" [1: 217]), he has given up everything else (his motherland, a life of comforts, and so forth). Echoing Rafael María Baralt's *Diccionario de galicismos* (1855), Recaredo critiques the French language's pernicious influence on Spanish. Although his poetics and aesthetics seem to be greatly indebted to the French Parnasse's "art for art's sake," he insists on preserving the purity of Castilian.

As Quintana saw in Spain (with the rise of Antonio Capmany and Leandro Fernández de Moratín to the position of the absolutist king's grammatical censors) and Sebastiano Timpanaro wrote about nineteenth-century philology, grammatical correctness and textual editing could all too often decline into the semiconscious repression of a foreign text's novel ideas. Caro often got away with this mystification in his paraphilological essays. By contrast, Rivas directed his reader's attention to Hugo's example: "Let us put aside the question of whether [what we read] are Gallicisms or not. As Victor Hugo says: 'That which has already been accomplished by new ideas cannot be undone by grammarians…An idea cannot have more than one form, which is its own. It is the idea's form par excellence—a complete, rigorous, and essential form which is born by the genius' brain at the same time as the idea'" (1: 221).[6]

In a memorable series of speeches given at the two legislative bodies during the liberal revolution of 1848, Hugo took a stand on several issues that at the time signaled the difference between radical-Liberal and Conservative politics, and not just in France, but in Spain and Colombia too. He spoke courageously against the rigors of the *état de siège* decreed in 1848, the curtailment of the freedom of the press, the government's indifference to the poverty and exclusion of the working classes, the permanent ultramontane threat to the Revolution's legacy of *laïcité,* the death penalty, and the practice of torture. As Hugo increasingly radicalized his positions, he also became a champion of universal suffrage and of women's rights in general, and helped bring about a more inclusive form of parliamentary democracy.[7]

In spite of the liberal leanings of Hugo's political writings since at least 1849, his later literary works also show some features more commonly associated with moderate conservatism. It was his poems and plays written before that date that built his reputation in Spanish America prior to the publication of *Les Misérables* in 1862. Bello owned this best-selling novel in the ten-volume French edition of 1865 and contemporary public figures as diverse as Hugo Chávez and Mario Vargas Llosa have singled it out as their favorite work of fiction.[8] Colombian theatergoers much preferred Hugo's dramas to Moratín's neoclassical comedies (*El sí de las niñas* addressed the perennial concern of the arranged marriage in a self-enclosed elite society), and many did not enjoy sitting through generally mediocre performances. Nevertheless, for the most part they acquiesced in pretending that there was some inherent good in a spectacle produced according to preexisting "rules" and restricted to the privileged few.[9]

The aspects of Hugo's writings that the reactionary lettered city could readily appropriate were, first, the poet's interest in—and use of—the topoi of Spanish heroism. Hugo spent part of his childhood in occupied Spain, was an avid reader of the *romancero*, and devoted about 200 pages of his epic cycle *La légende des siècles* to Spanish themes.[10] Second, as he lived through several wars, revolutions, and forced expatriations (in 1852 and 1870), Hugo became easily intoxicated with the emotional experience of losing himself in the pursuit of an irrational and often spiritual ideal. This is seen in his poems that rehearse the topoi of *amor patriae*, parental love, romantic love, and even divine love, which he saw as the subject's opening up to the mysteries of existence and transcendence, but not to the claims of Catholic dogma.[11] Third, and most important for my discussion, Hugo made a very ambiguous use of the conservative ideologeme of "prayer," a speech-act situation and motif that was already ubiquitous in the nineteenth-century Colombian literary system.[12] We may add to these circumstances Élisée Reclus's remarks on the resonant echo that *Les Orientales* (1829) had in Colombia: the Turkish and Egyptian landscapes could also be found in the New World, causing the traveler to admit that in America "l'imitation et la nature sont tellement confondues" (914). Vergara y Vergara expressed the same idea in his review of Jorge Isaacs's *María*, published—like the novel—in 1867: the "magnificent Cauca landscapes emulate oriental ones" ("Juicio crítico" 13). In fact, Vergara y Vergara went on to suggest that Isaacs "translated" his vision of nature and society into a tragic idyll whose semiotic code existed simultaneously both in Hugo's literature and in the Cauca's phenomenal world ("Juicio crítico" 12).

Quite predictably, of all Hugo's works, Caro hated *Les Orientales* the most, perhaps because it showcased nations of nomads and self-reliant mavericks. Like the Argentinian *gauchos* and the Venezuelan *llaneros*, these characters escaped the state's control and needed no organized religion for their survival. Hugo's detractors in Spain and the Americas repeatedly accused him of implementing a poetics of monstrosity, which conveniently provided those detractors with an occasion for defending Bello's taming of Hugo's exuberant imagination in his translations.[13] *Les Orientales* also disproved the theory that until 1830, Hugo had been monolithically Catholic and conservative. By contrast, the translations of Hugo that Bello produced in the early 1840s (among them "Los fantasmas," excerpted from *Les Orientales*) soon acquired an American life of their own, making their way through pious, pedagogical magazines in the Spanish-speaking world. They reassured Catholic educators that the work of "a romantic in literature and liberal in politics" could still be converted into a textbook for catechesis.[14]

Hugo was a *Chrétien sans Église*: he never tired of writing against ecclesiastical institutions, a tendency confirmed by the long, almost unmotivated digression on monastic and convent life that is Book Seven of *Les Misérables* (1862)—aptly titled "Parenthèse"—which even some modern English editions excise from the narrative, placing it at the end by means of an appendix.[15] At the same time, however, he extolled the incantatory power of prayer, which for him was simply a particularly spiritualized song that placed the speaker and his or her audience in the imaginative act of liturgical communion.[16]

If there was a Spanish American author capable of attacking the ecclesiastical establishment while searching for spiritual (and even religious) authenticity, it was the Chilean Francisco Bilbao. By his own testimony, he was greatly influenced by Félicité R. Lamennais, the former ultramontanist turned democrat who also convinced the Spaniard Larra—the translator, in 1835, of Lamennais's *Paroles d'un croyant* (1834)—of democracy's and popular sovereignty's status as the new Christianity. Bilbao was another former Catholic who felt Tocqueville's *place vide*, which left an imprint as powerful and inapprehensible as the eclipse of theo-political sovereignties that produced the *lieu vide* in Sieyès's democratic constitutions. Like Hugo, Bilbao could not fill that void save through his mystical raptures. The earliest example of this writing, which showed an exuberance, self-assurance, and intellectual range comparable only to Hugo's, was "Sociabilidad chilena" (1844), the article that provoked the closing down by the authority of Lastarria's *El Crepúsculo* after hardly one year of successful publication.[17]

The seeds of Hugo's theory of prayer appear in the "Préface de *Cromwell*" (1827), where prayers are explicitly opposed to Church liturgy. The passage in question is worth quoting at length:

> There you have the first man, the first poet. He is young, he is lyrical. The prayer is his only form of religion; the ode is his only form of poetry [*La prière est toute sa religion: l'ode est toute sa poésie*].
> This poem, this ode of the primitive times, was the Book of Genesis.

Little by little, however, the world outgrows its adolescence. Every realm expands; the family becomes a tribe, the tribe a nation. Each of these groups of people gather around a common center, and kingdoms make their appearance. The nomadic impulse is replaced by the social impulse. Camps give way to cities, tents to palaces, arks to temples. The leaders of these embryonic states are still shepherds, but shepherds of people; their shepherds' staffs are already starting to look like sceptres. Everything becomes settled and fixed. Religion assumes a form; rituals regulate prayers [*les rites règlent la prière*]; and dogmas organize the worship. Thus priest and king share the fatherhood of their people; a theocratic society replaces a patriarchal community. (*Théâtre complet, tome I* 411)[18]

In his booklength diatribe against Bentham, *Estudio sobre el utilitarismo* (1869), Caro silently rewrites Hugo's fable, presenting the priest—as proto-Vicar of Christ—as the original patriarch who willingly gave up his kingly authority to the temporal power on condition that the Church and the family be protected. The "moral sovereignty" [soberanía moral], from which all other forms of power derive, is thus made to reside in the Church (*Obras, tomo I* 169). Therefore, only the ecclesiastical authorities can educate and govern. Colombia's parents, teachers, and legislators are simply the appointed deputies of that power: "all power comes from God; the magistrate is a minister of his kingdom. To govern is to educate [*gobernar es educar*]; all good education, all education deserving of that name has at its foundation the moral truth, the religious truth. An atheistic ruler is a functionary incapable of performing his duty, he is a usurper. An atheistic government is a contradiction in terms" (*Obras, tomo I* 170).[19]

Caro posits here the coexistence of four interlocking forms of *potestas*: paternal, ecclesiastical, and civil in addition to the individual's self-possession ("man also governs himself…governing his passions"). Predictably, all four have their own limits, although the prerogative of *sacerdotium* is taken to be *primus inter pares*. He concludes with a question to which he provides the answer: "But, where is the supreme authority who establishes these limits, who establishes this harmony? This supreme authority is God" (*Obras, tomo I* 170). In the article "La religión y la poesía" (1882) Caro offered a substantive appraisal of Hugo. He did not try to conceal his disgust at the impiety found in much of the Frenchman's output. He dared to state (on the suspect authority of the noted antiromantic critic Gustave Planche) that Hugo's genius was best seen in his ability to produce 500 pages of verse—*Les Orientales*—without a single line of poetry in them (*Artículos y discursos* 327).

When a kinsman of Caro as well as Holguín, Julio Holguín Arboleda, published a sequel to "La religión y la poesía" of the same title in 1935, the magazine that carried it—*El Gráfico*—illustrated the text with a picture of U.S. combat aircrafts flying in V formation, as if modern warfare could provide the same epic tone found in religious and prophetic songs. This article discusses poems only by two of Holguín Arboleda's ancestors—his namesake Julio Arboleda and José Eusebio Caro—indicating explicitly that their religious output predates and surpasses Hugo's best. Several passages venture hyperbolic comparisons while cramming numerous errors in the evaluation of Hugo's achievement: "Arboleda's religious feelings shine in his political poems, which foreshadow Hugo's *Châtiments*, because *our compatriot* [he means, of course, *my ancestor*] was the first one to have the felicitous and timely idea of infusing his song with the content of a political ideology and to anathemize those who professed the opposing one" ("Religión y poesía [II]" 366; emphasis added). Holguín Arboleda proceeds to quote from the earlier Arboleda's "I am in jail" [Estoy en la cárcel], a dull piece cast in the form of a prayer of thanksgiving addressed to God, in which the speaker narcissistically rejoices in the symbolic sacrifice of his life for God and party.

In the poem, the incarcerated Arboleda seriously entertains the idea that a Liberal butcher will slaughter him—a "lamb"—in his cell now turned into an altar. Holguín Arboleda's paraphrase and gloss of the poem neglect to mention that Julio Arboleda was killed by one of his own bloodthirsty party comrades (a Conservative, not a Liberal). He also crucially omits the fact that in the civil war of 1859–1862, Arboleda imprisoned many principled Liberals (including fellow Cauca poet César Conto), whom he tried to humiliate by reciting to them passages from the *Aeneid* and other epics used by choleric victors to lash out at their captive enemies.[20]

Hugo equated himself with Moses and enjoyed being called Olympio; in Spain he was called the "Attila of poetry" because he destroyed the authority of the Old Regime as much as the rules of neoclassical decorum. He was also widely regarded as the new "Homer" because he echoed the spirit of a dying era and the dawning of the succeeding one without sparing the reader the messy and exuberant imperfections inherent in historical and cultural transitions. In "La religión y la poesía," Caro warned his reader against the stylistic and moral degradation to which Hugo's sinful bouts of impiety subjected him. This fallen side coexisted with an angelic one; the former "pleases the communist mob" [adula á la plebe comunista] instead of offering catechesis to "children and virgin girls" (*Artículos y discursos* 329–30). Caro saw the catechizing mission in "La prière pour tous," which he describes thus: "And *La Oración por todos* is (except for a few flawed passages) a page of Catholic theology translated into the language of fatherly love and domestic affections; it is a tender apology for the efficacy of prayer in the way we Catholics conceive of it, free and unencumbered by the ice chains of Protestant fatalism" (*Artículos y discursos* 328).

In 1889, Rivas Groot also tried to reconcile Hugo's writings in support of *laïcité* with his inspired condition as synthesizer of a tantalizingly protean and multiple world into a cosmic unit. He not only argued that Hugo transcended the distinction between romantic and neoclassical (i.e., between liberal and conservative)—Hugo was both—but he was now also something *other* or something *else*. In addition, Hugo could well be the Regeneración's guiding poet to the extent that his verbal and emotional alchemy reconciled opposing principles. For that reason, Rivas Groot also contended that it was possible for a literary genius—"a man-symbol"—to profess non-Catholic doctrines while keeping his Catholic feelings intact ("Estudio preliminar" lxxxviii–xcii, x–xiii, xl–xliii).

For Caro, Hugo's "La prière pour tous" originates in the Frenchman's appropriation of a theological speech-act consisting in naming God and his attributes, humbly asking him for his mercy at a time of distress. The blots in the prayers, which are erased in Bello's expurgated Spanish translation, would then reveal the work of *philologia sacra*, in which the original's imperfections are corrected in accordance with established doctrine. Hugo's *translatio secunda* was enabled by the combination of Bello's excisions and the body of commentary that Caro produced both on Hugo and Bello, taking the two versions of the texts as the quintessential expression of their respective authors' religious outlook on personal and social experience. To be fair to Caro and Bello, the latter had taken his share in eliminating non-Catholic contexts and contents from other Hugo poems. Although Bello was a connoisseur of Semitic literatures, he did not fully participate in the orientalist frenzy of his time. When confronted with a poem like Hugo's "Les Djinns" (from *Les Orientales* [1829]), Bello departed from the original, whose title references the supernatural creatures that in the Muslim tradition haunt (an may even possess) those who violate the liturgy and precepts of Islam. Hugo's speaker also mentions "des Arabes" and their "chants" as well as invoking one "Prophète!" reminiscent of Muhammad. Bello opted instead for a thorough Christianizing of the text, which he called "Los duendes. Imitación de Víctor Hugo" (first published in Santiago's *El Progreso* [July 19, 1843]). He inserted in it such exclamations as "¡Oh Virgen del Carmelo!" and "¡Jesus! ¡Jesus!" while situating part of the action in a Christian church.

Caro was also careful not to connect Hugo to nineteenth-century revolutions (Rivas Groot observed the same precaution). He knew that discussing Hugo's direct political influence—what he briefly if inexactly decried as his "communism"—would render impossible the projected canonization of prayer as literature's main genre. Caro had come to terms with the indisputable fact that Hugo was the most prolific and admired writer of literary prayers of the nineteenth century, perhaps of any century. The fellow *letrado* and self-styled theologian who insisted on connecting Hugo to the degradation of Spanish Catholicism in New Granada was Rufino Cuervo. Yet his son, the more cosmopolitan Rufino José, had the good sense of withholding publication of the *Vida de Rufino Cuervo y noticias de su época* (in which he and brother Ángel excerpt their father's writings) until 1892. By then, as stated by Lastarria in a citation given above, Hugo had been transformed into the epitome of French classicism and bourgeois respectability by the very force of history, which now moved quickly toward the advent of proletarian revolutions.

Rufino Cuervo's disdain for Hugo and his antiecclesiastical positions informs his attack in 1851 on an anonymous pamphleteer who had criticized Church abuses in the person of Manuel José Mosquera y Arboleda, the powerful Archbishop of Bogotá and brother of a bellicose president, Tomás Cipriano de Mosquera. Don Rufino intimated that the author of the presumed slander was as foul-mouthed and degenerate as the character of Jeahn Frollo du Moulin (Joannes Frollo de Molendino), the rowdy student in Hugo's *Notre-Dame de Paris* (1831) who continually swears against theologians and university professors with reckless abandon. In don Rufino's words: "He who wants to be acquainted with the violence and opprobrium of the most atrocious capital sins, as they are described by Sue, will find in this pamphlet Lucifer's pride and Cain's envy, set forth in the bitterly lascivious language used by Hugo's canon-law student Juan Frollo" (R.J. Cuervo, *Obras, tomo II* 1527). More than anything else, this passage tells us that Cuervo, notwithstanding his religious smugness, was reading the scandalous novels of Hugo and Eugène Sue, as was his son Rufino José.

Who Prays and to Whom: Hugo, Bello, and (José Eusebio) Caro

Caro's most daring reduction of Hugo to a Catholic fundamentalist consisted in the reprinting of Bello's "La oración por todos" in a cluster of shorter writings edited for the Colombian Academy's *El Repertorio Colombiano* (13.7 [1887]: 59–67). As part of the ongoing series "Lecturas paralelas en prosa y verso," this extensive cluster (pp. 41–84) featured the editor's ideal contexts for the reception of José Eusebio's religious writing and Bello's *translatio secunda* of Hugo's lyric. The cluster immediately followed Valera's essay on Hugo (pp. 36–41 of the same issue). It included four poems (by William Cullen Bryant, José Eusebio Caro, the Cuban-Spanish Gertrudis Gómez de Avellaneda, and the Mexican José Joaquín Pesado) and four pieces of doctrinal prose (by José Eusebio, Santiago José García Mazo,[21] Father Miguel Mir, who quotes from Donoso Cortés and Balmes, and Monsignor Bougaud—Vicar of Orléans—who cites Bossuet and de Maistre). These pieces are preceded by a fragment from Scripture (Luke 12:22–31) retitled by the editor "Providencia." In a paraphilological footnote, Caro indicates that he has used Felipe Scío de San Miguel's Spanish translation, which he has emended in two places employing Félix Torres Amat's slightly later *lectio.*[22] The rendering that Caro produces reads thus: "Therefore, seek primarily God's kingdom and its justice; and these other things [e.g., articles of material necessity] shall be yours as well" [Por tanto, buscad primeramente

el reino de Dios y su justicia; y todas esas cosas se os darán por añadidura]
("Lecturas paralelas" 44).[23]

Early in his career, Caro made the decision that he was to champion the
creation of a confessional state in which public institutions as a whole (the
state's legal, cultural, and educational apparatuses) would be placed under
the Church's supervision. For this purpose, he crafted a multisource doctri-
nal "vulgate" of his own, a downgraded mosaic of fragments and quotations,
mostly from Church doctrine but also from early modern Spanish prose
and contemporary counterrevolutionary thinking. The quotations gath-
ered under "Lecturas paralelas" were a miniscule example of his publicizing
efforts in this direction. What invested these exercises with cultural author-
ity was their appearance in such venues as the Colombian Academy's main
periodical, which not only ensured their circulation among the elite, but
also helped legitimate the fiction that all Colombians upheld the doctrines
expounded therein. "Lecturas paralelas" presented itself as a polyphonous
rescript implicitly endorsed by ecclesiastical and civil authorities across the
ages—by both the dead authors excerpted in the anthology of texts and the
living ones who occupied a seat at the Academy.

This presentation of paraphilological texts is done at the expense of phil-
ological acumen. Caro does not muster the rigor that he was expected to
observe in presenting texts from the past. The evidence that I have adduced
is almost self-explanatory. When Caro writes that he has collated two pre-
existing versions of the Bible (Scío de San Miguel's and Torres Amat's),
he is *seemingly* indulging in the accepted practice that textual criticism
calls *emendatio ope codicum* (emendation with the help of manuscripts—
published texts in this case). However, in not following the *lectio* of either
text mentioned in the note, he is implementing an *emendatio ope ingenii/
coniecturae* (emendation with the help of native wit), which as a layperson
he should not produce even if he warns the reader of this unorthodox textual
procedure. As Timpanaro wrote in his critique of philology's unfulfilled
promise to develop trustworthy protocols of research independent of the
editor's personal prestige, the history of the discipline is full of copyists and
editors who claimed to be collating older texts. In reality, however, many
of them frequently amended capriciously their base text by invoking the
practice of *emendatio ope ingenii* allowed only to particularly learned editors
(Timpanaro, *La genesi* 3–4).

At the center of "Lecturas paralelas" are José Eusebio Caro's two brief
compositions: the poem "The Baptism" [El bautismo] (1845) and the essay
"The Universality of Prayer" [Universalidad de la oración] (53–59). Miguel
Antonio does not date "The Universality of Prayer," perhaps because he
wishes to enhance the intemporality of its teaching and the argument it
advances, namely, that men and women of all faiths and races have in all

historical periods kneeled down before Jesus Christ to ask for his protection or to thank him for it. Because that liturgical practice is recorded in both the prophetic books and the Gospel, the author contends that it should be held as the basic doctrine of Catholicism. José Eusebio begins his shorter essay with these words: "People's prayers are the twofold acknowledgment of man's weakness and God's goodness and power followed by an imploration of God's goodness and power on behalf of man's weakness" (M. A. Caro, "Lecturas paralelas" 57).

"The Baptism" was written against those who equated the church-goer's excessive devotion to the liturgical aspects of religion with superstition. José Eusebio also contends that God grants equality of rights to his brethren because intellectual and economic disadvantages are not an impediment to moral regeneration and to obtaining God's grace. However egalitarian this may sound, José Eusebio explains in a related essay—"La cuestión moral" (1849)—that the poor need not envy the rich because it is also within their reach to obtain God's pardon for their sins but out of their reach to acquire wealth unless they receive providentially additional advantages (*Obras escogidas* 142–45).[24] He states further that the poor relate to prayer and other liturgical aspects in a vulgar way. Since they cannot understand the Latin formulae or the theological significance of symbols (their metaphorical meaning as it was given *secundum traditionem*), they participate in the liturgy through their "sensuality." In his opinion, the affluent elites who lose their faith but continue to attend religious services are demoting themselves socially by mimicking the plebeians' response. The Colombian reactionaries ostensibly shunned earthly possessions and the consolation of sensuous pleasures, which they denied the poor. At the same time, their writing also places the crucial political question of property rights and access to the franchise off limits, thus providing another textbook example of how lyric and catechesis carried out the superstructural work of making the legitimacy of proprietary institutions opaque to the masses.

The only text that is missing from Miguel Antonio's anthology, in which his father's writing shines through as the culmination of a theocratic discourse on sin and redemption, is Augustine's *On the Lord's Sermon on the Mount*. This text could not be included in "Lecturas paralelas" because it is even more candid than José Eusebio's letter to Arboleda in disclosing the ideological mystification behind the discourse on religious conversion, in which the material contexts underlying conversion are rendered alternately visible and invisible. For Augustine as for José Eusebio, the more the faithful crave for visible gifts, the more invisible and opaque will become the only gifts available to them. Propertyless individuals need to enact a "turning of the heart" [*conversio cordis*] through prayer so that they do not covet their wealthy neighbors' worldly possessions:

> God does not give heed to the ambitiousness of our prayers, because he is always ready to give to us his light, not a visible light but an intellectual and spiritual one [*dare suam lucem nobis, non visibilem, sed intelligibilem et spiritualem*]: but we are not always ready to receive it when we turn aside and down to other things out of a desire for temporal things. For in prayer there occurs a turning of the heart [*Fit ergo in oratione conversio cordis*] to he who is always ready to give if we will but take what he gives: and in that turning is the purification of the inner eye when the things we crave in the temporal world are shut out; so that the vision of the pure heart can bear the pure light that shines divinely without setting or wavering: and not only bear it, but abide in it. (*Opera omnia, Tomus tertius* 2.3.14; p. 1275)

In contrast with José Eusebio's Augustinian reactionarism, utilitarianism had long advocated that positive laws were corrective mechanisms used by the legislative branch of government to ensure that differences in wealth and education gradually shrink. This is what attracted Bolívar to Bentham's philosophy: the notion, as he put it in the "Declaración de Angostura" (1819), that the inequalities found in nature and society among individuals and classes could be corrected by the affirmative action of jurisprudence. For José Eusebio, however, the discourse on natural rights indeed *naturalized* those differences, making state intervention a tyrannical imposition upon the individual who thought of his praying routine as the righteous' quintessential legal transaction with God. The currency of this proposition at the end of the nineteenth century was shown by the Scottish legal scholar James Lorimer (1818–1890). In a popular handbook called *The Institutes of Law: A Treatise of the Principles of Jurisprudence, as Determined by Nature* (1872), he discussed "prayers" as one of the "secondary sources of positive law" (359–63). The strength of Lorimer's argument lies in its rigorous internal logic. Since only the faithful will pray to their deity, as a Christian, you can pray only in conformity with God's laws, or else your prayer will be a waste of breath and an infelicitous speech act:

> To pray for the alteration of laws which we assume to be perfect, is to pray for evil; whereas to pray for power and will to conform to such laws, is to pray for that which alone is wanting to our good; and the act of offering such a prayer is, in itself, no unimportant step towards its fulfillment. To pray that sin may be no longer sin, is to throw breath away; but to pray that we may not be sinners, is already to be sinless so far; and the frequent repetition of such prayer may end in the formation of habits of comparative sinlessness, or, in other words, of voluntary conformity with God's laws. (Lorimer 362–63)

In a letter to Julio Arboleda written during his expatriation in New York in 1852, José Eusebio set forth his views on the relation of religion to poetry, which anticipate those of his son Miguel Antonio. Poetry should contain neither "thoughts" nor "inventions"; instead, it should arise from the simple act of "singing" before and about God, or celebrating filial love and the virtue of women. "Prayer" and "action" constitute the high ideal of a verbose and bellicose publicist who could not stop catechizing others and who routinely slandered his political antagonists with his venomous prose (J. E. Caro, *Obras escogidas* 232–33). Together, prayer and action replace analysis and discussion, creating the conditions for a decisionist regime in which democracy is purged of *discordia*. Another key aspect of José Eusebio's creed was that "freedom," "right," and "truth" were theological dimensions of existence rather than political ones (it just so happened that one political party shared these assumptions with the Catholic Church). These concepts were good in themselves and need not be made contingent upon the benefits that they could bring to the individual. In other words, as long as we enshrine the words in a code of natural law (José Eusebio did not believe in codes of positive legislation despite holding a seat in Congress), we need not worry about guaranteeing that code's implementation since private virtues (the Christian's exclusive capital) precede and inform public ones (the citizen's).

This convoluted contention allowed José Eusebio to hypothesize that human beings are completely free in relation to other subjects and the state, and that governments should be as small as possible. One did not have to obey governments whenever their prescriptions contradicted the natural law that informed one's Christian thoughts. After all, one's full obedience was due only to God. He could thus kneel down before the "goddess" of Freedom as he did to worship God, by means of a "prayer" (J. E. Caro, *Obras escogidas* 127, 186). One need not be very astute to see that José Eusebio's ideas entail a complete reversal and subversion of Bentham's program for examining concepts not in themselves, but in the effects they have on the citizens' material well-being.

Like his son Miguel Antonio, José Eusebio also glorified women as mothers, daughters, and sisters. What made these female-gendered subject-positions very valuable for his reactionary discourse was that women were not yet allowed to acquire their rudimentary primary instruction outside the home or a few ecclesiastical establishments.[25] Their domestic subalternity was presented in the form of uxorial love. They were incessantly manipulated by priests and confessors to influence the political choices of their husbands, sons, and fathers (González Vigil, *Importancia* 81–83). José Eusebio knew firsthand that men were more likely to stray from Catholicism and embrace heretical ideas because they were better educated and spent less time in church and more in the agora or in pursuing their economic self-interest. To be sure, the centrality accorded to women made Hugo's poem all the more appealing to the Caros. In "La prière pour tous," the contrite speaker commemorates both his daughter and his wife, bringing their plight to bear upon his felt alienation and his resolve to be reconciled with God through the act of prayer and the acceptance of penance.

In the light of Caro's treatment of "La oración por todos" as the quintessential expression of Bello's thinking and of Spanish America's Catholic spirit, it is imperative that we ask the following question: Is there a sovereign deity in Hugo's poetry? Specifically, does "La prière pour tous" gesture in this direction? The moment of reckoning in "La prière pour tous" happens halfway through and concerns the status of the speaker's faith. Most crucially, it comes immediately after the line where Bello stopped translating. The suppressed half of the poem begins with this passage: "It does not fall upon me, my dove, to pray for all of humankind, for the living whose faith falters, for those who are trapped in their tombs; these tombs are the root of the altar! It is not me, whose soul is vain—full of errors, void of faith—who should pray for the human race, since my voice, Lord, is hardly enough [for me] to pray to you!" [Ce n'est pas à moi, ma colombe, / De prier pour tous les mortels, / Pour les vivants dont la foi tombe, / Pour tous ceux qu'enferme la tombe, / Cette racine des autels! / Ce n'est pas moi, dont l'âme est vaine, / Pleine d'erreurs, vide de foi, / Qui prierais pour la race humaine, / Puisque ma voix suffit à peine, / Seigneur, à vous prier pour moi!] (ll. 179–88).[26] Granting the possibility that "vide de foi" may signify that the speaker has momentarily strayed from the Christian path of perfection, or (this is the view taken by Saint-Beuve) that he has irretrievably lost his faith; either reading must have sounded very alarming to a churchgoer like Bello, who proceeded to its excision.[27]

In 1954 Henri Guillemin published an extract of a previously unknown journal by Hugo, found at the Bibliothèque Nationale, which spanned the years 1871–1872, a particularly difficult period in the writer's life. It contained an eight-line prayer in which the speaker asks a higher power (God is not invoked as such) that *It* may have pity for "ma pauvre petite Adèle" (who at the time was committed to an insane asylum; mentioned twice), for "mon fils Victor" (who became seriously ill in 1872 and died the following year; mentioned once) and for himself (who suffered a stroke and was expulsed from Brussels for sheltering revolutionaries during the Paris Commune; mentioned four times) (Guillemin 7). His other son, Charles, had died in 1871.

"La prière pour tous" became the text that Hugo could use in his later years to provide an emotionally meaningful closure to a life marked by losses as much as by triumphs. He saw the pattern of his life repeated in his two sons: François-Victor, the celebrated young translator of Shakespeare, and Charles, the advocate for the right of asylum, *habeas corpus*, the derogation of the death penalty, and several other worthy causes he shared with his father. In the prologue to François-Victor's *Œuvres de William Shakespeare* (1865) and in the best-selling short memoir "Mes fils" (1874), Hugo's meditations on translation became intertwined with the everyday reality of his expatriation and cultural estrangement (the narrative focuses on the years spent with his sons on the island of Jersey). He discovered that through the loss of his children, which had been strangely predicted in their early achievements and in his earlier losses, he had seen the children's invincible strength monumentalized. Likewise, through the loss of his faith he had become more profoundly religious; and through his self-estrangement in another language—English—his literary style became more aware of its own possibilities.[28] Among Spanish-speaking authors, only the Cuban José Martí, who translated "Mes fils" in 1875 and contributed his reflections on Hugo and translation by way of a preface, was able to see that Hugo demanded a translator who was able to experiment with the form of a text whose indomitable exuberance was its most salient ideological marker.[29]

At his philological best, Caro could be a thorough and fastidious textual editor, particularly of legislative texts, but also of literary ones when he so chose. He must have seen at a glance the discrepancy between Hugo's poem and Bello's version, which was missing lines 175–420 of the French original (about 56 percent of it). Nevertheless, this discrepancy did not take away from his enthusiasm about the Venezuelan grammarian's translating abilities. In 1860 he had Bello's partial version printed in *El Catolicismo*, the official newspaper of Bogotá's episcopal see. He did not feel then that he should try to explain to the reader the translator's reasons for the abridgment, and in fact, he even omitted Hugo's name from the publication. Upon Bello's death in October of 1865, Caro hurried to canonize him as a great Catholic poet. In the article "Bello era católico" (*La Caridad* 2.19 [January 5, 1866]: 298–99), he contended that Bello was not only "this century's first American poet and first Castilian philologist [el primer poeta americano y primer hablista castellano del siglo]," but also "the Church's obedient son." He accordingly believed in Purgatory and in the existence of guardian angels and fallen angels ("Bello era católico" 298–99). This enshrining was a serious affair. In the year of the centennial celebrations, 1881, at a time when Colombian grammarians who doubled as *letrados* were plotting—led by Núñez—their takeover of the secular state in the name of the Church, Caro wrote that "Bello's centennial…is a kind of apotheosis or popular canonization." In fact, Bello's conduct had by then made him worthy of a "beatification cause" [causa de beatificación] (*Escritos sobre don Andrés Bello* 326).[30]

Caro neglected to mention that Bello considered Spanish jurisprudence corrupt at its core and profoundly at odds with the democratic and increasingly egalitarian ethos of nineteenth-century constitutions. In fact, Bello did not hide his preference for France's civil code, which spared French professionals of the law the onerous task of learning Roman jurisprudence and Latin. The language of ancient Rome should be the province of the philologist and the scholar of jurisprudence, but not necessarily of the practicing attorney.[31] Despite this ideological disconnect, Caro persisted in his determination to use Bello as a model of Catholic piety, suggesting to his uninformed readers that the Venezuelan's daily churchgoing turned him into a proponent of theocentric polities.[32]

The contrast between the speaker's expression of disbelief in the French original and his presumed submissiveness to Christian dogma in the Spanish imitation proved to be unimportant for later commentators on the poem. With the exception of the Liberal journalist Fidel Cano, no one seemed puzzled by the fact that Bello left the second half of the French poem untranslated. When in 1902 Cano produced the first Colombian countertranslation of "La prière pour tous," he added a prologue in which he gently criticized Bello for ending his partial translation with two original eight-line stanzas besides inserting in his text some words and phrases from other Hugo poems such as "À ma fille Adèle." He also showed his discomfort with Bello's indulging in macabre imagery in the portrayal of the speaker's loved ones (Cano, "Al lector" 326–28, 332–33).[33] In spite of Cano's judicious remarks, later critics remained silent on the issue of the translation's literary unfaithfulness. Although some of these critics may simply have neglected to read the French original, some others deliberately skipped over the ideological contradiction that I have pointed out.

The most egregious case is that of Edoardo Crema, the author of the monograph study *Andrés Bello a través del romanticismo*, which was awarded the Premio Nacional Andrés Bello in Caracas in 1955 and subsequently published by Venezuela's Ministry of Culture. The book contains not one but two chapters on "La oración por todos," in which Crema argues inconclusively that Bello was able to improve on the original poem. Three years earlier, the often irreverent Chilean writer Hernán Díaz Arrieta (a.k.a. Alone), who was a friend and admirer of Neruda, had already stated the following in his *Historia personal de la literatura chilena*: "the translator's spirit has penetrated that foreign domain and taken complete possession of it, turning it into his own domain. If 'La oración por Todos' [*sic*] were not the work of a French autor translated in Spanish by a Venezuelan, it would be the best Chilean poem ever written…It appears as if in this poem the inscrutable sage were on the brink of disclosing his secrets" (150–51). Despite its vagueness, this is a valuable insight into Bello's personality. With the possible exception of Bolívar, no other nineteenth-century Hispanic author has proved as resistant to a global interpretation of his work and personality as Bello. Was he more a Benthamite or a Catholic? And while in Caracas, did he remain a follower of Miranda and Bolívar, or was he also secretly employed by Spanish royalists? Most important of all, were his deeper political convictions in Chile more in tune with the liberal *pipiolos* or the conservative *pelucones*?

If Alone chose not to follow up on his insights into Bello's personality, Crema decided to defend him to the point of placing his poetry above

Hugo's.[34] He states at the outset of his book that he is prepared to do what no one had done before: he will compare one by one all five sections of Bello's version with the original to prove that the Venezuelan is a better poet than Hugo, and that his romanticism is free of the ideological and formal imperfections found in "La prière pour tous." Although Crema claims to have done an exhaustive probing and collation of both texts, he mysteriously overlooks lines 175–84 of the French text, that is, the passage where the speaker expresses his disbelief. He felt he could do this because Bello did *not* translate those lines. Still unsatisfied by this first act of sabotage, in the concluding two pages of his study Crema states (like Caro) that Bello was able to "improve on the original" [mejorar el original] by means of "amazing corrections not only to the content but also to the expression [...] To the original's romantic contortions...Bello opposed the transparent simplicity of bare reality...he thus was able to eliminate some regrettable ambiguities besides clarifying he content" (179–80).[35] Unlike Crema, José Martí adopted the same opinions that Hugo had on translation, arguing that the question of style was always ideological. For him, translation could not be attempted on the basis of stylistic consistency alone if both the source and target languages were to be destabilized—if they were meant to bicker with each other like two opposing parties in a lawful debate (Martí 61: 159; see also Hugo's prologue to Shakespeare in Lafarga 400, 406). This commitment not to repress the asymmetries and dissonances created by the juxtaposition of two equivalent texts, *each* making its own claims on the meaning of what is presumably being communicated by *both*, is what a *liberal theory and praxis of translation* seeks to institute.

In fact, Hugo's republican understanding of translation involves pushing the limits of accepted notions of decorum, which is why his literary poetics is also a liberal politics. Martí suspended the distinction between "classicism" and "romanticism" that both Caro and Crema upheld very strongly so that Hugo could look more like an Old Regime writer. Martí welcomed "this revelation, this mysticism, this magnificence with which souls analogize one another, and worlds form a series, and life becomes lives, and everything is universal and potent, and everything is grave and majestic" [esta revelación, este misticismo, esta soberbia con que las almas son análogas, y los mundos series, y la vida vidas, y todo es universal y potente, y todo es grave y majestuoso] (61: 144).

Although he does not mention him by name, Crema seems aware that in 1954 a minor Colombian scholar and translator-poet, the always poisonous Enrique Uribe White, had raised a storm by pointing out the countless solecisms, nongrammatical usages, and poor metrical choices in someone—Bello—who was prone to prey ruthlessly on these very defects when found in other writers. According to Uribe White's exact calculations,

Bello's "La oración por todos" preserves about only 18 percent of the original poem's content, and so the Spanish text should more rigorously be treated as an example of "plagiarism" than an "imitation" (207).[36] Uribe White, a nephew of the assassinated Liberal *caudillo* Rafael Uribe Uribe, was an M.I.T.-trained engineer and had near-native fluency in English and French. No sooner did he launch his literary career as translator-poet than he became immediately aware of the enormous disparities between foreign poetic texts and their renderings in Spanish that circulated in Latin America.[37] He certainly had a point in lamenting that Bello and the other nineteenth-century translators had ruined Hugo for a Colombian audience by substituting their own ideas for those of the Frenchman and disposing of the rugged and sheer verbal imagery that flowed from his pen like a force of nature (202).[38] Since Bello soon acquired the authority of Scripture, the American scholar William H. Bohning could in 1945 bring his survey of Bello's versions of Hugo to a conclusion with these words: "[e]ach imitation reflects faithfully the central thought of Victor Hugo, and each imitation, with the exception of *Los Duendes*, reproduces his exact ideas and impressions" (67).

Crema, to the contrary, insists that Bello's poem belongs to a genre higher (not lower) than mere "imitation," a lesser literary mode involving variations on a set theme. For Bello, he concludes, "La oración por todos" was "the climax of a battle…fought for many years against the romantic school's exaggerations and deficiencies; romanticism, embodied in the 'Priére [sic] pour tous,' comes out of this climax in defeat" (180).[39] This construal of "La oración" as a text reflecting Bello's inner artistic demons is most interesting. It somehow underscores the trouble that conservative Spanish-American critics have had equating romanticism with either revolution or libelalism. Bello was attacked more than once in the course of his life for allegedly attempting to thwart the Revolution of Independence in Caracas.[40] Caro states that Bello did not do this, although the Venezuelan would not have supported an ungodly revolution either. He was also attacked, and often slandered, for his threefold role (as jurist, grammarian, and teacher) in the building of an authoritarian republic in Chile, which in turn would have stifled the talents of romantically inclined young lyrists.

In 1842 Sarmiento denounced Bello as a traditional intellectual, implicitly denying that he could be a *double agent* and even lamenting that Chile lacked the legal institution of "ostracismo" which could determine the sage's much-needed banishment from the land (*Sarmiento en el destierro* 68–69).[41] He placed Bello in the same category as the two Francophile Spanish grammarians Vicente Salvá (1786–1849) and José Mamerto Gómez Hermosilla (1772–1837), the latter receiving along the way the compliment of "retrógrado absolutista" perhaps on account of his three-volume pamphlet against liberalism titled *El jacobinismo* (*Sarmiento en el destierro* 68–69, 77) and the fact that Bello favored Hermosilla's *Arte de hablar* as his basic textbook in his early Chilean years.[42] This is a good measure of how devious and destructive the generally progressive Sarmiento could be at his most opportunistic. Salvá had been a liberal *diputado* at the Cortes in 1822–1823, assuming also the office of Secretary. He soon became the center of the Spanish community of political exiles in London (1823–1830), where he met Bello and set up a bookstore, moving afterward to France. Although he was able to return to Spain in 1835, he carried on his profitable and progressive publishing business on an international scale until his death in Paris in 1849. Salvá was guilty, if anything, of being a Spaniard and an acclaimed grammarian (the best in the language according to Bello), and one of the most versatile intellects of his time. He had been, like Gómez Hermosilla, a professor of Greek, and had, again like Gómez Hermosilla, José Marchena, and Bello, great expertise in Latin, Hebrew literature, the history of jurisprudence, and theology, among other accomplishments that Sarmiento generally lacked and often resented in others. Salvá also dared to edit and partially annotate Gómez Hermosilla's *Arte de hablar* in 1842, countering some of the absolutist publicist's opinions on the observance of rules, but also acknowledging that his was the most important book on the subject written in recent memory. Salvá lived and died a convinced liberal, which is perhaps more than what Sarmiento was able to say at the end of his life. It is interesting to note that Caro also attacked Salvá and especially Gómez Hermosilla. The latter was not just a reactionary atheist, but also the enthusiastic vernacular translator of Homer's *Iliad*.[43]

Despite his résumé, parts of which read like a facsimile of Caro's profile, Gómez Hermosilla remained a dangerous threat to ultramontanism because he was willing to speak realpolitik's crude language. Like Hobbes, he was not against religion—nor was he in favor of it—but argued instead for the implementation of an absolutist regime, secular or theological, that would keep human beings' material and instinctual drives in check. He had come to believe that the only stabilizing form of human association was the *pactum subjectionis*, which was also Juan de Mariana's position in *History of Spain* (*Historia de rebus Hispaniae* [1592; expanded 1605]; Spanish ed., 1601).[44] Gómez Hermosilla became theo-politics' unwitting foe from the moment he erased the text of religion (too irrational and discredited to be defended) from his initial justification of absolutism, which he construes in decisionist terms as the system of impositions and cessions by which the powerful minorities legitimate their acts of violence against the powerless. This opened the possibility for the appearance of a totalitarian lettered city in which grammarians and lawyers (as Quintana feared) would remain the first and only interpreters of social orthodoxies because of their exclusive intellectual skills.[45] Gómez Hermosilla questioned the existence of such a thing as Rousseau's "Contrato social" (he did this in the manner of de Maistre rather than Bentham), which had hitherto been rationally "explained and understood" [explicado y entendido] as "the alleged right of the people's Sovereignty" [el pretendido derecho de Soberanía popular]. He declared instead that there must have existed only a "tacit consent" [tácito consentimiento] in a "primitive contract" [contrato primitivo] that appears ex post facto, once the domination "by brute force or deceit" [por la fuerza ó el engaño] of the weaker by the stronger parts of society has been established (*El jacobinismo* 1: 181).[46]

Bello did appreciate Gómez Hermosilla's philological works, which he cites sparingly but almost always respectfully. Caro, by contrast, simply dismissed the Spaniard's translations as unsophisticated and never discussed his political tracts. He also arranged to have an expurgated version of the *Arte de hablar* published in Bogotá in 1883 (sixty years after it first came out in Spain), since the original contained, among other impious pearls, these three: first, it ridiculed the literati who insisted on writing in Latin and using the Scholastics' syllogistic reasoning when they could use the vernacular instead; second, it denied the divine origin of language, which in reality would have developed "mechanically" as the human kind also evolved; and third, it criticized epic poets for their sloppy handling of supernatural events (the author frowned upon their inclusion in any genre of writing), thus implicitly denying God's Providence.[47] It is a testimony to the strength of Gómez Hermosilla's convictions and the courage with which he made them public that he was able to include, however subtly and indirectly, these ideas in a handbook of literary rhetoric and style dedicated to a future Spanish queen.

For all his antitheological biases, Gómez Hermosilla did not believe in the people's sovereignty. For that reason, Caro directed his invectives instead against the belligerent Sarmiento, a more formidable rival because he had dared to quarrel with Bello, often bullying him into defensive positions in their polemics on orthography and romanticism. Even after Sarmiento reached the presidency of Argentina in 1868, Caro continued to depict him as an uncouth cowboy roaming the pampas and speaking substandard Spanish. He referred to him as a *llanero*, the appellation reserved in Colombia for José Antonio Páez, the mulatto Venezuelan *caudillo* who repeatedly challenged Bolívar's central authority and reached the presidency of his newly formed country in 1830.

In his defense of Hugo's romantic liberalism and the rapidly evolving American usages of Spanish vis-à-vis their Peninsular counterparts, Sarmiento adopted a take-no-prisoners approach. He knew that the authors who formed Spain's lettered city of translation (e.g., Marchena, Quintana, Moratín, Gómez Hermosilla, Salvá, Blanco-White) and its attending literary institutions had been primarily liberal. He also knew that some of these literati began to move away from their political radicalism first during the

Napoleonic invasion, and afterward during the Trienio Liberal (1820–1823). Sarmiento preferred to rely on authors whose biographical text unfolded in the opposite direction. Thus, he looked for examples of European public intellectuals, such as Larra and Hugo, who were able to outgrow their youthful Catholicism and royalism in order to *translate* themselves into the ideology of liberalism, attacking (like the good converts that they were) the self-complacency of conservative institutions.

This is also why Sarmiento liked the centrist Renan, whose *Vie de Jésus* (1863) was more radical than his—Sarmiento's—rendition of Kristoph Schmid's *Vida de Jesucristo, con una descripción sucinta de la Palestina* (1844). While Renan's book, which challenged the divinity of Jesus, caused the author to be expelled from the Sorbonne, Sarmiento's *refundición* of a German source text (using the French version) was incorporated into Chile's primary school curriculum, where it remained in place for at least one century.[48] Indeed, two of the most decisive intellectual experiences in Sarmiento's development were his discovery (through Bello) that Old Regime customs and institutions were still alive and well in Spanish America, and that the defeat in 1823 of Spain's liberal lettered city demanded of Americans that they effect a shift to the left, as Hugo did, toward both "romanticism" and "socialism" (Sarmiento's frequently used word for "radicalism" in his polemics of 1842).[49]

The amply documented and polemical intellectual exchanges between Bello and Sarmiento seemed to call for Caro's intervention. He aped derisively Sarmiento's ethnographic renditions of Southern Cone vernaculars (Caro uses what were then substandard Argentine words like the nearly untranslatable "cancha" in his attack). He acted in this manner not only because he was defending Bello as the paragon of classicist and philo-Spanish decorum, but also because, at his father José Eusebio's insistence, he had been privately and unnaturally educated in the Castilian variety of Spanish (like his father's friend, Julio Arboleda), which he could speak without an accent when he wished. The world's existing institution that he admired the most after the Roman Curia was Spain's Language Academy. The other charges leveled against Bello that Caro had to counter were that Bello may have been ambivalent about which side to take on the eve of the Independence in Caracas, and that he may have occasionally collaborated with royal authorities. Caro first read about these charges in the brothers Miguel Luis and Gregorio Víctor Amunátegui's shorter biography of their teacher, which came out in Santiago in 1854. There he found this revealing passage about the accusations made against Bello:

La ofensa [que se le habia inferido] era tan grande, tan dolorosa, que en lugar de quejarse ante los hombres [a quienes malos sentimientos suelen hacer sin

entrañas], solo tuvo fuerzas para implorar de Dios [que lee en todos los cora-
zones,] el perdón de los mismos que le habian difamado. En [una de sus
magnificas composiciones,] la *Oración por todos…* ha intercalado la siguiente
estrofa, que no se halla [Caro: está] en el orijinal frances:

> [Caro: Ruega, hija…]
> I por el que en vil libelo
> Destroza una fama pura
> I en la aleve mordedura
> Escupe asquerosa hiel. (Amunátegui and Amunátegui 97–98)[50]

Caro's attention was fixed on this passage, which he misquoted, as he often
revealingly did despite his philologist's impatience with the errors of oth-
ers (including Miguel Luis Amunátegui's) when he did not like what he
read. These lines in all likelihood reminded him of the journalistic attacks
to which he and his father José Eusebio were subjected, however justified
the attacks were in their case, given the denigrating style of their partisan
pamphleteering prose. Caro quotes at least twice elsewhere the same passage
from Bello that was highlighted by the Amunáteguis: in the first install-
ment of his "Contradiálogo de las letras," written in 1880 to defend Bello
from the charge of disloyalty to the Junta de Caracas, which was voiced
against him by the Venezuelan Juan Ignacio de Armas (*Escritos* 282), and
in the "Contestación" sent in a letter of April 8, 1881 to de Armas (*Escritos*
325). Referring his reader to the source in the Amunáteguis' sketch, Caro
points out that this early biographical study was published with Bello's con-
sent while the illustrious grammarian-jurist was still alive, implying that
the document carries the weight of a "confesión" and an eyewitness testi-
mony (*Escritos* 325–26). The autobiographical interpolation in "La oración
por todos" did not prevent Caro from considering it Bello's best work, and
granting it a special status. He added that the rest of Bello's better poetry,
particularly "The Agriculture of the Tropics" [La agricultura de la zona tór-
rida], was refreshingly "impersonal," dealing only with the propagation of
learning and the expression of *amor patriae*.

The Battle over Bello's Legacy:
Liberal and Conservative Constituencies

The most extraordinary thing that has been said about "La oración por
todos"—and it has been reiterated a few times—is that it is a quintessen-
tial distillation of the South American spirit, if indeed such a thing has
ever existed. In the light of the available textual evidence, this is, to be
sure, a shocking claim. For "La oración por todos," unlike Bello's original
didactic composition, "The Agriculture of the Tropics," does not contain
a single reference to South America's recognizably self-differentiated geog-
raphy—physical or human. It features a quaint and sentimental depiction

of a God-fearing herdsman and his kin, more in the rustic manner of the first José de Espronceda than in that of the exuberantly Anacreontic poet Juan Meléndez Valdés. In fact, Bello amplifies the references to rural mores and the rhythms of nature found in the French original, but this need not imply that he is nationalizing the poem as a specifically South American text.

The master image in the first two stanzas of "La prière pour tous" features a series of footpaths that become blurred in the twilight hour. The wayfarer-speaker has trouble finding the footpaths, while the herdsman and his flock voice a complaint that can also be heard in the wind beating against the scattered ponds and the cracks of an old tower:

> Furrows, paths, bushes, all commix and fade—
> The traveller hesitates which way to go.
> Day is for evil, hate, fatigue, and harm.
> Pray! Night is come—Night that is grave and calm.
> Old herdsmen, blasts that through torn turrets rove,
> The lakes, the flocks, with shrill discordant call,
> All suffer, all complain… (ll. 11–17; *Works of Victor Hugo: Poems* 1:200)

> Sillons, sentiers, buissons, tout se mêle et s'efface;
> Le passant inquiet doute de son chemin.
> Le jour est pour le mal, la fatigue et la haine.
> Prions: voici la nuit! la nuit grave et sereine!
> Le vieux pâtre, le vent aux brèches de la tour,
> Les étangs, les troupeaux avec leur voix cassée,
> Tout souffre et tout se plaint. (ll. 11–17)

Unlike this nineteenth-century English translator—Henry Carrington—Bello paraphrased freely Hugo's description of the rustics' widespread and afflicted toiling instead of aiming for a literal rendition. What follows is a close English translation of the passage in question in Bello's version:

> The old fortified tower trembles […] The rustic shelter is prepared and lit up for the dinner; and the peasant's wife and tender offspring wait on the threshold for his return. The shining blue sphere shoots one diamond after another; and hardly a hesitant wagon is heard in the distance. Everything sinks in the shadow: the mountain, the valley, the church, the shed, and the grange. And a traveler goes through the desert lands guided by the last glimmers of the twilight. The whole nature is but a moan: the wind on the trees, the bird in its nest, the sheep's quivering bleat, and the brook's fleeting course. Daytime hours are for evil and toil. (my translation)

> se ve temblar el viejo torreón. (l. 8)
> […]
> Para la pobre cena aderezado,
> brilla el albergue rústico; y la tarda
> vuelta del labrador la esposa aguarda

> con su tierna familia en el umbral.
> Brota del seno de la azul esfera
> uno tras otro fúlgido diamante;
> y ya apenas de un carro vacilante
> se oye a distancia el desigual rumor.
> Todo se hunde en la sombra; el monte, el valle,
> y la iglesia, y la choza, y la alquería;
> y a los destellos últimos del día,
> se orienta en el desierto el viajador.
> Naturaleza toda gime; el viento
> en la arboleda, el pájaro en el nido,
> y la oveja en su trémulo balido,
> y el arroyuelo en su correr fugaz.
> El día es para el mal y los afanes. (ll. 13–29)

Bello amplifies and embellishes Hugo's description of his rural setting at dusk. Not only does he sentimentalize the situation by populating the scene with a peasant and his family (absent from the original), who anxiously await the father's return, but he also multiplies the places designating forms of human habitation. Thus, we have the shelter, the church, the shed, and the farmhouse. Taken together, these additions constitute the georgic frame Bello devises in keeping with "The Agriculture of the Tropics," published in the London-based *Repertorio Americano* in 1826. This practice, however strategic, went against Bello's prescriptions for translating poetry, which he set forth in his posthumously published "*La Ilíada*, traducida por Don José Gómez Hermosilla," probably written in the 1830s and transcribed by Miguel Luis Amunátegui from the extant manuscript for its inclusion in the *Vida* (*Obras completas* 9: 418–22). Caro did not have any problem with Bello's licenses, as one of his main goals—and also a goal of the *ciudad letrada* generally, whether liberal or conservative—was to perpetuate the differences between the class of city-dwelling owners, whose ranks slowly but surely continued to increase as the extent of primary instruction and the suffrage also grew, and that of gradually impoverished small farmers. As trade and industry began to expand, so did the urban bourgeoisie's acquisition of large plantation estates to the detriment of the rural aristocracy.[51]

The invulnerability of Bello's translational liberties reaches its climax in Arturo Uslar Pietri's delirious paraphrase of "La oración por todos" in a speech called "Bello" (1965; pub. 1967), which seems to conflate this poem with "The Agriculture of the Tropics." Arguing that Bello "transplants" Hugo's poetry for the benefit of his Spanish-speaking audience, the Venezuelan novelist recontextualizes the verses quoted above in the following manner:

> At certain moments, the transplant resembles an ingrafted tree, making the new poem more lively and fecund, as happens in the *Oración por todos*, where

Hugo's French countryside and the Gothic bell towers found in Norman vil-
lages are transformed into the turret of a sugar plantation [torreón de trapi-
che], into a road filled with squeaking wagons and muleteers, and into a field
of sugarcane, coffee, and shade-trees beheld at sunset. (43)

Uslar Pietri transculturates both Hugo and Bello in order to claim Bello
back from Chile's Eurocentric cultural plurisystem, presenting his fellow
countryman instead as a vernacular Venezuelan icon. The landscape that
Uslar Pietri writes into "La oración" could well exist in the tropics, but not
in Chile.

The principal accounts of Bello given in Colombia and Chile in the
second half of the nineteenth century could not have been more differ-
ent. Bello's first important biographer, the Chilean *letrado* Miguel Luis
Amunátegui (1828–1888), was twice a cabinet member on national-front
governments and stayed for a long time at the helm of the central educa-
tional system. His career as pedagogue, author, and politician provides a
nice ideological contrast to Sergio Arboleda, whose life spans the same years.
In Amunátegui's time, Chile was still fighting the battle for *laïcité* and uni-
versal instruction. The prodigiousness of Amunátegui's work and his intel-
lectual versatility (eclipsed only by Bello's) turned him into Chile's most
trusted liberal technocrat and publicist of his generation.[52] He was Minister
of the Interior and Foreign Relations (1868–1870) in José Joaquín Pérez's
second administration. During the Liberal Federico Errázuriz's ensuing
presidency (1871–1876), which ushered in the end of the Fusión Liberal-
Conservadora, Amunátegui helped Diego Barros Arana (liberal Rector of
the Instituto Nacional) lead the fight against the intrusion of the Catholic
Church into primary instruction that the so-called Ley de Libertad de
Exámenes (promoted by the conservative Minister de Justice, Worship, and
Public Education, Abdón Cifuente [1871–1873]) would have made legal.
In the administration of the left-leaning Aníbal Pinto, Amunátegui occu-
pied first the same ministry held by Cifuente (1876–1878). As a theological
polemic regarding the government's right to nominate the new bishop of
Santiago broke out when the government rightfully claimed *ius patrona-
tus*, Amunátegui was again instrumental in not letting the Church appoint
a reactionary. He was then moved to the Ministry of Foreign Relations
(1879–1880).

Written also to counter Lastarria's criticisms of Bello in *Recuerdos lit-
erarios* (1878), Amunátegui's *Vida de don Andrés Bello* (1882) remains to
this day a sympathetic and intelligent treatment of the Venezuelan poet-
jurist's complex attitudes toward the role of the traditional intellectual. At
the time of the *Vida*'s publication, Amunátegui was the Secretary of Chile's
Consejo de Instrucción Pública. It was a trying time for *laïcité*, as the con-
troversial president Domingo Santamaría continued to battle the Church on

many fronts with the help of the radical liberals: for example, he decreed the opening of civil cemeteries [cementerios laicos] (where Protestants would not be segregated from Catholics) and promoted the replacement of the parish [parroquia] with the court registry [registro civil], which made civil matrimony an alternative to religious unions. As more and more Escuelas Normales were inaugurated across the Americas, Amunátegui felt the need to highlight Bello's educational ideas within the enormous legacy he had bequeathed to Spanish Americans. In his biography, he copies a lengthy portion of Bello's article titled "Educación" (*El Araucano* [August 5 and 12, 1836]) that summarizes the Venezuelan's liberal position on the spread of primary instruction:

> To foster public schools that target a small portion of the people is not to foster education; it does not suffice to train skilled men in the liberal professions; rather, we need to train useful citizens, we need to improve society, which cannot be achieved unless we open up first the field of studies to the majority. What good will it be to have orators, jurisprudents, and statesmen if most of the population is still trapped in the night of ignorance. They can neither do their part in the general economy, nor create wealth, nor even earn the dignified living that a nation's general population certainly deserves. (Bello qtd. in Amunátegui, *Vida* 380–81)[53]

Amunátegui also quotes at length from Bello's extensive review of José Ignacio Gorriti's *Reflexiones sobre las causas morales de las convulsiones interiores de los nuevos estados americanos, i exámen de los medios eficaces para reprimirlas* (*El Araucano* [May 6 and 13, 1836]). This piece argues that moral philosophy should take priority over religious worship. Amunátegui reminds his reader that Bello shared Jeremy Bentham's view that moral philosophy should be based on a principle of utility, and accordingly paraphrases the well-known utilitarian maxim—"seeking the greatest good for the greatest number of people"—as "one's true happiness…can never be in the way of the general public's happiness" (*Vida* 382). This amounts to an acknowledgment (against José Joaquín Ortiz and the Caros) that all moral criteria, including the Catholic one of fearing condemnation and seeking salvation in heaven, are ultimately linked to a principle of utility (*Vida* 382). Clearly, Bello is comfortable thinking through the criteria of pleasure and pain proposed by Bentham. For him, religious interdictions could be replaced by a strictly ethical imperative, namely, the "need to nurture one's conscience" within the system of rights and obligations that constitute a civil polity (*Vida* 381–82, 388). The advantage to this perspective on moral philosophy is that it does away with the principle of authority formerly monopolized by the Catholic Church.

The account given in Amunátegui's *Vida* of Bello's political ideology could not be more opposed to Caro's tendentious summary in "Ojeada a las opiniones políticas y religiosas de don Andrés Bello" (1881). It begins by stating that *El Araucano*—the journal Bello edited between 1830 and 1853—was the Conservative Party's official outlet. The journal's publication certainly overlaps in time with the period of conservative hegemony (1831–1861), but Bello was still able to advocate the suppression of censorship from its pages. He also advocated the opening of educational opportunities in the technical professions and the need for Chile to conquer its cultural autonomy. In the "Discurso pronunciado en la instalación de la Universidad de Chile" (1843), Bello wrote a sentence that Caro appropriates for his reactionary ideology in "Ojeada." This is Caro's shortened statement: "Morality, which I do not separate from religion, is society's living matter" [La moral, que yo no separo de la religión, es la vida misma de la sociedad] (*Escritos sobre don Andrés Bello* 106). And this is Bello's sentence quoted in full: "Morality, which I do not separate from religion, is society's living matter; freedom is the stimulus that gives social institutions a wholesome strength and a fertile activity" [La moral (que yo no separo de la religión) es la vida misma de la sociedad; la libertad es el estímulo que da un vigor sano y una actividad fecunda a las instituciones sociales] (Bello, *Obras completas* 21: 4). Bello clearly states here that his idea of morality is informed by Christianity. However, he does not imply that religion should be the core of both university instruction and morality, let alone that morality needs religion in order to exist, as Caro would have it.

Whenever acts of abusive power are committed by those who were supposed to govern democratically, acts of resistance ensue even from the party in power's potential friends. The Catholic questioning of Pius IX's anachronistic teachings in Caro's Colombia was led by the very conservative Rafael Pombo, whom Caro could never silence because Pombo's Catholic faith was beyond reproach and because he was Colombia's beloved and belated romantic poet besides being the child and grandchild of founding fathers. His symbolic and genealogical capital equaled Caro's. The relationship between Caro and Pombo illustrates the disciplinary role played by both translated and original poetry. The two authors were Catholic versifiers, but Pombo, unlike Caro, did not believe in the divine right of either *absolutist* presidents or *absolutist* popes. Pombo ridiculed the consecrated dogma of papal infallibility, which Caro invoked time and again in his journalistic prose of the 1870s, in the poem "La infalibilidad del Papa" (1877; *Poesías completas* 1113–24). Pombo's sonnet also mocks the form of the syllogism, and, by implication, two of the advocates of both syllogistic reasoning and the pope's infallibility: Caro himself and his future Minister of Education, Monsignor Rafael María Carrasquilla. Pombo antagonized Caro in ways more dangerous to him than he could envision at the time. His humanist argument revolved around the notion that the Christian person was entitled to use his or her reason and *liberum arbitrium* in making decisions regarding the good life and the salvation of the soul, and that the enlarged figure of the infallible Vicar of Christ questioned the very notion of human dignity advocated by Thomistic philosophy. "La infalibilidad" was the most irreverent among Pombo's "theological sonnets" [*sonetos teológicos*].

Also written in the mid-1870s, three related sonnets by Pombo that attracted Caro's fury were "La divinidad de Jesucristo" (on the redemption of the human condition through Christ's sacrifice) "Tota pulchra est" (on the mystery that "things of beauty" may awaken religious feelings) and "María" (on the dignity of women). All three advance variations on the same general argument, namely, what is good and beautiful in nature is so irrespective of God's claims over it.[54] This was by no means a schismatic position: Lorenzo Valla was its first paladin in the fifteenth century. The autonomy of morality from ecclesiastical control was potentially a subversive argument only in a society which had failed to enforce a true separation of Church and state and whose more educated members were turning in great numbers against liberal-democratic institutions. The two immediate corollaries of Pombo's position would be that the rights of man (for Pombo, but not for Caro, the rights of woman as well) existed independently of God's claims, and that there was no need to subject pagan texts to a *translatio secundum* since nothing could be aprioristically evil in texts that were not explicitly and militantly Catholic.

In "Ojeada a las opiniones," Caro summarizes Bello's response to Lastarria's tendentious denigration of Spain's cultural traditions (*Escritos* 123–25). For Bello, the study of Spanish literature and law was largely responsible for the Americans' vindication of their natural sovereignty during the French invasion of Spain. In contact with the French and North American revolutions, South Americans rediscovered Spain's traditions of municipal autonomy and parliamentary representation at the Cortes. Bello explains that the liberties characteristic of republican Rome and medieval Spain were gradually eroded by the institutions of absolutism and despotism in the early modern period. Caro deliberately doctors these sophisticated arguments to create the effect that Bello had no trouble disowning secular forms of representative government.

To summarize, Bello believed that the most valuable part of any religion was its moral philosophy, including the ideas of benevolence and philanthropy, which, at least since Francis Bacon (and later Benjamin Franklin, a major influence on Sarmiento), had been integrated into the rhetoric used to legitimate experimental science. Caro reverses Bello's privileging of the ethical over the liturgical, and of free examination over religious dogma, to argue instead that the Church's "principle of authority" [principio de autoridad] should never be questioned. In the same paragraph Bello goes on to add that the true enemies of the Catholic religion are neither empirical reason nor freedom of conscience, but the "suspiciousness shown by easily frightened personalities" [recelos de espíritus asustadizos] (*Obras completas* 21: 4). He also extols what he calls—in a passage reminiscent of Quintana—"the lights" [las luces], to which he attributes the revival of the Greek and Roman notions of freedom informing the "vast political movement" of the earlier nineteenth century, which could additionally be glossed as liberalism or representative government (21: 5, 6). There exists, he writes, "a close alliance between positivist enlightenment [revelación positiva] and that other universal enlightenment [revelación universal] that speaks to all of humankind from the book of nature" (21: 6). Therefore, conducting empirical research that satisfies the innate faculty of *curiositas* is analogous to the desire to discover and understand God's designs—both are forms of *inventio* as discovery through interpretation. Repressing such natural desires would entail denying "everything that is beautiful, generous, sublime, holy"; poisoning "the fountain of morality"; and debasing "religion itself" (Bello, *Obras completas* 21: 7).

We can use, as a third term of comparison, Marcelino Menéndez Pelayo's "Introduction" to volume 2 of the *Antología de poetas hispano-americanos* (1893), in which he adapts some of the ideas of Amunátegui and Caro, but is principally concerned with Bello's status as first Spanish American secular philosopher. It comes as a refreshing surprise that the conservative Ménendez Pelayo should silently concur with Amunátegui in labeling Bello a sui generis utilitarian, an empiricist (i.e., he favored direct empirical observation followed by inductive reasoning), a Benthamite, and even an "attenuated positivist" [positivista mitigado] (*Antología* cxxiii–cxxv). All this is consistent with Bello's critique of excessive use of the "syllogism" and the "belaboring of minutiae" characteristic, as he clearly states, of unimaginative grammarians and jurists, who may possess great "analytical" skills but tend to lack the "synthetic" powers found in the philosopher and the true poet (*Filosofía del entendimiento* [*Obras completas* 3: 529]).

Menéndez Pelayo specifically endorses the view that Bello's "highly Hispanicized imitations" [imitaciones muy castellanizadas] of Hugo are superior to the original poems and that the "Oración por todos" is not only Bello's greatest literary creation, but also the central text of nineteenth-century Spanish American poetry (*Antología* clvi). This opinion will be reiterated, particularly in Venezuela, where Uslar Pietri will go so far as to say that Bello describes in minute detail the tropical landscapes of their native country. (This is belied by the poem.) Menéndez Pelayo also subscribes to Amunátegui's notion that in his imitation, "Bello seizes the original thought and develops it in our language in accordance with our lyrical habits, the conditions of Spanish versification, and his idiosyncrasies as imitator" (2: clvi). This idiosyncrasy refers to Bello's antiromantic stance: "to do justice to modern poetry, he did not need to abjure his faith or burn what he had worshipped" [no necesitó, para hacer justicia á la poesía moderna, ni renegar de su propia fe, ni quemar lo que había adorado] (*Antología* cxxxiii).

The Grammarians' Republic: "To Govern Is to Educate"?

In their extremely cautious treatment of the religious question, Bello's poetry and pedagogical writings provided the reactionary lettered city with a justification for its sophistic arguments in favor of a return to the confessional state. This was in violation of August Boeckh's injunction, in his *Encyclopaedie und Methodologie der philologischen Wissenschaften* (1877), to keep philology separate from religion (25–26). Concomitantly, Bello's indefatigable efforts in favor of experimental science, positive jurisprudence, and educational opportunities for the urban underprivileged turned him into an apostle of cultural modernization even as he ostensibly placed his intellectual gifts also in the service of Chile's authoritarian conservative republic. At the opposite end of the political spectrum, another Venezuelan educator, the radical republican Simón Rodríguez, was the first to demonize, in *Sociedades americanas* (1828)—printed at the onset of Bolívar's Dictatorship—the office of the *letrado*. He argued that without an "agreement of feelings" [concordancia de sentimientos] from which a much-desired "unanimity of action" [unanimidad de acción] could ensue, the rising class of bureaucratic administrators ("Literatos" and "Escritores" schooled mainly in "Filología") would remain isolated from the general population's daily problems (Rodríguez 1: 286). As it was, the *letrados'* writing skills legitimated their social and economic promotion, enabling the pursuit of their self-interest more than anything else.

Rodríguez's view can be usefully connected to what Tocqueville (an author whom the two Caros cite occasionally) said about the white population of the United States: they would never rise against one another because they all uphold the national narrative of a providential arrival at a promised land and the collective writing of a paradoxical charter of rights that was explicitly Christian, but which also separated Church and state. The government system in place in the United States had made religious freedom compatible with mundane affairs. Its citizens had vast natural resources at their disposal to carry out their "pursuit of happiness" in a larger market than Colombia's without having to become involved in politics. Tocqueville was fascinated by the fact that the North American clergy, especially the Catholic priesthood, stood aloof from secular affairs and very rarely subordinated *amor patriae*, understood here in the strict sense of the citizens' obedience to the inclusive republican institutions legitimately established by the nation's *pouvoir constituant*, to *amor ecclesiae*, which I define as the priority given to imagined religious communities vis-à-vis civil polities.[55] Still, Tocqueville made two fundamental points, with which Bello and Caro (and Franklin, a notorious agnostic) also concurred: first, "[t]here is no religion that does not place the object of man's desires above and beyond the treasures of earth and that does not naturally raise his soul to regions far above those of the senses"; and second, "[r]eligious nations are…naturally strong on the very point on which democratic nations are weak," a circumstance that "shows of what importance it is for men to preserve their religion as their conditions become more equal" (*Democracy in America* 2: 23).

The differences between Bello, a moderate-liberal republican, and Tocqueville, a moderate-conservative republican who often bemoaned the passing of aristocratic societies, are certainly substantial.[56] Both authors, however, stand at the opposite end of the political spectrum from Caro, a reactionary defender of the absolutist monarchy. Tocqueville warns republicans of how onerous it would be for any religion to seal an alliance with a temporal government whose nature is by definition transitory:

> In proportion as a nation assumes a democratic condition of society and as communities display democratic propensities, it becomes more and more dangerous to connect religion with political institutions; for the time is coming when authority will be bandied from hand to hand, when political theories will succeed one another, and when men, laws, and constitutions will disappear or be modified from day to day…Agitation and mutability are inherent in the nature of democratic republics, just as stagnation and sleepiness are the law of absolute monarchies. (*Democracy in America* 1: 322–23)

Caro did not heed this counsel. Instead, as explained in chapter 2, he insistently exhorted modern states to organize themselves in conformity with the teachings of Pope Pius IX and vowed to let religious doctrines and ecclesiastical institutions determine his future acts in civil government. In *Estudio sobre el utilitarismo* (1869), he invented a fable in the manner of Hugo's fanciful account of the primitive and harmless prayer recited prior to the advent of theocracy. He did this with an ideological purpose in mind that was the antithesis of Hugo's attempt at democratizing religious experience by analogy with the downfall of Old Regime politics. Caro tried to show how the medieval monarchy was Aquinas's *communitas perfecta,* because the Catholic Church's *imperium,* being a form of shared sovereignty with each temporal prince, extended throughout the Western world. The medieval Catholic Church's political universality (a concept, which is a contradiction in terms) would have made the search for ideological differences irrelevant, at least until emperors began to refuse their subjection to Rome (*Obras, tomo I* 168–69).

In Caro's view, among Catholics who called themselves citizens of the *civitas Dei* and did not stray from the Vatican's teachings one was always going to find an "agreement of wills and thoughts" [conformidad de pensamientos y voluntades] (note the similarity in phrasing with Rodríguez's "concordancia de sentimientos" cited above). However, among Catholics as citizens of a secular republic (the mixed body of the *civitas permixta* always in danger of lapsing into a *civitas diaboli*), diverse "qualities and obligations" [calidades y obligaciones] that were of God's design also immediately arose.

(Note also that Bentham would have paraphrased "obligation" as "privilege.") These socioeconomic differences were legitimated by the dominant class' intellectual accomplishments. The primary and almost exclusive purpose of the elites' talents, and in general of "human reason," was to interpret divine Providence: "We must appeal to human reason qua interpreter of divine reason, that is to say, we must appeal to religion" (Caro, *Obras, tomo I* 171). It follows that the only good use to which human reason could be put was catechesis. In turn, this reduction explains the grammarian-presidents' indifference—in the course of the Regeneración—to the uneducated masses' need to acquire practical skills: "To govern is to educate [Gobernar es educar]; all sound education, all education worthy of that name presupposes a core of moral truth, a religious truth" (Caro, *Obras, tomo I* 170).[57]

Despite the generational and temperamental gap that separated Sarmiento and Rodríguez, they were *literatos* in the laudatory sense of someone who is attuned to the winds of innovation and change in culture and society.[58] Their fear of living in a republic of mostly unlettered citizens subjected to a belletristic and retrograde lettered city persuaded them of the need to build an inclusive educational system simultaneously with a more participatory system of government. For as long as the nation was not defined by its growing and consistent provision of a republican education and other nurturing state services to "destitute children" [niños pobres], the indispensable base of "citizens" required for a "nation" to recognize itself as such would not be created (Rodríguez 1: 286). Rodríguez made two additional remarks. The first one, which anticipates Caro's adage "to govern is to educate," lays emphasis on the need to indoctrinate the masses but to a contrary effect: "No project is too difficult or too vast when the mass of the population has been enlightened" [No hai *proyecto* que resista a los conocimientos difundidos en las masas] (Rodríguez 1: 322). The second one is that in sponsoring "Concordatos" rather than "Colegios," the creole elites were creating "Repúblicas sin Ciudadanos" (1: 286–87). The few existing schools of his time, to which the poor generally had no access anyway, "are making *letrados*…do no expect citizens" [están haciendo Letrados…no esperen Ciudadanos] (1: 285).

Rodríguez longed for the *strategic sacralization* of the Greater Colombia and the revolution that originated it as a precondition for the creation of a republican common ground on which everything could be discussed. The conquest made by the sword in the name of liberty had to be preserved and advanced by the pen. The writing of revolutionary conquests into coercive law was the way to consecrate the new nation's native freedoms as the transcendental *causa prima* that made up for the loss of the absolutist monarchy's theological foundation. Caro was able to reverse this narrative's ideological direction by simply substituting "providential" for "revolutionary." Rodríguez's expectations were soon frustrated by the Bolivian creoles' derogation of the 1826 Constitution and his ephemeral running of experimental schools for republican citizenship in Cuzco under the patronage of Bolívar's presumed successor, Antonio de Sucre, who was assassinated in 1828. The derogation of the quintessentially Bolivarian Constitution, coupled with the dismantling of the schools, amounted to an obliteration of the republican ethos that could in due time have effectively integrated larger sectors of the population into decision-making institutions.

As Rodríguez surmised, the acceleration of history that resulted from the revolution and its deconsecration of the divine right of kings had to culminate in a chronic state of civil and military strife, whose most noticeable index in Colombia was the promulgation of six very different constitutions between 1821 and 1886. This lack of a common ground was no doubt worsened by the factitiousness shown by radical Liberals and independents since mid-century, and their mutual antagonizing of conservatism in a series of regional and national civil wars. Caro saw in this state of affairs the symptoms of parliamentary democracy's fatigue in a nation that had not yet known an inclusive civil society. This conflicted social formation presented him with the opportunity to appropriate for his "Catholic Party" the institutions of political theology while also dissolving positivist philology into a re-Christianized and vulgarized *philologia sacra* for the Conservative elites' consumption. He reactivated these institutions in such a way as to make sovereignty reside in a strong executive office (supervised and sponsored by the Vatican Curia) to the detriment of civil government's legislative branch.

In the context of maximal instability of the signs denoting the sacredness of the temporal powers (the state), Caro conceived his grandiose scheme for legally instituting a totalitarian regime in which there was no separation among the different branches of government; no separation of nation, Church, and state; and no room for religious, political, and ethnic differences. The theo-political horizon articulated in the early modern period, in the context of the struggle for world hegemony between the pope and emperor, was resurrected in the nineteenth century in circumstances analogous to those of Colombia, as Claude Lefort has shown:

> Society is put to the test of a collapse of legitimacy by the opposition between interests of classes and various categories, by the opposition between opinions, values and norms [...] and by all the signs of the fragmentation of the social space, of heterogeneity. In these extreme situations, representations which can supply an index of social unity and identity become invested with fantastic power, and the totalitarian adventure is under way. (*Democracy and Political Theory* 233)

Lefort uses different lexical variations on "transfer," "translation," "reduction," "conversion," and even "regression" to signify the interpretive labor of forcing heterogeneity back into a union not just of the social body, but of the nation's material and spiritual life. Implicit in Lefort's choice of words is his conviction that the theologico-political has never ceased to be the foundation of legitimate power, and that "ideology" and "religion" (he tellingly conflates the two) each work through a series of obliterations—often only of strategic suspensions—of historical time. In Colombia, the projected new union would take place under a centralizing *monarcha* whom the people as a whole could see as their self-sacrificing ruler and their appointed deputy. Betrayed and vituperated by his own people yet later immortalized in majestic statues, poems, and histories, Bolívar is that *reigning* figure. Moreover, the proposed mystical union needs to reconcile the irreconcilable: not just experimental science and religious doctrine, as Bello's 1843 "Discurso prronunciado en la instalación" tried to do in a show of rhetorical finesse, but the triplicity of positive law, knowledge of causes, and transcendent justice. This is the original attribute of *imperium* and the kingly prerogative par excellence as seen in the medieval Spanish Cortes and the Solomonic tradition of *arcana imperii.*

The foregoing discussion makes redundant any other explanation of why the Regeneración felt so attracted to three Mosaic personalities—Bolívar, Bello, and Hugo—whose inspired prose converted everything they wrote into rescripts. They also inspired others to write compositions that could themselves be made into rescripts, like Bello's "La oración por todos" and the "Discurso" (1843) or Caro's "A la estatua del Libertador" (1883). Bolívar in particular seems to have functioned also as a Christological figure (even Caro calls him "semidiós"). The history of the Spanish American republics had to start necessarily with the violent assumption of sovereign representation by a previously underrepresented Third Estate.[59] We will see in chapter 4 how Bolívar was transformed into a sacrificial victim whose downfall was caused by local *caudillista* interests disguised in the form of their proto-Liberal federalism. This concealment was to enable and legitimate the reactionaries' desire for a centralizing and authoritarian regime identified with Bolívar's constitutionally correct Dictatorship. But few outside Caro's circle would readily embrace the rehearsal of this sacrifice, cast in the language of sin and redemption, as a symbolic return to political theologies. The Regeneración's appropriation of Bolívar in the year 1883, which marked the centennial of his birth, could not carry Núñez's future national-front government very far. The democratic body politic had by then already become the heterogeneous nation's modern incarnation, exposing in its fragmentation *pouvoir constituant*'s fictional nature and the related legal fictions involved in the delegation of sovereignty. In a field of power that was forever *political*, it was no longer possible to ascertain who was legitimated to rule, or by whom and for what purposes.

More so than Bello, Caro staked his literary career on the creation of a "canon" in the sense acquired by this word in the fourth century as a catalogue of interconnected Christian authors: "The formation of a canon serves to safeguard a tradition. There is the literary tradition of the school, the juristic tradition of the state, and the religious tradition of the Church: these are the three medieval world powers: *studium, imperium, sacerdotium*" (Curtius 256). In the year 1887, Núñez and Caro placed this projected canon of *studia* under the Vatican's control by signing a Concordat. In 1888 they issued the infamous Law 35 banning from all schools and universities the teaching of any work that contradicted Catholic doctrines (the law remained in place until the onset of the Liberal Republic in 1930), which in practice meant that only the economic elites could have access to secular philosophies outside the school system and the government-controlled press. Finally, in 1894 Caro appointed the self-proclaimed neo-Thomistic propagandist Monsignor Rafael Carrasquilla to the Ministry of Education. Since the bishop of Bogotá and the Vatican nuncio were at the time—following the signing of the Regeneración's Concordat—also given the prerogative of selecting the Conservative candidate at each presidential election, the canon of *studia* could potentially coincide with the canon of *imperium* and the canon of *sacerdotium*.[60] Only in a theologico-political system in which the invisible saints of the *civitas Dei* ruled over the state's contingent institutions, stripped as they were now of the legislative assemblies' *pouvoir constituant*, could the *translatio imperii* or providential transfer of dominion from a conquered nation to a conquering one be carried out without undermining the *translatio studii*.

Within this scheme, it was possible for Caro to contend that there was nothing wrong with the Spanish Empire's rule and institutions, and that the Revolution of Independence was not a revolution, but a civil war between *españoles peninsulares* and *españoles americanos*, the two sides of what Bello had designated as the "trans-Atlantic Iberia" [Iberia trasatlántica]:

> He who casts a philosophical eye on the history of our battles with the metropolis, will acknowledge right away that what has allowed us to prevail is undoubtedly the Iberian element. The native Spaniard's persistence has crashed against itself, against the innate persistence shown by Spain's children. The instinct of motherland revealed itself to the American souls, mimicking the prodigies of Numancia and Saragossa. The trans-Atlantic Iberia's veteran captains and legions were vanquished and humiliated by the improvised *caudillos* and armies from another young Iberia who, having abjured that name, still exhaled the old Iberia's indomitable breath in defending their homes. (Bello, *Obras completas* 19: 169)

Caro quoted these lines approvingly several times, including "Historia novelesca" (1872), "La Conquista" (1881), and "Centenario de Bello" (1881) (all three in *Artículos y discursos* 156, 187–88, 237), but did not mention the earlier part of the same passage. In it Bello states very candidly that the Spaniards' warlike energies, carried over from the medieval Reconquest and the sixteenth-century Conquest of America, constituted a legacy to be cherished however abusive or misdirected those energies may have been at times.

Nevertheless, the Spanish legal institutions that supported those colonizing efforts had to be disposed of:

> Such has been the Spanish-American revolution's character when considered as the spontaneous rising of a people; in it we need to distinguish between political independence and civil liberties. In our revolution, freedom was a foreign ally which fought under the banner of independence; even after independence it has had to go on fighting to consolidate itself and take root. The warriors' work is now finished but the legislators' will not end until the foreign ideas [la idea imitada]—the newly-arrived idea [la idea advenediza]—is able to penetrate the hard and tenacious core of Iberian beliefs. (*Obras completas* 19: 168)[61]

It was Bello who first invoked the interrelatedness of *studium* ("the reinstating of readings on the cloisters"), *imperium* ("new conquests [made] on the New World's soil"), and *sacerdotium* ("regenerated humanity") in his "Discurso pronunciado en la apertura del Colegio de Santo Tomás" (1848) (*Obras completas* 18: 26). Yet this speech was also Bello's almost desperate attempt to preach the republican ethics of public life to young boys who were likely to be indoctrinated instead in a variety of Catholic doctrines that naturalized class divisions, perpetuating the divide between the elite and the underprivileged. In the 1848 address, which was published twice in the course of that year, Bello repeated his idea, extolled by Caro, that morality had some legitimate claims on education, but omitted the same words that Caro highlighted to the greater glory of the Church. After championing the spread of primary education as the acquisition of both practical skills and humane learning (religion is conspicuously absent from this part of the piece), Bello concludes in an uncharacteristically impatient tone, which shows him also at his most Bolivarian:

> Some will say that this is *a dream, a chimera, a utopia*. I, however, have great faith in social perfectibility. I do not conceive of it without the nurturing of moral sentiments, which in turn I cannot conceive without the nurturing of one's intelligence. I cannot accept as an upsetting worry and nothing else the idea that the ignorance and degradation in which the great majority of humankind finds itself is an inheritance that cannot be repudiated.
>
> [...]
>
> This is among any people's sacred rights, whose importance cannot be overstated because it is required for the exercise of any other rights. Therefore, no government can forget this obligation, nor can the class that has been favored by fortune, the literary institutions, or, let me add as well, the ecclesiastical institutions. (*Obras completas* 18: 25)

According to Bello, literary institutions cannot fail to vindicate their independence from the superstitions and interdictions that civil and ecclesiastical governments have long imposed on them, making "ignorance" and "degradation" a socioeconomic rather than a theological reality for the nineteenth century. This daring statement in a year of such civil unrest as 1848 more than makes up for Bello's scruples and hesitations when in 1843 he did not live up to the task of producing a romantic-liberal version of "La prière pour tous." In defending Bello's translational liberties more than a century later, Crema unwittingly laid his finger on the crux of the problem that afflicted Spanish American literary criticism's historical dependence on *letrado* readings at a time when literature was not, and could not become, an autonomous artistic realm. It was not just that Bello's harmoniously abridged rendition was aesthetically more pleasing to him than the monstrously self-contradictory poem "La prière pour tous." In addition, Bello's translational act was an instance of *translatio secundum* and of *translatio fidei* to the extent that it brought Hugo back to the bosom of the Catholic Church at the same time as it made romanticism acceptable to the retrograde lettered city, first in Chile and later in Colombia. Conservative readers were comforted and reassured in discovering that—in the midst of social revolutions and the rise of atheism and socialism everywhere—Hugo periodically returned for his spiritual solace to acts of prayer. What granted additional significance to this gesture was the fact that Hugo was also one of the authors and politicians who did the most in his time to create an unrestricted public sphere in which all possible subversions of theo-political authority could at least be debated.

In the reactionary city of translation that emerged in Colombia under Caro's watchful monitoring, the symbolic acts of original sin and *remissio peccatorum*—in traducianist doctrine, *tradux peccati* and *translatio fidei*, respectively—provided a coherent framework for the exegesis of all future metaphorical writing that takes as its vehicle a foreign language.[62] If the medieval Church Fathers had appropriated the rhetorical categories of *interpretatio* and *conversio* of Quintilian and Cicero to make ancient wisdom conform to Christian doctrine, why would not Caro in turn think about literary translation from within theological institutions?

Yet, through his various translational efforts, Caro did more than simply reverse the ascendancy of literature over theology. As I explain in other chapters of this book, he also conflated "political" and "literary states of exception." Instead of authenticating the exceptional measures that he took as head of the executive branch through the evidentiary rhetoric of decisionism, he repeatedly invoked the linguistic authority bestowed upon the poet and the philologist to let political regimes be directed by grammatical regimes. This was his main point in the essay "A Light Ideological Excursus" [Ligera excursión ideológica] (1872) used as epigraph for the present book. Such discursive convertibility, made possible by the use of syllogistic reasoning, was exposed as mere sophistry in Locke's *An Essay concerning Human Understanding* and in Bello's *Filosofía del entendimiento*. In other words, Caro did not argue that Colombian rulers *could* promulgate the Constitution of 1886 *because* they defeated the liberals in the war of 1885. Rather, *he* was entrusted with writing the new charter *because* as philologist he was the main interpreter of the nation's *documentary as well as imagined* archive. The Regeneración's Constitution may have been the outcome of a carefully plotted plan to overcome chronic civil unrest and stop Liberalism in its tracks. At the same time, in foregrounding Catholicism as the decisive factor in the construction of Colombianness, it also subjected the nation to a *translatio fidei*. This collective religious conversion was authorized and naturalized by an uninterrupted *traditio* of Catholic literary works that surprisingly featured Hugo and Bello, and whose meaning was immediately available only to philologists and translators who happened to be also self-taught legists possessed of significant expertise in grammar and rhetoric.

It is in the interstices of translation, in the flow of signifiers and meanings that cumulatively constitute the writerly city or *ciudad escrituraria* within the reactionary *ciudad letrada* that texts can be returned not just to earlier stages of the language, but also to the orthodoxy of Roman Catholic doctrine. Both cities for a short time tried to tame the unmanageable *ciudad real*, which in Bogotá was at times almost successfully supplanted by the cornucopia of literary and pastoral texts produced by Caro and his coterie. Each text Caro edited or translated "on the second degree"—this is the meaning of *translatio secunda* or *translatio duplex* understood as a figure of polysemous metaphorizing—also advanced a *translatio secundum*, that is to say, a rendition "in conformity with" preestablished doctrines, carrying within it the attempt at sending New Granada back to colonial times. At the same time, the impression that these texts herald the advent of a millennial event was made all the more urgent and fateful by the proximity of the nineteenth century's end and the onset of the civil War of the Thousand Days, which broke out shortly after Caro produced his sonnet "Roma Dominatrix" and Valencia his apocalyptic "Anarkos" in 1898. The increasing isolation of the Regeneración governments seemed to echo the trials and tribulations experienced by the sudden eclipse of the popes' temporal power in the second half of the nineteenth century. In Rome as in Bogotá, the near annihilation of the visible symbols of the Church's earthly power seemed to be the ultimate omen of its certain, imminent triumph and the multitudinous conversions resulting from it. Some argued that the *translatio* and *regeneratio* of the unfaithful were close at hand.[63] Similarly, the interplay of the *civitas terrena* and the *civitas Dei* among an elite imbued with Augustinian doctrines legitimated the strikingly outdated literary productions just mentioned.

Caro's constant practice of rendering foreign-language poetry in Spanish and rendering Spanish-language poetry in Latin substantiates his legitimating rhetoric. In his almost desperate attempts at *converting* Hugo by eliminating any vestiges of liberal doctrines in Bello's translation, he went so far as to translate portions of Bello's "La oración por todos" into Latin, so that the palimpsestic trace of Hugo's original was erased not once but twice.[64] Alternatively, as he would have preferred to say, Hugo was *restored* or *regenerated* twice by two languages that were superior to French insofar as they had changed more slowly and were in keeping with Church doctrine, thanks to the efforts of grammarians like him.[65] The first anthology of Caro's neo-Latin verse was published as *Carmina et interpretationes a poetis nostratibus* in 1943. It was followed by Rivas Sacconi's edited collection *Versiones latinas* in 1951. Both volumes were drawn from Caro's two extant manuscripts, completed after he stepped down from the vice presidency: *Carmina latina* and *Latinae interpretationes*. Caro's purpose in producing Latin versions of such Spanish-Language poets as Garcilaso, Juan de Arguijo, Quevedo, Rodrigo Caro, Quintana, Bello, and Baralt in addition to his father, his grandfather (Miguel Tobar), his great-grandfather (the Spanish *letrado* Francisco Javier Caro), and even His Holy Father (Pope Leo XIII, whom he translated from the Italian) was to get these authors' words closer to the language of the Church and of revealed truth. The subtitle "carmina e poetis praecipue Hispanis, tum Italis, Gallis, Anglis, latine reddita" [songs by mainly Spanish poets, but also Italian, French, and English ones, *returned to Latin*] puts forth a hierarchy of national and transnational languages, among which Latin appears at the top and is posited as an absolute origin and an absolute end, that is, as the chief vehicle for building anew a *civitas Dei* of translation.

Appendix

Principal printings of Bello's "La oración por todos" in mainstream publications in the nineteenth century:

"La oración por todos (Imitación de Víctor Hugo)." *El Crepúsculo* [Santiago], vol. 1, no. 6 (October 1, 1843): 245–51.

América poética. Colección escojida de composiciones en verso, escritas por americanos en el presente siglo: Parte Lírica. Ed. Juan María Gutiérrez. Valparaíso: Imprenta del Mercurio, 1846. Pp. 85–88.

"La oración por todos. Imitación de Victor Hugo." *La Crónica. España y los pueblos hispanoamericanos* [New York], año 11, no. 56 (October 18, 1859): 387.

"La oración por todos." *El Catolicismo* [Bogotá] 7.453 (December 11, 1860): 845–47.

"La oración por todos. Imitación de Víctor Hugo." *Revista Literaria* [Caracas] 10–11–12 (1865): 159–60, 173–76, 191–92.

Colección de poesías originales por Andrés Bello, con apuntes biográficos por J. M. Torres Caicedo. París: Librería de Rosa y Bouret, 1870. Pp. 105–22. This may be the first nineteenth-century printing that offers the French originals of Hugo's poems alongside Bello's Spanish versions. The French text of "La prière pour tous" is truncated at line 178, leaving out sections

V–X (ll. 179–446). The *Apuntes biográficos* (pp. 5–19) mentioned in the subtitle is an earlier essay titled "Don Andrés Bello" and dated 1853. It reads like a draft of the longer essay (dated 1856) included in volume 1 of Torres Caicedo's *Ensayos biográficos y de crítica literaria sobre los principales poetas y literatos hispano-americanos. Primera serie* (Paris: Librería de Guillaumin y Cía, Editores, 1863), pp. 187–211.

"La oración por todos." *La Escuela Normal* [Bogotá] 2.37 (September 16, 1871): 591–92.

Colección de poesías originales por Andrés Bello. Con apuntes biográficos por J.M. Torres Caicedo. Nueva York: Librería e Imprenta de N. Ponce de León, 1873. Pp. 70–78.

Biblioteca de escritores venezolanos contemporáneos, ordenada con noticias biográficas por José M. Rójas, Ministro plenipotenciario de Venezuela en España. Carácas/Paris: Rójas Hermanos, Editores/Jouby et Roger, Éditeurs, 1875. Pp. 40–44. Like Torres Caicedo, Rojas includes the French original along with the Hugo imitations collected in this volume. An outstanding erratum changes the title of the Spanish text to "La oración por tarde."

Colección de poesías originales de Andrés Bello, acompañada de "La infancia y juventud de Bello" y de notas bibliográfica por Arístides Rojas (Edición del Centenario de Bello, aumentada y corregida). Caracas: Rojas Hermanos, Editores, 1881. Pp. 241–51. Edition printed in Paris by "Imprenta Motteroz."

Poesías de Andrés Bello (precedidas de un estudio biográfico y crítico). Ed. Miguel Antonio Caro. Madrid: Imprenta de D. A[ntonio] Pérez Dubrull, 1882. Pp. 95–104.

Obras completas de Andrés Bello, volumen III: Poesías. Ed. and Intro. Miguel Luis Amunátegui. Santiago: Impreso por Pedro G. Ramírez, 1883. Pp. 168–75. The fifteen volumes of the centennial edition came out in 1881–1892.

"La oración por todos." *El Repertorio Colombiano* [Bogotá] 13.7 (1887): 59–67. Included in a minicluster of readings in catechesis edited by Caro under the rubric "Lecturas paralelas en prosa y verso" (41–84).

Víctor Hugo en América (traducciones de ingenios americanos). Ed. José Antonio Soffia and José Rivas Groot. Bogotá: Casa Editorial de M. Rivas, 1889. Pp. 147–56.

Antología de poetas hispano-americanos, tomo II: Cuba, Santo Domingo, Puerto Rico, Venezuela. Ed. Marcelino Menéndez Pelayo. Madrid: Est. Tip. "Sucesores de Rivadeneyra," 1893. Pp. 340–48.

C H A P T E R F O U R

R E G E N E R A T I O N W I T H O U T R E V O L U T I O N — C A R O C O N T R A B O L Í V A R

Instituting the Exception: The Law and the Poets

A profound inquiry into the elegiac discourse of Colombian conservatism in the five decades stretching from 1883 to the 1930s should necessarily include the verse and prose poems of Rafael Pombo, Miguel Antonio Caro, José Asunción Silva, and Guillermo Valencia, the four most influential lyrists who began their careers in the last third of the nineteenth century. All the four devoted lyric texts to Simón Bolívar, taking as their pretext the Libertador's physical and political defeat in the last year of his life, which the first three contrasted with the commanding solidity of the marble and bronze statue inaugurated on Bolívar Square on July 20, 1846. Crafted by Pietro Tenerani (1789–1869), the pedestrian statue presides over the Cathedral of Bogotá and is physically and symbolically close to the Casa del 20 de Julio, where independence from Spain was hastily declared in 1810.[1] In the years 1848–1849, as the capitol building was under construction behind the statue, the nation's two most important political platforms consolidated their identities and their names: the Liberal Party, promoted by Ezequiel Rojas, and the Conservative Party, promoted by Mariano Ospina Rodríguez.[2] The two soon found in ambitious poets and journalists, such as Felipe Pérez and José Eusebio Caro, the requisite intermediaries between their attempts at indoctrinating the population in their respective political programs and *naturalizing* each program as part of a comprehensive national culture. Since analyzing in detail the poems to which I have just alluded would demand the format of a full monograph, in the present chapter I once again focus on Miguel Antonio Caro's writing. He shares with Simón Bolívar (1783–1830) two remarkable achievements: occupying the highest office in the nation—President of the Republic—and writing for it a fundamental law.

In his book *El culto a Bolívar* (1969), Germán Carrera Damas corrected the image of the prophetic and poetic Libertador shared by the generation of reactionary *letrados* that was in power at the end of the nineteenth century, and which Liberals interpreted as that of a stifling and totalitarian genius impervious to external influences. For Carrera Damas, on the contrary, Bolívar was first and foremost a careful political strategist (75–77). Three of the Regeneración's galvanizing agents—Caro, former Liberals Rafael Núñez, and José María Samper (1828–1888)—admired in him the oratorical and synthesizing qualities that all three also took pride in having. However, it is their shared office as legists that allows us to understand the complex relation that the three Regenerators established with the crafter of the Greater Colombia. One of my two initial hypotheses is that Caro's views on Bolívar derive largely from his disappointment with the Libertador's lawmaking acts. Moreover, the ode bearing the full title "To the Statue of the Libertador (on Bogotá's Main Square)" [A la estatua del Libertador: en la Plaza Mayor de Bogotá] (1883) constitutes its author's first quasi-legislative act insofar as he had by then been publicly accorded the privilege of interpreting Colombia's past.

After having occupied the nation's supreme executive office from 1880 to 1882, Núñez was elected president again in 1884 as the Liberal Party's moderate or *independiente* candidate, which meant that he already represented in that year a Trojan horse faction invested in preventing the radicals' return to power. Since the Conservatives did not enter anyone for the race, Núñez was able to defeat his only opponent, the radical Liberal Solón Wilches, by a sizeable margin, thanks to the Conservative vote that went his way.[3] Shortly afterward, in 1885, the radicals started an insurrection against Núñez on account of a muzzled succession to the presidency of the Sovereign State of Santander (the radical Wilches was this state's outgoing President). The insurrection quickly evolved into a civil war as radicals in other regions supported the rebellion on the well-founded suspicion that Núñez was sponsoring bipartisan alliances to defeat candidates of his own party elsewhere. With the help of the Conservative Party, Núñez created a national reserve army (until then the central government had a relatively small Guardia Nacional based in Bogotá with smaller garrisons scattered around the nation) that eventually defeated the radicals. The way was thus cleared for the Regeneración to carry out institutional persecution of radicalism in the open.

Núñez's short-lived coalition of disaffected contingents from the two main parties assumed the pompous name of National Party. He also obtained the support of most of the Catholic clergy and numerous speculators who hoped to capitalize on the promised centralization of the economy and the ensuing opportunities for monopolistic exploitation of national resources. The *nacionalistas* presented themselves as a *third-way* party rather than a bipartisan force. Caro joined the new organization as the only representative of the "Catholic Party," his way of referring—as pointed out in the introduction—to the undivided authority accorded to the popes' apostolic pronouncements and to Christian doctrines as infallible norms for civil government.

(Never mind that the dogma of infallibility applied only or primarily to spiritual matters.)[4] At this time, he was planning the centralizing Constitution of 1886, whose confessional and authoritarian tenets matched his famous ode's teachings and (according to the author) the mature Bolívar's opinions and decisions. The new charter of rights was issued by a Legislative Council [Consejo Nacional Legislativo] gathered in Bogotá in 1886, among whose members Núñez chose not to be included because of the retrograde spirit of Caro's proposals. In session in the nation's capital from November of 1885, the earlier Council of Delegates counted among its appointees Colombia's best-known jurist, José María Samper, who happened to be a prolific novelist

Figure 6 Frontispiece for inaugural issue of Alberto Urdaneta's *Papel Periódico Ilustrado* (August 6, 1881): p. 1. Composed by Alberto Urdaneta and engraved by Antonio Rodríguez.

Figure 7   Pietro Tenerani's pedestrian statue of Bolívar in Bogotá with Congress in the background. Author's collection.

and playwright in addition to being Bolívar's biographer. Invoking the newly approved constitution's polemical article 121 (on "extraordinary faculties" [facultades extraordinarias]), the National Legislative Council proceeded to promulgate the first exceptional measures.[5]

Prior to his writings honoring Bolívar, Caro had carried out another act of ideological appropriation. It was made possible by the one-hundredth anniversary of the quintessential *letrado*: the Caracas-born Andrés Bello. In 1881, Caro's opportunistic presentation of Bello as a preeminently conservative and Catholic founding father prepared the way for the ensuing reduction of Bolívar's creed to the tenets of philo-Spanish traditionalism. That very year a series of acts gave institutional consecration to the celebration of Bolívar's birth in conformity with the Regeneración's needs. Among those legislative acts, two stand out for different reasons: the "Law 84 of 1881 by which the celebration of the Libertador's Centennial is ordered" and the "Decree of July 24, 1881 by which, in order to commemorate the Libertador's centenary, the publication of the *Anales de Colombia* is ordered."[6] Just two weeks later, Alberto Urdaneta began publication of the *Papel Periódico Ilustrado*. This magazine featured in its inaugural issue the composition in which Urdaneta copies François Désiré Roulin's 1828 pencil profile of Bolívar, Pietro Tenerani's 1846 bronze statue, the conquistador's Gonzalo Jiménez de Quesada's sepulcher, and Bogotá's cathedral. These and hundreds of other documents were collected in the funeral crown prepared by Manuel Ezequiel Corrales: *Colombia's Homage to the Liberator Simón Bolívar in His First Centennial, 1783–1883* [Homenaje de Colombia al Libertador Simón Bolívar en su primer centenario, 1783–1883] (1884). Since the genre of poetry (whether it was previously published or not) is abundantly represented in the *Homage* and Bolívar's arresting oratory is a recurring theme in the volume's brief essays, one can conclude that the entire collection functions simultaneously as both a literary and a legislative instrument.[7]

My second hypothesis refers to the distinction that one should always make between the acts of *instituting* and *institutionalizing* the exception to the constitutional order. The act of instituting extraordinary measures seeks to grant administrative normalcy to a convulsed polity, whose three branches of government are only temporarily stripped of their habitual prerogatives. By contrast, the act of institutionalizing such measures leads to a de facto dictatorship.[8] Between 1886 and 1890, Núñez, Caro, and Carlos Holguín used article 121 of the 1886 *magna carta* to promulgate, from the cabinet's executive office rather than Congress, a legislation that exceeded the government's justified need to make quicker decisions and interventions during a state of emergency. The free expression of religious and political differences, and their articulation from accepted subject-positions in discourses on public life, were thus outlawed in the long run, although the charter of 1886 did not explicitly condemn other denominations. According to article 121, in cases of "internal commotion" [conmoción interior], the President could "declare the rule of law interrupted and the entire Republic or a part of it in a state of siege" [declarar turbado el orden público y en estado de sitio toda la República o parte de ella]. In this manner, without the intervention of multiple national constituencies represented in Congress, the President could implement "extraordinary measures or decrees of a provisionally legislative character" without previously consulting with the legislative branch.[9] It was remiss of Caro to derogate two of these "provisional measures" issued by the National Legislative Council under the constitutional appendix "Title XXI (added)" during his six-year tenure as head of state: article K, which empowered the executive branch "to thwart and repress the abuses of the press"; and article L, which allowed the President to extend in time any exceptional legislative acts that were ordered before the enactment into law of the Regeneración's Constitution "even if they may be opposed to it."[10]

Still more infamous was the Law 61 of 1888 or Law of the Horses [Ley de los Caballos], sponsored by the titular President Núñez and his *vicepresidente encargado*, Carlos Holguín Mallarino. This law granted the cabinet of ministers the ample faculty of suspending the already sparse liberties and constitutional guarantees. The first critique of the new law was Fidel Cano's "La Ley de los Caballos" (*El Espectador* [Medellín], no. 71 [July 4, 1888]; repr. in Felipe Pérez et al., *Periodistas liberales* 145–52), which expressed the concern that the extraordinary faculties assumed by the Regenerators would become permanent. In 1897–1898, near the end of Caro's term as head of the executive branch, the Liberal Miguel Samper and the Conservative José Vicente Concha wrote each an exposé of the ironically nicknamed "monarchical constitution" and the Regeneración's later legislation (especially Law 61). They both highlighted the contradictions between the letter of this *ley de leyes*, which was to be understood as *nomos* or fundamental law, and the many exceptions, already in place, to its universal application. Concha cleverly pointed out that Caro had strategically published his volume *Artículos y discursos* (1888) simultaneously with the promulgation of Law 61. *Artículos y discursos* included the Regenerator's speeches on "Facultades extraordinarias" and "Inmunidad del Presidente" (both given on May 27, 1886 before the Council of Delegates). Caro did not have much faith in his own constituent power. This is clearly indicated by the near synchronicity of the Constitution's promulgation in 1886, the theorization of exceptions to it, and the enactment of the first emergency measures into law without having previously developed some of the guaranteed freedoms outlined in the charter of rights. In Caro's estimation, however, his constitutional thinking of 1886 was not incompatible with the Regeneración's ensuing despotic laws.

For Caro, the reading of his *Artículos y discursos* in parallel with the recently instituted Constitution and Law 61 should yield the following interpretation: in order to save and perpetuate the *magna carta* of 1886, in which we all fervently believe, "I" had to create the mechanisms that would prevent insurgents from using the republican guarantees consecrated in it to their advantage. For a constitutionalist Conservative like Concha, the *lectio* that this joint reading invited was very different: the executive branch's exclusive reliance on its extraordinary faculties was illegitimate because the government's actions would thus become unpredictable and capricious. Just as important, such extraordinary legislation challenged the protocols of historical and legal hermeneutics. In Concha's reading, the legislator's intention needs to be illuminated through the study of the law's text. In doing this, the gap between an abstract philosophy of jurisprudence and its materialization in Congress in the form of universally accepted and applied legal guarantees will eventually be closed.[11]

For his part, Miguel Samper intelligently called Caro a "white Jacobin," explaining that the grammarian-president succeeded in carefully transforming a constitutionally legitimate state into a terrorist one. This metamorphosis was accomplished through the implementation of a hierarchical descending order of coercive acts inspired remotely by Caro's Augustinian discourse on evil and immediately by the need to move quickly from a liberal-parliamentary to a decisionist regime. Such legislative acts included the articles in the 1886 Constitution that allowed for its suspension; organic laws that explicitly contradicted the *magna carta* (such as Law 61); the abusive latitude with which presumably unconstitutional laws were interpreted; the abundance of presidential edicts or decrees that also undermined the notion of a parliamentary democracy;[12] and the arbitrary verbal orders issued by low-ranking government agents who could be thrice removed from those few qualified to assume extraordinary faculties in a constitutionally correct setting. Partisan literature committed to either party, like the increasingly active newspaper industry, also contributed to weakening the authority that New Granadans previously accorded to the law.

According to Marx, the building of ever-expanding state machineries since the advent of parliamentary democracy made it all the more tempting for legitimately elected governments to declare the state of siege as a way to assert an authority that both the general electorate and the opposition were likely to construe as contingent and temporary (*The Eighteenth Brumaire* 34–35, 121–22).[13] Local sentiments and interests exploded in Colombia as the colony's large administrative units became fragmented and polarized in the aftermath of the Independence. Reacting to this loss of effective control, the new centralizing administrations engaged in the production of countless legal interdictions. They made their frequent abuses of constitutional prerogatives look legitimate as long as they could be hidden behind legal subterfuges or correlated with derogated legal traditions that only philologists and antiquarians cared to know and could interpret. The public opinion manifested in the press was a deterrent to these abuses. To put it differently, a law promulgated during a time of restricted freedom of expression was neither discussed nor approved by the nation; it was rather imposed on it. Manuel Ancízar set down the new Liberal doctrine in 1848. For a government that called itself representative and democratic, to put limits to the freedom of the press, instead of prosecuting press-related breaches of existing legal dispositions like any other offense (namely, in a tribunal of justice), was equivalent to declaring the state of exception (Ancízar 61–66).[14]

Caro perceived himself as a founder and legislator of the exception in the early years of his literary career, as suggested in the poem that opens his first collection of verse, titled simply *Poesías* (1886). This "Canticle of Moses" [Cántico de Moisés]—renamed "The Crossing of the Red Sea" [El paso del Mar Rojo] in the edition of *Traducciones poéticas* (1889)—presents itself as a translation from the Old Testament. The second stanza says: "Showing his power to the world he became my Savior: I found in him my trust, my glory, and my strength" [Así ostentando su poder al mundo / Se hizo mi salvador: mi confianza, / Mi gloria en él, mi fortaleza fundo] (ll. 4–6). Further on, the theocratic regime established in the "holy dwelling" [morada santa] (l. 44) is identified as a "monarchy" [monarquía] (l. 45), a term which—as explained in chapter 2—in Aquinas already designates the sovereign *unus*' rule over the formless and divided *multitudo*. Of the thirty-four poems that compose the collection, at least eight declare themselves free translations or paraphrases of pagan texts or Biblical passages, while others (for example, "Ernest Renan") give expression to Caro's execration of positivist *laïcité* and his encomium of the confessional state. When paraphrasing pagan poems, such as Horace's Ode VI.4 ("Qualem ministrum")—retitled in Spanish "A Roma"—Caro underlines the providential destiny to which the people of Lazio make themselves deserving by means of the *translatio imperii* or assumption of a hegemonic position in the Mediterranean world upon the destruction of Carthage.[15] Similarly, the poems that deal with Spanish America's past do so from a patriotic and epic standpoint, which Caro picked up in Manuel José Quintana's anthologies and which became a constant in his work.[16]

It is worth examining briefly two more compositions from *Poesías*. The second poem is called "Miserere" and bears the subtitle "Paraphrastic Translation." One can describe it simply as a narcissistic prayer in which the subject requests God that he be delivered completely and violently from his "crimes" (l. 41): "Don't You let even a shadow of the guilt that tarnishes me: may my heart be seen renewed and resurrecting through You in a truer life" [Ni sombra de la culpa que me afea / Dejes: en ti a la vida / Resucitar se vea / Mi corazon, i renovado sea] (ll. 42–45). In a different tone, "To the War between Spain and Chile (1866)" [A la guerra entre España y Chile, 1866] develops the motif of the Cainite fight between the two offspring of the same ancestral family. It somehow anticipates the argument of such essays as "The Conquest" [La Conquista] (1881; repr. in *Artículos y discursos* 168–92; *Páginas de crítica* 255–80),[17] written in the year in which Caro was appointed Director of the National Library and bilateral relations between Spain and Colombia were reestablished after the signing of the Treaty of Paris.

A strand of philo-Hispanism or the Americans' post-Independence nostalgia for Spain's legacy underlies poems such as the already mentioned "To the Statue of the Libertador" (1883) and "The Reconciliation" [La reconciliación], a lyric-epic ballad included in the collective volume *Romancero colombiano* (1883).[18] In the year of the *Papel Periódico Ilustrado*'s founding, the first of the journal's several extensive dossiers on Bolívar featured two pages excerpted from José Manuel Groot's three-volume *Historia eclesiástica y civil de Nueva Granada* (1869–1870), in which Bolívar's piously Catholic death is described in detail (see *Papel*, no. 4 [November 1, 1881]: 66–67).[19] The main hero the other massive historical work of the period, Vergara y Vergara's *Historia de la literatura en Nueva Granada desde la Conquista hasta la Independencia (1538–1820)* (1867), is the publicist and patriot Antonio Nariño, on whose political doctrines a little has already been said in chapter 2.

In almost any biographical sketch by an author other than Vergara y Vergara, Nariño is discussed as a wealthy urban creole and able military leader whose centralist views on government did not prevent him from losing the presidential election to Bolívar at the Congress of Cúcuta in 1821. He was also the daring translator and printer of the French revolutionary Declaration of the Rights of Man (Declaración de los Derechos del Hombre y del Ciudadano) and the fleeting Governor President of the State of Cundinamarca (September 1813-May 1814), during which time he valiantly led an army of patriots against the royalist forces until he was captured and sent to prison in Cádiz. However, for Vergara y Vergara, he is primarily a pious Catholic, as Groot said of Bolívar and Caro said of Bello in the same decade. Of the nearly twenty pages that the *Historia de la literatura* devotes to Nariño, one-half is spent on the author's preparations for his own exemplary Christian passing, that is to say, Vergara writes a hagio-thanatography in which the doctrinal meaning of his subject's allegorical life is predetermined (2: 84–88; 3: 13–15, 47–58).[20] Caro's sonnet sequence "The Founding Fathers" (*El Repertorio Colombiano* 11.11 [July 1884]: 383–86) also belongs to this category of Catholic exegesis. It came out in the same year in which the author took up the position of Rector of the Catholic University and was voted, in a contest organized by the *Papel Periódico Ilustrado*, Colombia's most remarkable citizen (see no. 71 [July 20, 1884]: 370).

Although no archetype of Bolívar is included in Caro's *Poesías*, in "To the War between Spain and Chile" the author essentializes South American identities as an extension of Spanish traditionalism. The text seems to deny the legitimate attempts at self-differentiation that Bolívar had presented—albeit timidly—along ethnic, religious, and class lines:

Do not, Spain, claim entirely for yourself the ancient laurel that glimmers around your temples! And do not, America, insult Castile, as that offense twice degrades you!! Victor or vanquished, you are an Iberian, and so are you: you two share the same language, blood, and name

No tuyo entero clames / El lauro antiguo que en tus sienes brilla, / España! I tú no infames, / América, a Castilla; / Que ese insulto dos veces te mancilla!! / Vencedor o vencido, / Tú eres ibero, i tú: lleváis iguales / Habla, sangre, apellido.(ll. 61–68)

Rafael Pombo is the poet who consolidates the Conservative vogue of celebrating the statue made by Tenerani, which provided the occasion for honoring Bolívar as well. The late-romantic bard and author of children's books produced two translations of French poems originally published on the occasion of Bolívar's centenary in addition to his own sonnet titled "Bolívar" that came out also in 1883. Having trained as an engineer at the military school owned by the aristocratic and belligerent general Tomás Cipriano de Mosquera (president or dictator in 1845–1849, 1861–1864, and 1866–1867), the younger Pombo helped the volatile Mosquera revise his long manuscript, *Memoria sobre la vida del General Simón Bolívar, Libertador de Colombia, Perú y Bolivia* (pub. in 1853; third part written in 1870 and pub. in 1940). In his sonnet of 1883, the now mature romantic lyrist underlines the idea that the Colombian people never lived up to the Libertador's expectations of moral elevation. The final line, "so great a father of such small children" [padre tan grande de hijos tan pequeños] (333), subverts the well-known aphorism put forth by the last *claustralis* theologian, Saint Bernard of Clairvaux: *Pigmaei gigantum humeris impositi plusquam ipsi gigantes vident.* Caro will paraphrase it as "the smallness of human greatness" ([l]a pequeñez de la grandeza humana [l. 55]).[21] With his easy and extroverted expression, Pombo supported Caro's efforts at forging a new Catholic sentimentality in spite of repeated fallouts between the two. The newspapers in which he rendered such services were *El Tomista*, which he directed, and *La Siesta*, cofounded in 1852 with José Eusebio Caro (Miguel Antonio's father) and José María Vergara y Vergara.

In his ode "To the Statue of the Libertador" (1883; rev. in 1884 and 1886), Caro expresses the idea that the setbacks experienced by the Independence leader were rectified by the immortal majesty of Tenerani's bronze. This ode directly and immediately inspired the longest of the compositions honoring Bolívar that came out of the centennial celebrations. In 1885 the right-wing grammarian and legist Enrique Álvarez Bonilla, by then a member of the Academia Colombiana and the Consejo Académico de Colombia as well as an active contributor to the Ateneo de Bogotá's calendar of events, published an epic poem in twelve cantos titled *Santafé redimida*. This work would earn him high government offices at the end of the Regeneración such as director of the Biblioteca Nacional in 1888–1898 and 1905–1906 and secretary of public instruction and infrastructures, among others. The poem aimed to validate Bolívar as the subject of Colombia's national epic by analogy with Achilles: "I sing the sublime glory of the warrior who on the bondage in which he lived erected a whole world with strong arms that vanquished the hateful tyranny" [Canto la excelsa gloria del guerrero / Que de la servidumbre en que yacía / Alzó con fuerte brazo un mundo entero / Venciendo la ominosa tiranía] (p. 5; octave I).

In all fairness to Álvarez, the poem does not endorse in any explicit or implicit way Caro's efforts at reuniting Church and state under an authoritarian regime. Specifically, it does not speak to the executive branch's repeated attempts to reduce the separation of powers to a permanent state of exception, so that the task of government unfolds as the enforcement of arbitrary orders on a day-to-day basis. Although *Santafé redimida* describes Bolívar's Guerra a Muerte as a civil war rather than a revolution, the poem is also peopled by benign, saintly Spanish priests and missionaries in addition to the predictably indomitable patriots, while Bolívar is portrayed as a prudent strategist rather than an irascible *caudillo*. Toward the close of the last canto (octave XXV), Bolívar appears as the law-abiding citizen that he held himself to be, who nevertheless subordinates education and morality to the doctrine of the divine origin of political sovereignty. This is the part of his discourse on national regeneration that falls most clearly in line with Caro's design: "'Much more difficult than to reap laurels is to preserve them; be not so much the soldier as the worshipper of justice and the law; instead of fighting tremendous combats, educate the new nations for the common good. Safeguard your sacred rights; let us praise God's gift, let us devote our hearts to Him!'" ['Muy más difícil que segar laureles / Es saberlos honrar; más que soldados, / Ser á la ley y á la justicia fieles; / Más que librar combates denodados, / Para el bien educar pueblos noveles. / Vuestros derechos custodiad sagrados; / Bendigamos de Dios el beneficio,/¡Démosle el corazón en sacrificio!'] (p. 193; octave XXV).

José Asunción Silva (1865–1896) was the most gifted poet who sought to benefit, at the end of his short life, from an opportunistic conversion from his father's professed Liberalism to the Regeneración's program. After admitting in his poem "In Front of the Statue" [Al pie de la estatua] (1895) that Caro had already sung the epic Bolívar, Silva seems determined to recuperate the melancholy general's prophecy of defeat. To be sure, this image was more congenial to the *modernista* poet, who is described in the same poem as a "sickly offspring of a strong race" [enfermizo descendiente / de alguna fuerte raza] (52). Finally, the *historic* Conservative Guillermo Valencia (1873–1943), with whose career the line of public poets who double as presidential hopefuls extinguishes itself, identifies explicitly with Bolívar in a series of political discourses composed concurrently with the centennial of Bolívar's demise. This celebration follows shortly upon his second defeat at a presidential election in 1930.[22] In fact, Valencia intensifies the elegiac and melancholy aspects already present in the earlier poets.

Cornelio Hispano, a friend of Valencia—both hailed from the Cauca region—was the main commentator on Bolívar in the last years of Conservative hegemony. Hispano (a.k.a. Ismael López [1880–1962]) was one of the few Liberal *letrados* who had a distinguished literary career without frequently incurring the criticism of his political foes, not least because, unlike Valencia, he did not seek one of the higher offices of government. Their friendship provides one of many examples of *letrados* whose respective loyalties to mutually opposing parties could be suspended in a pastoral of literature. In this case, the pastoral impulse was enabled by their casting of their native Cauca as a bucolic and pristine natural world untainted by the *negotium* of party politics.[23] Hispano is a legitimate successor to Jorge Isaacs to the extent that he expresses repeatedly the idea that an author's love for his childhood paradise and his literary readings combine to create a sense of belonging analogous to the experience of nationhood. Although Hispano was neither a fervent Catholic nor a Conservative, his Hellenistic and cosmopolitan persona endeared him to Valencia.[24] Hispano was the best-known Liberal author who worked hard to keep his literary persona separate from his political loyalties (his use of a somewhat superannuated nom de plume is quite telling).

In 1912 Hispano brought out the first edition of the unabridged *Diario de Bucaramanga*, the work in which the French-born Bolivarian general Luis Perú de Lacroix (1780–1837)—or Jean-Louis-Michel Perou de La Croix Massier—had in 1828 allegedly set down the Libertador's most intimate thoughts during the Convención de Ocaña at Bolívar's request.[25] A more radical Bolívar emerges from reading the *Diario*, one who would have declared his disappointment at the way in which representative government was being instrumentalized by the proto-Liberal creole elites—the "demagogical party"—to ensure the type of domination denounced later on by Miguel Samper and Manuel Ancízar, among others. In Bolívar's words, this is what the Liberal lettered city would look like at its worst in the nineteenth century: "[I]n Colombia there is an aristocracy of rank, wealth, and office, which is equivalent in its pretensions and its pressure on the people to Europe's most despotic aristocracy of title and blood" (Perú de Lacroix 137). Anticipating Miguel Samper's later denunciation in *La miseria en Bogotá* (quoted in chapter 1), for Bolívar, the predictable outcome of preserving a rigidly hierarchical organization of society was "the bondage of the people, permanently oppressed by the military, the clergy, lawyers, and doctors" (Perú de Lacroix 136). Although some of these groups might pay lip service to "the most democratic Constitution," oppression of the people would not easily cease because of their own "limited education and deep-rooted customs" (Perú de Lacroix 137). Bolívar was quick to see that liberally inclined *letrados* wanted equality, which to many of them meant equality with the upper classes, not the lower.

The Colombian author who best represents the ambivalent feelings awakened by Bolívar's life and legacy in the years in which the Regeneración peaked may well be the already cited jurist and novelist José María Samper Agudelo (Miguel Samper's brother). Raised in a family of tradesmen from Honda, he went through an early manhood devoted to radical politics (he belonged to the "Gólgota" faction of Liberalism), in which he abhorred Bolívar, then was stigmatized by his party and by the Republican School, created in 1850. As time went by, however, his disenchantment became accentuated. He was particularly upset by the continual subordination of the nation's interests to *caudillo* politics and conflicts of jurisdiction among the three branches of government, and blamed the feuding nature of Liberalism's various factions for the impossibility of articulating a sense of national purpose. In the years stretching from the Revolution of Independence to the Regeneración, the creole aristocracy was concerned with maintaining its portion of influence and power at the local level. With this aim in mind, the elites took advantage of the autonomous nature of the United Provinces (Confederate

States since 1858), which the federation's central government proved unable to integrate fully as a single nation-state because of the peripheral territories' geographical inaccessibility and chronic litigiousness.

To follow Samper's story, his deconversion from federalist Liberalism, which led directly to the Regeneración (or at least was compatible with it), would have been completed in 1875.[26] In this year he wrote in Bogotá the first draft of *El Libertador Simón Bolívar*, a revised version of which appeared in Caracas in 1883, and subsequently, with an additional chapter, in Buenos Aires in 1884. Samper reads Bolívar biographically, explaining that both he and Bolívar went through a revolutionary youth before arriving at a moderate manhood and later at their more mature understanding of authoritarian regimes. This assessment is not completely unfounded. Once the emancipation process was completed, the Libertador's emphasis on the primacy of an undivided executive prerogative and on centralization would have transformed him, before the same citizens who supported him, into a founding father less reassuring than Santander, the more predictable "Man of the Law" [El Hombre de las Leyes].[27]

In the middle years of the nineteenth century, the later Bolívar's uncompromising centralism and the varieties of municipal self-government bequeathed by the viceroyalty were combined in new powerful ways. In the positivist-voluntarist discourse fostered by republican jurisprudence—already adumbrated by Antonio Nariño and taken up by Santander—individual states claimed respect for their self-differentiated identity irrespective of a larger juridical frame for the still shaky nation-state. The *santanderista* state may not have succeeded in claiming the monopoly over the legitimate means of violence or consolidating a public sphere conducive to the ensuing emergence of a civil society. It nonetheless ensured the transmission of a legal tradition in which the concept of territory bore upon the related concepts of people and culture (Palacios, *Parábola del liberalismo* 210–15). The creole culture sacralized the Spanish language's literary and oratorical registers without implementing the educational apparatuses that would allow other segments of the population to master the language's accepted standard. In this manner, the indigenous and black populations, and in general the laboring poor, were further alienated from public life.

In this model of the state, which favored tears in the social fabric most often identified with religious, ethnic, and class differences, legal inertia coexisted with the impulse to break away from the central powers. Such attempts were sheltered by a juridical order that increasingly alternated the recourse to the exception with the recovery of local rights vaguely inspired in the municipal autonomy of colonial times. The figure of the Libertador would have concealed the ideological contradictions between these mutually exclusive principles of government for the duration of the revolutionary process. To draw a parallel with the ancient stories to which reports of Bolívar's exploits were often analogized, the hero of a national epopee, however felicitous the latter may be, has to be banished after his final victory by the very community he has freed. Moreover, Bolívar had to become a "dictator" in order to free his people, as Bello held in explaining the political paradox resulting from the combination of a "foreign" emancipating impetus—a *principio extraño*—with the "native" resiliency—the *elemento nativo*—of the Spanish character (*Obras completas* 19: 170–71). The hero's inflexible character (his ethics) and exceptionality (his autonomy) pose a constant threat to the polis. In the case of aristocratic revolutions, recently liberated communities are often polarized in closed corporations formed by privileged individuals fighting for a hegemonic position. In the Venezuela of 1830–1840, the deceased Bolívar was depicted as "an insurmountable obstacle for the new organization of society," that is to say, as "the impossible citizen," reluctant to accept that postrevolutionary institutional life entails the appearance of endless debates on the nature and mission of the state (Carrera Damas 94).

The sudden transition from the moment in which the elitist revolution is instituted and the moment in which this founding gesture must be translated into government institutions not only legal, but also legitimate, establishes the reciprocal otherness of both moments: the second must repress the first. According to Samper, Bolívar was the perfect orator and military *caudillo*, and the most honest administrator possible, but he was also a mediocre statesman (*El Libertador Simón Bolívar* 24–25). The visionary general would have proved incompetent to navigate the complications of a postwar realpolitik; he was, in any case, less adept at this than at raising rebellious armies or managing a war economy. I have already indicated that Samper was then articulating his personal recantation of radicalism and any other challenge to the authority legally represented by an elite possessed of moderately Conservative convictions. For that reason, he affirms that Bolívar professed the creed of democratic republicanism (analogous to North American constitutionalism) in "the *language* and the *form*," but not in the *substance* (*El Libertador Simón Bolívar* 40). To his own regret, Samper did not gauge well Caro's intentions; he erroneously surmised that the Regeneración and the National Party would be shaped into an adequate platform not just for establishing a common political ground, but also for building a more inclusive society and state.[28]

A detailed comparative study of the above-mentioned lyric and romanticized texts by Samper, Pombo, Caro, Silva, and Valencia would reveal the gradual internalization of Colombia's modern history as a pastoral of defeat. The conservatism to which they all adhered, in different ways and at different moments, complemented a deficient discourse on nation building with the lyrical appropriation and transcendentalizing of a fragmented and ruinous patrimony. The Libertador first implemented a discipline of self-fashioning based on the related experiences of loss and recovery in his numerous (and often calculated) expressions of melancholy disillusion prior to his final relinquishing of power. The motifs of ruination and loss soon became central to Caro's production, allowing him and Valencia to project the premature death of their biological father (in Caro's case) or mother (in Valencia's case) onto the nation's more or less transitory crisis.[29] In Caro, this projection is more obvious insofar as he directly leveled two charges against federal Liberalism.

First, he blamed it for encouraging the administrative and ideological dismembering of the nation, which for him was a monolithic entity founded upon the exclusivity of Catholicism and centralizing decisionism. In contrast with federalism, Caro posits the historical continuity between the Spain's colonial heritage and Bolívar's exceptional powers of 1828–1830. Second, Caro also accused Liberalism (first in the person of the one-time radical Samper) of having persecuted his father. Caro thought that Samper might have pushed José Eusebio into exile in 1850 and into a premature death when he was coming back home in 1853. Although the son does not explicitly state this, José Eusebio could have become a second Bolívar after evolving from philosophical radicalism to Catholic conservatism and philo-Hispanism. This would also be in keeping with Caro's construal of the later Bolívar's imputed evolution from revolutionary republicanism to conservatism as set forth in the ode.[30]

At the risk of complicating further this family romance of parental figures that are alternately embraced and rejected, one must bring Miguel Tobar into the picture. He was José Eusebio's father-in-law and the legist who commemorated Manuela Sáenz's miraculous rescue of Bolívar from the assassination plot at the presidential palace in September of 1828, writing the Latin inscription sculpted in a marble plaque, which ends with the words: "pater salvatorque patriae / SIMON BOLIVAR / in nefanda nocte septembrina / Ann. mdcccxxviii" (Cordovez Moure 491).

No one so far has remarked on a coincidence that could not have escaped an author as prone to allegorize hagiographic and historicist narratives as Miguel Antonio. This is the fact that the Libertador and José Eusebio died in the same place: the surroundings of the Caribbean seaport of Santa Marta. The former died as he started on a journey of self-exile that would have taken him to Europe, while the latter was coming back from the United States, where he had fled to escape prosecution for slander and defamation. We can go a little further in suggesting that Caro enacts Bolívar's symbolic parricide at the hands of the first generation he emancipated. This constituency included the *erring* José Eusebio, although it was the latter's protector (the centrist Liberal Florentino González) who became actively involved in the assassination plot. Because since 1846 the very able González had been Secretary of the Treasury in Mosquera's so-called *ministerial* government, with José Eusebio acting as his Director of the Accounting Office, José

Eusebio understandably succeeded González in this position in 1848, but was summarily laid off upon engaging in a campaign against the administration that was employing him.[31]

Although the ritualizing of parricide is not consciously acknowledged as such in Caro's literary output, its traces appear in his use of the lyric topoi of the exile and the kingdom. To begin with, the ode "To the Statue of the Libertador" refers to the conspiracy to assassinate Bolívar in September of 1828. In addition to González and Ospina, it is widely believed that Vice President Francisco de Paula Santander could have approved of this conspiracy. The poem connects the betrayal that Bolívar suffered at home with the charity shown by the Spaniard (I translate in prose): "The obstinate brother stirred his dagger against your chest; and in the most remote corner of Colombia a Spanish nobleman offers you an honest roof in place of your motherland" (ll. 66–70). The documented circumstance that a Spaniard, Joaquín de Mier y Benítez, was the compassionate resident of San Pedro Alejandrino who hosted the declining Bolívar on his way to Europe, is mixed here with the act of betrayal by the Libertador's detractors.

Snapshots of an analogous psychological conflict are adumbrated in certain key episodes of Caro's public life. A good example is the extralegal persecution and banishment he decreed against former president Santiago Pérez (1830–1900). The longtime Liberal leader had preceded Caro in nearly every endeavor encouraged by the lettered city. He was a professional educator, the first grammarian-president in Colombia's history (1874–1876), and a substantial interpreter of Andrés Bello's linguistic ideas. Furthermore, he published a remarkable poem—"A la estatua de Bolívar" (repr. in Corrales iv–v)—which competes in its title with the ones written by the Regeneración's ideologists. Pérez's immolation came after Bolívar's banishment of Santander and the Liberal government's forcing of José Eusebio into exile during José Hilario López's presidency. This act may well have been the locus of a psychic transference, but equally important is the fact that it strangely justified the Regeneración's problematic return to the primal scene of the Libertador's disappointment in parliamentary regimes.[32]

One Hundred Years of Bolívar: Caro Confronts Restrepo and Rionegro

Upon Bolívar's demise in 1830, a short period of liberating catharsis ensued in Colombia. Signs of *fatherly* oppression by the founding figure had been announced in the copious body of denigrating poetry that surveyed the Libertador's actions and character.[33] The attacks on Bolívar in his lifetime cannot be subsumed in a dichotomy of liberal/conservative built upon the preference for a legislative branch of government conceived along federalist lines over a centralizing executive power, or for a Manchesterist, free-trade economy over an interventionist one. This simplification avoids the key question of the juridical inequality among groups that collectively are interpellated as subjects of the same process of emancipation from colonial rule. The attacks just mentioned would be the result, rather, of the conflict between participatory and nonparticipatory republican models of the state that traverses the history of Colombia through at least the first presidency of the populist Liberal Alfonso López Pumarejo (1934–1938), the time when the basic rights of manual workers were first given a full formulation (Tirado Mejía 337–39; Safford and Palacios 292–95).

On the one hand, Bolívar's transgressive republicanism would have foreshadowed liberalism at moments in which he advocated the elimination of monopolistic and protectionist practices that favored only the oligarchy's interests. The liberal ethos was most clearly anticipated by his envisioning of the gradual access to education and the suffrage ("universal, direct, and secret," as later radical democrats will add) by ample groups of the subaltern male population, or by his equitable taxation system that put a premium on great fortunes and estates, so that the state could help the poor become part of a nation of proprietors.[34] For many republicans, however, these interventionist measures were an affront to freedom. They believed that the aristocracy could lead by example and that little—if any—government intervention was needed to create a civil society.

On the other hand, Bolívar leaned toward conservatism to the extent that he often had trouble imagining the transition from a revolutionary regime (in which the executive prerogatives are temporarily augmented) to a proto-democratic regime (in which the legislative body of Congress limits the power bestowed upon the government cabinet). In any case, Bolívar could not rationalize the otherwise predictable disunion of the emancipated territories, since each of them was stirred by the interests of a particular oligarchy with its self-differentiated histories, capabilities, and desiderata. He looked at these internecine conflicts as proof that local differences needed to be acknowledged and reckoned with prior to the building of an encompassing national identity. The goal of keeping Colombia undivided could only be accomplished under the exception's strenuously constitutional regime. This reading modifies substantially Bello's early assessment, which he expressed in the course of his 1844 polemic with José Victorino Lastarria on the subject of Spain's colonial legacy. Bello wrote: "No one loved freedom more sincerely than General Bolívar; but he, like the rest of us, was surpassed by the nature of the events; the advent of freedom called first for independence, and the champion of independence was and had to be a dictator. The outstanding and necessary contradictions in his acts followed from this" (*Obras completas* 19: 170–71).[35]

It goes without saying that Bolívar was neither the only nor the first freedom lover to concentrate most government prerogatives in his person: the Athenian statesman Pericles, whom his hagiographer Thucydides called a *primus inter pares* or *princeps* [*pròtos anèr*] to distinguish him from some of his more authoritarian colleagues, was in fact a "tyrant." This office has been recently glossed by classical philologist and political historian Luciano Canfora as he who ruled in the assembly through a mixture of collective negotiations and personal decision making without necessarily being a despot. The only defining feature of the tyrant in ancient Greece was his "unbroken presence in power in a constitutionally correct setting" (Canfora 12–14). Bolívar strove to maintain the correctness of his first appointment to a dictatorial magistracy as dictator in February of 1824, when the Peruvian Congress temporarily placed in his hands *plenitudo potestatis* to counter more effectively the most recent advances of royalist troops. He accordingly held another Congreso Constituyente in 1825 and yet another in 1826, after which the Congreso Constitutional would be established in lieu of the *assemblée constituante* and the powers of dictatorship would be dissolved. In the paragraphs that follow, I explain why this plan could not be implemented in the terms set forth here.

Toward the end of his life, when holding the office of dictator longer than initially expected had brought him such bitter and adverse criticisms, Bolívar ostensibly downplayed his more honorific title of "Libertador." He much preferred instead—so he claimed—the designation of "Citizen." His early defenders found it offensive that he would be called a tyrant or a dictator rather than a liberator, but detractors were just as outraged for different reasons.[36] Similarly, in Rome Octavius favored his title of "princeps" (first citizen of the state) at the expense of "Augustus" or *Imperator maximus* (although he held the magistracy of *imperium maius* for life since 19 BC). Octavius managed to disguise for a long time his *coup-d'état* of 37 BC, when he illegally formed the Second Triumvirate with Antony (the Republic's declared enemy), de facto becoming dictator in 31 BC. In 27 BC he reached a settlement with a dissimulating and acquiescing Senate, to which he resigned—in a *traditio ficta*—all his exceptionally assumed powers on the understanding that he would get them back in the form of a legal transfer of sovereignty. This is Octavius's self-account in chapter 34 of his *Res gestae divi Augusti*: "having obtained power over all things [i.e., absolute power] by universal consent, I transferred the government of the state from my [consular] *potestas* into the control of the Senate and the people of Rome" [per consensum uniuersorum potens rerum omnium, rem publicam ex mea potestate in senatus populique Romani arbitrium transtuli] (24). Octavius does not renounce his *potestas soluta*, which he obtained *extra legem* through his ability to make juridical exceptions prevail over norms, but his instrumental control of government.

In assuming dictatorial powers at the request of a smaller assembly in the constitutionally unstable setting of the Convención de Ocaña, which had been summoned as a larger *assemblée constituante*, did Bolívar also appropriate for himself the rights that belonged exclusively to the people? Was the office of dictator the only possible recognizable form that *arbitrium* and *imperium* could assume before the eyes of a hopelessly divided nation? The ensuing series of lesser *caudillos* and military heroes who claimed to be following in the Libertador's footsteps suggests that in Colombia, as in Greece and Rome (if nothing else, this much at least New Granada had in common with the ancient world), the people continued to respond favorably to a charismatic authority. This larger-than-life leader presented himself as the guarantor of freedom in times of war even if the legal instruments used in this process were reminiscent of Old Regime institutions. The new consensus politics ushered in by the revolutionary process had been exposed as a republican politics of dilation in which decisions were not made quickly enough. When they finally happened, those decisions were often immediately challenged—invoking the republican right to resistance—and at times also reversed. However, countering the deconsecration of republican authority, as Bolívar certainly did, is different from arguing that the Libertador's acceptance of his exceptional executive faculties necessarily entailed an unstated reversion to doctrines of absolute power and undivided sovereignty.

When one wishes to argue, as this chapter does, that Bolívar's discourse on rights was neither monolithically nor primarily conservative, let alone despotic, one must first make at least three distinctions. The first one refers to the *décalage* between the letter of Bolívar's constitutional texts and the political careers of the creole magnates who adhered, with varying degrees of opportunism, to the personalist rule of the exception as the norm of constitutional government. Another important distinction is that which refers to the nineteenth-century concept of liberalism, which can assume very different meanings. In the first place, liberal projects can focus on the struggle for greater equality, which may in time become better represented (as the levels of education and income increase) in the legislative branch in which the nation's sovereignty resides.[37] The centralizing of power and the homogenizing of rights are often achieved at the expense of local privileges and interests (Tocqueville, *Democracy in America* 1: 314–17). Second, the liberal impetus can be realized in the struggle for the right of self-government and self-determination inherent in federalism—this may appear as a corollary in peaceful times of the struggle for emancipation. Finally, either one of these two philosophies of government can adopt (or not) the free-trade economic system, in which the state gives up in part the exercise of the protectionist and monopolistic prerogatives. These three distinctions are further complicated by the early proliferation of images of the Libertador that describe him by means of dichotomies founded more on impressionistic judgments than on a careful scrutiny of his ideas. Was he an optimist or a pessimist, an emancipating force or an oppressive one, an advocate for equality before the law or a believer in hereditary privileges?

No idea has done more damage to Bolívar's reputation than the allegation that toward the end of his life he began to favor the monarchical system.

By the middle of the nineteenth century, this had long been part of the character assassination carried out by Bolívar's partisan detractors, including Karl Marx, who in 1858 used these and other slanders of the Libertador found in French *légitimiste* literature as ammunition to attack Napoléon III. The notion was also easy to spread because in the late 1820s, Spain and France were already curbing their earlier revolutionary enthusiasms—that is. they were reverting to an appreciation for the monarchical institution—while the American Spaniards marched on toward the denouement of their Revolution of Independence. In their authoritative one-volume history, *Colombia: Fragmented Land, Divided Society* (2002), Frank Safford and Marco Palacios narrate the origins of Bolívar's black legend in a little over one page, reiterating the same point several times: in April of 1829 (less than two years before his death), Bolívar did listen to his council of ministers explain to him an unrequested scheme to establish either a British protectorate or a temporary monarchy that "would make Colombia more respectable in the eyes of European monarchies, thus helping to assure Colombia's external security" (127). Yet, "in July 1829 writing from Guayaquil, [Bolívar] pronounced firmly against it" (Safford and Palacios 128).[38]

In the República de Nueva Granada (called Confederación Granadina since 1858 and Estados Unidos de Colombia since 1861), the seminal work in the later cult of Bolívar is José Manuel Restrepo's monumental interpretation of the origins of Venezuela and Colombia: *Historia de la revolución de la república de Colombia en la América meridional* (1837; definitive ed., 1858). Later prose works include the biography already cited by General Mosquera and the brief text titled "Juramento en el Monte Sacro." Known also as "Juramento de Roma" and "Juramento del Monte Aventino," this is an account, recorded by the physician and writer Manuel Uribe Ángel, of the words Bolívar pronounced in 1805 in Rome before his mentor Simón Rodríguez, who set them forth for the historian in 1850. Both the "Juramento" and the equally apocryphal "Mi delirio sobre el Chimborazo" (pub. posthumously in Caracas in 1842) were included in Corrales's 1884 *Homenaje* (74–76, 35–36). As shown by Susana Rotker, these two documents have long functioned as rhetorical foundations of various nationalist discourses in Colombia and especially Venezuela. The Venezuelan counterparts to these early hagiographers were the functionary and diplomat Fermín Toro, who recorded the events of an important homage in *Descripción de los honores fúnebres consagrados a los restos del Libertador Simón Bolívar, en cumplimiento del decreto legislativo de 30 de abril de 1842* (1843), and the jurist Felipe Larrazábal, editor of the two-volume *Correspondencia general del Libertador Simón Bolívar…Precede a esta colección interesante la vida de Bolívar* (1865–1866). Among Colombian authors, the interim President José Fernández Madrid (1789–1830) was the first versifier to take Bolívar and other Independence heroes as the principal subject of the alternately celebratory and lyric-elegiac impulses of a national poetry. In the *Parte lírica* (pp. 453–502) of the anthology *América poética*, serialized in Chile in 1846–1847, some of his best-known patriotic poems and translations achieved wide circulation.[39] In 1816, the twilight year of the period known as the Patria Boba, Fernández Madrid succeeded Camilo Torres as first magistrate of the United Provinces of New Granada. The creole elites bestowed on him the dictatorial powers he needed to negotiate an honorable capitulation to Spain.[40]

Larrazábal and Restrepo are the two key *letrados* in the early liberal reception of Bolívar as the nucleus of the nations emerging out of the Greater Colombia. They were both less self-serving than the mercurial Mosquera although Bolívar had ambivalent feelings about Restrepo's eagerness to please him. Larrazábal praises the Libertador for achieving a kind of sublime martyrdom that makes him compatible with providentialist accounts of nation building. For his part, Restrepo often attempts psychohistorical interpretations of some of Bolívar's actions aided by his direct acquaintance with the revolutionary process: he was minister of the government in 1822–1827 and cosigned, as Secretary of the Interior, the Organic Decree of Dictatorship in 1828. Restrepo explains the Libertador's occasional authoritarian bouts as a result of the neurotic disorders provoked by the combined effect of illness, exhaustion, and the vituperative campaigns launched against him from within the revolutionary ranks as much as from outside.

The incipient movement of radicalism rejected Bolívar on account of the unpopular disciplinary measures that he took, from 1826 on, to counter the rise of *caudillismo* and the radicals' justified distrust of militaristic regimes. In particular, the assumption of dictatorial powers during the last stretch of the Convención de Ocaña (1828) was greatly censored.[41] The same happened with the Libertador's public repudiation of the Constitution of Cúcuta (1821); with his interest in recovering some of the institutions in place during the colonial period; and with his listening to proposals for the establishment of what would later be known as the "Bolivian presidency" or sovereign presidency with no time limits attached to it.

The advocates for the Cúcuta charter, led by Vice President Santander, opposed the Libertador's proposal that the Greater Colombia adopt the populist Constitution *for* Bolivia (1826), which concentrates the prerogative of making decisions in a strong executive office at the same time as it rescues the indigenous populations from their legal near invisibility. Since the original 1821 Constitution could not be derogated until it had had a ten-year run, this proposal went against the very essence of Colombia's legal order. The vote taken by several popular assemblies convened ad hoc across the Greater Colombia, during the Convención de Ocaña, to grant the Liberator dictatorial powers increased the political elites' frustration at the inordinate concentration of faculties. The illegality of these assemblies is far from clear, as even a noted critic of Bolívar, Jorge Orlando Melo, has acknowledged in recent years (21–22). Yet as important as this personalist turn in the balance of power was the contrast perceived at Ocaña between Bolívar's interest in forging a more horizontal society (which of course would require greater efforts at integrating ethnic minorities in processes of decision making starting from the bottom up) and Santander's preferred vertical organization.

Santander's scheme not only excluded the subaltern from the discourse on rights, but was also meant to neutralize the Venezuelan people's growing self-consciousness as a mulatto nation arbitrarily led by a white minority, which the *llanero* General Páez had already exploited to his advantage. Moreover, Santander argued against slave emancipation on the ground that those landowners who had supported the war against Spain could not be divested of their plantations' cheap labor force, and so requested of the Libertador that slaves not fight in the revolutionary armies. By contrast, Bolívar repeatedly held that freedom is not given to you. Rather, you have to earn it for yourself, convincing others of the moral need to expand the narrow inclusiveness of extant criteria and opportunities for citizenship even if that means antagonizing the minority in power. As an *idealistic pragmatist*, always ready to experiment with new formulae, he candidly believed that if the slaves fought shoulder to shoulder on the battlefields with the revolutionary creoles and against the royalists forces, the discourse on *rights for all* would be legitimated in the public's perception. This is an admittedly naïve yet thoroughly liberal-republican position to the extent that republicanism sets rigid limits to the law's inclusiveness, but allows the excluded minorities to advocate for the expansion of those limits. To his chagrin, Bolívar did not have much success in convincing the skeptical New Granadan slaves that *the* Revolution of Independence could also become *their* revolution of emancipation, that is, an opportunity for achieving citizenship for themselves through their effort alone. This would have happened despite most of the creole officers' racialized view of the struggle for independence from Spain, which the Libertador in general did not share.[42]

As early as 1824, the Frenchman Gaspard Théodore Mollien had suggested, in his *Voyage dans la République de Colombia, en 1823*, that the greatest opposition to the effective abolition of slavery would come from Venezuela and (Restrepo adds in his 1858 *Historia*) Colombia's Cauca, where half of the population was at the time either black or indigenous (Mollien 219–21; Restrepo 4: 196). If the Constitution *for* Bolivia may appear somewhat authoritarian owing to its emphasis on the executive branch's prerogatives, it also furnishes a revolutionary example of juridical inclusiveness since even the illiterate are granted the indirect suffrage (this was a provision until 1836, when only those who could read would be deemed fit to vote) so long as they are not servants (Tít. 3, capít. 2, art. 14; Tít. 4, capíts. 1 and 2). The charter's promulgation was accompanied by a series of affirmative-action and disentail decrees distributing state land among the Indians, abolishing the Indian tribute and implementing a progressive income tax in its place, as well as expropriating abandoned mines for its auctioning by the state. Such reformist measures met with strong resistance among political elites—who, for the most part, had not fought on the side of the revolutionary side— and accordingly were immediately reversed (Lynch 283–89). We could then say, with Hannah Arendt, that the juridical emancipation of an enslaved class, being often driven by the ruling class' paternalism, does not entail the cessation of political or economic exploitation. The freedmen's gradual access to the instruments of decision and representation ("liberation from tyranny"), to which only Bolívar, among the statesmen of his time, gave serious consideration, must be accompanied by the economic emancipation or "liberation from the yoke of necessity" that ownership of the land can bring about (Arendt 68–69). Only the combined effect of both conquests can bring about "freedom," which Arendt understands as the citizen's right to respond to the law's call upon him or her to participate actively in the economic and social life of their time and place. Only in this environment can decisions that are free of coercion be made (22–26).[43]

Bello had already addressed, from a different standpoint, the problem of political liberties disconnected from the mechanism of inclusion into the fold of economic emancipation. In 1844, in his polemic in Chile with Lastarria, he expressed an economically more progressive opinion than his radical opponent and disciple:

> Americans were much better prepared for their political emancipation than for the exercise of domestic freedoms [...] The monarch was stripped of its scepter, but the Spanish spirit was not: our congresses are unwittingly drawn to Gothic [i.e., conservative/reactionary] inspirations; Spain has shut itself up in our assemblies; the ordinances promulgated by the Carlos and Felipes have been preserved as the laws of the land; our warriors are bound by a special statute [fuero especial] that contradicts the principle of equality before the law, the cornerstone of a free government. The entire situation reveals that the ideas bequeathed by Spain, whose banners our soldiers trampled upon, continue to dominate us. (*Obras completas* 19: 170–71)

Conceptually (but not politically) the problem would be solved by the centrist Liberal Manuel Ancízar (1811–1882), who in 1848–1849 implicitly criticized the laissez-faire policy recommended by the elitist Liberal Florentino González following almost step-by-step the argument presented over one century later by Arendt (67–77). Ancízar lucidly understood that the *letrados'* fear of democracy (he mentions the red scare quickly spreading across Colombia in the year of the *Communist Manifesto*'s publication) clouded their judgment, making them a likely prey to hegemonic alliances and implicit pacts with Conservatives. Many self-proclaimed progressives could accept in the abstract the political equality of all Colombians, or even universal suffrage, but could not bring themselves to accept in their day-to-day practice that a civil society cannot relegate its newly emancipated citizens to a subaltern position. The question of economic justice for all was first raised by Bolívar among New Granada's high magistrates. It resurfaces intermittently, in the course of the nineteenth century, as the need for the state to develop more effective mechanisms of social inclusion, such as the creation of professional schools (the influence on Ancízar of Simón Rodríguez, "el filósofo de Colombia," here becomes apparent [Ancízar 40]). At some other times, these vindications take the form of the government's expropriation of land or the subsidizing of small industries through rural credit unions and the promotion of adult education, as advocated at mid-century by both Ancízar and the Peruvian González Vigil, among others.

Bolívar repeatedly stumbled upon the obstacles that the creole elites and his own officers created for advancing the republican ideal of equality before the law and the radically progressive one of guaranteed equality of opportunity. These early Bolivarians were mostly interested in taking the place of the Spaniards at the top of the power structure. In Bello's assessment, the subjects of the Spanish colonies in America had emancipated themselves from the metropolis, but did not immediately install a representative government based on freedom and equality, for which purpose they still had to reject the legacy of Spain's jurisprudence and administrative practices.[44]

The foregoing critique notwithstanding, the oversimplified notion of an aristocratic Bolívar poised against a liberal-democratic Santander has a certain basis in reality. The Libertador, whose forebears came from Spain's titled nobility, was in his own time cast as a Caesar-like figure, while his executive vice president had the aura of a paragon of republicanism who dressed like a common citizen and was not a *real* soldier: he was "the Man of the Law." (Bolívar caustically questioned that Santander could ever become a competent general since he was a Colombian rather than a Venezuelan, which automatically meant that he lacked martial heroism.) Aware that the ancestral Viceroyalty of New Granada was the only northern Andean territory with a majority of white Europeans, Santander welcomed the division of the Greater Colombia into three independent states—Venezuela, Ecuador, and the Republic of New Granada. At the same time, he adhered to the minority rule by an elite of *letrados* like himself whose enforcement of the law would ensure the uninterrupted transmission of a hierarchically descending social order. On the contrary, Bolívar regretted the fragility of political regimes founded on massive economic and political inequalities, a reality that was but a consequence of the plurality of races and its violent reduction to castes since the arrival of the Spaniards. As José María Samper explained, the model Bolivarian republic is built upon the optimistic Enlightenment foundation of human perfectibility. In it, time will witness the appearance of a "democratic and entirely American race, the fruit of the unrestricted cross-pollination [libre entrecruzamiento] of previous races: the Spanish, the indigenous and African, and the immigrant

European" (*El Libertador Simón Bolívar* 38). Samper changed the tone of this liberal discourse in his later autobiographical writings, which present environmental and biological determinism as the scientific factors explaining the different moral qualities shown by different races.

The inclusive yet hierarchical Constitution *for* Bolivia advocated the institution of an uncharacteristically strong executive branch as the best possible way to transform the gradual homogenization of rights and territories into a liberal-parliamentary state in which a civil society could one day emerge. Bolívar dreamed of a federation of American states that together would form a strong Greater Colombia. In this, he departed from Santander's views on developing a federal system exclusively for the independent state of New Granada. His emphasis on the need for a strong central power that would ensure the territorial integrity and legal homogeneity of the Greater Colombia becomes more accentuated as internal feuding within the multiregional or multinational megastate quickly escalated in the late 1820s. For this reason alone, it has been easy to demonize the Libertador as a Caesarian dictator alienated from the feuding, democratic creole bases who embraced federalism and other forms of local autonomy to varying degrees.[45]

According to Jacques Rancière, republican ideologies overcome the duality of "man" and "citizen" through the interpellation of a new subject of politics that exists in between the oligarchic privilege of the tax-paying citizen and the subaltern's "bare life" (57–64). While citizens are explicitly invited to abide by the limits of legal rights and representation, noncitizens can only implicitly test the limits of representation as they fight to become full members of the polis. Bolívar's Constitution *for* Bolivia was one such socially inclusive charter. In instituting a universal property tax and distributing state land among the indigenous peoples, the Libertador's ancillary legislation entailed a serious attempt at enabling the masses' transition from the dispossessed subalternity of bare life to the incipient citizenship of a class timidly interpellated as a subject of rights. Even if this interpellation had been more decisively enacted, it would have yielded only the instauration of the democratic game of hegemony or domination by consent.

Bolívar's inclusive discourse of gradually decreasing rights for all may sound self-contradictory. It did not initially pose a decisive threat to Bolivia's creole elites, since the charter prudently distinguished among enfranchising degrees of citizenship according to varying rights of representation. First, the unlettered majority was allowed to elect the minority endowed with full electoral rights (even indigenous males who were not literate could participate at the lowest level of this process). Next, there were those who could exercise direct suffrage (revealingly, the country's first legislative assembly was composed almost exclusively of landowning magnates and *letrados* trained at the colonial Pontifical University of Chuquisaca in Sucre), most of whom were not connected directly to the Revolution of Independence.

Finally, there were those who could be elected to the higher offices of the state (the same constituency as in the previous category). Republican regimes are malleable enough to enable the gap between bare life and organized politics to be bridged gradually without necessarily resorting to violent action. These regimes tend to be strict, if not also compulsive, in the institution of legal limits and exclusions, but they simultaneously create the conditions for those limits to be endlessly expanded through the dominated classes' organized struggle for self-emancipation.

During the Dictatorship of 1828–1830, Bolívar became the prototype of what Laureano Vallenilla Lanz called, in his *Cesarismo democrático* (1919), the "necessary policeman" [el gendarme necesario]. This was the figure of an astute decisionist who could use his personal charisma as the embodiment of the state's authority and the rescuer of the *nation's sovereignty* at moments in which popular democratic politics—that is, the *people's sovereignty*—had been abused (Vallenilla Lanz 89). The disciplinary policeman had another precursor—of the despotic and barbarous kind—in José Antonio Páez at the close of the revolutionary process. The future President of Venezuela subverted first Spain's imperial rule, and later Santander's legally established republican state, in order to launch an alternative national community. In this new status quo, trust rather than the law was employed to foster a sense of national cohesion in which one's personal loyalty to a higher-ranking person and the ownership of land upheld an alternative social order (Vallenilla Lanz 102). As in feudal regimes, the *llanero* magnate delegated to lesser lords the administration and exploitation of the territory on the assumption that the descending chain of command would always be legitimated by a superior figure's normalizing approval.

In the *caudillista* regime, previously disenfranchised individuals feel connected to a powerful lord, often of humble origins, who claims to dispense justice in person, as the medieval Castilian monarchs did to counter the feudal nobility's abuses. The need for the *caudillo* arises whenever the people find themselves defenseless against the abuses of another local power (for example, an aristocratic elite) or when they feel neglected by the central government's administration, or both. The trust established between the *caudillo* and the people forges a new *unwritten constitution* that takes on a quasi-scientific status ("trust [is] 'weak inductive knowledge,'" as Giddens reminds us in a paraphrase of Georg Simmel[46]) as the charismatic leader appears to attend to the people's demands for justice at least on the surface. Like the Castilian monarch, the *caudillo* legitimates himself not so much by his *imperium* as by his *maiestas* or much-publicized equanimity in the exercise of a sovereign justice. The policeman's "democratic Caesarism" is therefore a decisionist and populist solution. Thus, it employs bonds of fealty to gather a people around their particular and unique *iron surgeon* and the instances to which the latter delegates his power at the local level. This is different from the regime that Vallenilla Lanz dubbed "theocratic Caesarism" and attributed to New Granada's *nacionalistas*, from Núñez and Caro to Marco Fidel Suárez (president in 1918–1921), who for the most part governed with their backs turned on the masses' need for primary instruction and adequate channels for social promotion (118–21, 161–67).

In his poems and essays, Caro presents Bolívar's recantation of revolutionary republicanism as a poetics of baroque disenchantment (*desengaño*).[47] Since the translator of the *Aeneid* is very fond of Christianizing baroque literature and philosophy, he also transforms Bolívar into a sort of mystic body of the nation. Caro would like his constitutional reforms to assume Bolívar's moral authority; so much so that the Libertador is ultimately enshrined as the Regeneración's main precursor. The Constitution of 1886, which rechristens the nation as Republic of Colombia, restricts civil liberties more than Bolivia's Constitution of 1826. Its backwardness is even greater in relation to the federal Constitution of Rionegro (1863), in which the unwittingly ironic designation "United States of Colombia" was created. (The nation's division into "Sovereign States" comes first, as the main attribute of Colombia's *natural constitution,* while the political fact of the "union" is reduced to an adjectival quality: "Estados Unidos de Colombia.")

To be more precise, the prohibitory charter of 1886 evinces Caro's ability to have his particularly authoritarian views on positive legislation prevail over those of the then President Rafael Núñez. In founding the National Party almost coinciding with Bolívar's centennial, the former Liberal statesman gave up his earlier profession of agnosticism to attract Caro to the Regeneración, but was not prepared to counter Caro on the latter's preferred turf of fearmongering and apocalyptic politics. The 1886 charter was Colombia's first major retrogressive act of legislation since the proslavery Constitution of 1843, a by-product of the civil war of 1839–1842, in which the issue of emancipation played a key role.[48] As explained in chapter 2, the Regenerators relied on a combination of written legislation and verbal orders dictated by the executive branch to outlaw in practice any kind of association or opinion that would enter into conflict with the Catholic dogma or the public order. They also continued to exclude the majority of the population from the franchise.

Caro's ode employs other strategies to manipulate Bolívar's legacy, domesticating the aspects of his thinking that were incompatible with traditionalism. First, Caro undertakes the silent excision of undesired words such as "revolution" from the Libertador's writings. The general never tired of calling the project of independence—even at moments of dejection—a "revolution." This word had to be almost anathema for someone whose most influential periodical, founded in 1871, was called *The Traditionist* [El Tradicionista]. Whereas Bolívar writes, "He who serves a revolution ploughs the sea,"[49] the fastidious philologist that Caro claimed to be rephrased the sentence as the following: "Those of us who serve the cause of independence have ploughed the sea."[50] As if this was not enough, Caro begins his quotation from the *Historia de la revolución de la República de Colombia* (he conveniently abridges the title to *Historia de Colombia*) in the sentence immediately following an important mention of the word "revolution":

> It seems that Bolívar regretted his life's work, and that he was afraid that he had served poorly the South Americans by leading them to Independence. The crimes committed everywhere and the countless rebellions breaking out in the new republic so impressed his heart. [Restrepo: "soul"]![51]

In fact, Caro declares his philo-Spanish sentiments in the paratexts of "To the Statue of the Libertador," whose subtitle goes "On the Main Square of Bogotá." The poet restores the name of the agora, which in his own time was renamed "Bolívar Square." The change of name upon Independence expressed the creole rejection of the Viceroyalty of New Granada: in colonial times, unilateral orders and edicts were made public at the square often with little or no input from the locals, a practice that strangely foreshadows Caro's abuse of unconstitutional verbal orders. In other writings of a similar nature, Caro regularly describes the revolutionary process as a "civil war" in which the prodigal "son" (Colombia) abandons the authoritarian parental home (Spain) only to return to it as an equal. Both the ancestral home and the new nation place themselves under the Catholic Church's higher authority, which itself is built on a strongly hierarchized patriarchal order. Effecting a contrary movement, Bolívar had argued for the revolutionary character of his separation from the paternal home. To be sure, in the ode and in the two-part essay on "Dictatorships" [Las dictaduras] (1903; repr. in *La oda* 262–79) Caro seems to praise the Boyacá victor as well as his political achievements. At the same time, however, he transforms the Libertador into the Regenerators' precursor, who "made use, in times of war, of extraordinary faculties in keeping with the provisions of the Constitution and other laws" (*La oda* 272). In silencing the criticism of the stagnant political and social institutions inherited from the colonial regime, Caro in fact writes *contra* Bolívar.

Sculpting and Petrifying the Exception: What the Statue Said

"To the Statue of the Libertador" is an ode of romantic inspiration but neoclassical in shape. It is written in consonantal five-line stanzas (*quintillas*). Its episodic structure is held together by the conscious use of a powerful voice (that of the lyric "I") that interpellates a silent "you," which is but an external perspective (the sculptor Tenerani's). Although Tenerani does not himself speak, the speaker goes inside his consciousness, thus carrying out a sort of second-person ventriloquizing. In addressing also the Libertador, the authorial voice resorts to the apostrophe in the first and the last of the thirty-two stanzas: they begin, respectively, "¡Bolívar!" and "¡Libertador!" The poem adopts the structure of an address or allocution. Using the apostrophe, the object of the celebration becomes an interlocutor ("tú"= the sculpted Bolívar), turning now the sculptor (Tenerani) into an "él" whom the celebratory voice guides in his quest for a higher meaning. That is to say, although the entire poem is conceived as a public statement written on the occasion of a centennial homage, Caro speaks *in persona aliorum*, through Tenerani's mask. The artist's "he," who appears in the second half of the composition, when Bolívar is dead and all there is left of him is the sculpted form of Tenerani's bronze, becomes the strategy by which the speaker dissociates himself into a creative *other*, to whose art oracular powers are romantically assigned.

The first six stanzas insist on the precariousness of Tenerani's viewpoint, on everything the sculptor "neither knew" [no supo"] (l. 11) nor of course "heard" [oyó] (l. 17), let alone "saw" [vió] (l. 18). Indeed, Tenerani does not know the history of America, but he knows Rome, his city of birth, where in 1805 a young Bolívar would have taken his "oath"—the "Juramento del Monte Aventino" or "Juramento en el Monte Sacro"—to guide the movement of independence in the American colonies. In stanza 7, and in the manner of the baroque epistles of disenchantment, Caro makes Tenerani ponder *for him* the beheld ruins of Rome and the moral teaching contained in them. I quote the same lines from both versions of the poem:

> In the ruins of the Capitol he saw that you were, in spite of your youth, chosen by Heaven to experience a mind-stretching inspiration, and to dream of the Andean republics [Te vió, si adolescente, / Ya del cielo elegido, en las ruínas / Del Capitolio. Á inspiración potente / Dilatando la mente, / Soñar con las Repúblicas andinas...] (ll. 31–35 [1883])

> In the silence of the great ruin within Rome he saw that you were, in spite of your youth, grazing your mind, your dreamer's brow weighed down by a divine mission [Te vio, si adolescente, / Ya en el silencio de la gran ruina / Que Roma encierra, apacentar tu mente, / La soñadora frente / Doblada al peso de la misión divina...]. (ll. 31–35 [1886])

One need not insist on the difference in emphasis between the celebration of the envisioned "Andean republics" and the divine mission's *weightiness* that breaks and recontextualizes the original dream; or between the "mind-stretching inspiration" and the faux bucolic overtones implied by "grazing your mind." In the 1886 version, the younger Bolívar's consciousness grazes "in the silence of the great ruin." The mention of the "divine mission" situates the Libertador in the tradition of temporal empires (republican Rome's *hic et nunc*) merging into the otherworldly chronotope of salvation announced by the Church of Rome.[52] In this pastoral of ruins, the dreamer's brow is animated by a providential impetus, which leads directly into the "apacentar" reference to Church doctrine, where it appears in connection with Peter's keys to heaven as well as the actions of chaining and unchaining a captive people.[53]

The dreamer's "mind" accordingly makes the decision to emancipate the elect people who had until then been in chains. In this manner, two contrary arguments are introduced into the poem: the *translatio imperii*, which I presented in chapter 2 as a doctrine developed in the medieval Romania beginning in the eighth century; and the *pactum translationis*, a juridico-political concept popularized by such Jesuit thinkers as Francisco Suárez and Juan de Mariana since the later sixteenth century.[54] According to the first of these concepts, the illegitimate use of *dominium* by the Spanish Empire authorizes the transfer of such *dominium* from Spain to the same colonies, so that the movement westward that animates the *translatio* is thus continued. According to the second concept, the Americans would never have completely alienated the prerogative of *imperium* to their delegates in the metropolis' institutions of government. Rather, in their symbolic acts of reclaiming their sovereignty and declaring their independence from Spain, the American creoles would have vindicated their preexisting condition as self-determining subjects. This sovereignty enabled them to break their pact with a Peninsular, absentee monarch under certain circumstances, such as undergoing a delegitimation process on account of his absolutist rule and his arbitrary use of violence. Caro renders the opposition between the two forms of transfer irrelevant by assuming that in Colombia the Liberal emphasis on the threefold separation of government powers and the shrinking of the executive branch have already corrupted the providential use of *imperium* as undivided sovereignty (end of the *translatio*). He can thus make his second assumption, namely, that the transfer of sovereignty is inapplicable in a nation characterized by both the systematic atomization of all forms of authority and coercive power, and the seemingly irreversible state of chronic civil strife (end of the *pactum*).

In New Granada's relatively slow-paced Revolution of Independence, the main interpreter of the *pactum translationis* was Bogotá's well-off *letrado* and bibliophile Antonio Nariño, who in December 1793 published a Spanish translation of the Declaration of the Rights of Man (1789) in his Imprenta Patriótica. The ad hoc justification for breaking the contract entered between a sovereign people and their monarch took place in 1808, when the throne was left vacant upon Fernando VII's exile. Nariño was to write that "in a sudden state of revolution the people is said to claim back its sovereignty" (qtd. in Pombo and Guerra 1: 56). If the Peninsular subjects who favored a constitutional monarchy gathered themselves in a Junta Central and eventually agreed to the exiled king's return to Spain, the American subjects derogated the *pactum translationis* alleging that the throne had been unlawfully alienated, as becomes evident in the Acta de la Independencia de Venezuela (1811).[55] Likewise, Bolívar's "Juramento" reported by the ventriloquist Simón Rodríguez in 1850—some forty-five years after it allegedly took place—and published in Bogotá in 1884 leaves no room for the restoration of either the pact or Spain's absolutist claims.

Contrarily, Caro's ballad "The Reconciliation" [La reconciliación] (1883) advocates a new spiritual alliance between the metropolis and the former colonies. The remaining contributors to the *Romancero colombiano* include an inordinate number of self-taught jurists and legislators, and even a few corresponding members of Spain's Academy of the Language, all of whom enhance the covenantal and literary-legislative air that Caro wished to give the collection. The witnesses to Caro's covenant with Bolívar were the dependable translator-poet, publicist, and high-ranking government official Álvarez Bonilla, Núñez, Samper, José Manuel Marroquín, the former Liberal Jesús Casas Rojas (a member of the Council of Delegates in 1885–1886 and sometime cabinet member during the Regeneración), and two of José Eusebio Caro's fellow religious poetasters from the dawn of Colombia's literary and political counterrevolutions. These are José Caicedo Rojas (1816–1898), a Foreign Relations *letrado* and President of Congress in the eventful year of 1851 (when the radical-Liberal laws decreeing absolute freedom of the press and the expulsion of the Jesuits were issued with his signature in them), and José Joaquín Ortiz (1814–1892), the founder of the influential periodical *La Caridad* in 1864, a longtime congressman, and President of the Senate in 1890. José Eusebio, Caicedo Rojas, and Ortiz were physically or intellectually involved—in different capacities and to varying degrees—in the war of 1839–1842. All three *letrados* studied at either the San Bartolomé or El Rosario elitist seminaries and *colegios mayores*, in which liberal studies and civil law could be pursued in addition to theology and canon law. All three left without a degree, as happened with the most conspicuous members of the ensuing reactionary *letrado* generation, who were also generally trained at the seminaries rather than the universities. Their unaccredited status did not prevent these three capable dropouts from accepting high-ranking positions in the administration prior to the Olimpo Radical, for which purpose their family pedigree and rhyming skills *eminently* qualified them anyway.

Each contributor to the *Romancero colombiano* produces a bad patriotic poem while at the same time preaching to the choir of fellow elite *letrados* the notion that many (not all) of the lineages represented in their names are politically connected among themselves and to the Libertador (more so in 1850, when Bogotá had a population of only 29,000 people). The *Romancero* advances these existing alliances as it promotes the specific covenant that these versifiers will all support the promulgation of a confessional *magna carta* only three years later. This is a literary avatar of the *pactum translationis* in which the interpretation of the past is used to legitimate a specious return to Bolivarianism, an ideology now placed in the service of the Regeneración's program. The new pact is forged under the banners of "Hispanism," the "Latin race," and "Rome." In sum, Caro situates himself under the translating appellation or invocation (*translatio*) of Spanish traditionalism and Bogotá's archbishop. The tone used in the second half of "La reconciliación" leaves no doubts as to the nature of this mission: "From the smoking ruin the maternal banner rises…The two Spains came forward again wherever the Christian invocation rises to the Empyrean in a Castilian accent. Wherever the ocean sends its waves it embraces the reborn extremities of the immortal Nation" [De la humeante ruína / Se alza el materno lábaro; / […] / Resurgen las Españas / Doquier suba al Empíreo / En castellano acento / Cristiana invocación / Doquier sus ondas vuelva / Ciñe asombrado el piélago / Los miembros renaciente / De la inmortal Nación] (ll. 49–50, 57–64).

Unlike the ballad just mentioned, "To the Statue of the Libertador" exploits the effect of immediacy inherent in the evocation of the hero's personal feelings in his Andean epopee. The second half of the ode shifts its focus from the recollection of the general's military deeds to his experiencing of doubts, disenchantment, and repentance on witnessing the administrative dismembering of the Greater Colombia. To put it differently, if the first half of the poem features the war between Spain and Bolívar, quickly followed by the Libertador's dialectical reconciliation with the metropolis, in the second half, the poignancy of disenchantment and the ensuing expatriation replace the high drama of heroism. Through betrayal and martyrdom, Bolívar expiates his revolutionary excesses while his doctrines are purged of alien, non-Hispanic elements, a Catholic discipline and *reductio* that are carried out in the name of the divine power insistently invoked by the speaker.

The ode introduces twice the motif of "race" [raza], here understood as the historical or imaginary fact of an ethnically and spiritually homogeneous people. In the opening stanza, the speaker states that Bolívar's hand "avenges the Incas" (l. 5), which ironically contradicts his own views on the conquest (elsewhere Caro construes the subjection of the Indians as a "providential" event) and the colonial regime. In stanza 9, the speaking "I" takes up again the metonymic use of "hand," although the tenor of its attending metaphor is now changed: "With a compassionate hand to enslave Fortune in order to give back their native freedom to a captive race and the unhappy progeny it nursed" (ll. 41–45). The "captive race" corresponds neatly to the already cited "Latin race" (the Catholic creoles willingly submitted to Rome), the only one to which Caro would grant full membership in the republic.[56] He thus goes so far as to proclaim, in the fourth sonnet of the already cited lyric sequence—"The Founding Fathers" [Los padres de la Patria] (1884)—that Colombia is a country not only Spanish but Roman: "You must all love Spain and worship Rome" (l. 11). As evinced by his poetry translations from modern languages into Latin, the grammarian-president was intent on demonstrating the monolithically Catholic and Latin identity of the Romania's vernacular literatures. The two absolutist horizons of interpretation he puts forth—Hispanism and Catholic doctrine—are never inserted in a higher pluralistic framework that may help sustain a dialectical version of Colombia as a culturally autonomous nation still very much in the making. In this way, Caro denies ethnic and class *particularisms*, invoking in their place a transcendent corporation that is broken down into successive layers of privilege and decision making.

Caro did not compose his ode in a literary-historical vacuum, as I already explained when glossing the earlier vituperative literature produced in Colombia and Venezuela. The worship of Bolívar began timidly as the governance of the new republic deteriorated. The Libertador's truncated journey into self-exile quickly became symbolic capital for avid hagiographers upon his death. Only the continual fragmentation of the Greater Colombia's land and society could warm up the Colombians' hearts to nostalgic remembrances of a revolutionary past full of promise and unexplored opportunities. That past had a voice, which Caro alternately mutes and amplifies in his ode. Bolívar's incensed epistolary rhetoric, like his aborted or short-lived acts of legislation, falls within the genres of prophecy and utopia. Both are in keeping with the romantic fondness for pursuing the ineffable and what has not yet come into being. In the course of the nineteenth century, Bolívar will embody the true nation that is yet to be founded, the true law that is yet to be enacted, and the true destiny that is yet to be realized.

Institutionalized Exceptions and Literature's Extraordinary Faculties

"To the Statue of the Libertador" is a key work in the instituting of the Regeneración's ideological program. It was printed in different formats, in one of its three versions, at least ten times between 1883 and 1888. Carlos Holguín took an active part in procuring a reception for the poem amenable to Caro's nation-building designs, as becomes clear in the letters he exchanged with Caro and Pedro Antonio de Alarcón in 1884 (Caro, *La oda* 98–114). The publication of the text's definitive version in volume 1 of the canonizing anthology *Parnaso colombiano* (1886) coincides with the moment when Núñez, Caro, and Holguín derogate the radical-Liberal Constitution of 1863 and enact its centralizing opposite. Nevertheless, it soon became evident that Caro was particularly invested in fighting *laïcité*, freedom of speech, and the expansion of the suffrage slowly brought about by the equally slow-growing literacy rates.[57] In his search for arguments to attenuate civil liberties within the existing legal framework, Caro invents a Libertador who, in the years of his dictatorial regime, appears as the Regeneración's providentially anointed forerunner.

The ode's second half focuses on Bolívar's reaction to the adverse criticism received during the 1828 Convención de Ocaña, where he took the "extraordinary measures" that the Cúcuta Constitution authorized for "cases of serious internal commotion" (art. 128). This is also Bolívar as "necessary policeman," seeking an unlikely reconciliation with the Catholic Church as dispenser of theo-political legitimacy and making authoritarian decisions such as derogating the utilitarian-empiricist curriculum of studies instituted by Santander in 1825 under the influence of Bentham and Destutt de Tracy. The Organic Decree of Dictatorship (1828) includes a firm article 25, by which Bolivar will definitely ingratiate himself with Caro. It says: "The Government will support and protect the Roman Catholic religion as the religion of Colombian citizens."

Caro's vehemently antidemocratic persuasion is best understood as a typically post-1848 reaction to the instituting of feuding politics in liberal-democratic states with a tripartite division of powers and a federalist system in place, a type of administration that decentralizes further the prerogative of *imperium*. Such a response builds on Donoso and the early ideologists of the counterrevolution while foreshadowing Schmitt's thinking on the exception and decisionist regimes. For Schmitt—a well-known critic of the Weimar Republic (1919–1933)—parliamentary democracy is possible only in nations that are ethnically, religiously, and ideologically homogeneous and in which a theological horizon of interpretation overrides the inherently feuding character of mixed social bodies, which after Augustine are often called also *corpora admixta* or *corpora permixta* (*Legalität und Legitimität* 28–29; *Constitutional Theory* 289–90). Schmitt reminds his reader that Rousseau exposed the fragility of numerical majorities when he disapproved of the quantitative dominion of 90 corrupt men over 10 honest ones in a parliamentary setting (*Constitutional Theory* 280, 302–7).[58] Philo-Spanish traditionalists will increasingly denigrate the liberal-democratic state, in which the sovereign nation is represented by the numerical majority gathered in Congress.

Moreover, Colombian traditionalism depicts the modern republican system as a foreign creation at odds with the history and sensibilities of Spanish-speaking nations. To cite Caro again: "Our democratic institutions are [...] too cold, colorless, and improper for our buoyant and magnanimous feelings" ("La independencia y la raza" [*Ideario hispánico* 110]). Given the fact that in 1871 the "Latin race," in its restricted sense of Hispano-Colombian nation (what Andrés Bello memorably called "trans-Atlantic Iberia") is for Caro a "Roman-Catholic communion and collectivity" whose visible heads are the Roman pontiff and the archbishop of Bogotá ("La raza Latina" [*Obras, tomo I* 734]), the only democracy possible is that in which *all* publicly declare themselves Catholic. This would be tantamount to recognizing the Church's monopoly on virtue, not just on *virtus* in the Catholic doctrine, but on civic *virtù* in the humanist sense that Florentine republican thought gives this concept as the nucleus of the *vita activa* and *emulatio* ideals.

Caro's polemics with Rafael Pombo on whether Catholic laymen are entitled to write "theological sonnets" that deviate from the popes' apostolic *magisterium* underscore the fragility of that religious community. By Caro's ultramontane book, Pombo committed four sins that were deserving of his ire. First, Pombo's sentimental poetry often expresses the uncertainties, doubts, and spiritual crises that afflicted Catholics and post-Catholics alike in the nineteenth century, from José María Blanco-White (whose English sonnet "Night" Pombo translated from English into Spanish) and Victor Hugo to Rafael Núñez, Paul Verlaine, and Miguel de Unamuno. Second, Pombo expressly declared his displeasure at the way in which Caro (but not the majority of Regenerators, who for the most part knew better) demonized countless law-abiding, highly principled Liberals as if they were satanic creatures that had to be exterminated by any means possible. Colombia did not know this type of incensed rhetoric prior to José Eusebio's panicked diatribes against early radicalism, but Miguel Antonio surpassed his father's practice of hate speech because he lived a longer life and climbed higher on the political ladder than José Eusebio. Third, for Pombo, Catholicism was a religion of forgiveness rather than resentment and revenge in a period when these two destructive feelings materialized in the brutal repression of the defeated party at the conclusion of a civil war. Fourth, like the expatriate Rufino José Cuervo (another Catholic Conservative to whom Pombo remained a loyal friend over a span of some fifty years), he resiliently endorsed two of the core republican tenets espoused by his ancestors. These tenets were the separation of Church and state and the doctrine of resistance, namely, the notion that it was legitimate for a dissenter to resist a democratically elected civil authority by peaceful means. At the same time, the republicans' resistant citizen still had to accept the legitimate penal consequences of civil disobedience.[59]

Caro's political program fused the respective claims of Church and state into a series of repressive state apparatus that obliterated the republican creed espoused by Cuervo's and Pombo's illustrious fathers (and by Caro's grandfather, don Miguel Tobar). Three objective facts crucially marred the legitimacy of Caro's arbitrary and abusive acts in government. The first one (as already explained in a note in chapter 2) was that only municipal governments were summarily *consulted* on the constitutional *Bases* prior to this document's discussion by a Council of Delegates that was not voted at a popular election either. This explains in part why the Council featured neither *active* Liberals—radical or otherwise—nor *historic* Conservatives. Instead, nine *nationalist* Conservatives and nine *independent* Liberals who had little of the liberal militant left in them formed this body. These delegates exemplified the opportunistic compromises and deconversions that made Núñez's short-lived Partido Nacional possible.[60] Second, Caro's Constitution was not approved by the nation through a referendum; instead, it was summarily voted by the same Council of Delegates on the recommendation of a subcommittee that called itself "Comisión Nacional Constituyente" (not quite an *assemblée constituante*) and whose members were also Delegates. Third, the application of the 1886 Constitution in toto was suspended by the special prerogatives that the ongoing state of exception allowed the Legislative Council—the same *letrados* who formed the Council of Delegates, now headed by Caro—to issue important pieces of restrictive legislation upon the Constitution's *partial* enactment.[61]

Caro's patrimonialist and sectarian attitudes toward national politics were perhaps more germane to the neofeudal class than to the *letrados* proper, but both *letrado* and non-*letrado* Catholic literati—even non-Catholics like the Peruvian decisionist Felipe Pardo y Aliaga—often allowed for their poetry to be instrumentalized by authoritarian regimes. Caro could conceive of political representation only as the function of a restricted Catholic democracy in which the exercise of power rotated among the patrician elites and the relatively few upwardly mobile individuals who were regularly accepted into it. This acceptance often took place on the basis of the outsiders' previous or simultaneous membership in the literary field to which they contributed their dull retrogressive poems and philological pieces.[62] In 1888, in a passage that attacks the institution of the popular jury, Caro held that the "inferior social class"—the "plebeians"—"has never been nor is now an organized society, but rather a mass." Consequently, allowing this amorphous multitude to have any input in the main state institutions "would be illegitimate under the democratic regime" (Caro, *Libertad de imprenta* 114). That was the same year in which he wrote an electoral code that established majoritarian representation at all national and subnational elections (Law 7). This winner-take-all system favors larger parties with a strong propagandistic apparatus like the National Party. This law's efficacy was ably supplemented with the Regeneración's implementation of voting obstructions and fraudulent ballot returns. Combined with the Liberal Party's promotion of abstention as an ill-advised delegitimizing tactic, these circumstances yielded the following result: only two radical-Liberal representatives occupied seats in Congress between 1886 and 1899.[63]

Almost all of the Regeneración's literary and juridical enterprises carried out between 1883 and 1889 entail, to a lesser or greater extent, the appropriation of Bolívar, Bello, and other towering figures in Spanish republicanism for the project of redirecting the nation toward a providential destiny. In day-to-day practice, this grandiose design naturally conflicted with the shifting claims of public opinion and popular representation on the fallibility of all-too-human elected officials. Caro's fondness for providentialist narratives was in evidence in his Spanish renditions of Virgil's poetry, which show the Mantuan author as a proto-Christian prophet.[64] The same spirit presides over Caro's "To the Statue of the Libertador" and the epistolary documents that heralded its composition and publication; his indefatigable contributions to extremely right-wing periodicals, most often militantly Catholic ones; the sonnet series "Los padres de la patria" (1884) and other installments of patriotic and religious verse for *El Repertorio Colombiano*;

and the writing and defense of the Constitution of 1886. After the new charter's approval, he went on to direct the government's newly created organ of propaganda, the newspaper *La Nación*.

In his capacity as editor and translator, Caro also teamed up with Julio Áñez and José María Rivas Groot, whom he encouraged to pursue his pet project, the *Parnaso colombiano* (1886–1887), a two-volume anthology featuring an archaic canon of verse; he put the finishing touches on his collection *Traducciones poéticas*, published out of his second printer's shop and bookstore in 1889; he continued Bello's purge of Hugo's religious and political heresies, transforming the latter into an almost monolithically Catholic and monarchist lyrist; and he coordinated a modern *Romancero colombiano* (1883)—later renamed *Romancero bolivariano*—conceived once again with the nominal editor José Antonio Soffia's assistance. In this collection, Bolívar's main battles (e.g., Junín, Carabobo, Boyacá) are rehearsed and reinterpreted in verse not just by established Catholic writers, but also by some of the future members of the Council of Delegates who will approve the Constitution of 1886.[65] From this year dates also his edition of Julio Arboleda's *Poesías*. A prominent slaveholding landowner and Cauca politician, Arboleda (1817–1862) fought with José Eusebio in the war of 1839–1842 and had a remarkable *letrado* brother, the Conservative jurist, journalist, historian, and educator Sergio Arboleda (1822–1888).[66] Their two families intermarried with the Holguíns, thus giving shape to an expanding Caro-Holguín-Arboleda clan of enormous literary and political influence on the Cali-Bogotá axis to this day.

The poetry and historiography referred to in the preceding two paragraphs legitimated the Constitution of 1886 and were elevated by it to the status of "rescripts" [*rescripta*] or pastoral documents dispensed by a religious authority. In the rescript, whose main forms are the popes' encyclical letter and the bishops' pastoral letter, a *nomos* or spiritual norm arising from a *consensus fidelium* rather than a democratic vote acquires the force of a transcendent revelation. It goes without saying that Caro's propagandistic enterprise met with resistance across the board, as shifts from a conflicted and polyhedral historical formation to the institutionalization of the exception are inevitably gradual and conflicted.[67] Caro emphasized the experience of "belief" at the expense of "obedience" to the law because—like Tocqueville—he realized that beliefs and opinions spread faster and can be more easily manipulated to one's advantage than legal norms (*Democracy in America* 2: 27–28). In the serialized essay "Freedom of Worship" [La libertad de cultos] (1871–1872), Caro summoned his fellow Catholic literati to take up the study of civil law to supplement their knowledge of canon law. Since many of them could already boast a remarkable command of rhetoric, exegesis, philology, and the syllogism, their mastery of civil law would deal an important blow to the largely Liberal "aristocracy of pettifoggers" [aristocracia de los leguleyos]: "Among us, the lawyers, and formerly the military, have exclusive control over the exercise of all branches of government" [Entre nosotros, los abogados, y en su día los militares, monopolizan el ejercicio de todos los poderes públicos] (Caro, *Obras, tomo I* 799). The pious men called to hold "the government of the state" are "obliged to acquire a solid theological training while the common citizen is obliged to abide by the just ordinances that the Church and the state jointly promulgate" (*Obras, tomo I* 797–98).

The goal of these studies was not only "to convert the government" [convertir al gobierno], understood here as a cabinet elected for a limited term, but also to move the state as a whole from the system of popular representation to a system of "permanent triggers" [resortes permanentes] that would leave no room for parliamentary democracy understood as a network of mutually responsive interlocutions. Democracy was to remain in place only as a mechanism of representation that is "impersonal and alternative" [impersonal y alternativo] (Caro, *Obras, tomo I* 796). This design was made all the easier by Caro's fraudulent electoral practices, which purged Congress of Liberal representatives right to the end of his term in office with the Liberals' willing collaboration when they boycotted elections. In its most sublimated expression, Caro thought of this permanent trigger as God's Providence, which indeed happens as a disruption of the expected order of events in sacred history. In its darkest and most self-serving expression, the trigger that made the state of exception permanent was the endless series of arbitrary edicts and verbal orders that Schmitt, no less than Caro, placed at the base of his equally formidable constitutional edifice. Spurred by these teachings as well as the example of the ode "To the Statue of the Libertador," the Regeneración's coterie promulgated a literary canon in conformity with the imperatives of the new theo-political order. Religious and epic poetry continually featured acts of divine Providence and happily self-withdrawn rustics who did not care for the *negotium* of politics, while acts of prayer became the preferred speech act.

The widespread protest against the regime of the exception inaugurated in 1886 resonated abroad as much as at home. In France, the lawyer and former Supreme Court justice Rafael Rocha Gutiérrez (1842–1912) published *The True and False Democracies* [La verdadera y la falsa democracia] (1887).[68] There he held that public life cannot do without the voices of dissent from government orthodoxies, including those of the defeated at an election. The inclusion of these voices in the debate not only illustrates the true liberal ethos, but also helps even an "autarchic" order look legitimate if not exactly democratic (Rocha Gutiérrez 384, 393–94). At home, 1886 also witnessed the creation in Bogotá of the Universidad Externado de Colombia, promoted by the pedagogue and publicist of Herbert Spencer's ideas, Nicolás Pinzón (1860–1895). The inauguration took place in the same year in which Caro persuaded Holguín and Núñez to set up a Ministry of Public Instruction whose main purpose was to purge all levels of public education of pernicious secular influences. Moreover, it happened right before the National Party derogated the freedom of instruction by signing a Concordat with the Vatican on December 31, 1887 and began to box into a corner the public system of *escuelas normales* or teacher's colleges to which Dámaso Zapata (1833–1888) dedicated much of his professional life and which President Núñez had long supported.[69]

In his short literary career Pinzón contributed minor poems and translations to widely circulated anthologies, such as the above-mentioned *Víctor Hugo en América* and *Parnaso colombiano* in addition to *La lira nueva* (1886), published by the industrious Rivas Groot.[70] In the latter collection appears the sonnet "A Nariño," dedicated to former Liberal President Santiago Pérez, who was then exiled in New York. As a living example of republicanism's pedagogical traditions, Pérez was the legendary teacher of numerous Liberal, Conservative, and Regeneración *letrados*. He was also celebrated by his political rivals, such as the *historic* Conservative José Manuel Marroquín, who would eventually antagonize Caro.[71]

Beginning approximately in 1871 the Catholic Conservative intelligentsia intensified their literary interventions in order to gain support for Caro's reclaiming of a providential *imperium* for his projected confessional state. Among these activities are the translation of lyric poetry from other Latin nations; the composition of original patriotic and religious verse; and the writing of grand historicist narratives articulated around a divine purpose. These various undertakings often overlapped. The individuals who undertook the work of cultural propaganda were the same ones who carried out the philological work of producing grammars and definitive editions of canonical poets, as Caro did with Bello. Caro was able to work simultaneously on a Spanish Virgil and a massive body of commentary in the same years in which he launched his ambitious ultramontane forum, *El Tradicionista*. The contamination of genres and modes of writing reached its climax with "To the Statue of the Libertador," revised several times in the course of five years (1883–1887) and turned into a simulacrum of collective rewriting by the whole nation through the pages of the Colombian Academy's official publication, *El Repertorio Colombiano*. A similar legitimating goal was fulfilled by the public celebrations, monuments, and epigraphic Latin inscriptions scattered around Bogotá. In conclusion, literature took on an extraordinary lawmaking power in support of the state of exception that Caro longed to make permanent. As Emilio Castelar wrote, "the statues, the centennial celebrations, the symposia, the worship of the great men gradually produce the sacred almanac of History and yield exempla for us to imitate on account of their luminous teachings" (*Papel Periódico Ilustrado*, no. 30 [November 28, 1882]: 83).

In the slow production of the sacred almanac of history, the people's sovereignty is undermined each time the act of instituting the exception is perpetuated through its quick institutionalization. Caro's writings about Bolívar appear to communicate very much the opposite idea: first, he claims that the Libertador never tampered with "the legal order for the transmission of power" ("Las dictaduras" [*La oda* 270]); and second, he contends that the revolutionary leader had converted to the ideology of conservatism prior to issuing the Organic Decree of Dictatorship in 1828. While the first point is well taken, the passages from the *Diario de Bucaramanga* cited in this chapter belie Caro's second presumption. The Libertador opposed the idea of establishing the Dictatorship without the sanctioning of an *assemblée constituante* and an appropriate constitutional charter. Only this legal setting could ensure the same lawful transmission of power that did not worry Augustus (Octavius) in Rome to the same degree. However, he also conceived of the president's dictatorial powers as a way to free the Greater Colombia from the imminent threat of fragmentation. Unlike Caro, Bolívar avoided praising the institution of dictatorship because he did not wish to undermine directly the executive's right to use the sovereignty alienated to it through a constitutionally legitimate process that should not be reversed except as a last resort. A second revolution of emancipation, in keeping with the arguments of Simón Rodríguez, Manuel Ancízar, and Hannah Arendt for bringing freedom from necessity and eligibility for the franchise to the majority of the population, certainly did not occur in New Granada in the course of the nineteenth century. Nevertheless, Bolívar was the only early statesman imaginative enough at least to *consider* undertaking it on moral grounds and pending more favorable circumstances because it would have benefited the republic as a whole.

Through a calculated series of public celebrations and literary-legislative acts, Caro made the translation of Bolivarianism into Liberalism almost impossible. In assigning a nontransitory nature to Bolívar's last government decisions, which of course contrast with the imputed transitoriness of the exceptional powers, centralization was from then on perceived as a Conservative, potentially reactionary tenet of government. It is equally important to note that Caro also prepared the way for Colombians' gradual and partial acceptance of a more disturbing doctrinal body in which the exception became the norm. The restrictive Constitution of 1886 and the self-undermining dispositions contained therein partially covered up the arbitrary and partisan interpretations of the law found in the Regenerators' subsequent acts in government.

Conclusion

On Lettered Cities and the Writing of Lyric

I began this study with a reconsideration of Rama's interpretation of lettered-city policies in post-1810 Latin America. According to this critic, one such virtual polity was made possible by the nationalization, in the aftermath of Spain's colonial rule, of existing bureaucratic apparatuses now charged specifically with systematizing and publicizing the new republics' self-legitimating body of knowledge (scientific, juridical, literary, sociological, etc.). In Rama's view, the hypertrophy of the institutions of writing that thrived within those apparatuses was designed to produce ultimately a robust centralizing state in which the modernizing forces of secular progress (public education, transportation, industrial development, etc.) would slowly yet steadily eradicate the traces of religious superstition, Spanish traditionalism, and the so-called indigenous "barbarism."

In the eyes of its promoters, this project did not contradict the notion that the *Latin* European nations and their American offspring would continue to be primarily Catholic. The legal formulae that legitimated revolutionary constitutions more often than not were self-conscious reconceptualizations of existing structures of thought and rights of instituting in place during the Old Regime. In their turn, the theo-political underpinnings of monarchical absolutism had a conflicted republican and parliamentary ancestry whose roots went back to ancient Rome and the medieval Spanish kingdoms, which were nonfeudal, moderately centralizing regimes. The same was true of the Vatican Curia: it could present itself as the Roman Empire's surviving avatar at least in part because it was just as interested in suppressing the democratizing aspects inherent in its *parliamentary* assemblies. In Spain's case, these assemblies were the episcopal councils that legitimated the Visigothic monarchy; they foreshadow the networks of negotiated interests that the medieval Cortes typically rehearsed.

The reactionary *letrados* whose orbits circled around Caro tried to manufacture the people's assent to their policies through the production of epic and theological poetry and the complete revamping of the nation's past, for which purpose they had to invest grammarians and authors with para-legislative faculties. However, this program was carried into practice when elsewhere literature was claiming its autonomous status from the demands made on it by the state powers. In Rama's chronological chart, around 1870 the lettered city gave way—in such privileged locations as the River Plate region, Cuba, and Mexico—to the "modernized city" [*ciudad modernizada*] (71), which he connects specifically to the *modernista* poets and essay writers' attempts to conquer an autonomous sphere for literature and art without renouncing their prerogative to guide society in less tangible ways than the *letrados* proper had done from the bureaucratic field. It did not occur to Rama that the battle for *laïcité* and a secular legal order was far from over in most Spanish American republics at this time. Instead, he assumed that in the three decades of what he considered the *ciudad modernizada*'s apogee (1870–1910), liberals and conservatives produced different yet complementary versions of the same modernizing projects. As they alternated in the government of their respective countries, the two ideologies underwent scrutiny (under different names) by an increasingly independent contingent of writers who wanted their output to remain socially relevant, but who were no longer positioned at the center of political life.

Much of the *longue durée* just described was anticipated in the writings and career of Manuel José Quintana, an early advocate for the fostering of an independent public opinion and of *liberum arbitrium*. Colombia does not easily conform to Rama's interpretation to the extent that a *ciudad internacionalizada* could not emerge in Bogotá, Medellín, and Cartagena without the appearance first of larger constituencies of better-educated and more prosperous middle-class readers. Other factors that increased this delay were: Bogotá's diminutive size and economic underdevelopment in contrast with Havana and the River Plate metropolis; the focus of much writing prior to 1886 on the issues of secular education and the internecine struggles within Liberalism; literary production's subsequent refocus, after 1886, on the Regeneración's themes of the reconciliation with Spain's colonial rule; and the catechizing celebration of Catholic virtues in a new print environment controlled directly by Caro and the Catholic Church.

Rama did not ask himself how the lettered city's commendable projects, which in his book remain by and large a liberal-democratic construct despite their varying disciplinarian strains, were thwarted in Andean countries such as Ecuador or Colombia as early as the late 1860s. It was then that important contingents of ultra-Catholic *letrados* began to reverse the tide of secular progress, slowly transforming the state bureaucracy and its literature into an antiquating force. In "Freedom of Worship" [La libertad de cultos] (1871–1872), Caro called upon conservative Catholic poets to take up the study of jurisprudence without giving up their Latin and Church doctrine so that they could fight the legally minded Liberal governments on their own turf. The fragmentation of sovereignty in the federal system of government promoted by Liberalism had long encouraged the training of legists and bureaucrats who were not literati. Caro realized early on that knowledge of the law was needed to dismantle existing legislations, but that it was insufficient in itself. Expertise in Church doctrine, rhetoric, and literature was just as necessary to turn public opinion away from an appreciation for the Constitution of 1863 and in favor of a new one. He wanted to fight radical Liberals at the same time as he evangelized those Conservatives who had *not yet* let go of their ancestors' secular republicanism.

The Constitution of 1886 culminated the intense, protracted Catholic refashioning of the revolutionary-republican legacy in coordination with the elevation of philology and translation to the status of untranscendable horizons for both interpreting the nation's past and projecting its future. As public education and the censorship machinery were returned to the hands of the Church, priests once again occupied important posts in the administration. In this hypertrophied textual environment in which genre boundaries had long been blurred, literature and textual criticism assumed exceptional powers. They were granted faculties so extraordinary that they not only influenced the writing of the new *magna carta*, but also convinced many Colombians of the superiority of textual editors of sacred texts over secular jurisprudents. Caro went so far as to argue that theories of sovereignty were easily analogized to theories on the origin of language, which only philologists could legitimately assess. In form if not in spirit, Colombia reversed temporarily—and legally—to a theocratic, neocolonial regime in which some of the most cherished republican conquests, such as the freedom of the press or the right of the accused to confront the persecuting state in a court of law, were summarily suspended.

The failed Revolution of 1810 and Bolívar's later movement of national emancipation certainly did away with Old Regime government structures, but could not erase many of the social hierarchies and habits of thought underlying them. Conversely, the Regeneración's authoritarian legislation and its attendant exceptional measures did not eradicate seventy years of resistance to absolutist designs. This is yet another reason why the life of letters remained central to the well-being of New Granadan society: literature was still a privileged locus for the improvisation and negotiation of contradictory subject-positions in which fictional personae (political and otherwise) could be alternately assumed and put down. Literature furnished an outlet for attempts at launching revolutions and counterrevolutions in a century that witnessed scores of both. What goes often unnoticed, even by lettered-city scholars, is the literary productivity of *letrados* while they stayed in office. The conclusion to be drawn from this evidence is that they spent most of their time writing a lot of literature and a little policy, and made the implementation of those policies a secondary endeavor.

Aware that *The City of Translation* presents a bleak yet faithful picture of Colombian society and politics, I have provided a few examples of peaceful coexistence and collaboration among *letrado*-poets from the two main parties. Some of the literary periodicals and *tertulias* were bipartisan for the self-evident reason that Liberals and Conservatives continued to belong to the same hegemonic social class even when one of the parties retained exclusive control of the central government for long periods. Their children regularly intermarried, did business together, and declared themselves Catholic whether they could agree to the enforcement of *laïcité* or not. The principal bipartisan publication founded at mid-century was *El Mosaico*, whose resonantly paralegislative title—like its resonant first day of publication (December 24, 1858)—seemed to augur well for the possibility of a new cultural and social order. *El Mosaico* was in its later years organized by Monsignor Carrasquilla's father. This was the educator, poet, and Catholic publicist don Ricardo (1827–1886), who called himself a collateral descendant of the founding father Antonio Nariño.[1] Reactionaries such as José Joaquín Ortiz, José María Vergara y Vergara (coeditor of *El Mosaico*), and José Manuel Groot graced the pages of this publication, as did the Liberals Salvador Camacho Roldán, Medardo Rivas, and Santiago Pérez. Except for a brief spell as bureaucrat at the Treasury (he had José Eusebio Caro as one of his colleagues there), which ended when the radical Liberal José Hilario López took over the presidency in 1849, don Ricardo did not join the ranks of the *letrados* and lived a modestly dignified life.

In chapter 4, I briefly touched upon the friendship between two grammarian-presidents, the Liberal Santiago Pérez and the Conservative José Manuel Marroquín, who used the periodical *El Mosaico* as a cultured *locus amoenus* in which their mutually opposing views on the nature of representative government and the place of Catholic traditions in modern society could be for the moment left behind. Here, too, poems of reciprocal appreciation could be recited and published. At mid-century, escapist literature became yet another type of exception by which the norm (hostility among party factions) could be suspended. At venues like *El Mosaico*, politics reverted to the older yet inauthentic notion of a Colombia organized as a more homogeneous corporation in which the literati with the right social pedigree could greet one another as the children and grandchildren of the same founding *letrados* who sat at the Congress of Cúcuta in 1821 or served in an important capacity in any of Bolívar's administrations. On admittedly more rare occasions, literature could also effectively counter the power of executive orders in certain contexts in which the disputing parties involved were at the same time members of the republic of letters and citizens of the increasingly divided federal polity.

Ricardo Carrasquilla was the protagonist of one of these rare episodes. In 1862 the young Liberal novelist, *letrado,* geographer, and future publisher, Medardo Rivas, issued an executive order as Governor of Cundinamarca, then a sovereign state with its capital city set in Bogotá. Medardo's father-in-law—José Manuel Groot, the celebrated author of the *Historia eclesiástica y civil de Nueva Granada*—was known for expressing Catholic convictions as deep as don Ricardo's, but was possessed of a more sanguine temperament. A copy of the order sent to Carrasquilla requested that the latter contribute a "silla" (a riding horse) to the government's militia in the midst of the civil war that transformed the Bolivarian general and landowner Tomás Cipriano de Mosquera from a regional president into an antiecclesiastical dictator. Mosquera marched triumphantly with the powerful Cauca army into the poorly defended federal capital. Bogotá had at the time only a small Guardia Nacional whose main function was (according to Conservative detractors) to help the radicals commit fraud at the elections. Rivas knew that Carrasquilla had a large family and little money, and that he was a model citizen. The two corresponded in verse, Carrasquilla requesting an exemption from the executive order's enforcement at a time of enormous emotional and financial strain for all, and Rivas granting the petition (by means of a *décima*) on the basis of the petitioner's poignantly self-belittling humor. Rivas's text mocks the administrative register of Spanish; it takes on the title "Resolution," begins with the line "Gobernación del Distrito," and moves on to its conclusion-decision with the conjunction "Therefore" [Por tanto]. Rivas had all these words printed in upper case. Calling himself the "undersigned," the speaker ends the poem with a warning to his addressee, exhorting him not to help his fellow Conservatives' militia: "THEREFORE: Do not hand a horse over to me, but have the good sense of not giving one to the guerilla either."[2]

Had Colombians engaged more often in this type of symbolic negotiation, in which the two interlocutors' intellectual prestige, mastery of the *captatio benevolentiae* topoi, and service to the nation overrode factional politics, the two parties may have fought fewer regional civil wars. Or would they? The bellicose *caudillo* Julio Arboleda was a master of the lyric harangue and lawsuit. He used his generally overrated versifying skills to frighten prisoners (as he did with César Conto), arouse his insurrectionist troops, or litigate with Popayán's council members on the matter of his fiscal responsibilities.[3] Be that as it may, *El Mosaico* was one of several prestigious venues in which some of the economic capital accumulated by the entrepreneurial Liberal families (e.g, Samper, Camacho Roldán) was invested in the hope that a new public sphere could be created for the professional writer to appear. Although *El Mosaico*'s publication was made possible by the subsidizing of Catholic Liberals, much of the writing was done by Catholic Conservative laypersons, among whom Carrasquilla was perhaps the most financially in need.[4] How Carrasquilla's son—the presbyter and educator Rafael María—came to adopt a more right-wing position than his father remains the subject of conjecture.[5]

El Mosaico was quick to recognize past and present Liberal administrations' limited yet tangible achievements in education. Its frank endorsement was tinged with a more self-interested rationale: if the number of competent readers multiplied, the number of subscriptions might also rise more quickly, enabling the longed-for advent of independent professional writing. Don Ricardo could thus dream of sustaining himself and his family by the pen, something that few others had been able to do: Caro and Rafael Pombo succeeded in nearly becoming full-time professional writers because of their wondrous productivity across genres and their partial ownership of some of the venues in which they regularly published their articles and poems.[6] But Pombo was a proverbially frugal bachelor and did some teaching, while Caro worked intermittently as a private tutor and university lecturer when he was not part of the Regeneración's propagandistic apparatus and administration. To encourage further subscriptions and attract investments, periodicals and book publishing houses printed their lists of subscribers and stockholders. This was also a way in which patrons and readers could show allegiance to literary-cultural enterprises that had a clear counterpart in party politics. The holder of a subscription to a given periodical regularly cast a vote of confidence—presumably at times also a ballot—in support of the ideas advocated by writers who were likely to become candidates at the next important election to public office.[7]

As this book proceeds chronologically, it moves from the impact of eighteenth-century ideas on late colonial societies—which I explore especially in chapter 2—through the conflicted legacies of Bello and Bolívar and to the remarkable career of Miguel Antonio Caro, who remains the book's focus from beginning to end. In a booklength sequel to *The City of Translation* currently in progress, I chart in detail Guillermo Valencia's equally eventful literary career, in which translation, poetry, politics, and religion also form a conflicted discursive continuum. That second study shifts its focus from the debates about the lettered city to the debates about the autonomy of literature at a time when Spanish American readerships began to expand at different speeds depending on the country in question. The new expansion came as a result of the spread of public education and growth of an urban middle class composed of artisans, tradesmen, professionals, and government functionaries.

Translation and poetry continued to play a key role in Colombia's cultural plurisystem after the period of Conservative hegemony—the government of the grammarian-*letrados*—came to an end in 1930. The gradual eclipse of the *letrado*-grammarian-poet, though slow in coming, greatly improved the quality of Colombian literature. The lettered city's stiflingly culturalist bearings slowly gave out, so that vernacular cultures could achieve greater visibility even at the price of being subjected to lettered-city mediations. Today Caro's reputation is seriously damaged despite the fact that an institute for philological research was created in his and Rufino José Cuervo's honor in 1942. Long controlled by right-wing groups and Colombia's

Catholic Church, the Instituto Caro y Cuervo published numerous editions of Caro's works between 1947 and 1988 to complement the eight volumes of *Obras completas* (poetry and literary criticism) published by the government's Imprenta Nacional between 1918 and 1945 under the coeditorship of Víctor Caro, one of the author's sons. José Manuel Rivas Sacconi's editions of Caro's translations from Spanish into Latin were the Instituto's first major publishing enterprise (and a telling choice this was). They were padded with an unfriendly critical apparatus written also in Latin, setting the tone for the Instituto's later publications, which also included a more accessible *Boletín* and a scholarly journal—*Thesaurus*. The journal's true character was shown in its numerous articles written in Latin or about Latin and neo-Latin literature (often by prelates), which helped preserve the fiction that Colombia's national culture was monolithically neo-Thomistic and theocratic in nature. Yet, some Thomistic thinkers would have found both attributes in conflict with each other and not just with the prospect of an emerging civil society.

These publishing enterprises were carried out under the assumption that a cloistered city of reactionary literati could still thrive within Bogotá's manifestly multiethnic and pluricultural urban space. The República Liberal (1930–1946) timidly tried to bring this previously unacknowledged diversity into the mainstream through the recovery of regional fiction, the compilation of popular *romanceros* and *cancioneros* (where another, less retrogressive *natural constitution* than *ius naturale* lay hidden), and the creation of research institutions and periodicals devoted to the study of vernacular folklore. The Liberal Party strategically tried to mobilize the subaltern population on its behalf by actively promoting upward social mobility at an admittedly slow and irregular pace. They proceeded from below, by boosting literacy rates and acknowledging the centrality of a vernacular counter-*traditio*—independent of Church doctrine—to Colombia's national identity. This experiment was short-lived, as the divisions within Liberalism, the assassination of populist leader Jorge Eliécer Gaitán in 1948, and the onset of La Violencia were to prove. The Instituto Caro y Cuervo attempted almost quixotically since its creation in 1942 to slow down—if possible, to neutralize—the progress made by popular culture, which in certain ways correlated with the progress also made by inclusive government policies, if not exactly with the effective democratizing of state institutions. The first three scholarly books published by the Instituto were Rufino José Cuervo's *Obras inéditas* (1944), Caro's Latin-language edition and neo-Latin translation of *La "Canción a las ruinas de Itálica" del licenciado Rodrigo Caro* (1947), and José Manuel Rivas Sacconi's *El latín en Colombia* (1949).

The Instituto's early ventures coincided with the publication of Octavio Quiñones Pardo's well-known anthologies of *cancionero* and *refranero* cultural production sponsored by the República Liberal's Comisión Nacional de Folklore in the mid 1940s. The República Liberal's popular book fairs and mass market editions of middlebrow authors (some of whom deliberately used substandard Spanish in their writings) also helped discover a multicultural Colombia that had remained hidden by Bogotá's changing fictitious appellations, from the "Athens of New Granada" and the "relegated city" (Élisée Reclus), to the "withdrawn Santafé" and the "heavenly city" (Vergara y Vergara), and on to the "colonial cloister" (Henao and Arrubla).[8] Likewise, universal primary instruction and adult education made great strides for the first time since the Olimpo Radical, thanks to the opening of the Escuelas Aldeanas and the programming of radio broadcasts with a cultural literacy component.[9] Yet, as Eduardo Posada Carbó has argued in a recent historical interpretation of modern Colombia's crises in national consciousness, the promotion of literacy and professional education exacted a high price from the advocates for state intervention. The same *letrados* who formed the ranks of the República Liberal soon realized that Colombia was not a nation-state by any stretch of the imagination and could not easily become one. This was certainly the case with the psychiatrist, grammarian, and racialist thinker Luis López de Mesa (appointed Minister of Education in 1934 and Minister of Foreign Relations in 1938) and the novelist and journalist Eduardo Caballero Calderón, who served as congressman and diplomat, and even as mayor of a small municipality (Posada Carbó 216–30). For them, Colombia was integrated by a series of smaller countries that Bolívar had artificially assembled together following the centralizing designs of Spain's colonial administration for fear that decentralization would make the smaller administrative units weak and belligerent.

The mid-nineteenth-century experiments with federalism proved that the natural impulse of the sovereign states was to break away from the union, most often because of the local elites' economic self-interest rather than a well-articulated consciousness of substate national differentiation. In such works as López de Mesa's *Escrutinio sociológico de la historia colombiana* (1955) and Caballero Calderón's *Cartas colombianas* (1949) and *Historia privada de los colombianos* (1960)—all published or at least thought out during the years of La Violencia—Colombia comes across as a conglomerate of ruined fragments which had not composed an organic whole in the first place. Posada Carbó neglects to mention that these two *letrados'* glance at their country's past and present woes may have been representative of a liberal generation's disenchantment with the failed politics of progressive populism, but that it was not necessarily upheld by the majority of intellectuals. In fact, the crowning historiographical work written by a New Granadan at mid century—Fernando Guillén Martínez's monumental *La torre y la plaza. Un ensayo de interpretación de América*—celebrates not just the unity of all Spanish American republics, but their common historical destiny shared with Spain. *La torre y la plaza* symbolizes in its title the author's disturbing yet dazzling attempt at making ecclessiastical power (the tower) compatible with municipal freedoms (the square). The book was published in Madrid by Franco's Instituto de Cultura Hispánica in 1958, the year after the *golpista* General Gustavo Rojas Pinilla stepped down from power in the face of massive opposition to his rule of four years. An urban legend has it that the poet and diplomat Eduardo Carranza offered to negotiate secretly the terms of his exile in Spain.

Only with the promulgation of the 1991 Constitution (which derogated Caro's Constitution and its various major reforms over the years) were New Granadans interpellated by their fundamental law as citizens of a multicultural state. Understandably, this development spelled trouble for the Instituto Caro y Cuervo. Incorporated first into the Ministry of Education (2001), and later into the Ministry of Culture (2003), it languished for much of the present decade (it was temporarily closed down) until it was restructured and reopened in 2008.[10] Its current structure boasts various book series and research groups devoted to indigenous and creole languages in addition to languages in contact, all of which allows the Instituto to use the phrase "lengua española" as little as possible for the sake of political correctness.[11] The Instituto was once again in the spotlight after obtaining the Premio Bartolomé de las Casas from Spain's Ministry of Culture in 2001 for its diffusion of Colombia's understudied indigenous languages. The award may have made Caro turn in his grave, given his famous polemics with Jorge Isaacs on the subject of the Indians' unlettered and heathen condition.

Quite predictably, the better part of the Instituto's major publishing has been to this day in the area of nineteenth-century reactionary thought, an endeavor in which Spain's Instituto de Cultura Hispánica (along with its Colombian branch) also played a central role under Franco. As my works cited list shows (and as I diligently set down in the acknowledgments), the Instituto's painstaking elaboration of philologically annotated editions of otherwise hard-to-find minor works by the Regeneración's main authors has made my book possible. We have long had copiously annotated editions of works not only by Rufino José Cuervo and Miguel Antonio Caro, but also by José Manuel Marroquín, José Eusebio Caro, Marco Fidel Suárez, José María Samper, Rafael Pombo, Rafael Núñez, and Guillermo Valencia, among other precursors and contemporaries of the Regeneración.[12]

As I write this conclusion, a major exhibit titled "Miguel Antonio Caro (1843–1909)" has run its course in Bogotá. It was inaugurated on August 6, 2009 and remained open through the end of November. It celebrated Caro's intellectual legacy on the one-hundredth anniversary of his passing. Since this book places great emphasis on the centennial celebrations of Bello's and Bolívar's births, it is only fitting that I end with some remarks on the lasting effects of the Regeneración's politics of the exception on contemporary Colombia.

The parallelisms between Núñez's and Álvaro Uribe Vélez's defections from the Liberal Party are well known. Each led an authoritarian reaction to the fragmentation of sovereignty in Spanish America's global climate of liberal-democratic politics on the assumption that Colombia risked becoming a failed state for lack of a stronger, decisionist executive branch. The main challenge faced by the two presidents was how to monopolize and implement effectively the legitimate means of corrective violence.[13] In doing this, both Núñez and Uribe risked the prospect not so much of heading a failed state, but of instituting a failed democracy in which the earlier institutionalizing of congressional debates (the political "rule" in mature parliamentary democracies) was de-emphasized by declaring a chronic state of "exception." While Núñez delegated his power first to the very right-wing but able Carlos Holguín Mallarino, the equally right-wing Carlos Holguín Sardi (a former Senator, President of the Conservative Party, and Minister of Justice and the Interior [2006–2008]) long entertained the idea of succeeding Uribe, who sponsored the legislative initiative in Congress in 2004 that allowed him (despite a constitutional interdiction) to be reelected in 2006.

Could a new Caro have emerged after the inauspicious interregnum of another "Carlos Holguín" or anyone like him? This unlikely scenario was frustrated in early 2009 by former President Andrés Pastrana's call to the Conservative Party to enter a younger, more progressive candidate at the 2010 election. This candidate turned out to be Noemí Sanín, a moderate Conservative who once headed an alternative party, and has shown remarkable skills as an administrator and negotiator. She is the daughter of a prestigious *letrado*-writer, the hard line conservative Jaime Sanín Echeverri.

The election turned out to be a relatively close contest between two other candidates. The first one was Juan Manuel Santos Calderón, a seasoned technocrat and journalist, and Minister of Defense (2006–2009) during Uribe Vélez's second term. He comes from the ranks of Liberalism, but in 2005 cofounded a new party, the generally right-wing Partido de la Unión Nacional. The Santos family still has partial ownership of the legendary newspaper *El Tiempo* and its media conglomerate, although since 2007 their majoritarian owner has been Spain's Grupo Planeta. Santos Calderón is the grandnephew of a president in the years of the República Liberal (the moderate Eduardo Santos Montejo [1938–1942]), who once had exclusive ownership of *El Tiempo* and slowed down President Alfonso López Pumarejo's Revolución en Marcha [1934–1938]). He is also first cousin of Francisco Santos Calderón (Uribe Vélez's vice president in 2002–2006 and 2006–2010). Note that Juan Manuel and Francisco share their two last names but are only first cousins. Their respective fathers—Enrique and Hernando Santos Castillo—married each a Calderón *bon parti* (the sisters Clemencia and Helena Calderón Nieto). With Juan Manuel Santos in power, little is likely to change, as was shown by the example of López Pumarejo's son—the novelist and former radical Alfonso López Michelsen, who became president in 1974 after defeating the children of two other former presidents.

Moving from a *república de los cuñados* (the rule of the brothers-in-law—Holguín Mallarino, Caro, and Súarez, who married one of Caro's cousins) to a *república de los sobrino-nietos* (the government of the presidents' grandnephews—Holguín Sardi and the two Santos cousins) does not augur too well for the future.

Entering the last week of the campaign, the candidate who led at the polls by the narrowest of margins (in a virtual tie was Santos) was Antanas Mockus, the Green Party's nominee. Mockus seemed the preferred choice among many true independents and disenchanted liberals who wish to move beyond the two-party system but who at the same time reject Uribe's authoritarian regime and its inaction in promoting much-needed socially minded policies. Mockus is a mathematician of Lithuanian descent and the former Rector of the Universidad Nacional de Colombia (1990–1993) and Mayor of Bogotá (1995–1997, 2001–2003). His immensely popular civic interventions in the municipal government have many Colombians convinced that the advent of an inclusive, egalitarian, and peaceful civil society is still possible. This prospect will be put on hold for now. At the May 30 election, Santos received 46 percent of the vote—only four points short of the 50 percent that would see him dispense with the need for the run-off race scheduled for June 20. The polls showed that Mockus might still make up his twenty-five-point deficit if he could swing the votes of the eliminated left-wing candidates in his favor. As it turned out, at the run-off contest Santos obtained more than two-thirds of the vote. His landslide victory confirms the preponderance in Colombian politics of family pedigrees and direct connections to the culture and media industries, which have been central to this book's arguments. The electoral results also underscore the difficulty that New Granadans have historically experienced accepting such social-democratic platforms as the ones currently in power in Ecuador, Venezuela, and Bolivia. These are the three South American countries that were once also part of Bolívar's Greater Colombia and recently forged—with Cuba and Nicaragua—the Bolivarian Alliance for the Americas.

To this day numerous New Granadans continue to reminisce nostalgically on a not-so-distant era in which the nation could be justly called the *república de los cuñados* or the *república de los gramáticos*. Belonging to certain families or clans and identifying publicly with philo-Spanish culture, the Catholic Church, or counterrevolutionary ideologies has historically multiplied Conservative *letrados'* chances of reaching Colombia's highest elected offices. This book's two main purposes have accordingly been to contribute to the ongoing critique of that nostalgia and to examine critically the nineteenth-century historical events that enable that suspect reminiscing about the past.

Notes

Introduction

1. See Rama 41–42, 94.
2. Among political historians of nineteenth-century Spain and Spanish America, this assumption can be found in Guerra (31, 173); Palti (65–76); Fernández Sebastián and Fuentes (23–36). Their main theoretical inspiration is Reinhart Koselleck's "history of concepts" [*Begriffsgeschichte*] (*The Practice of Conceptual History*, esp. 4–7).
3. Rama made this mistake when characterizing Colombia's hypertrophied grammatical production as the lettered city's self-legitimating cultural apparatus, which in his hurried assessment was ancillary to the *letrados*' "effective" modernization of the state (82–83). The regime of grammarians modernized neither the state administration nor linguistic institutions. Unlike their Liberal counterparts (which were just as prone to confuse their class interests with those of the disenfranchised population at large), Colombia's Conservative *letrados* did not include any sociologists, economists or self-reflexive educators of note. Their vast linguistic enterprise is also fatally marred by an excessive emphasis on etymology and worship of the archaism; by their oversight of the arbitrariness and mutability of the linguistic sign (a trait, however modern, which did not go unnoticed by Jeremy Bentham, among other materialist philosophers); and by their adherence to the doctrine of the divine origin of language.
4. Within pactist or contractualist theories, another distinction must be made between the *pactum societatis*, by which the people freely constitute themselves into an assembly of delegates, and the *pactum subjectionis*, by which the right of conquest or the claims of the stronger over the weaker parts of society are legitimated as law *ex post facto* rather than the arbitrary imposition of force. The *pactum*, which originally appears in opposition to the divine right of kings, could thus paradoxically be used to uphold the institution of the absolute monarchy, particularly when it was argued (as did seventeenth-century theorists Hugo Grotius in *De jure belli ac pacis* and Samuel Pufendorf in *De jure naturae et gentium*) that the people completely alienated their sovereignty to the monarch. This position was rendered untenable by both Locke and Rousseau while Hobbes tried to rethink the *pactum societatis/ pactum subjectionis* binomial by contending that the subjected ones never conceal their condition as slaves to the stronger power to which they have capitulated. For a useful overview, see Fataud and Bartholy (12–15), who neglect to incorporate into their discussion the contributions to this ongoing debate by the Spanish Jesuits of the later sixteenth century and by Johannes Althusius.

5. An informed discussion of μεταφορά/ *metaphorein*/ *metafora* in relation to *translatio* must ultimately go back to Aristotle and look ahead to Thomas Aquinas. In medieval Latin translations from Aristotle, the Greek μεταφορά is most often rendered as either *metafora* or *translatio*. In Boethius's Latin version of Book Six of Aristotle's *Topics*, as in the alternative translation by an anonymous twelfth-century author (both edited by Lorenzo Minio-Paluello), a number of terms alternate to designate the principle of dissimilar similitude, which in the translators' minds overlapped with their efforts to hierarchize and redeem the fallen order of pagan words: *secundum translationem*, *secundum metaforam*, *metafora*, *transferentes secundum*, and *similitudinem transferunt*, among others. What separates these translators from Quintilian is that they make more explicit the transcendent purpose behind *translatio* qua *metafora* by adding the adverb *secundum*, which means (as noted above) "according to" or "in conformity with." I follow the text of the Latin versions collected in Minio-Paluello's *Aristoteles Latinus, V.1–3* (115–16, 256–57).

6. In this new textual environment of maximal semantic undecidability, terms such as the adjective *duplex* and the adverb *dupliciter* were used in discussions of how to translate theological works in various interrelated ways. First, each word translated from one language into another could designate the same entity, as in Augustine's example of the *bos* (i.e., "ox") discussed in *On Christian Doctrine* [De doctrina Christiana] (42–43). Literary and vernacular metaphors in the English language may evoke the animal's attribute of strength without necessarily making one think of the ox itself. But, as Augustine also remarks, as a Christian one always has to consider as well the occurrences of *bos* in Scripture (Deut. 25:4) and their apostolic interpretations (1 Cor. 9:9; 1 Tim. 5:18). A related discussion appears in another work whose Augustinian eschatology I will also be referencing in chapter 2, the twelfth-century Bishop Otto von Freising's *Chronica, sive historia de duabus civitatibus* (446–51). If translation for the theologian is always twofold or threefold, for the philologist who deals with multiple sources of the same utterance (the *traditio*) it is tantalizingly manifold. Since Jeremy Bentham's philosophy of jurisprudence will play an important part in this study, let me add that the Benthamite terms "pain" and "punishment" can be both translated into Spanish as "pena," which is a capaciously polysemous noun. Being the nucleus of much fifteenth-century *cancionero* poetry and sentimental fiction, the noun "pena" can mean at one and the same time emotional affliction, physical punishment, and penance.

7. Quoted from p. 1265 of the *Index in libros moralium et homilias* (these are indices of works by uncertain authors) included in Gregorius I's *Opera omnia, Tomus secundus*.

8. These arguments have already been developed in my two articles "Sobre héroes y urnas" and "Valencia's Verlaine." The second of these two articles answers—via Bourdieu—the call made by various critics to address the increasing opacity and ambiguity of Spanish-American literature as it begins to claim its autonomy from other state-sponsored discourses (Alonso 289–90; Ramos 59–61).

One   The Colombian Lettered City— Philology, Ideology, Translation

1. See de la Campa (47–48) on the centrality of discursive convertibility to Rama's concept of the lettered city. See also Rama 50.

2. See Foucault, esp. 50–71. For a survey of twentieth-century theories of translation vis-à-vis theories of discourse, see Rodríguez García, "Literary into Cultural Translation."

3. I use the lowercase "liberal" to designate a political creed or platform that upholds such tenets as the limited yet gradual spread of electoral and educational rights; the separation of Church and state; the citizens' equality before the law; the freedom of the press; and the priority of the legislative branch of government over the executive and the judiciary. I reserve the uppercase "Liberal" to refer to militants of a Liberal Party in Colombia or elsewhere, or to a period of Liberal rule.

4. I understand "the theologico-political" or "theo-politics" as an interpretive framework in which the question of religious salvation becomes inseparable from the question of organized government, so that the absolute claims of theology are extended into the realm of politics. For a survey of alternative definitions, see de Vries 25–29. My use of "return" is meant to suggest theo-politics' irreducible latency even in confidently secular regimes, as Jules Michelet in France, Domingo Faustino Sarmiento in Argentina, and Francisco Bilbao in Chile realized early on. In the nineteenth century, the political reactivation of religious interpretation frequently took place at social junctures in which parliamentary democracy failed to efface the marks of its arbitrary self-legitimation.

5. For two accurate early assessments of this dynamics, see Cané 148–50; Uribe Uribe, "Ensayo sobre las cuestiones teológicas y los partidos políticos en Colombia" (pub. 1911; repr. in *Obras selectas* 1: 73–83).

6. This "right of patronage" was derived from the "Real Patronato" of colonial rule, which in turn took its name from the *ius patronatus* or legally regulated grant made by the Church, including Church benefices or gifts of land bestowed on its benefactors. In the sense used in this book, the *Patronato* was more or less the opposite, namely, a concession made by civil governments to the Church of Rome, allowing bishops and priests to conduct their evangelical work within the state and paying them a salary out of gratitude for this service, but also in exchange for their subordination to legally elected civil authorities. In modern times, Congress—*la Nación*—retained the originally "royal" privilege to propose episcopal appointments to the pope. For a brief exposition of jurisdictional issues raised in several Spanish American republics by the *Patronato*, see Beneyto Pérez 566–70, 630–32. Tirado Mejía discusses its abolition by the Liberals through the Law of June 15, 1853 in the context of other anti-ecclesiastical government measures including the secular Constitution of 1853 (360–365). Because the Colombian state paid the salaries of the priests, the clergy could function at times as ecclesiastical *letrados*. They became disaffected intellectuals after that patronage was revoked in 1853. See Guillén Martínez (*El poder político en Colombia* 484–92) for an intriguing interpretation of the extravagantly theo-political Concordat of 1887. According to this historian, the Regeneración consciously attempted to use the clergy as a "socializing bureaucracy" that placed the moral oversight of manual workers in the hands of a corporation completely autonomous from the state's body of positive legislation.

7. On the alarms set off by the founding of the first important Sociedad Católica to influence the vote and mobilize public opinion against President Francisco de Paula Santander's secular policies, see "Observaciones sobre la sociedad formada en Bogotá con el título de Católica," *La Bandera Nacional,* no. 49 (September 16, 1838): 218–20. Soon the Sociedades Democráticas would be founded to counter

the Católicas from a radical-Liberal position. In a series of articles and letters to the editor of this newspaper, which was published between 1837 and 1839 by Lorenzo María Lleras (an ancestor of Liberal presidents Alberto Lleras Camargo [1958–1962] and Carlos Lleras Restrepo [1966–1970]), the terms "partido progresista" and "partido retrógrado" were popularized to refer to the organized groups that only in 1848–1849 would call themselves officially Liberal and Conservative, respectively. Not all Conservatives were retrogrades, but all retrogrades professed a conservative sociopolitical creed and claimed to put the Church before the state.

8. On the need for spiritual *regeneratio* from the sins transmitted or translated through biological *generatio*, see Augustine, *The City of God* 4: 506-9. For Caro's adaptation of this antiliberal imperative as one of the lettered city's main goals, see "El Partido Católico" (1873; repr. in *Obras, tomo I* 866). The term "regeneration" was also used by proponents of representative government to signify their nations' need to bounce back from centuries of absolutist rule. It is found in Sieyès, Quintana, and Colombia's founding father Francisco Antonio Zea's "Copia de las propuestas hechas por los comisionados de Venezuela en Londres" (1810), where it occurs in conjunction with the even more frequently used "reconciliation." I have consulted Zea's text in the multiauthored popular anthology listed under Bolívar et al. (*Bolívar, Camilo Torres, Francisco Antonio Zea* 247, 249, 252–55, 278).

9. Although Caro was able to close down *El Correo Nacional*, the newspaper that Martínez Silva and his brother Luis founded in 1890 to denounce the Regeneración's abuses, he could not do the same with *El Repertorio* because the very influential Conservative literati in control of the Academy (the cofounder José Manuel Marroquín and Rafael Pombo are the two best known) were also now positioned against Caro's rising theocracy.

10. The word "reactionary" as used in this book designates a person who not only shuns the democratizing impulses of liberalism, positivism, and universal instruction (many conservatives would adhere to this program), but who also wishes for a return to the hierarchical order implicit in the Old Regime's invocation of Providence and the divine right of rulers. Most Catholic Conservatives who still recognized themselves as "republicans" did not uphold the divine right, let alone the dogma of papal infallibility. Reactionary becomes thus roughly synonymous with my other preferred term, "ultramontanist," that is, he/she who believes that the temporal powers of a Catholic nation must subject themselves to the pope's instructions on civil government, as Joseph de Maistre and Caro did. Furthermore, the distinction between republican conservatives and ultramontanists correlates imperfectly with the accepted designations of "Conservadores históricos" and "Conservadores nacionalistas" in Colombia's party politics. Caro, Holguín, and Marco Fidel Suárez became "nacionalistas" while Marroquín and presidential hopeful Guillermo Valencia were "históricos."

11. The concept of "sovereignty" plays a key role in this book. It corresponds to both "*potestas/potestad*" (Sánchez Agesta) and "*imperium*" (Palti). This alternation indicates an ongoing shift in emphasis: on the one hand, *potestas* may be highlighted to indicate—in Diego de Covarrubias's formulation—that the sovereign is one who does not recognize anyone legally higher than himself [qui superiorem neminem habet in eius principatu] (the decisionist version of Covarrubias's notion is Jean Bodin's *potestas soluta*—the *puissance souveraine*

that is independent of the law). On the other hand, *imperium* seems to have been used more often to designate the delegated nature of sovereignty as it is exercised by deputies or magistrates in a correct constitutional or theo-political setting (from the Roman magistrate to the divinely anointed Holy Roman Emperor). The scholar concerned with the origin and transmission of sovereignty—especially with the emergence of the people, the nation, and the legislative assembly as sovereignty's depositaries—is more inclined to favor the term *imperium*, as did the Jesuit jurists and theologians studied in chapter 2, and encouraged to do so by Cicero's use of *summum imperium* and *imperia et potestates* as equivalent phrasings.

12. For a surprisingly candid exposition of these ideas, see Sergio Arboleda, *La República en la América española* 148, 240–41, 257–60. The author's shocking notion that Colombia, as a monolithically Catholic nation (although the Constitution of 1863 suggested otherwise by not naming a single form of worship and decreeing the separation of Church and state), should actively persecute religious dissenters is qualified in a later passage (262). About one-half of the pieces composing Arboleda's book first appeared in the Conservative newspaper *La República* in 1869. The remaining articles were first published in a variety of venues in the ensuing years through 1874, showing that his ideas predate the articulation of Regeneración politics and were congenial to it.

13. Various surveys conducted around this time showed that virtually all Neogranadines identified themselves formally as Catholic, which was not incompatible with their wanting—in very great numbers—the separation of Church and state. Art. 41 of the 1886 Constitution established that "Primary instruction will be free of charge at state schools and compulsory only to the extent that the law so decrees." Art. 3 of Law 39 (1903), promulgated under the grammarian-educator José Manuel Marroquín's presidency, made the marginalization explicit: "Primary instruction financed by the state will be free of charge and noncompulsory [no obligatoria]" (*Compilación de disposiciones* 7, 12). Additional laws (35 of 1888; 34 of 1892; 44 of 1918) and constitutional reforms ensured that the majority of children remained unschooled through 1936 and that all public instruction be conducted "in conformity with the Catholic religion" as still indicated in the edition of Colombia's *Código civil* published that year (5).

14. Stirner qtd. in Calasso (55); Núñez qtd. in Valderrama Andrade (15). Núñez pronounced these words as President of the Senate, where he was charged with investing Julián Trujillo with the office of president of the republic. He declined the interim presidency in 1882, upon the death of the incumbent (he was the first in line of succession or *primer designado*). He did this so that he could run for President of the Sovereign State of Bolívar, which would secure him at least one of the nine state votes that were at stake in the subsequent election to the country's highest office. Each federated state carried a single electoral vote, which was formally issued by its Legislative Assembly, but which often represented more narrowly the regional president's preferences. This circumstance made it very tempting for the central government to intrude in the affairs of each state (militarily or politically) despite the provisions against intervention consecrated in the Constitution of 1863.

15. Although admittedly a less frequent occurrence, individual members of a well-known Liberal or Conservative family could come to profess a political creed

at odds with their lineage, as happened with the Arboledas, the Mosqueras, the Sampers, or the Rivas.

16. Former (and future) heads of state were not exempted from these penalties, as was the case with Caro and Santiago Pérez. The rationale behind such penalties was the alleviation of the fiscal crisis at the root of each war, which the armed conflict normally worsened.

17. Between 1877 and 1880, Antioquia had a series of three Liberal presidents imposed by the central government on the Legislative Assembly after the Conservative defeat in the war of 1876. It was merely an interruption in a long period of Conservative regional hegemony (Antioquia was a cradle of conservatism). If Isaacs had proceeded to the battlefield, he would have had to fight two *antioqueño* generals, the Conservative Gregorio Vergara and the independent Liberal Tomás Rengifo (President of the Sovereign State), who had Holguín's and Núñez's support respectively because their common enemy was the radicalism now represented by Conto and Isaacs.

18. Many years later, in March of 1897, Martínez Silva also wrote in *El Repertorio Colombiano* that the unused paper confiscated by Núñez's government upon arbitrarily closing down in 1885—through a verbal order—Santiago Pérez's *El Relator* was ironically used "to reprint the first part of the *Código civil*" (first issued in 1886), in which "the Title of the Constitution featuring individual rights and social guarantees is reproduced" (2: 418). The Regenerators' decision was a belated act of revenge on Aquileo Parra's order—Parra succeeded Pérez to the presidency in April of 1876—to confiscate the equipment of Caro's insurrectionist periodical *El Tradicionista* in October of 1876 to pay off Caro's enforced debt to the Treasury. Among on-site chroniclers of Colombia's Regeneración years whose writing is now collected in book form, I have favored Martínez Silva over all the rest (including his Liberal counterpart in the fight against Caro's regime, Rafael Uribe Uribe, and the belligerent Director of *El Constitucional*, Juan Bautista Pérez y Soto) because of his moral imagination and perspicacious attention to textual and contextual details.

19. Text reproduced in Santos Molano 202–3.

20. This is the thesis advanced by Guillén Martínez (*La Regeneración* 35–42). By *étatisme* I mean the opposite of laissez-faire, namely, the practice or doctrine of giving a centralized government control over economic planning and policy. A more balanced account of the Regeneración's takeover of financial and cultural corporations and institutions, with which I substantially agree because it pays more attention to the role of existing reactionary platforms in legitimating the government takeover, appears in José Fernando Ocampo's recent essay, "Regeneración y hegemonía política." I also agree with Ocampo's scathing critique of Indalecio Liévano Aguirre's and Alfonso López Michelsen's hagiographic treatments of Núñez.

21. Ortiz had recently published his edition of José Eusebio Caro's *Poesías* (1886) and had proven instrumental (with Sergio Arboleda) in helping Caro make the connection between the reactionary romanticism of the 1840s and 1850s (that of the deceased Julio Arboleda and José Eusebio in addition to Ortiz and José Manuel Groot), Pius IX's *Syllabus errorum* (1864), and Caro's insurrectionist and so-called *ignorantist* efforts of the 1870s. Groot (1800–1878) was the son of a *letrado* in Antonio Nariño's inner circle and succumbed to proto-Liberal temptations in his youth. He withdrew from active politics after his daughter,

Rosa Groot, married the moderate Liberal polymath and *letrado* Medardo Rivas in 1859. Although Groot continued to write as a Catholic controversialist and produced a book against Ernest Renan (pub. in 1865 and 1869), he left Ortiz almost alone (among José Eusebio's surviving *letrado* coevals) to wave the banner of romantic ultramontanism in Congress through the end of the century.

22. In Spain, Menéndez Pelayo began to use the term "regeneración" in Book Six of the *Historia de los heterodoxos españoles* (1882) to signify Spain's need to immerse itself in its own past and be reborn into the achievements of sixteenth-century humanism, a project in which he predates Unamuno (Laín Entralgo 114–16).

23. See Palti (127–41) on the dialectics of *vacatio regis* and *vacatio legis*, which enabled patriotic writers, in the early stages of the independence process, to foreground theories of the *pactum societatis*—as a replacement of the *pactum subjectionis*—as well as Sieyès's concept of *pouvoir constituant.*

24. Palti remarks that many of the Spanish delegates gathered in Cádiz, who eventually produced the text of the Constitution of 1812, did not think at the time that they were going to deal a terrible blow to the Old Regime, and in general did not feel authorized to do this nor did they want to (65–66). They were thus gradually unsettled by their unprecedented course of action: first, they would reassume the sovereignty in order to create a new *magna carta* (the most advanced of its time) instead of reviving the ancient institution of the medieval Cortes; and second—and most important—they became intoxicated by their own daring to challenge theo-political reason.

25. According to the later Sieyès, it will take a long time before the "magic of words" [magie des mots] can radiate its power, as the sun king did, to the last confines of the republic. The French Constitution may not yet fill the emptiness left by the theo-political with the people's sovereignty, which (always according to Sieyès) had been greatly exaggerated by the democrats to the detriment of preventive and negative forms of power, that is, the balance between the branches of government and the overseeing power of public opinion (*Opinion* 2, 6–7).

26. This is Roberto Calasso on what Talleyrand called "the mysterious strength of legitimacy" found in French *légitimisme*'s historical arguments: "A vicious circle: Legitimacy is the only force that guarantees the continuance of a government; but for a government to become legitimate, it must already have lasted a long time" (53). Just as revolutions can be *staged* politically only after significant changes in a nation's economic and social structure have already taken place or are well under way (as François Furet, Claude Lefort, and Octavio Paz have argued), so do state apparatuses and forms of representation achieve consecration in a twofold movement involving an *instituting* moment followed by its *institutionalizing.*

27. Bogotá was to be described too by later commentators, such as historians José María Henao and Genaro Arrubla as a "colonial cloister" [claustro colonial] (2: 630). Sarmiento's Córdoba featured a "people educated by the Jesuits and cloistered [enclaustrado] by nature, education, and art" (*Facundo* 168).

28. See Sieyès, *Opinion* 2; Lefort, *Democracy and Political Theory* 17–19, 39.

29. In the 1870s, Holguín edited the periodical *La Ilustración* (1870–1873) while contributing articles to many other ephemeral publications whose main purpose was to gather support for the insurrectionist effort. As explained by

Holguín in an article printed in the newspaper *La América* (August 18, 1873), he had launched *La Ilustración* as the "constitutionalist" arm of what Caro called the "Partido Católico." Caro launched *El Tradicionista* (1871–1876) as its politico-philosophical arm, arguing for the union of Church and state and the resistance to civil authority, which resulted in its formal closing by Aquileo Parra's radical government. Finally, José Joaquín Borda, who at the time edited the more widely circulated *La Caridad* (1864–1882), focused his attacks on secular education, which was also one of Caro's chief targets. In the same article, Holguín referred to the reactionaries' multigenre writing, which was to be deployed for an entire decade, as a carefully planned division of intellectual labor (Rausch 123).

30. The Latin quotations are given in Book I, Tit. II of Justinian's *Institutes* (12). Gaius insists that the primary distinction in Roman law is between written and unwritten norms (see Justinian 8–9).

31. In a recent essay, Jean-Luc Nancy speculates on the meanings of the term *ecclesia*, which he understands as a heteronomous and dissenting community in relation to the autonomous civil polity that requires all the citizens' tacit and explicit assent: "The sovereign state is the state that must derive its legitimation for itself" (107). Contrary to the secular state, the *ecclesia* is predicated upon "the law of Jesus or the law of love" rather than the "legal law" (106, 112). Confessing his disenchantment with the perceived failure of the French Republic's paradoxical religion of *laïcité*, Nancy foregrounds the tropes of "affect" and "touch" as markers of the ethical dimension inherent in the religious subject's willingness to exist in a state of "resistance" to the "gathering" [rassemblement] that characterizes the impossible coexistence of the autonomous and the heteronomous, the Church and the state (111–12). Note that the present book does not share Nancy's objections to *laïcité*, which make little sense in assessing the contested nineteenth-century transition from a theocratic Old Regime to liberal-democratic politics.

32. Bello, *Obras completas* 8: 493; Camacho Roldán 47.

33. Bello's main nineteenth-century sources were the *Code civil des Français* (with the commentaries by jurists Delvincourt, Rogron, Duranton, Troplong, and Marcadé); the Austrian code of 1812; Louisiana's 1822 civil code, which incorporated Spanish and French sources and whose version was completed in French in 1808; and García Goyena's *Proyecto de Código Civil Español* (1851). He also used what were already studied by some as paraphilological rather than strictly juristic texts, among which was the *Corpus Iuris Civilis*, Alfonso X's *Siete Partidas* (which was a favorite text among Colombians because in it the *Wise* monarch fashioned for himself the persona of a proto-*letrado*), and the *Fuero Real*.

34. At the climax of the Olimpo Radical's federal regime, the central government also enacted the *Código civil* in 1873, but its implementation remained in dispute until the Regeneración issued Law 57 of 1887, which officially adopted it as the entire nation's standardized compilation of laws once the 1886 Constitution derogated the federated states' individual bodies of legislation.

35. According to Monsignor Carrasquilla's antimodernist position, one's "philosophical" understanding of the law requires eight years of Latin and three of Greek in addition to mastering the original sources of jurisprudence: the *ius*

naturale and canon law that decisively inspired the tradition of Spanish legislation. Any positive code that contradicts either *ius naturale* or canon law delegitimizes itself and should not be obeyed; a legist who does not have Latin and theology may indeed "read" and "know" Colombia's civil code, but he cannot "interpret it" (*Lo nuevo y lo viejo en la enseñanza* 32–36). This philological understanding of jurisprudence was exactly what modern positive codes were designed to render unnecessary. As indicated by Beneyto Pérez, in nineteenth-century Spain too the "positivization of the political regime" (achieved through the reiterated promulgation of constitutions in public law and of civil codes in private law) was instantly followed by the reactionaries' futile attempts to "purge the public Administration of its regulations and ordinances [reglamentos]" (512–13).

36. The poet Rafael Pombo's father, don Lino (1796–1862), was a mathematician and a geographer, one-time Secretary of the Cauca University, and the organizer of President Santander's fiscal and foreign policies for the duration of the latter's term in office (1832–1837). He served on the cabinets of three other presidents (Márquez, Mosquera, and Mallarino) and in the Senate, and was a diplomat in Venezuela. Don Lino wrote a biographical study of his mentor, the celebrated astronomer, natural scientist, and patriot Francisco José de Caldas.

37. Carlos IV enacted the *Novísima Recopilación* following closely upon Napoléon Bonaparte's promulgation of the *Code civil* the year before. Carlos III sponsored an earlier *Novísima Recopilación* in 1768. Rufino José Cuervo defended both royal codes in 1892 despite the fact that they were promulgated by absolutist monarchs and on the argument that they were not being explicitly derogated or superseded until Lino de Pombo produced his *Recopilación* and various sovereign states adopted a civil code (*Obras, tomo II* 914–15).

38. This is vintage Bentham, as seen in the following quotation, which I cite from Marx and Engels's *The Holy Family*: "The interest of individuals…must give way to the public interest. But…what does that mean?…Individual interests are the only real interests" (179).

39. Here I am not concerned with the alternative meaning of *traditio*—in Roman private law—as a transfer of property carried out on the basis of an intention expressed in a contract, and to which Bello's *Código civil* (unlike its French predecessor) devotes an extensive section.

40. Caro's most original discussion of the *traditio* occurs in "El darwinisno y las misiones" (serialized in *El Repertorio Colombiano* in 1886–1887), where he contends that the theory of evolution is a hoax because no one can summon witnesses (in the juridico-philological sense) who attest to any nation's belief in the "simian tradition." As this belief has left no poem, ritual, or script of any kind—it has no *traditio*—then it is ruled false within the paradigm of patristics. By contrast, the creationist myths can boast a hypertrophied *traditio* transmitted through the generations (Caro, *Obras, tomo I* 1069–70). This is a variation on de Maistre's and Gómez Hermosilla's critique of Rousseau's social contract: no one can point out the exact moment when the first *pactum translationis* was enacted by two or more parties, and no traces of that original contract have been preserved. The notion that *traditiones* exist and that they should command cultural authority allowed Monsignor Carrasquilla to

attempt the syllogistic demonstration of God's existence on the sole ground that every people has left everywhere testimonies of their belief in a higher being ("Sobre el estudio de la filosofía," *El Repertorio Colombiano* 7.38 [1881]: 146–60).

41. Bello did not realize that the fourteenth-century apographic manuscript quotes Per Abbat as having dated his copy 1207. Menéndez Pidal later dated it 1140, and this was accepted for a long time. Today the date is somewhere in the 1200s, and therefore closer to Bello's conclusions than the Spaniard's. After the demise of Menéndez Pidal's *control* of the Cidian field, Bello's dating (albeit not using Per Abbat) is not a weak position anymore.

42. To the extent that Bello does not collate existing editions with manuscript sources, he does not produce a critical edition per se. As Menéndez Pelayo noted, Bello was a practical man and a utilitarian synthesizer. For this reason, "more than on [studying] pure philosophy, he insisted on its practical applications; more than on *ius naturale* [Derecho Natural], on positive law [Derecho positivo]; more than on philology proper or higher criticism, on grammar. His times demanded this, and he wisely accommodated his intellectual priorities to his times" (Menéndez Pelayo, *Antología de poetas hispano-americanos, tomo II* cxxi).

43. For the opinions of a disenchanted Spanish liberal who came to see the *romancero* as the bearer of a *derecho consuetudinario* more authentic than any positive legislation in the years coinciding with the launching of the Regeneración, see Joaquín Costa's *La vida del derecho. Ensayo sobre el derecho consuetudinario* (1876) and *Introducción a un tratado de política sacado textualmente de los refraneros, romanceros y gestas de la Península* (1881). The ideas paraphrased in the preceding sentence are cited from his anthology *Ideario* (118–23), which spans the main political themes in Spain's Regeneracionismo movement. For an early critique of the philological fragment as an artificial text that is neither a synecdoche of the complete work nor a self-sufficient part of it—it is rather an "artificial fragment"—see Vossler, "Carta española a Hugo Von Hofmannsthal" (1924; repr. in *Algunos caracteres de la vida española*), esp. 15–20.

44. See Jaksić (*Andrés Bello* 79–84, 247–56) for a stimulating short presentation of the contexts in which Bello carried out intermittently his research on El Cid for some fifty years.

45. This is evidently not an accurate assessment of the *romancero*, much less of the factionalist *cancionero* poetry of Castile's civil wars in the later Middle Ages. It is even less applicable to New Granada's autochthonous *romanceros* and *cancioneros*, like the ones collected by the Liberal jurist and Congressman Antonio José Restrepo (*El cancionero de Antioquia* [1929]) and especially by Octavio Quiñones Pardo. The latter's *Interpretación de la poesía popular* (1945) features representative attitudes of peasant resistance to abuse by *gamonales*, government bureaucrats, and the Church, among them the ballad "Romance del indio que desconoce su origen remoto" (40–42), which echoes some of the motifs found in Medardo Rivas, Candelario Obeso, and the twentieth-century indigenous leader Manuel Quintín Lame. In Spain, the nineteenth-century vogue of traditions and legends (which romanticism exploited from Byron and Hugo to Zorrilla and Bécquer) was given particular attention in Manuel Milá y Fontanals's *Observaciones sobre la poesía popular, con muestras de romances catalanes inéditos* (1853) and *De la poesía heroico-popular castellana* (1874).

46. See his note to line 1087, in which he directs the reader's attention to a surprisingly large amount of emendations made on the basis of his theory of assonant rhyme and the *Crónica*'s authority (*Poema del Cid* 235). This is the only work by Bello that I cite from the first edition rather than the *Obras completas* that began publication in 1951. I do this to engage Bello's work more directly on the terms of nineteenth-century philology and jurisprudence. Interestingly, Bello also proceeds on the assumption that Per Abbat would have wanted to follow the same rules if he had known them; that Per Abbat's deviations from those rules indicate that either he made a mistake or a later copyist did; and that a version of the poem that showed greater linguistic homogeneity on the synchronic axis should once have existed. In sum, for Bello any correction may be ruled legitimate, even advisable, if it clarifies the poem's meaning, enhances its rhythmic patterns and metrical regularity, and does not significantly depart from the *Crónica*.

47. For instance, his eighteen-line terse note on the fictive "Infantes de Carrión" references over a dozen sources and witnesses to the poem's composition process that either confirm or disprove these two characters' existence (as do the middlebrow *romancero*, the *Crónica general*, the *Crónica del Cid*, other *crónicas fabulosas*, and what Bello calls sources of *opinión vulgar*), as do the main highbrow Latin history of El Cid (the *Chronica Roderici*), the Archbishop's chronicle, and in general all the archives and monuments consulted by earlier scholars (*Poema del Cid* 261).

48. As indicated above, although in textual criticism *recensio* and *traditio* are at times conflated, strictly speaking, the *recensio* is the organization of the textual tradition into a stemma.

49. The international popularity of Falck's writings is shown by the English version from which I have just quoted as well as the French translation published in Paris in 1841. Heinrich Ahrens (see biographical note below) also acknowledged his indebtedness to Falck.

50. A strict coeval of Falck (1784–1850), the philologist August Boeckh (1785–1867) started from the opposite end to reach the same conclusion. In writing about the need for philology to become an overarching and comprehensive science of culture capable of meeting the demands of nineteenth-century nation-building projects, he emphasized his discipline's convergence with jurisprudence (17).

51. The two phrases that encapsulate the *irrationalist* reaction against the popularization of vernacular Bibles are "the harder reading is better than the easy" [proclivi scriptioni praestat ardua] and "the hard reading is more powerful" [difficilio lectio potior]. See Sheehan (97–99, 106–17) for a detailed account of attempts at rephilologizing the Latin Bible, publishing it with a complete critical apparatus that required expertise in textual criticism. The two Spanish Bibles that Caro favored (Felipe Scío de San Miguel's and Félix Torres Amat's) offered—at least in their lavishly produced printings for elite readers—a bilingual text (the Latin Vulgate accompanied by its Spanish translation on facing columns) followed by numerous glosses and textual notes.

52. In the more specialized matter of regularizing toponyms and patronymics, the argument was also made at the time for eschewing custom and tradition in favor of orthographic and etymological rules on whose application all could agree, as in the application of a civil code. See Conto and Isaza's comments in the prologue to their *Diccionario ortográfico de apellidos* (xxviii–xxxi).

53. As Colmenares points out, the conflict between the "Christian republic" (what I dare to call "the *civitas Dei* of translation") and the "profane republic" (the *civitas terrena* over which the *civitas diaboli* was always hovering) was a sublimation of the privileged *vecinos'* "moral duties" as they became gradually replaced by the *ciudadanos'* "abstract" rights. Through the end of the century, the Liberals' "utopian" invocation of "intangible" positive legislation fought an ongoing battle with the realistically tangible "coercion of 'customs'" (Colmenares, "La ley y el orden social" 18–19). This book highlights the significance of *unwritten constitutions* enacted and upheld by *caudillos* and caciques to ensure the domination of their subalterns *extra legem*.

54. The decisive attack on nineteenth-century doctrines of inequality did not come from anarchist or socialist writers, as is commonly believed. It came from the writings of a professor at Brussels and Graz universities, Heinrich Ahrens (1808–1874), whose *Cours de droit naturel, ou de philosophie du droit* (first published in French in 1838; German ed. pub. in Vienna in 1851) had by 1868 undergone nineteen editions (three in Spanish) in all the major European languages except English and was soon taught at the principal universities in Chile, Perú, and other Spanish American republics. Ahrens theorized the equality of all citizens, including the notion that manual labor was as important as intellectual labor of the highest order. The two should be publicly rewarded and used to ground the workers' equal rights of citizenship. See Lorimer (313–21) for relevant passages from Ahrens's *Cours* in which these controversial arguments are presented followed by Lorimer's conservative counterarguments. What made Ahrens acceptable to conservatives and reactionaries, from Lorimer to Caro to Schmitt, was that he did not take issue with property rights and did not write against religious metaphysics. This is what separated Ahrens from Bentham, perhaps the most influential philosopher of jurisprudence before him. Nietzsche's aristocratic voluntarism and Schmitt's nationalist decisionism constitute each a different adverse reaction to Ahrens.

55. See Bonald (48–56) for an instance that predates Caro's frequent correlations. See also Marco Fidel Suárez, *Obras, tomo II* 154–55, 1278.

56. With few exceptions (e.g., Lorenzo María Lleras, César Conto, Santiago Pérez), Colombian grammarians who reached a high office professed retrogressive ideas and had not been formally trained as lawyers. Instead, they generally underwent private instruction in rhetoric, grammar, elocution, and versification at the homes of private Catholic instructors. The lives of both Liberal and Conservative patricians also regularly crossed through their children's private education: to give a few examples, Rafael Pombo studied at General Mosquera's military and engineering academy; José María Samper studied at José Manuel Groot's Catholic school; and future president Alfonso López Pumarejo (whose father worked for the Samper family in Honda) received private lessons in Caro's home after the latter stepped down from the executive vice presidency.

57. See Rama 6, 12, 46, 49. Later scholars have echoed Rama's general ideas on nineteenth-century Colombia (this country is not highlighted in his book) without necessarily adopting his categories or acknowledging a possible debt to him. See von der Walde Uribe; Palacios, *La clase más ruidosa* 148–49, 172–80; Poblete 303–6; Rojas 49–63. Colombian *letrados* were, in Gramsci's classic formulation, "traditional intellectuals" insofar as they were centrally interested in ensuring the domination of the uneducated majority of the population by a bookish elite at the same time as they adopted a paternalistic attitude toward the subaltern classes.

58. See García Canclini 244–54.

59. Ramos rightly points out that Bello envisions the field of culture in the same way as the field of politics (23–40, esp. 33–37). While the Venezuelan seems to uphold the notion of popular sovereignty, which he analogizes to the creative unfolding of language usage (for him a "natural right"), he also argues for disciplining the masses and hierarchizing the transmission of knowledge within state apparatuses, in a manner reminiscent of Enlightenment *letrados* Jovellanos and Meléndez Valdés in Spain. Yet Bello seems less conservative to us than he did to his younger contemporaries (particularly Sarmiento and Lastarria) because of his emphasis on the inevitability of change (linguistic as well as political). I cannot fully endorse González Stephan's extreme Foucauldian reduction of the first Spanish American constitutions, grammars, and conduct manuals to state technologies used to form "a subjectivized police corps, a repressive agency in each individual" (86).

60. These elites had already used the Revolution of Independence to seize enormous extensions of communal land and were now preventing large groups of the population from assuming their rights of citizenship. The excluded ones were the vanquished at the Battle of Lircay (1830)—the decisive event in the Conservative Revolution of 1829—the rural banditry communities, and the native *araucanos*, who could not be integrated into the "nosotros" of the nation-state, to which Bello variously referred to as the "parcialidad dominante" of the "clase de propietarios." See Jaime Concha (153–57) on the grounding of Bello's synecdochical appropriation of the nation in a series of legislative interventions.

61. He did this without downgrading French culture, let alone the French language, and without discouraging others from engaging in linguistic innovation, as seen in his negative review of fellow Venezuelan Rafael María Baralt's *Diccionario de galicismos* (1855). There Bello advocated the need to upgrade Spanish scientific discourse through the coining of neologisms on the basis of Latin and through sensible analogies with French (Bello, *Obras completas* 5: 185–219). He was an Anglophile and an admirer of commonsense and empiricist philosophies, which is why Ménendez Pelayo called him a "conservative in the English manner, like our Jovellanos," for whom the "traditional element" in Spain's culture was not inherently or monolithically outdated (*Antología de poetas hispano-americanos* cxxi).

62. While his appointment as censor (along with Mariano Egaña, already mentioned as the principal writer of the 1833 Constitution, and Ventura Marín) happened in 1832, from 1833 he began to advocate the complete abolition of censorship, an event that took place only in 1878. As an example of a less compromising *letrado*—in fact, a prototype of the public intellectual—we have Hugo, who had the advantage over Bello of enjoying the returns of an immense literary capital that ensured his financial independence, allowing him to turn down the political bribes known as state pensions.

63. In 1884, Cané already made this point (176–77). On numerous indices of material and social progress, Colombia remained the most underdeveloped nation south of the Panamá isthmus through the end of the nineteenth century. According to Safford, "the goal of technical progress tended to have a phantasmatic unreality. In the context of nineteenth-century Colombia, material improvement was an ideal abstraction [...] Politics and political aspirations...were much more palpable." For this reason, Safford goes on, the main

caudillos of peripheral areas "turned easily to military-political enterprise" (231). As I argue in this book, in Bogotá they turned to *literary-political enterprise.*

64. A moderate-Liberal intellectual who had started out as a radical (like his more famous brother, José María), Miguel Samper epitomized Colombia's small enlightened bourgeoisie. He unsuccessfully ran for president in 1898, in a half-hearted attempt to stop the Regeneración's disastrous rule of twelve years.

65. A working distinction can be made between the liberal and the conservative lettered cities in the post-Independence years. The former is best represented by the educator Domingo Faustino Sarmiento (1811–1888), who became President for the years 1868–1874, and the jurist and publicist Juan Bautista Alberdi (1810–1884) in Argentina, and by the Samper, the Zapata, and the Pérez brothers (Santiago Pérez served as President in 1874–1876) in Colombia. The conservative city is best represented—in its reactionary variety—by the Caro-Tobar-Holguín and Urdaneta-Arboleda-Valencia clans. While Colombia's Catholic Conservatives were interested in translating and publicizing mostly religious literature, as I show below, the Argentine and Colombian "radicals" were committed to the implementation of a utilitarian system of education that would stimulate critical thinking and scientific progress. Cané intelligently notes that Colombia's political-intellectual plurisystem during the Regeneración was to the far right of Argentina's when he writes: "One of our demagogues would pass for a conservative over there; and an Argentine conservative would be called a communist by Colombians of that persuasion" (148).

66. Among nineteenth-century social and educational reformers who were accomplished classicists, but who nevertheless believed that instruction at all levels should take place in the nation's vernacular language, are Quintana, Bello, and Wilhelm von Humboldt.

67. The expulsion of 1850, signed by José Hilario López under radical-Liberal pressure, was carried out on the dubious legal ground that Carlos III's banishment order of 1767 was still in effect. This is a perfect example of a legal fiction.

68. For two different yet complementary takes on the teaching and the concealment of grammar as a powerful ideological practice, see Waquet 230–56; Lefort, *The Political Forms of Modern Society* 212–13.

69. For related yet differently argued positions, see Villacañas Berlanga (169–74) in addition to my presentation of Lefort's concept of ideology at the end of this chapter. The *locus classicus* for modern discussions of *pouvoir constituant* is Sieyès's *Qu'est-ce que le tiers état?* (70–73)—Villacañas highlights Kant instead—which also plays a central role in Schmitt's theory of sovereignty. For an additional statement by Sieyès, see the complete text of "Limites de la souveraineté" (ca. 1791; reproduced from the extant ms. in Pasquino 177–80).

70. See *Parábola del liberalismo* (14). The city is where Colombians can invoke the sanctity of a law with no real jurisdiction over the nation's dismembered territory while continuing to push for economic modernization. Although this argument refers specifically to today's Colombia, where guerilla warfare and other forms of systemic violence have repeatedly exposed the weakness of the state, it is applicable also to the nineteenth century. Avelar (107–54) offers a stimulating Weberian interpretation of nineteenth-century Colombia's cultural plurisystem mediated by his readings in the canon of regional fiction and by Palacios's scholarship.

71. Among contemporary authors, the Argentine constitutionalist and human rights jurisprudent Germán José Bidart Campos (1927–2004) devoted a monograph, inspired by Ortega y Gasset's *La rebelión de las masas*, to showing the fictionality of democracy, equality, and the people's sovereignty. Titled appropriately *El mito del pueblo como sujeto de gobierno, de soberanía y de representación* (1960), this disturbing little book must be read in the context of the rise of populist movements in Argentina. Its main contention, which I find reminiscent of nineteenth-century reactionary thought, is that the uneducated masses should let themselves be led by a technocratic caste of "specialists" (e.g., in government, the law) whose legitimate monopoly on decisions is never to be questioned by the nonspecialists provided that the meritocratic elite abides by the law. "Popular democracy" is for Bidart a social "pathology" while the masses' civil "insubordination" exemplifies the crisis of authority that has afflicted modern society in other realms as well (100–2).

72. Bentham went so far as to deny the existence of any form of "social contract" in *Tratados de legislación civil y penal* (1821–1822). For his indictment of Hobbes's, Locke's, and Rousseau's respective versions, see Bentham, *Tratados de legislación* 84–86, 92. I cite from Ramón Salas's Spanish translation of Étienne Dumont's original compilation in French from the extant English manuscripts (*Traités de législation civile et pénale* [1802]), which was the text used in Colombia's educational system.

73. "In morality as well as legislation, a reasoning that cannot be translated into the simple terms of *pain* and *pleasure* remains an obscure and sophistic reasoning for which we have no use" (Bentham, *Tratados de legislación* 48).

74. Ortiz, Caro, Arboleda, and Rufino José Cuervo used the derogatory term "sensualismo," instead of "sensismo," to convey Destutt de Tracy's and Bentham's emphasis on sense perception. Bentham was a notoriously sober reformer (and a chastiser of Catholicism's sensuous idolatry) whose thinking drew upon the somewhat heretical Condillac and the very respectable and commonsensical British empiricists. Even conservative proponents of *ius naturale*, such as James Lorimer, used the honorific phrases "objective school" and "sensationalist method," instead of "sensualism," to characterize Bentham's philosophy of jurisprudence. Uribe Uribe was, despite his bellicose instincts, a serious legal scholar and did not think much of Bentham; he nevertheless favored the more accurate term "sensismo" (*Obras selectas* 1: 78). While conceding that Bentham might be called a "sensualista exagerado" and a "demócrata" in the early nineteenth-century sense of a radical leftist, Juan Valera (*Obras completas, tomo II* 1483, 1473) considered that the Catholic reactionaries were also indebted to Condillac's and Helvetius's brands of "sensualismo," since they paid exaggerated attention to the form and materiality of discourse to the detriment of its abstract meaning. With his opportune talent for always finding the right label, Valera called de Maistre and Donoso "sensualistas tradicionalistas" and "neocatólicos serviles" (*Obras completas, tomo II* 1331, 1385, 1472–73). For further elaboration, see continuation of paragraph in main text after this note.

75. However, Bentham was not prepared to answer the question of why modern societies that have instituted the emancipating discourse of universal rights do not accept the validity of "paraphrasis." In fact, Bentham does not bring into his discussion a sophisticated understanding of the reticulation of economic and political interests and their correlation with class divisions. For him to envision ideology in the way we do today, he needed to have known Marx's work.

76. Compare this alternative definition of paraphrasis: "The finding among propositions having respectively for their subject the name of a real entity, some *alethosemantic* appellative, some one that will be of the same import with a proposition having for its subject the name of a fictitious entity, some *plastosemantic* appellative" (Bentham, *Deontology* 78–79). Elsewhere Bentham explains that his efforts at turning verbal connotations into denotations are often hindered by his inability to find the "name capable of occupying the place of a substantive in a sentence" so as to strip this statement of its mystifying ideology. In such cases, it is unavoidable that "fabricate[d]" names may consist of "two or three words brought together" or that an alternative type of "circumlocution" be implemented (*A Fragment on Government and An Introduction to the Principles* 400).

77. A characteristic example of the translation of a fiction into the terms of real entities is the word "title," which disguises the fact that most proprietors do not have the strength "[t]o *possess*, to *have* [their property] in a physical sense." To "*possess a title*" is a meaningful, nonfictitious proposition only insofar as it can be "translated into other words," namely, "to occupy the thing, or to be able to occupy it (*posse, potes*, to have power over it)" (*Theory of Fictions* cxxxii–cxxxiii). Like many of his coevals in the business of philosophy and the law, Bentham was an etymologist, a circumstance that must also have driven Caro crazy since Bentham was always prepared to argue historically the soundness of his translations and paraphrases.

78. See José Eusebio Caro, *Obras escogidas* 141–44; Sergio Arboleda, *La República en la América española* 159, 174–77.

79. Let me add immediately that Lefort's model tries to avoid confusing the order of the "ideological" with the order of the "symbolic," as Marx had allegedly done in treating ideology as a product of bourgeois society instead of seeing ideological formations as being coconstituted simultaneously with the social order (*The Political Forms* 195).

80. Revealingly, Caro focused much of his animadversion upon Liberalism on two *letrados* whose aristocratic, debonair personae and moral strength in the face of adversity made them a threat to the ultramontanists' politics of fear. These two men were Santiago Pérez and Manuel Ancízar.

81. Marx and Engels also analyze the concept of "right," which in their estimation conceals the world of "privilege" sanctioned paradoxically by the abolition of slavery, monopolies, and estates as Old Regime privileges gave way to the citizens' gradual equality before the law (*The Holy Family* 157). The three Colombian authors who most insistently vindicated the legitimacy of "right" (*derecho*) as opposed to "the law" (*la ley*) were José Eusebio Caro, Sergio Arboleda, and Miguel Antonio Caro.

Two   The Regime of Translation in Caro's Colombia

1. A passing reference must be made here to the founder of modern Colombian literary criticism, Baldomero Sanín Cano (1861–1957), who was a republican or moderately liberal politician (he held mostly diplomatic posts and was elected to Congress in 1924) and the literary mentor of the Conservative translator-poet Guillermo Valencia. In 1944, he ventured the hypothesis that the superabundance of philological works among his coevals and the members of the previous

generation stemmed from the oppressive feeling of geographical isolation and cultural insecurity that the Bogotá elite experienced since independence from Spain (*Letras colombianas* 158–60). To this hypothesis, one should add the elite's fear of the upward social mobility of the subaltern classes and the above-mentioned fact that the grammarians started out as relative outsiders to the university establishment (as I indicated in chapter 1, Marroquín, Cuervo, Caro, and Suárez did not have university degrees). Sanín Cano was also the author of a textbook for second-language users of Spanish: *An Elementary Spanish Grammar* (Oxford: Clarendon Press, 1918).

2. The tradition begins, no doubt, with Simón Bolívar and Francisco de Paula Santander, who combined an immense talent for bureaucratic administration (they both seemed to have enjoyed it a great deal) with an inspired oratorical prose, made most evident in the copious correspondence between the two. Later heads of state, presidential hopefuls, and party founders who upheld an authoritarian philosophy of government and left a significant literary output include the following: the frustrated tyrannicide Mariano José Ospina Rodríguez (president in 1857–1861); Tomás Cipriano de Mosquera (titular president or dictator in 1845–1849, 1861–1864, and 1866–1867); Rufino Cuervo (Rufino José's father, a vice president "charged with" (*encargado de*) directing the executive branch in Mosquera's absence in 1847 and presidential runner-up in 1849); José Eusebio Caro (sometime congressman and Miguel Antonio's father); Rafael Núñez (executive president in 1880–1882 and 1884–1886, and mainly nominal president in 1886–1894); Miguel Antonio Caro (all-powerful vice president in 1892–1894 and interim head of state—nominally still a vice president—in 1894–1898 upon Núñez's death); José Manuel Marroquín (president in 1900–1904); Marco Fidel Suárez (president in 1918–1921); Guillermo Valencia (presidential runner-up in 1918 and 1930); Miguel Abadía Méndez (president in 1926–1930); and Caro's brother-in-law, Carlos Holguín, who acted as Núñez's deputy head of state (*vicepresidente encargado*) in 1888–1890 and as the permanent *designado* or substitute president of the cabinet in 1890–1892 after his investiture in Congress. Among the Liberal politicians who professed the life of letters are Santiago Pérez (president in 1874–1876), César Conto (president of the Cauca Sovereign State in 1875–1877), Rafael Uribe Uribe (Liberal Party leader, congressman, and head of the armed rebellion of 1899), Lorenzo María Lleras (a longtime congressman and Bogotá councilman in the middle years of the nineteenth century), Alberto Lleras Camargo (president in 1958–1962), Alfonso López Michelsen (president in 1974–1978), and the controversial revisionist historian Indalecio Liévano Aguirre, who was López Michelsen's right-hand man.

3. For a brief history of this institution, see Marco Fidel Suárez, "Cómo se fundó la Academia Colombiana" (*Obras, tomo I* 747–54). The national presidents and vice presidents who at some point in their careers also served as members of the Academy include, in the early years, Caro, José Manuel Marroquín, Santiago Pérez, Abadía Méndez, and Suárez.

4. See Agamben (*Mezzi senza fine* 89–90) for another Schmittian take on sovereignty understood as the indivisible prerogative to hide the "undecidable link between violence and right" [nesso indecidibile tra violenza e diritto] and between "being and language" [vivente e linguaggio] behind a juridical form of decision that annuls all previous decisions.

5. Schmitt uses chapters VIII and X in Book One of Jean Bodin's *Les six livres de la république* (1577; rev. 1583) as his main authority in arguing that sovereignty cannot be divided when the state of exception takes place: "by referring to the emergency [and] by considering sovereignty to be indivisible, [Bodin] finally settled the question of power in the state" (*Political Theology* 8). Bodin favored the Latin term *maiestas* (interchangeable with *souveraineté* and *puissance souveraine*) at the expense of *merum imperium* to refer to the supreme, absolute, and perpetual power held over citizens and subjects (1–5). In an important survey of early modern theories of the state, Luis Sánchez Agesta held that Spain had been left out of the gradual transformation of the exceptional faculties into the normal functioning of royal *imperium/potestas* because Castilian law prevented royal absolutism from dismantling the administration of justice embodied in the bureaucratic state (81–88). See Maravall (1: 283–87) for a penetrating critique of both Schmitt's ventriloquizing of his decisionist project through Bodin's voluntarism and Sánchez Agesta's privileging of *imperium ex lege* over *legibus solutus*. In Maravall's words, as the "royal will" [voluntad real] overpowers the estates' claims for "justice," the "limited" or "corporate monarchy" [monarquía limitada/monarquía corporativa] gives way to the "absolute monarchy" [monarquía absoluta].
6. "Facultades extraordinarias" denotes in Spanish a greater concentration of power than the concept "plenos poderes" ("pleins pouvoirs" in the French tradition and "plenitudo potestatis" in Roman law). The closest equivalent in the Anglo-Saxon legal tradition is "emergency powers." A similar terminological indeterminacy underwrites the concept "state of emergency," which Agamben prefers to translate as "stato di eccezione" by analogy with the German "Ausnahmezustand." For a useful yet inconclusive brief presentation of the Italian "decreti di urgenza," the French "état de siège," and the German "Notstand" or "state of necessity," see Agamben, *Stato di eccezione* 12–15.
7. Only municipal governments, as the smallest legally constituted political units in the nation, were summarily *consulted* (this is an overstatement) on the *Bases de reforma constitucional* prior to this document's discussion by the Council of Delegates in 1886. Caro acknowledged this irregularity by exaggerating its true significance, calling it a "plebiscito municipal…unánime y solemne" and a "mandato imperativo" (*Estudios constitucionales* 91). In reality, Núñez and he strategically mobilized their followers at the local level to create this fiction of unanimity. It is doubtful that the people of Panamá would have spontaneously voted for Caro—who never left Cundinamarca—to represent them at this extraordinary assembly. Caro also admitted that it was the Council of Delegates' decision to call itsef a "legítimo poder constituyente" (*Estudios constitucionales* 93). In his 1888 self-anthology *Artículos y discursos*, he tellingly rechristened the "Consejo Nacional de Delegatarios" as "Consejo Nacional Constituyente" (369), a designation that resonated with Valderrama Andrade and other hagiographers. Caro and his fellow delegates arrogated to themselves a *pouvoir constituant* that could come from the nation represented in Congress alone (in revolutionary France, the slogan "La Nation, la Loi, le Roi" replaced the Old Regime's divine-right motto "Une Foi, une Loi, un Roi"). The Regenerators thus assumed an office closer to what Schmitt would call a "sovereign dictatorship" (*Die Diktatur* 184–89).
8. Théodore Reinach, whose *De l'état de siège* (1885) is strictly contemporaneous with the Regeneración's quasi-decisionist Constitution of 1886, reminded his

readers that already in Rome "the expeditious concentration of power in the hands of just one man" [l'énergique concentration de pouvoirs…entre les mains d'un seul homme] was intended to "suppress factious fickleness" [réprimer les velléités factieuses], most often (as with the Colombian radicals in favor of secularism and free trade policies) "the demands of the common people" [les revendications de la plèbe] (16–17).

9. These retrogressive ecclesiastical institutions came under fire even among the liberal-minded clergy, as shown by the Peruvian Francisco de Paula González Vigil (1792–1875), whose works will be referenced in the remainder of this study.

10. Until the close of the century the Liberals often referred to the Regeneración's first and second administrations as a permanent coup d'état and to its decisionist praxis as a state of emergency.

11. In 1209, Pope Innocent excommunicated John the Landless after the English monarch resisted appointing to the episcopal see of Canterbury the candidate chosen by the pontiff, who did not have this prerogative according to the English council of bishops. The "symbolic" reappropriation (*translatio legati*) of John's kingly tenure in England, which since Constantine I's Donation of his powers to Pope Sylvester naturally belongs to each new pontiff, was a juridical fiction (he did not take possession of the English realm) based on two earlier fictions that have no basis in Scripture or the Church Fathers: that Constantine had alienated his temporal *imperium* and that popes could be temporal and spiritual rulers at the same time. Note that I am not claiming that Roman pontiffs did not act as temporal rulers most of the time; my point is that this appropriation of prerogatives had been in dispute since the early years of the Church. For a position diametrically opposed to González Vigil's, see Groot, "El poder temporal de los papas" (*Obras escogidas* 182–98).

12. Citizens of the United States have been hearing time and again in the past few years the Nixonian "If the president does it, it is not illegal," a variation on the ancient principle *licet si libet*—if the king wants it, it is not illegal.

13. Caro repeatedly expresses the idea that those who are not practicing Catholics and do not pledge unconditional obedience to the ecclesiastical authority should not enjoy electoral rights, much less be eligible to hold any kind of office. In a tirade against the institution of the popular jury, he adopted a characteristically denigrating attitude toward the "inferior social class" [clase social inferior], which "neither has been nor is an organized body, but a mass" [no ha sido ni es sociedad organizada, sino masa]. Therefore, the appointment of "plebeians" [plebeyos] to positions of responsibility "would be illegitimate under the democratic regime" [resulta ilegítimo bajo el régimen democrático] (*Libertad de imprenta* 114). This notion continued to be pursued by other Regenerators, attracting Martínez Silva's dignified sarcasm in September of 1897 as Caro sought reelection on the ground that he was one of only "two" Colombians who could head up a "gobierno de los doctos" in which no room was left for the people's electoral participation (2: 70–72). Whether he deals with the expansion of the suffrage, the institution of the jury, or the history of the Indian's Catholic redemption by the benign Spanish conquistador, Caro's democracy presupposes a *concordia ordinum* among the citizens regarding the vertical organization of society and the subordination of all state powers to the Vatican Church and its local representatives.

14. See Arciniegas (52–62) for a short, informative account of Caro's persecution and denigration of Isaacs.

15. See Bobbio (*Liberalismo e democrazia* 30–34) on how democracy and liberalism could be reconciled organically, in a process that involves reducing the totality of the state to a minimum and reassembling its constituent parts in a contract among particular private powers. A similar model of democracy, made possible by the new "decision making ability of the multitude" found in Empire's immanent "biopolitical…social organization," appears in Hardt and Negri 336–40. Hardt and Negri's "Empire" designates the growing interdependence of capitalist interests and information networks that undermine the sovereignty of weaker nation-states and citizen rights generally while also creating opportunities for global resistance.

16. See Palacios, *Estado y clases sociales en Colombia* 87–148; *Parábola del liberalismo* 81–97, 141–236; *La clase más ruidosa* 133–53.

17. Moreover, the Liberal regime failed to fulfill the three basic criteria for the emergence of a legitimate state authority since Max Weber: the monopoly on the legitimate means of violence; the creation of reliable tax-collecting instruments in a well-regulated economy; and the implementation of an interest-free dispensation of justice.

18. This is what in modern times has prevented the country's transition from a repressive state into a civil society, in which consensus gradually replaces coercion. See Bobbio (*Stato, governo, società* 23–42) for a discussion of the interplay between these two forms of community in modern Western history.

19. Caro's Latin version, preceded by the fourteen-line fragment from Baralt's "A España," is included in his *Versiones latinas* (310–11). The complete Spanish-language poem—the ode titled "A España"—won the second prize at a literary contest in Madrid in 1846 and was published in *El Tiempo* in the same year. I have consulted the full text in Baralt, *Obras literarias* (46–48).

20. Dante quoted from Pinsky's bilingual text. Baralt's Spanish original may indeed have been conceived as a sonnet—taken separately, the ode's beginning fourteen lines are a particularly fine lyric piece—in the manner of Garcilaso's sonnet "A Boscán desde La Goleta," the principal Golden Age short lyric in the *translatio imperii* mode.

21. This pronouncement reverses Bello's position on the subject. Álvarez Bonilla (*Tratado de retórica y poética* 63) tops Caro's imaginative flights when he doctors Horace's famous dictum—he gives it as "usus est jus et norma loquendi"—contending that Horace could not mean by language usage anything other than the literary standard—"uso literario"—sanctioned by such institutions as "Spain's Language Academy."

22. We need not emphasize Bentham's and Destutt's well-known breaks with the past. For a representative selection of passages illustrating the historicist-reactionary position, see de Maistre, *Considérations sur la France* 102; Caro, *Artículos y discursos* 159–69, 350. Besides Humboldt (78–79), other middle-of-the-road positions are represented by Quintana and by Martínez Marina (*Discurso* 225) in Spain, and, quite predictably, by the older Lastarria in Chile (264–65), who had in the 1870s become more or less reconciled to Bello's possibilist approach to the philosophy of history and jurisprudence.

23. See Timpanaro (*Sul materialismo*, esp. chapters 1 and 4) for a stimulating discussion of the contemporary claims that both history (positivism/empiricism) and theory (structuralism/rationalism) have made on social

and linguistic-anthropological research since the late nineteenth century. Timpanaro and fellow Italian Luciano Canfora are among the few contemporary philologists who have used their primary discipline of research to think about totalitarian politics in ways that are both stimulating and conceptually rigorous. Timpanaro's main quarrel is with structuralism's cavalier disdain for empirical research and the material environment (biological, biographical, and so forth) in which text production always takes place, a critique that one can extrapolate to various poststructuralist approaches.

24. Among the recent commentaries on the political "delegate" and cultural "intermediary" as an "expert" who administers an economy of *both* communication *and* separation (and, in the case of the Catholic Church, also of service [*ministerium*] and domination [*imperium*]) in increasingly participatory regimes are those of Bourdieu, esp. 201–19; Godzich 236–42; Martín Barbero 117–22.

25. The text of the Concordat is reproduced in Santos Molano's anthology of documents (210–18).

26. In post-Reformation theories of the pact, it is required that the state be progressively transformed into a civil society, that the *vis coactiva* (the Weberian state's prerogative) and the *vis directiva* (the Church's prerogative) be kept apart. In modern Colombia, however, they have regularly invaded each other's territories.

27. In this he is like the translator-poet and the literary critic, who use the source text (the translator does) and primary text (the critic does) only as a pretext for the writing of their own work. For a stimulating discussion of these issues, see Paz 15–16. Significantly, the composition that Caro placed at the front of his first collection of poems was a paraphrase from the Old Testament entitled "Cántico de Moisés" (*Poesías* 5–7). Núñez wrote a poem just as bad—"Moisés (fragmento)" (*Poesías* 82–86). The two poets and lawmakers also dedicated several poems to both Rome and Bolívar (the quintessentially Mosaic figure of Spanish America).

28. Originally published as "Los Padres de la Patria," *El Repertorio Colombiano* (11.11 [July 1884] 383–86); repr. in Caro, *La oda "A la estatua del Libertador"* 138–42.

29. Although he refrains from citing Jaime Balmes, these ideas read almost like a paraphrase from the Catalan prelate's article "Lo que no se quiere y lo que se quiere" (1844). Balmes, the main spokesman for the Partido Monárquico Nacional at the Spanish national election of that year, rejected the notion of "the people's sovereignty." Instead he called for a "sovereign king" and a new constitutional charter in which the spirit of the century would allow Isabel II's Catholic monarchists [i.e., *el elemento tradicional español*] to remain "hegemonic" (*preponderancia* is the word in the Spanish original) without alienating the ultramontane *carlistas* or contradicting "Spain's national temperament" [*el temperamento de la nación española*] (752–53).

30. Caro stressed the practice of "plebiscitary legitimacy" to the detriment of "the legality of the legislative state" (see Schmitt, *Legality and Legitimacy* 62). However, the Colombian's popular consultations did not happen at the polls, but rather took the shape of what can be called (paraphrasing Martínez Silva) "telegraphic plebiscites." These were the fabricated newspaper reports of an intense traffic of telegrams informing one-half the people—as represented by the newspaper-reading public opinion—that the people's other half—the parishes and small municipalities that Caro had never visited—were spontaneously

and unanimously declaring for him as their permanent president. For a contemporary trenchant critique of Caro's newspaper article and of his absolutist and monarchical style of government, see Martínez Silva 2: 420–23, 411–13. Martínez Silva is very adept at mocking the Thomistic-Aristotelian language of essence and accident that informs Caro's doctrinal sophistry.

31. As explained by Sánchez Agesta (98–103), *princeps legibus solutus* (the *infra legem* doctrine explicitly defended by Fernando Vázquez de Menchaca [1512–1569] and Francisco de Vitoria [ca. 1483–1546]) is the opposite of *princeps absolutus a lege* (the *extra legem* doctrine explicitly condemned by Diego de Covarrubias). However, Agamben (*Stato di eccezione* 89) reads *princeps legibus solutus* as an *extra legem* confirmation that the prince is juridically immune—and etymologically absolved—from the law's constraints. This interpretation is the least plausible of the two in the history of Spanish political thought.

32. Bellarmino polemicized with James IV & I as well as with William Barclay on the allegiance that bishops owed to the Roman pontiff to the detriment of their local temporal princes.

33. The otherwise thought-provoking argument for the derivation of positive jurisprudence from theology and theo-politics has been a bit overstated not just by Schmitt, but by such liberal political philosophers as Kantorowicz (115–20, 143–64) and Villacañas Berlanga (169–79). But consider Gaius (*Digesta* 1.4.1): "that which the emperor deems fit has also the force of law" [quod principi placuit, legis habet vigorem] (qtd. in Justinian 10). Largely treated as the most felicitous aphoristic enunciation of the *lex regia*, this adage reveals the transformation of Rome's republican regime into a monarchy. The figure of the emperor is all-powerful *only because* two previously existing branches of government, each the result of a *pactum translationis*, have now been united in a single office that is also susceptible of transmission by hereditary succession. The monarch shows in his person two prerogatives: first, the proconsular *imperium* transferred on to him by the Senate or by the military qua nation raised up in arms in times of war (a residue of republican institutions); and second, the tribunal *potestas* that comes directly from the *populus'* plebeian assemblies (another relic from the past). After the third century, beginning with Diocletian and Constantine, references to these historical origins gradually disappear, so that three centuries later, when the absolutist monarch Justinian commissions the *Instituta*, he can represent the emperor's prerogatives as the outcome of a rational decision rather than ad hoc improvisations made possible by the combination of *actiones fictitiae* and historical opportunity.

34. In the Hebrew Bible, "Covenant" designates the agreement between God and his people in which God makes certain promises and requires certain behavior from his people in return. It is the customary word used to translate the Hebrew term *berith*. The Hebrew Scripture certainly features instances of covenants entered by mortal beings alone. In Biblical theology, the Old and New Covenants stand for two different Christian adaptations of Israel's primitive Covenant with God, but this need not mean that the *lex regia* can not be treated (in the objectivist spirit of Hobbes, Bentham, and Gómez Hermosilla) as the sublimated and "civilizing" refinement (I am consciously employing Norbert Elias's term) of an arbitrary act of physical coercion.

35. González Vigil became such an eccentric yet popular figure in Spanish America at mid-century that the elder Rufino Cuervo, in his conflicted republican defense of ecclesiastical privileges (*Defensa del Arzobispo* [1852]), mistakes him for an advocate (à la Bossuet) for "absolutist governments based on *divine right*,

to whom abject writers granted divine honors, wishing that the Church's undivided authority would thus be broken into two" (repr. in Rufino José Cuervo, *Obras, tomo II* 1563). Because of the novelty of González Vigil's formulation, don Rufino was unable to grasp that numerous aspects of ecclesiastical jurisprudence are a copy, imitation, or adaptation of a preexisting institution in public civil law. He could not fathom either that the popes' self-proclaimed spiritual decisionism is perhaps best understood by analogy with the absolutist civil regimes he also decried. Just as the people's sovereignty—the only legitimate source of power in González Vigil's opinion—was strategically usurped by the *imperator/rex* (by Octavius in the first century BC, and by the centralizing monarchy in the twelfth and thirteenth centuries), so were the priests' and bishops' faculties appropriated by the Roman Curia. Once again, this is the opposite of what Schmitt knowingly preached in *Political Theology*. González Vigil can be described as an *ecclesiastical federalist/cantonalist* thinker: each bishop and each priest was a sovereign subject of the Church while the pope was not *primus inter pares* in the council of bishops since, technically speaking, the election to the papacy did not in principle have attached to it the office of Bishop of Rome. The Peruvian's other scandalous proposition is that bishops and priests should work first to ensure the material well-being of the dispossessed masses according to an Enlightenment program of universal education, job training, and small loans (this made González Vigil a natural ally of the liberal lettered city). Only *after* this has been accomplished should they worry about the spiritual salvation of this new republic of small owners.

36. Among the early critiques of this ecclesiastical *pactum subjectionis* is Fidel Cano's "El Concordato" (*El Espectador,* no. 50 [March 8, 1888]; repr. in Felipe Pérez et al., *Periodistas liberales del siglo XIX* 142–47). According to Cano, who was well known for both his Liberalism and his Catholicism, the Concordat aimed to reduce Colombia to a nation of kneeling penitents forced by the Roman Curia's temporal rule to pray for atonement for their unspeakable and ineffable theological crimes.

37. See also Bellarmino 230. Among early critiques of modern constitutionalism, the analogy first occurs in the sixth paragraph of Joseph de Maistre's 1797 *Considérations sur la France* (2–3), from where Schmitt most probably took it.

38. This argument becomes less eccentric once we realize that by "people" Martínez Marina does not mean a nation's total population or even the uneducated masses vis-à-vis the nation's corporate elites. He means rather the representatives of small municipalities—the sum total of "towns" [pueblos] represented at the Cortes.

39. René-Moreno provides a wonderfully nuanced account of the public debates held in the Alto Perú (today's Bolivia) by the new archbishop of La Plata, the Catalan Benito María Moxó, who argued in favor of the dynastic rights of Fernando VII, by a "free and well thought-out pact" [por un pacto libre y meditado], and the creoles who defended the idea that they had never entered into a pact with the Bourbons. The creoles were aided by presumably Jesuit theologians who "consulted by heart St. Thomas's *Summa*" [estudiaban de memoria la *Suma* de santo Tomas] to prove that the "inalienable sovereignty of the people" [soberanía inalienable del pueblo] was stronger than the "feudal law of perpetual dominion by hereditary privilege" [lei feudal del señorío perpetuo por privilejio hereditario] (René-Moreno 2: 260–61). Note that Castilian law, which took shape as a systematic legal corpus through Alfonso the Wise's *Siete*

partidas in the thirteenth century, had historically been nonfeudal. Thus, René-Moreno concluded that the "doctrine of the primitive dynastic pact" [doctrina del primitivo pacto dinástico] was confirmed by the *ius gentium*, the historical method, and the success of the French Revolution and American democracy (2: 261). Later in his narrative, René-Moreno uses the word "traducir" to refer to Moxó's attempt at representing performatively the *American Spaniards'* legal obligation to support Fernando VII and the word "trasplantamiento" to refer to the fantasy of carrying the Bourbon dynasty over to America following the westward movement of the *translatio imperii* (2: 305). One of the Enlightenment patriots who acted as transmitters of key political concepts between sixteenth-century Thomistic theorists and René-Moreno was the Peruvian Jesuit Juan Pablo Viscardo y Guzmán (1748–98), whose widely circulated *Letter Addressed to the American Spaniards* [Lettre aux Espagnols-Américains] (1791) echoes the idea of the people's sovereignty as a divine concession long preserved in a visible tradition dating back to the medieval Cortes and legislation, to which the king could not do violence without risking an insurrection (82–83). See Colmenares (*Las convenciones contra la cultura* 190–98) for a brief assessment of René-Moreno's avoidance of grand narratives in favor of a theater of power and an ethnographic approach to symbolic objects and ceremonies, which today we would call a "thick description."

40. Caro was the main publicist of the cultural movement called "Hispanismo colombiano," which spans the years 1865–1905. The broader ideology of Hispanismo (as it was called in the Americas) or Hispanidad (as it was called in Spain), achieved such currency at the turn of the nineteenth century, marked by the Cuban-Spanish-American War, that the word "hispanidad" found its way into the 1934 *Webster's New International Dictionary, Second Edition*, where it is defined in contradistinction to the earlier Monroe Doctrine that justified the invasion and recolonization of Puerto Rico in 1898: "A movement based on assertion of the spiritual unity of Latin culture in Europe and America and the doctrine that Spain is destined to control Latin America."

41. Bishop Otto (ca. 1111–1158) tends to structure each book of the *Chronica* as a series of momentous events in the history of the world, moving at the close of the book into a mournful reflection on the fallen condition of life on earth. In this he follows closely Augustine's doctrine of the two states, as expounded principally in *De civitate Dei*, although he also echoes the ideas of Orosius concerning the misery of the world. Otto highlights the conflict between the *civitas Dei* and the *civitas diaboli*, between the children of God in Israel and the *cives Babyloniæ mundique amatores* (citizens of Babylon and lovers of the world). After Christ's coming, the conflict changes into a tension between Christianity and paganism. However, once the complete victory of Christianity has taken place, Otto treats almost exclusively of the *civitas Dei*, which then merges into the Church of Rome. It is to Otto's credit as an ethically minded writer that he chooses to represent the Church in its earthly incarnation as a *corpus admixtum*, in which the chosen ones must live and act side by side with the outcasts.

42. The language of "perfection" pervades Aquinas's discussion of government in the *Summa Theologiæ*: "Since the carrying out of government is for the sake of bringing the governed to their perfection, that form of governing will be better which communicates a higher perfection to the governed. Now there is more

excellence in a thing's being both good in itself and a cause of good in others, than in its simply being good in itself" (I: 103.6). Following the established manner of citation, references to Aquinas's work will be by part, question, and article number rather than page number. I will only give the Latin original when complex concepts are being mentioned.

43. In a similar vein, in his discussion of contracts in *Leviathan* (1651), Hobbes states that the "tradition," "translation," or "transferring of Right" (all three are synonymous) has to be "voluntary" for a contract to take effect, and that contracts—a "renouncing" of rights—most often arise out of one of the contractors' necessity (73–75).

44. The two quotations from Mariana's Latin original are reproduced in Moore's scholarly "Introduction" to his English translation (26 n2). I think Suárez and Mariana feel authorized to argue thus because Aquinas left his announced discussion of the right to resistance in the *Summa Theologiæ* unfinished, avoiding any conclusive pronouncement on the topic. After stating that the "multitude" [multitudo] is best governed by the rule of "one" [unus] and that "those who are subject to one ruler may be in disagreement among themselves only because of the ineptness, stupidity or incapacity of their ruler" [ea quæ gubernantur ab uno a se invicem non dissentiunt nisi propter imperitiam aut insipientiam aut impotentiam gubernantis] (I: 103.3), the Angelic Doctor went on to state that "a king does not justly punish those who do not rebel against his commands. Therefore, if nothing makes resistance to God's command, God could not justly punish anyone" [nullus rex juste punit eos qui ejus ordinationi non repugnant. Si igitur nihil contraniteretur divinæ ordinationi, nullus juste puniretur a Deo] (I: 103.8). Aquinas puts forth a more forceful argument in chapter 10 of *On the Governance of Rulers* [De regimine principum] (ca. 1267–1271): "So God does not permit tyrants to reign a long time, but after the storm brought on the [sinful] people their agency; He restores tranquility by casting them down, as we read in Eccli. (X.17)" (83).

45. Very similar ideas are found in *De iustitia et iure* (1602) by Luis de Molina (1530–1600).

46. Although Pérez-Sarmiento's work was announced as a multivolume publication, only volume 1 appeared in 1914. The year before, Castro y Rossi published his anthology of documents produced during the gathering of the Cortes de Cádiz, in which the argument just cited is echoed in the pamphlet *Cartas de Juan de la Nación y Juan Vecino, escritas para la instrucción del pueblo, sobre la soberanía y sobre el Rey* (1810). According to the pamphlet's author, Damián Tubiolls y de Gorgo, the people cannot alienate their sovereignty to the king because it does not belong to the present generation only; it is also the patrimony of "los que han de poblar la Nación en adelante," which means that the Cortes' obedience to the king is always a "juramento inútil" and "contra la justicia" (Castro y Rossi 1: 314; phrasing adjusted). Both Nariño's "Declaración" (1793) and his "Defensa ante los tribunales" (1795) are included in *Escritos políticos* 37–40, 41–92. Although Nariño's unauthorized printing of the Spanish-language Rights of Man seems to have taken place in December of 1793, several scholars have used 1794 as its date of publication because this was the year when the viceroyalty's authorities experienced a general legitimation crisis. See Safford and Palacios (70–74, 83–84) for a succinct overview of Nariño's career between the crisis of 1794 and the failed revolution of 1810.

47. The state attorney's philological diligence is confirmed by Albert Dérozier, the first modern scholar to collate "A España, después de la Revolución de marzo" with issue no. 3 of the *Semanario* (September 15, 1808). See the notes to Dérozier's edition of Quintana's *Poesías completas* (320–22). The ode intratextualizes several passages in at least three newspaper articles. This coincidence suggests Quintana's exclusive authorship of the most important chronicles of the Cortes sessions included in the weekly magazine.

48. In reality, *España libre. Odas* was not a single composition, but an opuscule containing two poems: "A España, después de la Revolución de marzo" and "Al armamento de las provincias españolas contra los franceses" (I am giving the later titles favored by Quintana rather than the original ones). This *plaquette* came out in Madrid in June or July of 1808, but its title page indicated no date or place of publication. The two odes were reprinted a few months later in the volume *Poesías patrióticas* (Madrid: Imprenta Real, 1808) along with "A Juan de Padilla," "A la invención de la imprenta," "El Panteón del Escorial," and "A la expedición española para propagar la vacuna." They were preceded by an "Advertencia" in which the author explains that some of these poems (e.g., "A Juan de Padilla") had been written eleven years previously but were left unpublished for fear of retaliation.

49. Quintana's position on the American colonies' independence is further complicated by the fact that he was the writer of the "Proclama del Consejo de Regencia de España e Indias a los americanos españoles (14 de febrero de 1810)," which was published across the Americas (I have consulted the reprint in the *Gaceta de Buenos Aires* [June 9, 1810]: 1–7). Two years after Quintana wrote this document, Nariño was still mocking the terms of the address in his periodical *La Bagatela*, no. 32 (February 9, 1812): 123. However, in the poem "A la expedición española para propagar la vacuna en América bajo la dirección de don Francisco Balmis" (1806), Quintana had advised Balmis to stay in America because in Spain the "light" of "reason" and "virtue" has been extinguished; only in America "sagrado asilo/ Tendrán la paz, la independencia hermosa" (*Obras completas* 5–6). Quintana also plagiarized himself—that is, he intratextualized this poem—in "A Spaniard's Address" [Discurso de un español a los Diputados de Cortes] (pub. in *El Observador* [September 21, 1810]), but this time he argued that the "lights" did not need to exile themselves from the "Continent" to America, in a sort of *translatio libertatis*—"freedom" did not need to "abandon a people that did not deserve it"—but rather could flourish again on native soil (Castro y Rossi 1: 145). In the "Editors' Note" to the chronicle published in issue no. 41 (January 17, 1811) of the *Semanario Patriótico*, Quintana stated that he favored treating the Americans on the basis of "equality with the metropolis in the principle of representation." At the same, however he contended that discussing now how many representatives each American province could have was pointless, given the fact that the Americans had other long-standing complaints against the metropolis and the extraordinary Cortes could not change the terms of representation without violating the principle of representation on which the *assemblée constituante* had been established (Durán López 165–66).

50. Caro uses the same quotation—*Non est potestas nisi a Deo*—without referencing Saint Paul or Cuervo in *Estudio sobre el utilitarismo* (*Obras, tomo I* 141).

51. In the quotation from Bolívar's letter to General Juan José Flores of November 9, 1830, which Caro uses as one of his epigraphs in the ode "A la estatua del Libertador," the word "revolution" found in the original letter was silently

replaced by the word "independence." See Caro, *La oda "A La estatua del Libertador"* 49, 54 n1.

52. Patrilinear and patriarchal models of government, which originated by analogy with the authority derived from biological procreation, run through most Aristotelian political philosophies (including Scholasticism). John Locke, in his *Second Treatise on Government* (1690), dismisses this authority as illegitimate on the basis that it takes place independently of the principle of consent on which he anchors civil government. See Bobbio (*Stato, governo, società* 68–70) for a good summary of "paternal power" [potere paterno] debates.

53. Interestingly, Caro was not particularly drawn to Dante, perhaps because *De monarchia* comes close to arguing for the separation of Church and state and declares that as a temporal ruler the Holy Roman Emperor derives his sovereignty from the people although sovereignty comes ultimately from God. This argument anticipates some of Francisco Suárez's doctrines. Caro nevertheless *returned* Canto II of Dante's *Inferno* to the theologically more conducive Latin language that the Florentine should have used in writing his spiritual epic in the first place. This is the canto that controversially conflates Aeneas with Saint Peter and his "successors"—the popes—as the providential holders of Rome's temporal *imperium* (Caro, *Versiones latinas* 328–37).

54. This he may have learned from the bitter experiences of two of his illustrious namesakes: Emperors Otto I, who was the first king of Germany to be crowned Holy Emperor in Rome in 962, and Otto III, who challenged Pope Gregorius VII's claim to have absolute rule over the bishops of Germany and over emperors even in the temporal *civitas mundi*.

55. For a modern critique by a historical theologian, see Chenu 265–68. The explanation set forth in this paragraph is my own.

56. See Frankl's article for a useful discussion of Jiménez de Quesada's complex ideology, which draws on both the Scholastic defense of the Indians and the absoluteness of the Augustinian *civitas Dei*.

57. According to a widely accepted liberal doctrine, there was no *imperium* above and beyond the state, whose sovereignty was embodied by a parliament formed upon the completion of a free electoral process (often carried out through an indirect suffrage) in which increasing numbers of the adult male population were to enjoy the right to vote. Federalism complicated this regime by splitting the legislative prerogative between local and central sovereign powers.

58. The text in which the dogma of infallibility was made public, the "First Dogmatic Constitution on the Church of Rome," is reproduced as an appendix on pp. 746–51 of Arthur's work. As Arthur explains, while he was writing his book (1876–1877), the papacy recognized that the only head of state who had implemented the *Syllabus errorum* was Ecuador's dictator Gabriel García Moreno, who ruled the country with the help of the Church and the landowning class between 1861 and 1875, the year of his assassination (236).

59. In the 1903 sonnet "Search for Him in Rome" [Buscadle en Roma], which also transvaluates Quevedo's Roma sonnet, the object of the pilgrim's awe is not the ruins of the Eternal City, but the figure of the captive pontiff—surrounded in 1903 by the *civitas diaboli* of the Liberal dominated and corrupt Kingdom of Rome—referred to as "Majestad cautiva" (Caro, *Obras poéticas: Sonetos—Cantilenas* 155). The fixation with the early modern poetry devoted to Rome's ruins was passed on to Cuervo, who collected a handful of lesser-known European texts in 1908.

60. Caro's reference is to article 80 of the *Syllabus*, which stigmatizes as an error the view that "[t]he Roman Pontiff can and ought to reconcile himself to, and agree with, progress, liberalism, and modern civilization" (Arthur 732). In 1873 José María Samper had attacked the *Syllabus* in print, accusing Pope Pius IX of trying to assert his "temporal power" at a time when he could no longer effectively claim control over the city of Rome and the Papal States. A recent convert from disbelief to Catholicism, and at the time still a moderate Liberal (he would eventually lend his support to the Partido Nacional in the early stages of the Regeneración), Samper also argued vehemently for reconciling technological progress with the teaching of the Gospels in a country that should nevertheless continue to honor the freedom of worship (*Los partidos en Colombia* 117–21). Samper married a reactionary publicist and textbook writer, Soledad Acosta de Samper. As late as 1888, and with the belligerent Colombian Church recently reenergized after Holguín and Caro had the Concordat signed, the wealthy and refined Acosta de Samper continued the Conservative tradition of ranting against economic interest and earthly pursuits in her unfortunate book of catechesis, *Domingos de la familia cristiana*, which collected her contributions to the popular magazine *El Domingo de la Familia Cristiana*. Published in Bogotá in book form in 1889, it was preceded by the endorsements from five Colombian prelates. The book was reprinted in Paris by Garnier Hermanos in 1896, in an expensive edition that would certainly not reach any of the barely literate poor children to whom it was addressed as an exercise in missionary oral catechesis.

61. Ortiz devotes a chapter of *Las Sirenas* to interpreting the entire course of human history as an entropic process of irreversible sickness and degeneration unto death using as his only authority the account of Adam's fall found in Genesis. Original sin would have made impossible the Benthamites' pleasure-seeking existence: "Let pagan and sensualist philosophies…explain this complete and radical degradation, to which Christian doctrine finds an easy solution in the concepts of original sin and the transmission of guilt [la transmisión de la culpa]" (*Las Sirenas* 43). See Arrieta (117–20) for a mocking yet lucid critique of Ortiz's obsession with suffering, penance, and the expiation of sins.

62. Aquinas refuted generationism in *Summa Theologiæ* I: 90.2; I: 98.2. A slightly different doctrine, called "traducianism," to which Augustine was also drawn (he was characteristically torn between the two), stated that the body and the soul had been created at the same time, and so were also carried over together in a *traductio*. For a full discussion of the tropes *tradux peccati* and *peccatum ex traduce* in Augustine, see Beatrice, esp. 41–46, 98–104.

63. See also Donoso Cortés 2: 595.

64. See especially Schmitt's *Political Theology*, where he defines "sovereignty" as "the authority to suspend valid law" (9), and "sovereign" as "he who decides on the exception" (5). The "exception," in turn, "is that which…defies general codification, but…simultaneously reveals a specifically juristic element—the decision in absolute purity" (13). An alternative definition of sovereignty based on Sieyès's concept of *pouvoir constituant*, which an agent of the state can claim for himself instead of acting simply as its deputy, appears in *Die Diktatur* (194). Schmitt hastily states that decisionist models of sovereignty were widespread in the seventeenth century. I have provided enough evidence above showing that in the Spanish world the doctrines of the *pactum* were just as central to debates about sovereignty.

65. Donoso Cortés's two main phrasings are these: (1) in the long "Carta al director de la *Revue des deux mondes* (15 de noviembre de 1852)" he writes

"feuding nations" [razas disputadoras] (2: 777); and (2) in the "Carta al director del 'Heraldo' (30 de abril de 1852)" he writes, "peoples single mindedly devoted to arguing" [pueblos…*puramente discutidores*] (2: 741; emphasis in the original). Schmitt adapts these phrases as "clase discutidora": "Die Bourgeoisie definiert er geradezu als eine 'diskutierende Klasse', una clasa [sic] discutidora" (*Politische Theologie* 52). With the same spelling mistake, the phrase reappears in a later essay (*Donoso Cortés in gesamteuropäischer Interpretation* 35). Most likely, Donoso's coinage comes from Joseph de Maistre's *Du Pape* (1819–1821). In the first Spanish edition of this work, published in 1824, we read: "The Catholic Church is not litigious by nature; rather, it has faith without feuding" [La Iglesia católica no es disputadora por su naturaleza; sino que cree sin disputar] (1: 15). Another possible source would be Jaime Balmes's 1844 short essay "La discusión y el gobierno" (447–50).

66. For the complete composition and publishing history of Caro's translations of Virgil, begun in 1861, see Rivas Sacconi, *El latín en Colombia* 356–57 nn11–12. His Spanish rendition of the Latin poet's complete works appeared in 1873–1876. His other volumes of translated poetry published in his lifetime were *Traducciones poéticas* (1889) and *Poesías de Sully-Prudhomme* (1905), both collected in *Obras completas, tomo VIII.*

67. I quote from Plessis and Lejay's *Œuvres de Virgile (texte latin)* 377–78. For Caro's translation, I have consulted the 1901–1902 Madrid reprint.

68. Note the author's shift from the first person to the third.

69. Nariño's influence is seen in the final text of the Constitution of Cundinamarca (1812), whose article 1 makes the following three points regarding the legal status of *soberanía*: (1) sovereignty resides in the "totality of the citizenship" and is "one, indivisible and inalienable"; (2) no portion of the people can arrogate to itself this sovereignty; and (3) he who would try to do this should be treated like a tyrant (Pombo and Guerra 1: 311). "That sovereignty is inalienable" and "That sovereignty is indivisible" are the respective epigraphs that Rousseau used in the first two chapters of Book II of *The Social Contract* (69–72). Other constitutions produced in the same year as Cundinamarca's, such as the one promulgated by Cartagena de Indias, omitted any reference to "sovereignty," preferring instead the word "power" [poder], a faculty derived from the people as a whole but which was temporarily administered by "agents and substitutes" [agentes y substitutos] accountable to the people (Pombo and Guerra 1: 397). "Agent" [commissaire] is also a word favored by Rousseau to designate the person who has the authority to carry out the orders of a larger corporation but not to make any decisions in the people's name.

70. Quotations from *The Social Contract*'s English text come from Cranston's translation. The words in the original French are taken from Grimsley's modern critical edition of the 1762 *editio princeps*. Note once again that early democrats like Sieyès realized immediately how dangerous Rousseau's reservations were for the cause of liberalism and the future of representative government (*Des manuscrits* 510).

71. In addition to my earlier comments on Caro's arguments to this effect in *La libertad de imprenta*, see his "Cartas al Señor Doctor Ezequiel Rojas," where he denies that congressmen are entitled to legislate "in the people's name" [en nombre del pueblo] rather than "in God's name" [en nombre de Dios] (*Obras, tomo I* 387–88).

72. See Arango for a line of argumentation that complements my own.

73. For an illuminating rehearsal of this desire, see the poems "The Maternal Voice" [La voz maternal] (1879) and "Motherland!" [¡Patria!], both collected posthumously in *Obras poéticas: Sonetos—Cantilenas* (1928).

74. The paradoxical idea of the physical wound whose purpose is to heal a fractured spirituality can also be related to Georges Bataille's and Roberto Esposito's negative conceptualizations of sovereignty as expiation through self-immolation. In Esposito's account, which I find interesting mainly as a melancholy symptom of the partial eclipse of radical-liberal and Marxist ideologies, the possibility of sovereignty arises for the subject in his/her exposure to the experiences of crisis and defeat. Yet, in this scheme sovereignty would manifest itself not as the action of a subject that seeks self-perpetuation as an institution (e.g., the state, the Crown), but as the subject's response to the call of an *other* that is pure exteriority and nonaction. According to Esposito, the nothingness of this new subject of sovereignty often finds its literary realization in the imagery of ruination, martyrdom, and open wounds (87–111). This imagery pervades Colombian literature in the Regeneración and *modernista* periods.

75. The last two sentences are indebted to Todorov, esp. 163–70.

76. Hispanic scholars often draw attention to the temporal priority of Caro's attribution to Virgil of a proto-Christian eschatology in 1866–1867 over analogous ones by Gaston Boissier, J. C. Sharp, and Guglielmo Ferrero. The claim is also often made that he was a better interpreter of Virgil than Saint-Beuve. See Gómez Restrepo 26–32.

Three   Hugo, Bello, Caro

1. The French original quoted here is taken from Hugo's *Œuvres poétiques, tome I* (791–803) while the Spanish text comes from Bello's *Obras completas* 1: 238–45.

2. Additional poems featuring a prayer are "Ora, ama" and "L'Enfant," among several others.

3. Nietzsche is thinking of Aristophanes, Petronius, and Machiavelli, who share with Hugo these untranslatable characteristics: they show a preternatural capacity for producing "the most delightful and daring nuances of free, free-spirited thought"; they "cannot help presenting the most serious affairs in a boisterous *allegrissimo*"; and they are "master[s] of *presto* in invention, ideas, words" (59–60). It seems to me that the delicate balance of lightness, exuberance, and depth contained in this description fits Hugo's best poetry to a tee.

4. He also referred to the cultural field of the French *âge classique* as a *literary Old Regime* in the poem "Réponse à un acte d'accusation" (1834; included in *Les Contemplations* [1856]), which contrasts "ancien régime" words to the idiom of "la Révolution" and "la république." Responding to mounting accusations that he was ruining the French language with his plebeian words, imaginative excesses, and repeated violations of neoclassical decorum, he writes: "Oui, de l'ancien régime ils ont fait tables rases" (l. 134). Noble words reside at Versailles and the Académie, and have "le décorum pour loi" (l. 44). Needless to add, the speaker sympathizes with the colloquial and substandard registers of the language, whose place in society foreshadows that of the upwardly mobile valet, Ruy Blas: "J'ai, contre le mot noble à la longue rapière, / Insurgé le vocable ignoble, son valet" (ll. 143–44). I quote from *Œuvres poétiques, tome II* 494–500.

5. In a later essay, "*Ensayos literarios y críticos* por Don Alberto Lista y Aragón" (1848), Bello took up the same argument apropos of another liberal turned reactionary, Alberto Lista, who was the teacher of both Espronceda and Pardo y Aliaga, and Gómez Hermosilla's colleague at the Colegio de San Mateo. Lista had also collaborated with Quintana and especially Blanco-White, whom Bello befriended in London, and had to leave Spain in 1814 because of the Frenchified ideas he opportunistically espoused in 1810, when the French army occupied Seville. Bello gently corrects Lista's partisan linkage of republicanism and romantic love with the disappearance of individualism and morality. At the same time, he agrees with the Spanish critic's denunciation of much bad writing produced in the name of romantic freedom from convention. Against Lista's specious invocation of historical precedent (*autoridad*) and "nature," which was the reactionaries' only argument against representative government, Bello champions the dignity of human reason and feeling: "The poetry of all centuries and countries is characterized by the discovery of new materials and free discovery of forms, which admits no subjection except to the eternal laws of intelligence and the human heart's noble instincts. Therefore, romanticism, which is the poetry of our age, has emancipated itself from conventional rules and classifications, and has adapted itself to the demands of our century" (*Obras completas* 9: 459).

6. See Bourdieu (58–59) for some incisive comments on the French elites' interest in preserving Old Regime institutions through the publicizing and enforcement of the literary standard and of grammatically correct usage in everyday contexts. Bourdieu also cites Hugo's writings as the banner of romantic rebellion against traditionalism. Rivas devotes a few pages of his French travelogue to a penetrating contrast between the Institut de France and the Académie, which in his estimation was then still a *légitimiste* and reactionary corporation in contrast with the republican and positivist Institut (2: 461–66).

7. See Pena-Ruiz and Scot for an up-to-date survey of Hugo's politics, which contextualizes and excerpts numerous documents illustrating the fights just mentioned and their relevance for present-day civil societies. Hugo mentions some of these human rights causes, for which he fought like a happy warrior with his children—their premature deaths illustrated the heroic "joy of self-sacrifice" [alegría del sacrificio]—in "Mes fils," from which I quote in Martí's Spanish version (61: 153, 178).

8. Hugo's *Les Misérables* (1865) and Lamartine's *Histoire des girondins* (1847; serialized simultaneously, in Spanish translation, by Cartagena's *El Porvenir* and Medellín's *El Censor* in 1848–1849) were two best sellers in the genre of prose. José María Samper could thus tell Lamartine that he, Dumas, and Hugo were Colombia's three French literary idols (*Historia de una alma* 387). Those who opposed Hugo's naturalist descriptions of urban brutality and isolation sought the authority of French reviewers, who were also quickly translated. See "*Los misérables*: novela de Victor Hugo, juicio del señor Doupanloup, obispo de Orleans, sobre este libro" (*La Caridad*, vol. 2, no. 19 [January 5, 1866]: 290–93). The triad of mid-nineteenth-century authors just mentioned seemed to represent the canon favored by liberal-leaning Colombian readers, who also read Zola. Conservative *letrados*, such as Caro, Marroquín, and José Joaquín Casas, praised Pereda's *Peñas arriba* (1894)—a bucolic depiction of robust rustic life in Cantabria, which the author first attempted in *Escenas montañesas* (1864)—as the greatest novel of their century (Casas 138–39). Not surprisingly, Pereda was

a lexicographer, a political reactionary, and a staunch Catholic in addition to a landowner and an influential member of Spain's Language Academy.

9. This is how I interpret Cordovez Moure's reports—in *Reminiscencias de Santafé y Bogotá*—on theatergoing in the late 1840s and early 1850s (56–63). In Spain, critics such as Larra praised the innovations of Alexandre Dumas's theater over Hugo's, which explains in part why Hugo's stature as a playwright did not match his reputation as poet and novelist. Bello translated Dumas's *Teresa* in the 1830s and had it produced in Santiago in 1839 long after it circulated in manuscript among the capital's cultured elites. It was subsequently published in that city in 1846 and 1849. Since respectable Colombian women refused to work as actresses even in amateur productions for fear that their reputation be tainted, "effeminate men" [hombres del género *promiscuo*] normally played the female roles (63). Note the highbrow euphemism: the primary acceptation of *género promiscuo* is the grammatical category of nouns that can designate simultaneously an individual of the male or female gender without having to take alternately male and female articles (e.g., *la víctima*; *el estandarte*).

10. Not everyone was pleased with Hugo's fascination with Spain's cultural *alterity*, to put it mildly. The French poet was criticized by the Spanish Liberal expatriate, José Joaquín de Mora (1783–1864), in a poem titled "A Victor Hugo," in which he asks the person addressed in the title that he not focus on such unfortunate realities as the Inquisition or Spain's brutal colonization of the Americas (repr. in Mora, *Poesías* 188). Mora became a *letrado* in the administrations of Francisco Antonio Pinto in Chile as well as Andrés Santa Cruz in Bolivia and Perú). One major reason why the French *Encyclopédie* and the practical publications for the professions emanating from it were long delayed in Spain was the affront to Spain's honor contained in the polemical article "Espagne," which somehow corroborated Hugo's assessment. Mora's complaint is borne out by the fact that one of Darío's best lyrical pieces (included in *El canto errante* [1907]) is a paraphrasis of Hugo's "Les raisons du Momotombo" (from *La légende des siècles*)—the Nicaraguan also produced a literal prose translation and a newspaper chronicle devoted to this Central American volcano—a poem about Indian sacrifices of human life that were somehow syncretically validated by the Catholic Church and that greatly contributed to Spain's black legend in the romantic period. Darío had succumbed to the temptation to exoticize Spanish America for both Spanish-speaking and French-speaking audiences in whom Hugo had excited a craving for magical-realist figurations.

11. As pointed out by Rivas Groot, Colombian Conservatives loved *La légende des siècles* for the reasons just cited ("Estudio preliminar" lxxvi–lxxvii, lxxxiv–lxxxvii).

12. The Venezuelan José Antonio Calcaño (1827–1897) published a book of religious poetry in which each poem features the calculated simplicity of a bucolic setting to celebrate God's creation in a prayer. It is called *El ruego de la inocencia* (*Leyenda católica*) and came out in Liverpool in 1876, preceded by a congratulatory note (the equivalent of today's dust-jacket blurb) signed by five Spanish literati, including the conservative politician Cándido Nocedal and the playwright Manuel Tamayo y Baus, to each of whom a poem is diligently dedicated. Calcaño translated numerous poems by Hugo, some of which were collected in *Víctor Hugo en América*. Caro brought out an edition of Calcaño's *El canto de primavera* and *La Fornarina* in his Imprenta de "El Tradicionista" in 1873.

13. A very useful document to understand Hugo's place in the Spanish imaginary is Juan Valera's essay "Victor Hugo" (*El Repertorio Colombiano* 13.7 [1887]: 36–41), which was drawn from his *Apuntes sobre el nuevo arte de escribir novelas* [1887], pp. 191–99). The pages extracted in *El Repertorio* are located in the book's ongoing discussion of Quintana's atheism, Hugo's revolutionary drive, and the notion that poets have been anointed by "divine right" with a special "grace" whose use only the Creator can judge. Furthermore, in *Apuntes sobre el nuevo arte*, the passage on Hugo is followed, with no transition, by a long discussion of Zola's *Germinal* (1885), whose reading Valera found repugnant and accordingly could not finish. Among the Regeneración's Peninsular contemporaries, Valera was, along with Menéndez Pelayo, the most interested in Spanish American letters, as testified by his two volumes of criticism: *Cartas americanas* (1889)—where he inserted a new essay titled "Sobre Victor Hugo," dated February of 1888 (pp. 1–10)—and *Nuevas cartas americanas* (1890). In both pieces on Hugo, Valera voiced his disagreement with the Frenchman's opinions on religious, political, and social issues, but added that the author of *Les Orientales* was the greatest literary talent of the century notwithstanding his feverish imagination. The "polémica del romanticismo" waged between Sarmiento and the coterie of Chilean critics organized around Bello, which centered on Hugo's *Ruy Blas*, is also instructive.

14. For two examples of the type of venue in which Bello's other translations of Hugo appeared in Bogotá, see "Los fantasmas (Imitación de una de *Las orientales* de Victor Hugo)," *La Caridad*, vol. 2, no. 46 (July 20, 1866): 727–30; "Moisés salvado de las aguas (Traducción de Victor Hugo)," *La Escuela Normal*, vol. 2, no. 32 (August 12, 1871): 510–11. Other "imitators" include Gregorio Gutiérrez González, "Traducción de Victor Hugo," *El Mosaico*, vol. 3, no. 11 (March 26, 1864): 85; José Joaquín Borda, "Bardo (Imitación de Victor Hugo)," *El Mosaico*, vol. 2, no. 15 (April 2, 1859): 116–17; anonymous, "De Victor Hugo [Una flor a una bella mariposa…]," *El Mosaico*, vol. 4, no. 27 (August 12, 1865): 212. Núñez published a new translation of this last poem under the title "La flor y la mariposa" when he was President (*Papel Periódico Ilustrado,* no. 95 [July 24, 1885]: 373), as part of this magazine's homage on the occasion of Hugo's death.

15. Yet Hugo's antiecclesiastical stance was not an obstacle for the strategically decontextualizing appropriation of passages of this nature by Catholic newspapers. See Hugo's "Los conventos," *La Caridad*, vol. 4, no 36 (March 11, 1866): 567–68.

16. See Malavié for the significance of the various prayer scenes in *Les Misérables*.

17. See Lastarria (194–99) for a succinct account of the *Crepúsculo* venture and Bilbao's philosophical profile.

18. Hugo is stylizing here the same shift that Marx and Engels describe in *The German Ideology* (1846): the passage from an undivided "herd-consciousness," in which man is different from animals only in that "his instinct is a conscious one," to the division of labor that produces "'pure' theory, theology, philosophy," that is, the discourse by means of which consciousness "conceiv[es] something without conceiving something *real*" (20).

19. He reiterated the same ideas in the writings of 1882–1886 used to legitimate the imminent advent of the Regeneración and its Catholic Constitution.

20. Conto was made prisoner at the Battle of El Cabuyal. This captivity provided the occasion for Isaacs, who was then still a Conservative enthusiast in Julio Arboleda's army, to befriend Conto. The latter was in turn friends with one of Julio's kinsmen, Simón Arboleda y Arboleda (1824–1883), who during the war fought on the side opposing the Conservative Julio—that of General Mosquera (Julio's uncle). Like his *letrado* brother José Rafael (1832–1890), Simón started out as a *mosquerista*. He then moved closer to Liberalism as Mosquera also enacted a shift to the left. José Rafael later acted as secretary to former radical-Liberal president José Hilario López and finally became a *nuñista*. Conto dedicated to Simón the postwar poem "The Homecoming" [La vuelta al hogar], written in 1864 (included in *Versos* 69–72). Patronymic combinations such as "Holguín y Holguín," "Valencia y Valencia," or "Muñoz y Muñoz" (all aristocratic lineages) are not infrequent in Colombia's history since members of the aristocracy often tried to marry close relatives to ensure the clan's ownership of the land and to keep their genealogy's symbolic capital off limits for the parvenus.

21. García Mazo's had recently published a *Catecismo de la doctrina cristiana explicado; o, Explicaciones del Astete que convienen también al Ripalda* (París/México: Ch. Bouret, 1882).

22. The version of the Latin Vulgate published in 1790–1793 by the Escolapian Father, Felipe Scío de San Miguel (1738–1796), proved to be both successful and controversial. He was responsible for reorganizing religious primary instruction in Castile (for that purpose he wrote a *Método uniforme para las Escuelas Pías* [1780]). This service earned him the appointment as preceptor to the future king Fernando VII and the bishopric of Segovia in 1795. A theologian, publicist, and pioneering historian of Catalan literature, Félix Torres Amat (1772–1847) became bishop of Astorga in 1835 and senator for Barcelona in 1837. Both Carlos IV and Fernando VII asked him to produce a new translation of the Scripture. The first edition appeared in 1821–1823.

23. The Latin Vulgate and Torres Amat's translation read: "Por tanto, buscad primero el reino de Dios y su justicia; que todo lo demás se os dará por añadidura" [Verumtamen quaerite primùm regnum Dei, et justitiam ejus: et haec omnia adjicientur vobis].

24. This is also the argument of his 1840 poem "El pobre" (*Obras escogidas* 7). Perhaps the best-known poem about "Charity," regarded by Colombian retrogrades as a theological virtue *only* (i.e., if you are not Catholic, your helping the needy is *not* Charity), is Julio Arboleda's "La Caridad" (repr. in *Papel Periódico Ilustrado,* no. 15 [May 12, 1882]: 245–46). José Manuel Groot went even further in his article "La sociedad y el Evangelio" (*El Catolicismo* [October 15, 1850]), arguing that it was heretical to embrace "socialist" or "communist" ideas in imitation of "the latest Paris revolution" because in the Gospel, Jesus—by a "divine oracle"—justified the need for any Christian society to preserve the numbers of the poor so that they could be saved all the more easily while the rich could continue to exercise the virtue of Charity (*Obras escogidas* 135–42). Miguel Antonio edited important collections by his father, Arboleda, and Groot.

25. The most candid expression of this opinion was, as always, Sergio Arboleda's; for him the Republic's "felicitous neglect" of female instruction had prevented America from turning entirely into a "materialist" continent (*La República en la América española* 115–16). Not all Catholics shared this opinion, as seen in

Medardo Rivas's shorter essays of 1869 ("La escuela ayer") and 1874 ("La escuela hoy"), which praise the Liberals' reform of primary education, and particularly the intellectual elevation of women through the founding of Colombia's first women's teacher-college [Escuela Normal] (1: 323–32).

26. The Spanish translator Pedraza y Páez, whose undated version must have come out ca. 1912, produced an extremely literal prose rendition of this passage: "no me corresponde a mí, cuya alma está llena de errores y vacía de fe, rezar por el género humano, porque mi voz es deficiente acaso, Dios mío, para rezar por mí mismo" (Hugo, *Rayos y sombras* 293). One important reason why Bello may have been drawn to "La prière pour tous" is that he lost an eight-year-old daughter, Dolores Isabel, in January of 1843, the same year in which he composed his Spanish version. Hugo's other daughter, Léopoldine, also drowned in a boat accident in 1843.

27. For a sampling of these early responses, see the editor's summary in Hugo, *Œuvres poétiques, tome I* 1395–96 n.1.

28. See Hugo, "Prologue à *Œuvres* de W. Shakespeare" (bilingual text repr. in Lafarga 400); Martí 61: 143–48.

29. An earlier Spanish version of "Mes fils" was published the year before in book form: *Mis hijos (Por Victor Hugo. De la cuarta edición francesa)*, trans. Eduardo Marquina (Madrid: Dirección de La España Literaria, 1874). It was reissued in 1876.

30. In "Ojeada a las opiniones políticas y religiosas de don Andrés Bello," he states that the American creoles had no desire to be independent, but rather, in the absence of a legitimate king, "asumie[ron] accidentalmente el ejercicio de la soberanía" (Caro, *Escritos* 116). Writing about Francisco José de Caldas, a martyr of the failed Revolution of 1810 and friend of Alexander von Humboldt who was equally committed to experimental science and the cause of Independence, Caro reduces his life to the attempt to advance the *imperium* of the Church in a united Greater Colombia (*Obras, tomo I* 850–52). As I explain in chapter 4, Vergara y Vergara subjected Nariño's life to the same kind of depoliticizing treatment.

31. This was the habitual position among men of letters left and right, including Gómez Hermosilla, Sarmiento, and Quintana, who wanted instruction to be in Spanish, so that the vernacular would be developed and strengthened in all possible intellectual contexts, and because they opposed obscurantist professional jargons. In "Latín y derecho romano" (1834), Bello also foresaw the eclipse of Latin as soon as Spanish-speaking nations have a civil code analogous to France's, in which case Roman law would cease to be the main ancillary tool for interpreting the anachronistic repository of relics that Spanish legislation was (*Obras completas* 8: 493). For the contrary position, namely, the notion that one could become a good lawyer or physician without attaining a complete mastery of Latin, see Rafael María Carrasquilla (*Lo nuevo y lo viejo en la enseñanza* 32–40).

32. Jaksić has intelligently remarked that Bello "sometimes needs to be defended from his defenders" ("Introduction" xxxiii).

33. See also the authoritative opinion of John Locke, one of Bello's acknowledged masters: "In traditional truths, each remove weakens the force of the proof: and the more hands the tradition has successively passed through, the less strength and evidence does it receive from them" (*An Essay* 4.16.10).

34. One of the first literati to argue before a Venezuelan audience that Bello had improved on Hugo's poems, surpassing any achievement seen in the

French-language originals, was the Spaniard Manuel Cañete. His 1863 essay on Bello (originally published in Madrid's *La América*) was featured in José M. Rojas's *Biblioteca de escritores venezolanos contemporáneos* (1875). Cañete ranks "A Olimpio" as the best of the imitations while "La oración por todos" is in his estimation the "least felicitous" of all five (13). However, for him "La oración" rises to unprecedented heights of Catholic devotion in its understanding of prayer as an infallible consolation for all human afflictions (8–16). It seems obvious that Cañete influenced greatly Caro's and Crema's respective readings of "La oración por todos."

35. In 1882 Caro had already stated—contra Cañete—that this was "Bello's greatest and most admirable poem, as many have already said: in it the imitator greatly improved on the original [mejoró extraordinariamente el original]" (*Escritos sobre don Andrés Bello* 93). Menéndez Pelayo followed suit in 1913: "no Spaniard who has read those melancholy and sobbing stanzas will ever glance at the French original again without finding it notoriously inferior" (*Historia de la poesía hispano-americana, tomo II* 392).

36. In reality, Bello labeled his versions "imitations." They vary from virtual independence from the source text ("Los duendes") to accurate paraphrasing ("Los fantasmas") to faithful translation ("Moisés salvado de las aguas"). The most interesting cases are "A Olimpio" and "La oración por todos," in which Bello tries to find metrical patterns equivalent to Hugo's, but follows a mixed mode in the degree of freedom used in each rendering. As Bohning put it, "in *A Olimpio* and *La oración por todos*, where the techniques are similar, we discover important differences in the proportions of literal translation, close rendering, and complete independence" (66).

37. During his stay in Popayán in the early 1930s, Uribe White befriended Guillermo Valencia, whom he helped translate Keats's ode "On a Grecian Urn" and Wilde's *Ballad of Reading Gaol*. Both renderings were published in 1932. Yet because he could not resist a literary challenge, he also eventually produced his own versions of the two English poems. Although Uribe White was a Liberal Party member and held various positions in the República Liberal's administrations (1930–1946), he worshipped Valencia, whom he considered his literary mentor. Together they conceived of translation as a form of jousting in which the aggressiveness of parliamentary life and journalistic prose was sublimated into a polite competition for literary prestige.

38. Without making any of these judgments explicit, Anderson Imbert's short note of 1956 on one of the opening stanzas of "La oración por todos" makes a similar point. For him, Hugo's poem has pantheistic overtones, positing the contiguity of cosmos, nature, and person as overlapping dimensions of an organic totality, whereas Bello sees nature as a "simple marco mental" for the "hombre" who is the poem's chief protagonist (78).

39. Simply put, Bello did not produce a romantic composition. His text does not aim to destabilize social structures or the lyric subject's identity. The subject does not strive to reach an ineffable meaning nor does he welcome religious doubt or guilt as an occasion for a transvaluation of values. Hugo's speaker, in contrast with Bello's, does all of this in showing that the experience of doubt can be more authentic and profound that the experience of belief. For a brief overview of the main social and identiary features of high romanticism, see Rodríguez García, "The Avoidance of Romanticism," esp. 93–94.

40. According to Caro, a particularly vindictive accuser was José Domingo Díaz, author of the 1829 *Recuerdos sobre la rebelión de Caracas* (*Escritos sobre don Andrés Bello* 282). Another important accuser was Mariano Torrente, who paraphrased Díaz in his *Historia de la revolución hispano-americana* (1829–1830). Caro found this information in the Amunátegui brothers' shorter biography (96). In Chile, the first important ad hominem attacks on Bello took place in 1834, when the liberal José M. Infante construed Bello's interest in the teaching of Latin as an antirepublican bias. In 1830 José Joaquín de Mora had already criticized the abundance of French texts used at the Colegio de Santiago, thus initiating the first of many engrossing polemics in which Bello was involved in Chile against his will.

41. For two valuable accounts of Sarmiento's animosity toward Bello, see Rodríguez Monegal 258–76; Ramos 23–24, 34–37. See also Kristal for a balanced overview of how much Sarmiento, Bello, and Lastarria needed one another (despite their constant polemics in Chile) in their common project of consolidating a society headed by *letrados* rather than *caudillos*. In the fateful years 1899–1903, a similar polemic would be waged by the Spaniard Juan Valera (a cosmopolitan moderate-liberal who paradoxically defended the immutable unity of the language) and the Colombian expatriate living in Paris, Rufino José Cuervo (a Catholic Conservative who was resigned to incorporating language variation in codification processes). These are the years stretching from the outbreak of the civil War of the Thousand Days to the secession of the department of Panamá, two obvious instances of national fragmentation. In "Historical Linguistics and Cultural History," del Valle has set forth the terms of the exchange between Valera and Cuervo besides tracing the Colombian lexicographer's intellectual development.

42. Lastarria explains that Amunátegui's biography misstates the facts when saying that Bello outgrew Gómez Hermosilla's teachings on rhetoric very soon. For Lastarria, the *Arte de hablar* would have remained Bello's "predilect textbook" (159), which in turn might lead one to suspect (as Sarmiento and Lastarria did) that their master could look more liberal than he was in the Chilean's estimation.

43. Having been introduced to Enlightenment ideologies through the French encyclopedists while he was teaching Greek and rhetoric at the Colegio de Santo Tomás, Gómez Hermosilla became a supporter of the centralizing reforms dictated by Napoléon I. Upon the French invasion, he occupied the post of chief of division at the Ministerio de Policía General and acted as secretary to Pablo Arribas, the police superintendent for Madrid. His services and his literary works earned him the Orden Real de España, which he received from José I. Between 1814 and 1820 he was exiled in France. Back in Madrid, he wrote for *El Sol* in 1820, collaborated with *El Censor* (1820–1822), and was a regular contributor to *El Imparcial* (1821–1822). The *Arte de hablar en prosa y verso* (1826) expounds a neoclassical poetics and uses a living author (the translator-poet and recanting *Frenchified* Liberal Leandro Fernández de Moratín) as the paragon of the good style, something that infuriated the likes of Sarmiento. A Real Orden turned this manual into an official textbook until the year 1835. Gómez Hermosilla brought out a verse translation of Homer's *Iliad* in 1831 and *Principios de gramática general* in 1835. His most important work of posthumous appearance is *Juicio crítico de los principales poetas españoles de la última era* (1840), published in Paris by Vicente Salvá.

44. In his anthology of Spanish authors from the sixteenth and seventeenth centuries who upheld the doctrine of the people's *immediate* sovereignty, Quintana included the passage in Mariana's *Historia de España* (Book XVII, Chapter 15) in which the Hobbesian *pactum subjectionis* between the strong and the weak is articulated (*Obras inéditas* 238). Mariana was well known for providing a legal frame for legitimate regicidal acts as well as for his criticisms of Felipe III's corrupt ministers and the Jesuit Order's dysfunctions. Caro still ranked him as one of Spain's three greatest prose writers because he was a priest and a master of both Latin and Spanish. Mariana translated himself from Latin into Spanish and from Spanish into Latin.

45. See Hobbes's classic account of the time when "every man is Enemy to every man" in chapter XIII of *Leviathan* [1651] (68–72) and Gómez Hermosilla's recasting of this passage in *El jacobinismo*, which does not mention Hobbes (1: 148–59, 236–40). The Spaniard's preference for the language of domination over the language of rights/privileges to defend absolutism places him simultaneously in the company of decisionist philosophies and in that of materialist exposés of legality as a justification of domination after the fact.

46. Reversing Gómez Hermosilla's denigrating approach, in *En torno al casticismo* Unamuno coined the concept of "immanent pact" [pacto inmanente] or "intrahistorical social contract" [contrato social intrahistórico] to designate the members of a polity's evolving consensus on their unreflecting cultural assumptions, one which is based on a "community of interest" and the "shared external pressures" on their daily life across the generations (41–42). The model for this is not the absolutist theological *constitution* (as in de Maistre) or the naturalistic one (as in Hobbes or Gómez Hermosilla), but rather the development of vernacular speech in contact with other vernaculars and with more standardized languages. Unamuno's choice of phrasing is further clarified by Menéndez Pidal's related concept of "romanesque plebiscite" [plebiscito romancístico] (see *España y su historia* 1: 84), in which (as in Unamuno) one can detect the intertextual presence of Ernest Renan's "daily plebiscite" [plébiscite de tous les jours]. Unamuno connects the questioning of seamless linguistic laws to the making of ad hoc vernacular constitutions that are neither more nor less legitimate than a nation-state's or an empire's *magna carta*.

47. *Arte de hablar* 2: 58–59, 73–74, 179–80. References will be to Vicente Salvá's annotated two-volume edition of 1853, which omits Salvá's name from the title page and the text of the book. Salvá must have had mixed feelings about associating with an absolutist grammarian after he acted as secretary of both the Trienio Liberal's Cortes of 1822–1823 and the *assemblée constituante* of 1836–1837, a political fiction whose legitimate existence Gómez Hermosilla did not acknowledge. In a later edition of *Arte de hablar* that I have consulted, published by Garnier Hermanos in Paris in 1883, the year 1842 is given as the date when Salvá wrote his notes and the editor's name appears on the title page. In one of these lengthy notes, Salvá contradicts Gómez Hermosilla in stating that the rules of rhetoric and poetics are not to be faithfully heeded, but used only as general guidelines (*Arte de hablar* 2: 173–75).

48. Bello reviewed Sarmiento's translation in *El Araucano* (1845), praising both the Argentine and Schmid, and taking that opportunity to offer a theory of Bible translation in which he argues for treating Scripture as poetry rather than doctrine. For that reason, he says, the Vulgate's Spanish version by Father Scío

is preferable to Bishop Torres Amat's. Scío may be more difficult to understand because he preserves the rough, synthetic shape of the Latin original (which in turn is still *faithful* to the Hebrew) as well as its "Oriental tropes." In thus letting his Spanish syntax and idiom be foreignized, eschewing all rules of "grammatical correctness," Scío enshrines the prophetic books' "exalted" lyricism (*Obras completas* 9: 445). Bello is here speaking like a true romantic critic, going out of his way to use the Hugolian epithet "Oriental." He is indeed thinking through the same dichotomous concepts as Friedrich Schleiermacher in "Über die verschiedenen Methoden des Übersetzens" (1813). For the German hermeneuticist, foreignizing translations, in preserving traces of the source language, can function as an incentive for readers to explore new possibilities of expression in their native language. Such translations let readers discover their own language's unused and seemingly inexhaustible indigenous potential, preventing them from adopting excessive foreign terms or sentence structures (Schleiermacher's bilingual text repr. in Lafarga 324–41). Within these cultural coordinates, the native language becomes more its own by being constantly reminded of how flexible it is but also how different from other languages with which it comes into contact.

49. As I show in chapter 4, Caro implemented the same recuperative strategy, but starting from the opposite end of the political spectrum. As he tried to present Bolívar as a believer in quasi-absolutist regimes, he enlisted the authoritative voices of former liberals such as Joseph de Maistre and Donoso Cortés, as well as the example of the later Quintana, all of whom allegedly *converted* to monarchism after a period of fiery republicanism.

50. I have left this quotation untranslated to convey to my reader a sense of Caro's habit of silently doctoring his quotations from other authors. The brackets that I have inserted indicate phrases that Caro eliminated when he copied from the Amunáteguis' text or his substitution of a synonym for the Amunáteguis' original word selection, or even his interpolation (as in the last bracket) of an additional line from Bello's poem.

51. See Rama 94–95.

52. Colmenares also considers Amunátegui to be one of the finest historians in nineteenth-century Spanish America, praising especially his analytical skills and his ironic treatment of heroic topoi (*Las convenciones contra la cultura* 81–82, 157–59, 168–69). His major work is *Los precursores de la Independencia de Chile* (1909–1910).

53. The same idea appears in the 1843 "Discurso pronunciado en la instalación de la Universidad de Chile" (*Obras completas* 21: 9–11).

54. See Pombo, *Poesías completas* (887-89). The theological sonnets that stirred up the controversy date from the mid-1870s and were supplemented by a religious pamphlet called *El 8 de diciembre*, which was the primary focus of Caro's attack. Caro recited his first diatribe in verse against Pombo, under the name "Aurelio," in the *tertulia* held at his Librería Americana in 1881. Pombo responded under the poetic persona of "Florencio." These compositions were published in various periodicals. They are reproduced in "Páginas olvidadas: Ataque y defensa de la prosa teológica en sonetos," *Santafé y Bogotá*, vol. 2, no. 17 (May 1924): 301-12. A second polemic erupted in 1883 after Pombo entered a sonnet at the literary contest organized by the *Papel Periódico Ilustrado* to commemorate Bolívar's centennial. Caro found a lexically faulty line, which he used as an

excuse to write a seventy-six-line invective that was printed in *El Repertorio Colombiano* 11.11 (July 1884): 400. I have not been able to consult Pombo's response, defending the maligned verse, which appeared almost immediately in the newspaper *El Comercio*. The relationship was never repaired, as shown not just in Pombo's correspondence with the Cuervo brothers, but also in his criticisms of Caro's insatiable power ambitions in the political sonnet "Junta de médicos (el lío electoral Caro-Reyes)," which Carlos Martínez Silva included in his "Revista política" serialized in *El Repertorio Colombiano* 16.1 (June 1897): 67–80. Pombo's poem is reproduced on p. 76. Caro also attacked Pombo's sonnets in his own sonnet aptly titled "Justicia inquisitorial" (*Obras poéticas: Sonetos—Cantilenas* 82).

55. *Democracy in America* 1: 310–26; 2: 28–29. His acquaintance with American Catholic priests must have made him reconsider the long-standing conflict between the Gallican Church and Ultramontanism in France.

56. According to Jaksić, Bello's correspondence with Blanco White shows that in 1820 the two authors—both were living in London at the time—were disenchanted with the young republics' inner conflicts and began to favor the monarchical form of government (*Andrés Bello* 74–77). But by 1824 Bello had changed his mind enough to accept his appointment as Secretary of the Colombian Delegation in the English capital.

57. In a particularly mean-spirited article, "La religión y las escuelas" (1872), Caro ranted against the group of Liberal congressional representatives (he called them the "instructionist party") who signed a document endorsing "the tenet of universal and free education" [el principio de la educación gratuita y universal] (qtd. in *Obras, tomo I* 1320). Caro found this desideratum deceitful on several counts. Education in Colombia should not be free of charge because to propagate "conocimientos puramente humanos" using Catholic taxpayers' money was an "impious task" [impío trabajo]. And it could not be universal either because it was not "católica" (Catholicism being *the* "universal" Church) and would only reach a fraction of the nation's children (*Obras, tomo I* 1320). During his presidency, Caro did nothing to increase the number of public schools since he supported only private education under the auspices of the Church. He also held that it was not worth investing resources in primary instruction for all because only a few had the leisure and the money to explore the life of the mind. Citing his own study of Latin grammar and invoking the authority of reactionary publicists de Maistre and Balmes, Caro contended that just as the acquisition of property required a "providential" combination of talent and hard work, so did the acquisition of culture: "Let us not deceive ourselves: the same providential law that presides over labor in general also presides over schooling and studies. Except for free transmissions, property must come into being as the outcome of labor; if this providential law applies to the entire economic order, why should it not apply to the sphere of education too?" (*Obras, tomo I* 1315). The same opinions on property, education, and the Scripture's injunction to keep the poor in the same condition in which they were created providentially, were expressed in Argentina by ultramontane *letrado* José Manuel Estrada soon after Sarmiento—as Director of the National Council for Education during Roca's presidency (1880–1886)—drafted Law 1420, which made "mandatory primary instruction" universal, secular, coeducational, and free of charge for all citizens. See Estrada's 1884 lecture "El liberalismo y el pueblo" (repr. in Romero and Romero 263, 268–69).

58. Caro and Sarmiento illustrate the Argentine's shrewd distinction between the American "archeologist" [arqueologista] and the American "man of letters" [literato], who is also a "fastidious thinker" [pensador concienzudo], "enlightened man" [hombre de luces], and a "writer of his time" always alert and responsive to the progress made by "modern civilization" (*Sarmiento en el destierro* 109).

59. For two related takes on this argument, see Colmenares, *Las convenciones contra la cultura* 94–96; Guerra 360.

60. As noted by Koselleck, in *De civitate Dei* Augustine attempted to keep *imperium* (which resided in the city of Rome, a place enjoying no special status *qua* civil polity) separate from *sacerdotium*, which resided in the Church (*The Practice of Conceptual History* 79). Implicit in this decision is a willingness to accept the separation of Church and state since the state itself cannot be redeemed: *ne regeneratus est*.

61. Interestingly, this was the same position adopted by José María Samper before his conversion to Hispano-Catholicism in 1867. See his *Ensayo sobre las revoluciones políticas* (170–71).

62. In *De praescriptionibus adversus haereses omnes*, Tertullian uses the phrase *tradux fidei et semina doctrinae* to signify the providential correction of *tradux peccati*. He was, to be sure, a traducianist (like Donoso Cortés, Ortiz, and Caro), implying in *De anima* that human regeneration into virtue is arduous. It is challenged continually by the many opportunities for sinning afforded by the company of other fallen souls. In *De praescriptionibus*, the centrifugal evangelical movement involves the founding of a new congregation (offshoot/*tradux*) out of an existing one and the planting of true doctrines into fertile soil (*Opera omnia, Pars secunda* 32). The editors of Tertullian's works for the Patrologiae acknowledge in their "Comentarius" that the third-century Carthaginian theologian put forward an unexpected metaphor that linked *tradux* (here understood as uninterrupted transmission of guilt through intercourse) to its cognate *traducere* (understood as the opportunity for finding new sacred meanings through prophetic apostolicity).

63. See also Sergio Arboleda, *Las letras, las ciencias y las bellas artes* 55–56.

64. He translated lines 37–48 of "La oración por todos" under the title "Orandum pro parentibus" [Praying for the Parents], and seems to have rendered also lines 85–90, which are not extant, under the title "Preces medicina malorum" [Prayers Are a Cure for Afflictions]. They have been included in Caro, *Versiones latinas* 124–27; *Escritos sobre don Andrés Bello* 356–59.

65. The earliest substantive text in which Caro developed jointly his two arguments on the French language's insufficiencies and the illegitimacy of all poetry that is not Catholic is "Frenchified Literature" [Afrancesamiento en literatura] (1864) (*Obras completas, tomo III: Estudios literarios* 18–35). Compare Bello's more cautious remarks in the "Prólogo a la *Gramática de la lengua castellana*" (1847) (*Obras completas* 4: 11–12), which welcomes much-needed French loans to help take account of "the prodigious advancement of all the sciences and the arts as well as the diffusion of intellectual culture and political revolutions."

Four   Regeneration without Revolution—Caro contra Bolívar

1. Tenerani had already executed in Rome a famous marble bust of Bolívar, dressed in military uniform, in 1831–1832, three years after the Libertador posed for him in Bogotá. This bust is now at Popayán's Panteón de los Próceres. At roughly

the same time as Caro and Pombo published their original poems setting forth the message communicated by Tenerani's statue, a young Conservative critic in Caro's coterie, José María Rivas Groot (1863–1923)—the coeditor of *Víctor Hugo en América*—won the official poetry contest commemorating Bolívar's centennial with the composition *Canto á Bolívar*, published as a separate volume in 1883.

2. Both Rojas and Ospina were involved in the failed plot against Bolívar's life in September of 1828, and for the same reasons: the subordination of New Granadan patriots to Venezuelan leaders; the growing concentration of power in one military *caudillo* whom they considered to be a "tyrant"; and the excessive number of military officers in charge of civil administration at the expense of *letrados*. For a complete roster of *septembrinos*, as these young conspirators were soon called, see Hispano, *El libro de oro de Bolívar* 261–75.

3. In the federal system consecrated by the radical Constitution of 1863, the president was not elected after computing the cumulative popular vote obtained in all nine sovereign states by each of the candidates. Rather, each state's legislative assembly issued only a one-unit vote for the candidate who won there. Thus, in 1884 Núñez defeated Wilches 6 to 3 because he carried six states. Political control of the five least populated states could thus theoretically deliver the presidency to one candidate who may not have been widely favored by the general electorate.

4. Caro was not affiliated with the Conservative Party, of which his father José Eusebio had been cofounder with Mariano Ospina Rodríguez, because, among other reasons, in his opinion there were leaders in this party who did not abide by the pope's dogma of infallibility in temporal affairs. Moreover, at the 1880 and 1884 presidential elections, he did support the agnostic Rafael Núñez, whose new *possibilist* project for national "regeneration" and stability included protecting the Catholic Church and signing a new Concordat with the Vatican. When in 1886 Núñez saw his presidential term extended through 1892, in an extraordinary way, by the Legislative Council, he was already the visible head of the National Party, whose policies would soon be dictated by Caro. In 1888 Núñez handed over his presidential faculties to a trusted *designado* or substitute president voted to that effect by Congress. This was Carlos Holguín Mallarino, Caro's brother-in-law and the nephew of another substitute chief of the executive branch: Vice President Manuel María Mallarino (acting president in 1855–1857). Carlos's brother, the General Jorge Holguín Mallarino, would become *designado* in 1909 (after Rafael Reyes's resignation) and 1921–1922. He replaced the resigning Marco Fidel Suárez after having served as Governor of Cundinamarca in 1898–1899. Carlos Holguín Sardi (1940–), who distinguished himself as General Secretary of the Conservative Party, is a three-time senator, former Governor of the Valle del Cauca (1976–1978 and 1992–1994), and Alvaro Uribe's ex-Minister of Justice and the Interior (2006–2008). Holguín Sardi is Carlos Holguín Mallarino's grandnephew. Another Carlos Holguín Holguín, whose two last names capture beautifully the endogamic and nepotistic nature of Colombian politics to this day, was also Governor of Cundinamarca in 1957–1958. Soon after his last reelection in 1892, Núñez delegated his full powers to Vice President Caro (*vicepresidente encargado del poder ejecutivo*).

5. See Restrepo Piedrahita, *Las facultades extraordinarias*, esp. 66–67. The *Proyecto de Constitución* came out with the Imprenta Nacional in 1886, coinciding with

the publication of the comprehensive anthology of verse *La lira nueva*, compiled by Rivas Groot. The *Proyecto* lists on its title page the names of Miguel Antonio Caro (who was its main author), Felipe Fermín Paúl y Vargas, General José Domingo Ospina Camacho (a minister in both Holguín's and Caro's cabinets, and Governor of Cundinamarca in 1895), Miguel Vives Orrantía, and Carlos Calderón Reyes.

6. This official publication would eventually be named *Anales Religiosos de Colombia* (November 1883–December 1886). Caro directed it from 1884 until its interruption upon the promulgation of the 1886 Constitution, which made the opinions held by the journal carry nearly as much weight as legislative acts. Caro then went on to direct *La Nación*, the openly propagandist organ of the National Party in power at the time.

7. In addition, Corrales collects the edicts and agreements issued by various sovereign states, departments and municipal governments instituting celebrations in schools, theaters, and newspapers; the two poems by Caro (the ode "A la estatua del Libertador" and the ballad "La reconciliación") as well as Rivas Groot's prize-winning *Canto*—all three first published the previous year; extensive sections from Samper's book discussed in this chapter; one poem and one proclamation by president Núñez; a representative text by historian Manuel Uribe Ángel; and numerous examples—apocryphal and otherwise—of the Libertador's romantic oratory.

8. As pointed out by Bidart Campos, the exception's extralegal normativity first appears in the form of an everyday facticity—that which "is"—or at least is tolerated advisedly as such by those on whom it is forced (*Doctrina del estado democrático* 104–5). As the facticity begins to occupy the regulatory sphere formerly framed by the constitution, which is gradually turned into a fossil, the need is created again for that facticity to be consolidated into a new, *extra legem* or *contra legem* set of norms that are now endowed with a history, however extralegal this may seem. In a related argument, Restrepo Priedrahita calls this process the state's "deconstitutionalizing" [desconstitucionalización], a term he borrows from Bidart Campos (*Las facultades extraordinarias* 71 n76).

9. This document can be consulted in Restrepo Piedrahita's compilation *Constituciones políticas nacionales de Colombia* (341–88), which also features the texts of the reforms to Caro's Constitution enacted between 1894 and 1986. The charter issued by the Regeneración was not derogated until 1991, when the Liberal president César Augusto Gaviria sponsored the present *magna carta*.

10. The exceptional measures decreed by the Regeneración's governments and the permanent state of exception that Álvaro Uribe Vélez attempted to institute in 2003 show important points of contact. Minaudier (186–91) lists and discusses briefly other decrees promulgated during the retrograde years 1886–1890.

11. See Concha, "Las facultades extraordinarias" (repr. in the multiauthored anthology *Oradores conservadores* 46–49). See also my brief comments on Bello's and Caro's takes on how to interpret the legislator's "intentions" in chapters 1 and 2 of this book, respectively.

12. The executive branch's reiterated usurpation of the legislative prerogative first became a serious problem in post-Bolivarian Colombia in 1861, when Mosquera seized the presidency upon his victory in the civil war. For the specific passages quoted or paraphrased in this paragraph, see Miguel Samper, "Las reformas y el cesarismo" (*Selección de escritos* 279–87).

13. See also Marx (*The Eighteenth Brumaire* 118–19) for a brief discussion of the economic interests served by the state of siege, which could be used to plunder the purse of the republic, creating along the way a new class of opportunistic parvenus who remained faithful to the despot only on that account. The measures taken since 1886 by Núñez, Holguín, and especially Caro—without carrying out a *coup d'état*—closely parallel those taken by Louis Bonaparte in France after his coup of December 2, 1851. A main difference between the two cases is that "Napoléon le Petit" carried out his subversion of republican institutions without the willing support of the Catholic Church.

14. The law sanctioned by President José Hilario López on May 31, 1851 declares that "the expression of thoughts in the press" is "completely free." Its implicit derogation took place in the "Bases de la reforma" or "Bases constitucionales" of 1885 under the flexible limit put on it, namely, any attacks "against the social order or against public peace." Both documents are reproduced in Santos Molano (185, 205).

15. As pointed out in chapter 2, he did likewise in his versions of the *Aeneid* and the *Georgics* as well as his essays on Virgil's work.

16. In his Traducciones poéticas (1889), Caro warns that his translations from Latin authors are drawn from an unpublished book manuscript entitled *Flos poetarum*, which be printed only in *Obras completas, tomo I* (1918). The poets featured in the collection are Catullus, Tibullus, Propertius, Pseudo-Gallus, Ovid, and Horace.

17. The editor of Caro's posthumously anthology *Páginas de crítica* (1919), Antonio Gómez Restrepo (1869–1947), used this fragment on the conquest, which belongs to a longer essay, as colophon to the collection. The anthology was published concurrently with Gómez Restrepo's important short essay "Relaciones con España" (*El Gráfico,* vol. 9, no. 501 [October 1919]: 2–3), which publicized the movement called "pan-latinismo," a more fluid reelaboration of Caro's earlier "hispanismo colombiano." "Relaciones" reproduces a facsimile of the 1881 Treaty of Paris' last page, a document that resulted in Carlos Holguín's appointment as first Minister of Colombia in Madrid. See also Gómez Restrepo, "Sobre el acercamiento intelectual latino americano" (*El Gráfico* vol. 12, no. 613 [September 2, 1922]: 194–95).

18. The ode's original publication took place in the *Papel Periódico Ilustrado,* no. 46–48 (July 24, 1883): 380–81. The definitive version was printed in Áñez (1: 93–98) and in *El Repertorio Colombiano* 13.10 (October 1887): 339–44.

19. Perú de LaCroix's *Diario de Bucaramanga* (posthumously pub. in 1912) records several instances of Bolívar's professions of atheism, his impatience with those who called him a savior sent by Providence, and his disdain for the clergy's double standards, all of which did not prevent him from attending mass daily to please both the troops and the Church who supported him (87, 119, 212–13). In other words, the Libertador was careful not to vacate completely the place of sovereignty still occupied by theo-political symbols.

20. In 1888 the Cuban José Martí also took Vergara y Vergara to task for reducing Colombia's violent history and multicultural reality to a romanticized image of "ecclesiastical Spain," turning the colonial rule's abuses and legacy into a sustained idyll (20: 153–54).

21. In his sonnet "A Nariño" (included in Rivas Groot's anthology *La lira nueva* [277–78]), the Liberal educator and jurist Nicolás Pinzón undertook the

subversion of this topos, calling his prominent coevals (the allusion to the likes of Caro, Núñez, and Samper seems clear) "esta vil generación de enanos" (l. 12). Unless otherwise indicated, references to Caro's ode "A la estatua del Libertador" will be to the 1883 text, which differs in several passages (ll. 66–70 is one of them) from the 1884 version (repr. in Corrales iii–iv) and 1886. The critically edited 1883 and 1886 texts are included in Caro, *La oda* (45–95), but the 1884 text is left out. The two translations from the French referred to above are of poems by Leon Duplessis (a section from *Erostrate* [1882]) and Louis Ratisbonne (the sonnet "Simón Bolívar" [1883]) and can be found on pp. 1368–76 of Pombo's *Poesías completas*. The sonnet is built on the guiding idea that the Libertador avoided combat only in 1830, when "he banished himself" [se expatrió a sí mismo] (l. 13) upon realizing that (note the hyperbaton and the preposition) "his glory threatened the temple *of* liberty" or "threatened the temple *with* liberty" [su Gloria amenazaba *de* libertad el templo] (l. 12). The Bogotá-based magazine *Papel Periódico Ilustrado* had been printing, since its inaugural issue of August 6, 1881, lavishly illustrated stories and poems about the Libertador. Between 1883 and 1886, the magazine serialized five translations (one in prose and four in verse) submitted to an in-house literary contest consisting in rendering in Spanish Ratisbonne's already cited sonnet. See *Papel Periódico Ilustrado*, no. 53 (October 28, 1883): 75; no. 72 (July 24, 1884): 394; no. 103 (October 28, 1886): 98. Among the translators were José A. Soffia (a Chilean diplomat serving in Bogotá and a writer who variously collaborated with Pombo and Caro through the Academy's *El Repertorio Colombiano* and in the celebrations of Bello's centennial), Jorge Roa, José Joaquín Casas, Tito C. Lesmes, and Rafael Pombo. Urdaneta's publication also printed, among other poems, Caro's ode (no. 46–48 [July 24, 1883]: 380–81) and José Joaquín Ortiz's "Un húsar de la guardia del Libertador" (no. 72 [July 24, 1884]: 386–88).

22. The abbreviated titles of the three main speeches on Bolívar are: "Todo es sagrado aquí," from 1924 (*Discursos* 1: 36–41); "Aquí se extinguió el genio-relámpago," from 1930 (*Discursos* 1: 49–52); and "Imprecación al padre," from 1932 (*Discursos* 1: 68–72). See Rodríguez García ("Sobre héroes y urnas," esp. 179–88) for a detailed discussion of these speeches in relation to Valencia's poetry of ruins and the Conservative Party's debacle of 1929–1930.

23. Each produced a translation of Keats's ode "On a Grecian Urn" and both admired Renan's work, which Hispano also translated.

24. The two late-*modernista* authors idolized Silva (Hispano kept for many years the suicidal poet's death mask in his custody); both lived simultaneously in what Hispano called the "real motherland" [patria real] (i.e., the Gran Cauca) and the "ideal motherland" [patria ideal] (i.e., Greece) at the same time as they pursued their public careers as *expatriates* in Bogotá and (in Hispano's case) in several embassies abroad; both succumbed to the spell of Bolívar's charisma and to the necessity of embracing him in order to rebuild the nation (in this project they foreshadow Enrique Uribe White, Bernardo Arias Trujillo, Indalecio Liévano Aguirre, and other younger Liberals who began their writing careers in the 1930s and 1940s); and both took part in the efforts at solving diplomatically the border conflict that broke out in 1933, when Perú occupied the river port of Leticia. Hispano was an expert in international jurisprudence. His writings on the Colombo-Peruvian conflict are collected in *De París al Amazonas* (145–241).

25. The first fragmentary edition was published posthumously in Paris in 1869, in the aftermath of the 1868 revolution, under the lengthy and colorful title *Raciocinios del libertador Simón Bolívar sobre religión, política, educación y filosofía, con su juicio imparcial sobre varios que le acompañaron en la empresa de libertar á Venezuela, Nueva Granada, Ecuador, Perú y Bolivia, ó, Diario de Bucaramanga, por La Croix.* Hispano also published *El libro de oro de Bolívar* (1925), which was selected by the Liberal Daniel Samper Ortega for the popular book series Biblioteca Aldeana de Colombia in 1936.

26. In 1879 Samper helped produce the Partido Conservador's political program. His earlier conversion from agnosticism to Catholicism happened in 1864, prompting him to give up the presidency of Congress and attracting him the understandable criticisms of his former supporters (modest artisans as well as *letrados*) who had fought by his side in the civilist battle for *laïcité*. Interestingly, the account of the conversion was first published as a sequel to the author's *Historia de una alma. Memorias íntimas y de historia contemporánea, 1834–1881* (1881), during the celebrations of Bolívar's centennial, in the Colombian Academy's journal: "Mi conversión religiosa," *El Repertorio Colombiano* 10.2 (October 1883): 97–123. Samper was inducted into the Academy in 1886.

27. Among recent strong vindications of a democratically inclusive Santander vis-à-vis an authoritarian and aristocratic Bolívar is Melo's prologue to his anthology of Santander's *Escritos políticos.* This historian overemphasizes the Libertador's fear of the suffrage besides his frustration at the masses' lack of democratic and patriotic instincts (15, 22). To Melo's credit, he also acknowledges that Santander's behavior was not always as mindful of legality as the popular cult that grew around his figure in Colombia made him out (20–21).

28. Two sections of Samper's book on Bolívar are reprinted, without acknowledgment of its source, in Corrales's edited volume under the titles "Bolívar hombre público" (246–50) and "Bolívar poeta" (307–9), respectively. He also contributed a hagiographic, intensely Catholic piece titled "Bolívar" to the *Papel Periódico Ilustrado* (no. 46–48 [July 24, 1883]: 379–80), in which America becomes "a new and continental Palestine" and the Libertador an "instrument of God" and a "new Moses of the American world."

29. See Schivelbusch (19–20, 142–47) on the culture of bloody hecatombs and territorial losses, by which a nation or a party sublimates defeat into a sign of moral superiority and a promise of revenge. The Colombian Catholic Church preached violent retaliation each time it supported morally (if not also materially) one of the armies going to war (Jaramillo Castillo 300–1, 305–6).

30. In reality, José Eusebio left Colombia as a lawsuit was brought against him involving his repeated slandering (from the pages of the pamphleteering newspaper *La Civilización*, whose directorship he shared with fellow Conservative and future president Ospina Rodríguez) of Camilo Rodríguez and Samper, who was then a brilliant young jurist and orator. Although he does not explicitly state the same, the well-documented account given by Miguel Antonio Caro's modern biographer and editor, Carlos Valderrama Andrade, invites the reader to draw this conclusion (*Miguel Antonio Caro y la Regeneración* 37–54). For an early hagiographic treatment of José Eusebio, see Cordovez Moure (806–9). But see Camacho Roldán (64–67) for a nineteenth-century perspective that coincides with my assessment of his literary output and his destructive role in Colombian politics.

31. In his early youth, José Eusebio professed an idiosyncratic brand of antimilitaristic utopianism (understandably, *letrados* most often feared and disdained revolutionary armies) marked by Enlightenment readings (Voltaire, Bentham). He went on to represent Bogotá in Congress as a proto-Conservative (1843–1846) and to launch in 1848 the Conservative Party with Ospina Rodríguez (President in 1857–1861), who had been working on the articulation of a usable program during the previous decade. Both González and Ospina were among the plotters against Bolívar's life in September of 1828, which may have caused Miguel Antonio a great deal of anxiety, given his father's closeness with both politicians. Two recurrent motifs in José Eusebio's poetic output are the pains of exile and the father's death, which Miguel Antonio took up in a monologue in five-line stanzas called "El parricida o crimen y expiación" (*El Repertorio Colombiano* 4.22 [April 1880]: 283–89).
32. This paragraph is indebted to Freud, esp. 69–76, 170–74, 208–12.
33. For a survey of these attacks, see the anthology prepared by Rodríguez Demorizi.
34. To be sure, the opinion in favor of the freed slave's social promotion does not originate as a philosophical dogma, but rather is a consequence of the obligation to publicize revolutions as emancipation processes across the board, rewarding along the way the services of the limited slave contingents that fought on Bolívar's side. At the same time, creating a larger body of propertied citizens would be beneficial for the commonweal since the new owners would feel more inclined to defend the new country against external attacks, specifically from Spain. About a half-century later, when disentail laws had considerably weakened the landed aristocracy in both Spain and Colombia, reactionaries would continue to insist that the propertyless or otherwise impecunious masses should not be enfranchised. Lacking enough wealth, they could not sincerely care for the commonweal's well-being. This argument appears prominently in Antonio Cánovas del Castillo's and Sergio Arboleda's writings of 1869–1870.
35. Bolívar's republicanism manifests itself (if his dictatorial lapse of 1828–1830 were to be excluded) in the importance given to the balancing of the executive branch of power (the appointment to the president's office for life) and the aristocratically conceived legislative body (the hereditary Senate inspired in the English Parliament) through their accountability to a special chamber and the sponsoring of an active (if at first minimal) participation of all estates in the political life of the nation. The "Discurso de Angostura" (1819) and the Constitution *for* Bolivia (1826) encapsulate the Bolivarian ideal of maximal popular representation and maximal balance of power within a realistically proto-liberal framework. Both texts are optimistic about the declared purpose to "correct the physical and moral inequality" [corregir la desigualdad física y moral] in which citizens of ethnically diverse republics are born (Bolívar 2: 82–83). For a succinct account of Bolívar's mixture of optimism and pragmatism, which made him think hard and long on ways in which the black slaves' emancipation could be beneficial for both the white elites and the slaves, see Lynch (210–12), for whom the Libertador was too much of an "idealist"—the right word in the context of my discussion would be "proto-liberal"—for his fellow creole patriots.
36. One of the judgments that should carry more weight is that of don Rufino Cuervo (in "Actas de Guayaquil y Quito" [1826]), whose defense of republican

institutions from a center-right position (his more conservative side always surfaced when he felt that Catholicism was being attacked) made him denounce the insufficiently constitutional setting in which the Andean republics' political life unfolded. This important text is reproduced in Rufino José Cuervo, *Obras, tomo II* 1143–51. For don Rufino, Bolívar's tenure as dictator (in Perú or elsewhere) could only be legitimated by a preexisting fundamental law that regulated this extraordinary magistracy, which in turn needed to be issued by an *assemblée constituante* representing the entire nation. But this new charter of rights would be impossible to approve without violating the people's sovereignty since decisions made through *pouvoir constituant* have to be reached by unanimity according to classical republican doctrine.

37. Yet one should avoid idealizing the democratizing impulse behind the "plebeian revolution" advanced by the series of progressive federal administrations nicknamed Olimpo Radical (1861–1878), which was often in conflict with everyday reality (Palacios, *Parábola del liberalismo* 223). Through the Constitution of 1853, the Liberal Party instituted direct and universal suffrage (for married men of age 21 and older) at the election to Congress of that same year (at which they lost important ground to conservatives) and the presidential plebiscite of 1856, which they lost partly because of the well-organized work of proselytizing, under the guise of literacy campaigns, carried out by the Church among the working classes. For a candid and compassionate account of the moral reasons why the Liberals could not strip the common people of their electoral rights in anticipation of a massive shift of opinion to the right at the 1856 election (won by Ospina Rodríguez), see Manuel Murillo Toro's article "El sufragio universal" (1855; repr. in *Obras selectas* 89–96).

38. Safford and Palacios repeat this point three more times in the ensuing two paragraphs of the same page: "Bolívar also rejected the idea of a European monarch" (128) and "Bolívar's refusal to cooperate killed the monarchy project. It had, nevertheless, several negative consequences. Although Bolívar had opposed the project, opponents blamed him for the scheme and his reputation suffered" (Safford and Palacios 128). Other hereditary institutions outlined in the Constitution *for* Bolivia also had a republican notion at their root. For Urueña Cervera, the Libertador's "hereditary senate" was a compromise solution to the problem of "how to introduce in a republican Constitution that central element known as the neutral power, embodied by the king in a monarchical Constitution" (94), a solution that Bolívar shared with two other republicans of the Coppet group: Benjamin Constant and Madame de Staël (202–5). A related point that I should probably make here is that the late 1860s saw in the Hispanic world the emergence of the doctrine called "accidentalist republicanism," a position that argues that the ideals of freedom, mixed sovereignty, equality before the law, and separation of Church and state characteristic of classic republican regimes can also exist under the form of a monarchy (Fernández Sebastián and Fuentes 626).

39. The selections from Fernández Madrid's poetry included in Ortiz's *El Parnaso granadino, tomo I* (1848) appropriately begin with the most popular among these compositions: "Al Padre de Colombia i Libertador del Perú" (269–73).

40. The other anthologized versifiers in *América poética* who devote poems to the Libertador are Ricardo J. Bustamante, José Antonio Maitín, Juan José Olmedo, and José María de Pando.

41. See Bushnell (163–84) on the dictatorial regime's authoritarian lineaments and the numerous social goals it accomplished. Lynch summarily denies that the Dictatorship (legally extended from October 1828 to April 1830) had any despotic elements to it (255).

42. On Bolívar's and Santander's differing views on the moral and political grounds for slave emancipation during the revolutionary process, see Lynch 210–12; Liévano Aguirre, esp. 259–68. Santander voiced an economic objection against slave emancipation that echoes his coeval Thomas Jefferson's arguments in the 1820s, although the state of war in the Greater Colombia would have allowed the government to free the slaves in a legal manner—and without compensation to the owners—unavailable to Jefferson (Hardt 48–51). On later political programs, left and right, which have severely impaired some historians' evaluation of the progressive and retrogressive aspects found in Bolívar's and Santander's respective ideologies, see Bushnell 163–67; Safford and Palacios 112–23. On the basic tenets of Colombia's dawning liberalism before the Liberal Party came into being as such, see Molina 14–34 (esp. 26–32). Among the texts by Santander that contributed to the Liberals' early rejection of Bolívar is the widely circulated letter to Alejandro Vélez (March 17, 1828), written during the Ocaña Convention (399–401). Santander states there that the Libertador surrounded himself only by "sworn friends of a perpetual dictatorship or the Constitution *for* Bolivia" (399).

43. Bolívar's document that is closest to Arendt's concerns is the "Discurso de Angostura" (1819), in which the Libertador defends the hereditary Senate and the Moral Power as two high-officialdom institutions committed—to varying degrees and in with different emphases—to monitoring the other public servants' abiding by the fundamental law. Bolívar was, like Rousseau, very apprehensive about both the threat of political corruption and the possible manipulation of the masses by their deputies. For this reason, he wished to have in place institutions that would help him "curb the general will" [moderar la voluntad general]—as expressed in the elected legislative branch of power—and "limit the public authority" [limitar la autoridad pública]—as expressed in the executive branch (Bolívar 2: 95). The "Discurso" specifically figures the transition from revolution to nation building as an ongoing "movement for freedom" [movimiento para la libertad] in which equality before the law and the right to a free education may ensure the people's desire to assume fully their citizenship rights and responsibilities (Bolívar 2: 77).

44. Simón Rodríguez was more specific when he referred to the end of the war of Independence as an "armisticio" or "suspension de la guerra" that marked the military defeat of the enemy (Spain), but also exhorted Americans to destroy the instruments of domination (the institutions) that the enemy had left standing (1: 272–73).

45. Triana Antorveza enumerates and comments upon Vice President Santander's edicts by which he attempted to "reduce" the "savage" inhabiting the frontier, who as yet lacked citizen rights. The Man of the Law promoted compulsory evangelizing as a stepping-stone to the Indians' peaceful relinquishing of their lands to the Bogotá commercial class, eager to invest their profit in large country estates. Pressured by the Treasury's mounting public debt and his own idealized vision of Colombia as a white nation, Santander allowed his fellow liberals from Bogotá to seize communal lands, a trend which did not slow down as the

century drew to a close (Triana Antorveza 130–33). For a critique of the economic elite's opportunistic capitalizing on the demographic and legal changes that took place between 1820 and 1850, see Palacios, *Estado y clases sociales* 115–17.

46. The continuation of the Giddens quotation defines "trust" as "a form of 'faith,' in which the confidence vested in probable outcomes expresses a commitment to something rather than just a cognitive understanding" (26–27).

47. In the article "Rasgos de historia antigua y moderna" (1903), Caro cast Santander in the same interpretive light, comparing him to Bolívar: "El *hombre de las leyes*…le fue a los alcances en desengaños…Traía la autoridad del que por largo tiempo ha ejercido el mando, la aureola que dan los padecimientos, las luces, la mayor experiencia que había adquirido" (*La oda* 238; italics in the original).

48. Colombia abolished slavery for good in 1852. In 1843 a law had been passed that authorized the export of slaves (a trade banned in 1821) to enable the landowning aristocracy to recover part of their investment in slave labor before the emancipation would become a reality. The ultra-Catholic and refined Arboledas used this time to sell their human capital overseas instead of gradually emancipating their slaves, which drew intense criticism even from Conservatives.

49. "Carta al general Juan José Flores, de 9 de noviembre de 1830" (Bolívar 1: 635).

50. "Ojeada a las opiniones políticas y religiosas de don Andrés Bello" (pub. in *A la memoria de Andrés Bello en su centenario* [1881] and repr. in Caro's *Escritos sobre don Andrés Bello*) is the essay in which the paradox of a traditionalist "revolution of independence" is theorized. This event would have got under way in 1810 and proceeded through the logic of *translatio imperii* that certifies Spain's willing transfer of sovereignty over the Americas once the metropolis became aware of its inability to advance further the joint ideas of "progress in tradition" and "conquest understood in a moral and Christian way, untainted by brutality" (*Escritos* 118, 122). In "Non verbo, sed opere" (1872), Caro contended that in every document of what he now dared to call the "revolución de independencia," one can see "the oath of allegiance to the Catholic Church unanimously and constantly reproduced" [unánime y constantemente repetido el juramento de fidelidad a la Iglesia católica] (*Obras, tomo I* 851). Caro obviously could not have read François-Xavier Guerra, Elías José Palti or Reinhart Koselleck on the *transculturating* need experienced by eighteenth-century constitutional republicans to preserve Old Regime formulae in their documents to avoid showing the *lieu vide* in which their new theories of sovereignty were being launched.

51. See Restrepo 4: 602 n.18. In the texts of 1886 and 1887 Caro omitted the epigraph featuring the passage from Restrepo while adding a note explaining that line 3 ("Sobre el collado que a Junín domina"), now in italics, came from the poem by the Ecuadorian Juan José Olmedo (1780–1845) titled *La victoria de Junín: Canto a Bolívar* (1825). The quotation from Restrepo begins by stating that the catalyst for this fleeting repentance was a nervous breakdown provoked by the illness, exhaustion, and slander that the general had to endure in previous weeks. The historian and former cabinet member goes on to add that Bolívar pulled himself together right away and issued a much-cited memorandum— one which I have not been able to locate—in which he communicated his decision to call Congress to convene (as promised the year before) at the same time as he invited Gran Colombians to participate in a poll on the citizens' preferred form of government for the republic (Restrepo 4: 191–92).

52. I once again refer my reader to Caro's Latin version of Baralt's fourteen lines featuring the *translatio imperii* topos, which was discussed at the opening of chapter 2. Caro's fondness for the poetry of ruins is evident in his Latin renderings of such baroque poems as Rodrigo Caro's [no relation] "A las ruinas de Itálica," Quevedo's "A Roma sepultada en sus ruinas," and the anonymous "Epístola moral a Fabio," all three collected in José Manuel Rivas Sacconi's edition of his *Versiones latinas*. Rufino José Cuervo also became interested in the poetry of ruins at approximately the same time (see "Dos poesías de Quevedo a Roma" [1908]; repr. in Cuervo, *Obras, tomo II* 683–90). For additional poems on the topos of *reliquae Romae*, see Caro, La *"Canción a las ruinas de Itálica"* 213–229.

53. González Vigil discusses the *apacentar las ovejas* metaphor at length (*Compendio de la defensa* 4–7). The point of his extensive treatment is that Jesus Christ did not grant Peter sovereignty over the totality of the faithful (Peter is not an archetype of the pope but of the bishop of Rome), much less *plenitudo potestatis*, a concept that he also deconstructs philologically and etymologically (*Compendio de la defensa* 46–47). In González Vigil's antiabsolutist thinking, every priest is a sovereign representative of incommensurable spiritual gifts—and only spiritual—which were individually bestowed upon him by the Creator, a *traditio* demonstrated by the priest's ability since antiquity to pardon sins and administer the last sacraments.

54. This paragraph summarizes arguments fleshed out in chapter 2. Since the eighth century, the concept of *translatio imperii* posits the transfer of dominion or global hegemony from one declining nation to an emerging one after the former has misused this providentially acquired prerogative (Curtius 27–30; Gilson 4–12).

55. See especially paragraphs 9–10 and 20.

56. In this he is in agreement with his father José Eusebio, who in a letter of 1851 to his wife Blasina Tobar from his New York exile bitterly complained about the Liberal Party's [el partido salvaje] mobilization of the "slave," "savage," and "degraded" race, which no longer wants to "return to the habits of obedience to, and respect for, the superior class" [volver a los hábitos de obediencia y respeto a sus superiores] (*Epistolario* 151).

57. A more extensive right to vote remained in place in the election of councilmen and members of the departments' assemblies. These corporations had some influence upon the indirect suffrage by which the representatives to the National Congress were elected. The goals of returning the monopoly of education to the Catholic Church and restricting access to literacy and the suffrage appear *in nuce* in items 4, 6, 9, and 10 of Caro's "Programa Católico de *El Tradicionista*," the colophon to his article "El Partido Católico" (*El Tradicionista*, vol. 1, no. 3 [November 21, 1871]: 22–23; repr. in Caro, *Obras, tomo I* 758–60).

58. The contrary opinion appears in Sieyès, *Qu'est-ce que le tiers état?* 73–75.

59. For the text of Rufino Cuervo's discussion of the Catholics' right to resist a civil authority and obligation to resign themselves to the ensuing consequences (*resistencia/resignación*), see his son Rufino José Cuervo's *Obras, tomo II* 1564–77. Hardt has recently defined republicanism in Jeffersonian terms, which are not incompatible with Rancière's discussion, as "a government of freedom, which must be…a government that allows for and even promotes the primacy of resistance over sovereignty" (66).

60. Núñez shrewdly promoted two fictions of democratic participation in the making of the 1886 Constitution. The first one was cast in the form of a Mosaic and

evangelical president's response to his people's concerns—a rescript—and published in *La Nación*, the government newspaper directed by Caro, on September 15, 1885. It stated that a spontaneous referendum had already taken place in the local governments and in the countless telegrams and letters addressed to him daily, so that the proposed constitutional "reform" had been "approved before hand by the municipalities' infallible ballot [sancionada de antemano por el voto inequívoco de los pueblos]." The second fiction (issued as an executive order—Decree 594 of September 10, 1885) was that he would let the governments of the nine Sovereign States choose their own delegates at the Council of Delegates. Núñez's two texts are reproduced in Caro, *Estudios constitucionales y jurídicos* 490–92.

61. There was nothing illegal in Caro's appointment to the vice presidency, or in Núñez's entrusting of the executive branch to him as *encargado*. However, given Caro's well-established reputation as a bigot and a fearmonger, it is very unlikely that he would have been elected to the vice presidency (let alone the presidency) in a truly participatory election in which both the Liberal and the Conservative parties would have entered a strong candidate, which was not the case in 1892. He resisted being formally appointed president of the republic in 1894, at the death of the titular president—Núñez—in order to capitalize on the related ideas that a deceased former Liberal was *still* the El Cid-like president and that he—Caro—was *still* eligible to run for that same office in 1898.

62. The best example is Marco Fidel Suárez (1855–1927), who pulled himself up by his bootstraps to become a largely self-taught grammarian and one of the true masters of Colombian prose. After Caro took him under his wing in 1881, he received all the political appointments that came with philological prowess and made it all the way to the presidency in 1918. A similar yet less successful and dramatic case (he was not raised in the same extreme poverty as Suárez) was that of the aforementioned Enrique Álvarez Bonilla (1848–1913). He went from obscure journalist and school teacher in Chiquinquirá (Tunja) to academician, law professor, and high-ranking bureaucrat in Bogotá (he was *secretario* several times in the Regeneración governments and served as Bibliotecario Nacional in 1888–1898 and 1905–1906, as did Caro in 1880–1885 and Suárez—*ad interim*—in 1884). Álvarez Bonilla's promotion took place on the basis of his early *Tratado de gramática castellana* (third ed., 1881) and his ability to produce speedily *compendia* and *refundiciones* of previously existing handbooks across the curriculum (in jurisprudence, history, rhetoric, and moral philosophy) as well as translations of epic poetry (Tasso, Milton). Caro wrote an important preface for Álvarez's abridgment of Gómez Hermosilla's controversial yet massively influential *Arte de hablar* in 1883. The main media attack launched by Caro's pundits against General Rafael Reyes—a self-made man and war hero of humble origins—was that his proficiency in grammar was not good enough to steer the nation's destiny. As indicated in chapter 1, the decorated general's condition of *iliterato* only became an issue after Reyes abandoned the Regeneración in order to launch a presidential campaign of his own.

63. To put it in the terms favored by Álvarez Bonilla, who mentions the Frenchman Claude Aubry's writings on civil law, Caro would have substituted the majority's "right to decide" [derecho de decisión] for the minority's "right of representation" [derecho de representación] in which the majoritarian vote lawfully silences the dissenting voices (*Elementos* 100).

64. The first edition of the collected poetry in Spanish translation came out in 1873–1876. The complex history of the translations' composition and publication is set forth in Rivas Sacconi (356–57 nn.11,12).

65. Between 1885 and 1888, Núñez was prodigiously prolific as literary *auctor patriae*. He saw through print an anthology with commentary titled *La rebelión. Noticias de la guerra* (1885), consisting of telegrams, edicts issued by local governments, and reports from the war front, all of which seemed to confirm radical Liberalism's intolerant positions (3). This book was followed by a two-volume compilation of articles arguing in favor of constitutional reform. The articles exploit such binary oppositions as "cisma"/"reconciliación," "degeneración"/"regeneración," and "abismo"/"luz." Simultaneously, the radical iconoclast José María Vargas Vila (1860–1933) wrote his caustic chronicles of the war and Núñez's reforms, which were published in Maracaibo in 1887 and 1889, during his exile in Venezuela.

66. Don Sergio's work is excerpted in chapter 1 as a counterpart in Popayán to Caro's journalistic efforts in Bogotá.

67. On the advent of historical change through the resolution of multiple forces into clearly defined positions of power, see Williams (115–20).

68. This work was finished in Paris and printed there the following year. It is divided into four parts, the first three having each the length of a monograph. Their subtitles are descriptive enough: first, a "Discurso preliminar"; second, the "Doctrina constitucional"; third, a "Proyecto de Constitución para la República de Colombia," written in 1885; and fourth, a coda titled "La nueva Constitución autoritaria (examen crítico del proyecto)" (383–97), which dissects the Regeneración's *Proyecto de Constitución* published in 1886.

69. For a brief summary of Zapata's career, see Rausch 89–90.

70. However, for his intended pedagogical reforms Pinzón leaned on numerous progressive intellectuals who had also been his teachers, among whom were Pérez and the sociologist and publisher Salvador Camacho Roldán. It was the Librería Colombiana Camacho Roldán y Tamayo that published Rivas Groot's *Parnaso colombiano*—favorably reviewed by Juan Valera in his *Cartas americanas* in 1888—a further indication of the suspension of political enmities around specific literary events. Camacho Roldán and Medardo Rivas were the principal Liberal intellectuals who owned a successful publishing house. Unlike the reactionary Imprenta de "El Tradicionista," the Librería Americana—both were owned or part-owned by Caro at different stages in his career—they regularly published literary-legislative work by members of the two feuding parties. The right-wing Imprenta de "La Luz," the Imprenta de Zalamea Hermanos, and the Imprenta Oficial (called Echevarría Hermanos until the state purchased it in 1893) were the main recipients of the Regeneración's government publication contracts.

71. Marroquín had previously celebrated Pérez as his beloved "friend" in the eclogue "La vida en el campo" (*El Mosaico*, vol. 1, no. 10 [February 26, 1859]: 74; repr. in 1887 in Áñez 2: 67–70). Utterly dismayed at the belligerence shown by both radical Liberals and the Regeneración's incipient repressive apparatuses in the armed confrontation of 1885, Pérez left Colombia of his own accord in 1885, settling in New York. He returned in 1892 to teach law at the Externado and lead the Liberal resistance to Caro's authoritarian regime. He was banished from Colombia the following year and died in Paris in 1900 (Hernández Peñalosa 89–91).

Conclusion   On Lettered Cities and the Writing of Lyric

1. A member of the Colombian Academy like his son, the impecunious don Ricardo founded, with the reactionary Ortiz brothers, the private school Instituto de Cristo, and, with Ignacio Gutiérrez Vergara, the Liceo de la Infancia, a more successful religious primary school that established him as Bogotá's best-loved private educator. An author of children's literature, a religious versifier, and a benign satirist (in all three capacities he resembled Rafael Pombo), he wrote a brief "Apuntes para mi biografía" in verse, which was posthumously published in full under the title "Una curiosa auto-biografía" in *Santafé y Bogotá,* vol. 2, no. 21 (September 1924): 168–69. José María Samper contributed a substantive biographical sketch upon the poet's passing to the *Papel Periódico Ilustrado,* no. 107 (January 1, 1887): 162–66. In the same venue, Pombo also published a poem paying tribute to his friend (p. 176 of the issue already cited); its last octave begins by calling the year 1886 a "black date ushering in furor and fright" [negra fecha de furor y espanto], perhaps a reliable indicator of how frightened Pombo—an ardent Catholic—was by the recent enactment of Caro's retrogressive Constitution.

2. In the same year of 1862, don Ricardo, who did not own a horse, had to borrow one from his distant relation and close friend Marroquín to go on an outing organized by José María Vergara y Vergara. As the horse was returned in pretty bad shape, Marroquín added his own mocking poem about Carrasquilla's troubled relations with equines. The texts by Marroquín and Carrasquilla are printed, along with Rivas's ten-line poem, in *El Mosaico,* vol. 3, no. 7 (1864): 52–53. A slightly different version of Rivas's poem was reprinted in volume 1 of his *Obras* (412).

3. This last example—litigating in verse—is given in Torres Caicedo's lengthy early hagiography of Arboleda (*Ensayos biográficos y de crítica literaria...Primera serie* 2: 34–35). Arboleda was the nephew of Torres Caicedo's mentor and patron, Archbishop Manuel José Mosquera.

4. "Suerte de mis versos," *El Mosaico,* vol. 1, no. 2 (January 1, 1859): 12.

5. The same story is repeated in the son of don Ricardo's fellow literary jouster: José María Rivas Groot.

6. "La instrucción de los colombianos," *El Mosaico,* vol. 10, no. 2 (February 9, 1871): 10.

7. The names of the investors in Caro's "Imprenta y Librería de *El Tradicionista*" are proudly listed, "by order of seniority," at the front of José Eusebio's *Obras escogidas* (1873). The list includes the names of Sergio and Rafael Arboleda, José Joaquín Ortiz, Mariano Ospina, Rufino José Cuervo, and José María Urdaneta in addition to several presbyters. What they invested in the bookstore and printing house was more than financial capital: by lending their support to Caro's publishing ventures, they expected to obtain political returns, for themselves or their already illustrious families, once Caro's counterrevolution seized power.

8. See Reclus 917, 918; Vergara y Vergara 2: 135, 140; Henao and Arrubla 2: 630. Caro also used the phrase "relegated city" [ciudad relegada] and condemned the comparison with Athens, which he knew Reclus could not have meant seriously, given Bogotá's social, economic, and cultural underdevelopment in 1867 (Caro, *Obras, tomo III* 1172–73). Núñez was of the same opinion (*Diccionario político* 35–36).

9. For my comments on the República Liberal's cultural policies, I am indebted to Renán Silva's *República Liberal, intelectuales y cultura popular.*

10. All my attempts to contact the Instituto in writing (by letter, fax, and e-mail) to vet this information and request updates on its ongoing activities have sadly been ignored.

11. Its first assignment was the preparation of the *Diccionario de Construcción y Régimen de la Lengua Castellana*, the work that Rufino José Cuervo undertook intermittently between 1872 and 1911. At his death, he was still halfway through letter "E," having reached the adversative conjunction "however" [empero]. The eight-volume dictionary was later conceived as Colombia's main contribution to the five-hundredth anniversary of Columbus's first crossing. Although the dictionary was not ready for publication in 1992, it was awarded Spain's prestigious Premio Príncipe de Asturias in 1999.

12. In all fairness, the Instituto's book lists have occasionally included titles devoted to progressive authors such as Tomás Carrasquilla—no relation to don Ricardo and Monsignor Rafael María Carrasquilla—and Candelario Obeso, the Afro-Colombian poet who wrote (like Carrasquilla) in a stylized version of the vernacular, but who also excelled in the use of the literary standard and produced academic translations from various European languages.

13. Civilist statesmen Belisario Betancur—the last Conservative head of state prior to the 1991 Constitution—and Andrés Pastrana Arango—Uribe's Conservative predecessor in the nation's highest office—still presided over administrations organized within the frame of liberal parliamentarism with all its advantages and limitations.

WORKS CITED

A la memoria de Andrés Bello en su centenario. Homenaje del "Repertorio Colombiano" en su centenario. Bogotá: Librería Americana, 1881.

Acosta de Samper, Soledad. *Domingos de la familia cristiana. Evangelios, prácticas y conversaciones sobre religión.* Paris: Garnier Hermanos, 1896.

Agamben, Giorgio. *Mezzi senza fine. Note sulla politica.* Milano: Bollati Boringhieri, 1996.

———. *Stato di eccezione: Homo sacer II, I.* Milano: Bollati Boringhieri, 2003.

Aguilar, Federico C. *Colombia en presencia de las repúblicas hispano-americanas.* Bogotá: Imprenta de Ignacio Borda, 1884.

"Alone" [Hernán Díaz Arrieta]. *Historia personal de la literatura chilena. Desde don Alonso de Ercilla hasta Pablo Neruda.* Santiago: Zig-Zag, 1954.

Alonso, Carlos J. "*Rama y sus retoños*: Figuring the Nineteenth Century in Spanish America." *Revista de Estudios Hispánicos* 28.2 (1994): 283–92.

Álvarez Bonilla, Enrique. *Elementos de derecho público interno (Lecciones dictadas en la facultad de Derecho y Ciencias Políticas de Bogotá).* Bogotá: Imprenta Nacional, 1904.

———. *Santafé redimida.* Bogotá: Imprenta de Medardo Rivas, 1885.

———. *Tratado de retórica y poética.* Bogotá: Imprenta de Vapor de Zalamea Hermanos, 1893.

Amunátegui, Miguel Luis. *Vida de don Andrés Bello.* Santiago: Impreso por Pedro G. Ramírez, 1882.

Amunátegui, Miguel Luis, and Gregorio Víctor Amunátegui. *Biografías de americanos.* Santiago: Imprenta Nacional, 1854.

Ancízar, Manuel. *Editoriales del "Neo-granadino."* Bogotá: Editorial Minerva, 1936.

Anderson Imbert, Enrique. "Neoclasicismo y romanticismo." *Sur* 236 (September–October 1955): 77–78.

Áñez, Julio, ed. *Parnaso colombiano.* Intro. José M. Rivas Groot. Bogotá: Librería Colombiana Camacho Roldán y Tamayo, 1886–1887. 2 vols.

Aquinas, Thomas. *On the Governance of Rulers (De Regimine Principum).* Trans. Gerald B. Phelan. Rev. ed. London: Sheed & Ward for the Institute for Mediaeval Studies, 1938.

———. *Summa Theologiæ.* Bilingual ed. New York/London: McGraw-Hill/Eyre & Spottiswoode, 1963–1975. 60 vols.

Arango, Rodolfo. "La construcción de la nacionalidad." *Miguel Antonio Caro y la cultura de su época.* Ed. Rubén Sierra Mejía. Bogotá: Universidad Nacional de Colombia-Facultad de Ciencias Humanas, 2002. 125–53.

Arboleda, Sergio. *Las letras, las ciencas y las bellas artes.* Bogotá: Ministerio de Educación Nacional/Editorial Minerva, 1936.

Arboleda, Sergio. *La República en la América española.* Bogotá: Banco Popular, 1972.

Arciniegas, Germán. "La vida de un poeta revolucionario en el siglo XIX." Vergara y Vergara et al., *A propósito de Jorge Isaacs y su obra* 15–80.

Arendt, Hannah. *On Revolution.* 1963. Rev. ed. New York: Viking, 1965.

Arrieta, Diógenes A. *Colombianos contemporáneos, primera serie: Joaquín José Ortiz.* Caracas: Imprenta de "La Opinión Nacional," 1884.

Arthur, William. *The Pope, the Kings, and the People: A History of the Movement to Make the Pope Governor of the World by a Universal Reconstruction of Society from the Issue of the Syllabus to the Close of the Vatican Council, by the Late William Arthur.* Ed. W. Blair Neatby. London: Hodder & Stoughton, 1903.

[Saint] Augustine. *The City of God against the Pagans.* Bilingual ed. Latin-English. Trans. George E. McCracken et al. London: William Heinemann, 1956–1957. 7 vols.

———. *On Christian Doctrine.* Trans. D. W. Robertson. New York: Macmillan, 1958.

———. *Opera omnia, Tomus tertius.* Ed. J.-P. Migne. Paris: Petit-Montrouge, 1841.

Augustus (Octavius). *Res gestae divi Augusti. Hauts faits du divin Auguste.* Trilingual ed., Greek-Latin-French. Trans. and ed. John Scheid. Paris: Les Belles Lettres, 2007.

Avelar, Idelber. *The Letter of Violence: Essays on Narrative, Ethics, and Politics.* New York: Palgrave Macmillan, 2004.

Balmes, Jaime. *Obras completas, tomo VI: Escritos políticos.* Madrid: Biblioteca de Autores Cristianos, 1950.

Baralt, Rafael María. *Obras literarias.* Ed. Guillermo Díaz-Plaja. Madrid: Atlas, 1967.

Beatrice, Pier Franco. *Tradux peccati. Alle fonti della dottrina agostiniana del peccato originale.* Milano: Vita e Pensiero/Publicazioni della Università Católica del Sacro Cuore, 1978.

Bellarmino, Roberto. *Scritti politici.* Ed. Carlo Giacon. Bologna: Nicola Zanichelli Editore, 1950.

Bello, Andrés. *Colección de poesías originales por Andrés Bello (con apuntes biográficos por J. M. Torres Caicedo).* Paris: Librería de Rosa y Bouret, 1870.

———. *Obras completas de Andrés Bello.* Ed. Comisión Editora de las Obras Completas de Andrés Bello. Caracas: Ediciones del Ministerio de Educación, 1951–1986.

———. *Poema del Cid.* Vol. 2 of *Obras completas.* Santiago: Impreso por Pedro G. Ramírez, 1881.

Beneyto Pérez, Juan. *Historia de la administración española e hispanoamericana.* Madrid: Aguilar, 1958.

Bentham, Jeremy. *Deontology; Together with A Table of the Springs of Action and Article on Utilitarianism.* Ed. Amnon Goldworth. Oxford: Clarendon Press, 1983.

———. *A Fragment on Government and An Introduction to the Principles of Morals and Legislation.* Ed. Wilfrid Harrison. Oxford: Basil Blackwell, 1948.

———. *Theory of Fictions.* Ed. C. K. Ogden. London: Kegan Paul, 1932.

———. *Tratados de legislación civil y penal.* Trans. with notes by Ramón Salas (1821–1822). Ed. Magdalena Rodríguez Gil. Madrid: Editora Nacional, 1981.

Bidart Campos, Germán José. *Doctrina del estado democrático.* Buenos Aires: Ediciones Jurídicas Europa-América, 1961.

———. *El mito del pueblo como sujeto de gobierno, de soberanía y de representación.* Buenos Aires: Abeledo-Perrot, 1960.

Bobbio, Norberto. *Liberalismo e democrazia.* Milano: Franco Angeli, 1985.

———. *Stato, governo, società. Per una teoria generale della politica.* Torino: Giulio Einaudi, 1985.

Bodin, Jean. *On Sovereignty: Four Chapters from* The Six Books of the Commonwealth. Ed. Julian H. Franklin. Cambridge: Cambridge University Press, 1992.

Boeckh, August. *On Interpretation and Criticism.* German ed., 1877. Trans. and ed. John Paul Pritchard. Norman: University of Oklahoma Press, 1968.

Bohning, William. "Andrés Bello's Imitations of Victor Hugo." *Hispanic Review* 13.1 (1945): 60–67.

Bolívar, Simón. *Simón Bolívar fundamental.* Ed. Germán Carrera Damas. Caracas: Monte Ávila Latinoamericana, 1992. 2 vols.

Bolívar, Simón, et al. *Bolívar, Camilo Torres y Francisco Antonio Zea.* Bogotá: Ministerio de Educación Nacional/Editorial Minerva, 1936.

Bonald, Louis-Gabriel-Ambroise, Vicomte de. *Essai analytique sur les lois naturelles de l'ordre social, ou du pouvoir, du ministre et du sujet dans la société.* 1800. 3rd ed. Vol. 1 of *Œuvres de M. de Bonald.* Paris: Librairie d'Adrien Le Clere, 1836.

Bourdieu, Pierre. *Language and Symbolic Power.* Trans. Gino Raymond and Matthew Adamson. Ed. John B. Thompson. Cambridge, MA: Harvard University Press, 1991.

Bushnell, David. *Simón Bolívar: hombre de Caracas, proyecto de América (una biografía).* Buenos Aires: Editorial Biblos, 2002.

Butler, Judith, Ernesto Laclau, and Slavoj Žižek. *Contingency, Hegemony, Universality: Contemporary Dialogues on the Left.* London: Verso, 2000.

Calasso, Roberto. *The Ruin of Kasch.* Trans. William Weaver and Stephen Sartarelli. Cambridge, MA: Belknap Press of Harvard University Press, 1994.

Calcaño, José Antonio. *El ruego de la inocencia (Leyenda católica).* Liverpool: Edward Howell, 1871.

Camacho Roldán, Salvador. *Memorias.* Bogotá: Librería Colombiana Camacho Roldán y Tamayo, 1923.

Cané, Miguel. *En viaje (1881–1882).* Buenos Aires: "La Cultura Argentina," 1906.

Canfora, Luciano. *La democrazia. Storia di un'ideologia.* Roma/Bari: Laterza, 2004.

Cano [Gutiérrez], Fidel. "Al lector: crítica a la traducción de 'La oración por todos' de Bello." *Lecturas Populares* [Bogotá] (17 January 1914): 325–33.

———, trans. *La oración por todos.* By Victor Hugo. Medellín: Tipografía Central, 1902.

———, trans. "La oración por todos (Victor Hugo)." *Lecturas Populares* [Bogotá] (17 January 1914): 335–54.

Cañete, Manuel. "Ligeros apuntes acerca del insigne venezolano Andrés Bello." *Biblioteca de escritores venezolanos contemporáneos ordenada con noticias biográficas.* Ed. José M. Rójas. Carácas/Paris: Rójas Hermanos, Editores/Jouby et Roger, Éditeurs, 1875. 1–25.

Caro, José Eusebio. *Epistolario.* Ed. Simón Aljure Chalela. Bogotá: Ministerio de Educación Nacional-Revista "Bolívar," 1953.

———. *Obras escogidas en prosa y en verso, publicadas e inéditas, ordenadas por los redactores de "El Tradicionista."* Bogotá: Imprenta y Librería de "El Tradicionista," 1872.

Caro, Miguel Antonio. *Artículos y discursos*. Bogotá: Librería Americana, 1888.

Caro, Miguel Antonio. *La "Canción a las ruinas de Itálica" del licenciado Rodrigo Caro, con introducción, versión latina y notas por Miguel Antonio Caro*. Ed. José Manuel Rivas Sacconi. Bogotá: Instituto Caro y Cuervo/Editorial Voluntad, 1947.

———. *Escritos sobre don Andrés Bello*. Ed. Carlos Valderrama Andrade. Bogotá: Instituto Caro y Cuervo, 1981.

———. *Estudios constitucionales y jurídicos (primera serie)*. Ed. Carlos Valderrama Andrade. Bogotá: Instituto Caro y Cuervo, 1986.

———. *Ideario hispánico*. Ed. Antonio Curcio Altamar. Bogotá: Instituto Colombiano de Cultura Hispánica, 1952.

———. *Libertad de imprenta. Artículos publicados en "La Nación" en 1888*. Bogotá: Imprenta de "La Nación," 1890.

———. *Obras, tomo I: Filosofía, religión, pedagogía*. Ed. Carlos Valderrama Andrade. Bogotá: Instituto Caro y Cuervo, 1962.

———. *Obras, tomo III: Estudios lingüísticos, gramaticales y filológicos*. Ed. Rafael Torres Quintero. Intro. Carlos Valderrama Andrade. Bogotá: Instituto Caro y Cuervo, 1980.

———. *Obras completas, tomo I: Flos poetarum, El cinco de mayo, de Manzoni*. Ed. Víctor E. Caro and Antonio Gómez Restrepo. Bogotá: Imprenta Nacional, 1918.

———. *Obras completas, tomo III: Estudios literarios. Primera serie*. Ed. Víctor E. Caro and Antonio Gómez Restrepo. Bogotá: Imprenta Nacional, 1920.

———. *Obras completas, tomo V: Estudios filológicos y gramaticales. Segunda serie*. Ed. Víctor E. Caro and Antonio Gómez Restrepo. Bogotá: Imprenta Nacional, 1928.

———. *Obras completas, tomo VIII: Sonetos de aquí y allí—Traducciones poéticas—Poesías de Sully-Prudhomme*. Ed. Antonio Gómez Restrepo and Eduardo A. Caro. Bogotá: Imprenta Nacional, 1945.

———. *Obras poéticas: Sonetos—Cantilenas*. Bogotá: Imprenta Nacional, 1928.

———. *Obras poéticas: Musa militante—Sátiras—Lira cristiana*. Bogotá: Imprenta Nacional, 1933.

———. *La oda "A la estatua del Libertador" y otros escritos acerca de Bolívar*. Ed. Carlos Valderrama Andrade. Bogotá: Instituto Caro y Cuervo, 1984.

———. *Páginas de crítica*. Ed. and intro. Antonio Gómez Restrepo. Madrid: Editorial-América, 1919.

———. *Poesías*. Bogotá: Imprenta de Foción Mantilla, 1866.

———. "Roma Dominatrix." Bilingual ed. Latin-Spanish. Trans. Antonio Gómez Restrepo. Ed. José J. Ortega Torres. *Revista de estudios eclesiásticos. Organo del Centro de San Francisco de Sales*, no. 9 (1941): 329–330.

———. *Traducciones poéticas*. Bogotá: Librería Americana, 1889.

———. *Versiones latinas*. Ed. José Manuel Rivas Sacconi. Bogotá: Publicaciones del Instituto Caro y Cuervo, 1951.

———, ed. "Lecturas paralelas en prosa y verso." *El Repertorio Colombiano* 13.7 (1887): 41–84.

Carrasquilla, Rafael María. *Lo nuevo y lo viejo en la enseñanza*. Bogotá: Imprenta Eléctrica, 1909.

Carrera Damas, Germán. *El culto a Bolívar. Esbozo para un estudio de la historia de las ideas en Venezuela*. Caracas: Instituto de Antropología e Historia-Universidad Central de Venezuela, 1969.

Casas, José Joaquín. *Semblanzas (Diego Fallon y José Manuel Marroquín)*. Bogotá: Ministerio de Educación Nacional/Editorial Minerva, 1936.

Castro y Rossi, Adolfo de, ed. *Cortes de Cádiz*. Madrid: Imprenta de Prudencio Pérez de Velasco, 1913. 2 vols.

Chenu, M[arie]-D[ominique]. *Nature, Man, and Society in the Twelfth Century: Essays on New Theological Perspectives in the Latin West*. French ed., 1957. Trans. and ed. Jerome Taylor and Lester K. Little. Chicago: University of Chicago Press, 1968.

Código civil colombiano (y leyes adicionales y reformatorias). Ed. J.A. Archila. Bogotá: Editorial Cromos, 1936.

Colmenares, Germán. *Las convenciones contra la cultura. Ensayos sobre la historiografía hispanoamericana del siglo XIX*. Bogotá: Tercer Mundo Editores, 1987.

———. "La ley y el orden social: fundamento profano y fundamento divino." *Boletín Cultural y Bibliográfico* 27.22 (1990): 3–19.

Compilación de disposiciones sobre régimen de universidades 1888–1952. Bogotá: Ministerio de Educación Nacional/Imprenta Nacional, 1952.

Concha, Jaime. "Bello y su gestión superestructural en Chile." *Revista de Crítica Literaria Latinoamericana* 43–44 (1996): 139–61.

Concha, José Vicente. "Discurso pronunciado en la Cámara de Representantes el día 9 de agosto de 1898, sobre 'facultades extraordinarias.'" *Oradores conservadores*. By José Vicente Concha et al. Bogotá: Ministerio de Educación Nacional/Editorial Minerva, 1936. 39–63.

Conto, César. *Versos*. London: Printed by Gilbert & Rivington, 1884. Appears to be an edition published at the author's expense.

Conto, César, and Emiliano Isaza. *Diccionario ortográfico de apellidos y de nombres propios de personas, con un apéndice de nombres geográficos de Colombia*. 5th ed. London: Moffatt & Paige, 1897.

Cordovez Moure, José María. *Reminiscencias de Santafé y Bogotá*. 1893–1913. Ed. Elisa Mújica. Madrid: Aguilar, 1957.

Corrales, Manuel Ezequiel, ed. *Homenaje de Colombia al Libertador Simón Bolívar, en su primer centenario, 1783–1883*. Bogotá: Imprenta de Medardo Rivas, 1884.

Costa, Joaquín. *Ideario*. Ed. J. García Mercadal. Madrid: Afrodisio Aguado, 1964.

Crema, Edoardo. *Andrés Bello a través del romanticismo*. Caracas: Ministerio de Educación, 1956.

Cuervo, Rufino José. "Dos poesías de Quevedo a Roma." *Revue Hispanique* 18 (1908): 432–38.

———. *Obras*. Bogotá: Instituto Caro y Cuervo, 1954. 2 vols.

Curtius, Ernst Robert. *European Literature and the Latin Middle Ages*. German ed., 1948. Trans. Willard R. Trask. New York: Bollingen/Pantheon, 1953.

Dante Alighieri. *The Inferno of Dante*. Trans. Robert Pinsky. New York: Farrar, 1994.

de la Campa, Román. "El desafío inesperado de *La ciudad letrada*." *Ángel Rama y los estudios latinoamericanos*. Ed. Mabel Moraña. Pittsburgh: Instituto Internacional de Literatura Iberoamericana, 1997. 29–53.

del Valle, José. "Historical Linguistics and Cultural History: The Polemic between Rufino José Cuervo and Juan Valera." *The Battle over Spanish between 1800 and 2000*. Ed. José del Valle and Luis Gabriel-Stheeman. London: Routledge, 2002. 64–77.

Destutt de Tracy, [Antoine]. *Elementos de verdadera lógica. Compendio ó sea estracto de los Elementos de Ideología*. Trans. and ed. Juan Justo García. Madrid: Imprenta de Don Mateo Repullés, 1821.

de Vries, Hent. "Introduction." De Vries and Sullivan, *Political Theologies* 1–88.

de Vries, Hent, and Lawrence E. Sullivan, eds. *Political Theologies: Public Religions in a Post-Secular World*. New York: Fordham University Press, 2006.

Donoso Cortés, Juan. *Obras completas*. Ed. Carlos Valverde. Madrid: Biblioteca de Autores Cristianos, 1970. 2 vols.

Durán López, Fernando, ed. *Crónicas de cortes del* Semanario Patriótico *(1810–1812)*. Cádiz: Fundación Municipal de Cultura-Excmo. Ayuntamiento de Cádiz, 2003.

Esposito, Roberto. *Nove pensieri sulla politica*. Bologna: il Mulino, 1993.

Fataud, Jean-Marie, and Marie-Claude Bartholy. "Préliminaires: L'horizon de la réflexion politique de Rousseau." Jean-Jacques Rousseau, *Du contrat social ou principes du droit politique*. Ed. Fataud and Bartholy. Paris: Bordas, 1972. 3–15.

Fernández Sebastián, Javier, and Juan Francisco Fuentes, eds. *Diccionario político y social del siglo XIX español*. Madrid: Alianza, 2002.

Foucault, Michel. *The Order of Things: An Archaeology of the Human Sciences*. French ed., 1966. No trans. listed. New York: Vintage, 1973.

Frankl, Victor. "Agustinismo y nominalismo en la filosofía de la historia según Gonzalo Jiménez de Quesada." *Estudios Americanos* 16.82–83 (July–August 1958): 1–32.

Freud, Sigmund. *Moses and Monotheism*. Trans. Katherine Jones. New York: Knopf, 1939.

García Canclini, Néstor. *Hybrid Cultures: Strategies for Entering and Leaving Modernity*. Trans. Christopher L. Chiappiari and Silvia L. López. Minneapolis: University of Minnesota Press, 1995.

Giddens, Anthony. *The Consequences of Modernity*. Stanford: Stanford University Press, 1990.

Gilson, Étienne. "Humanisme médiéval et Renaissance." *Revue Trimestrielle Canadienne* (March 1930): 1–17.

Godzich, Wlad. *The Culture of Literacy*. Cambridge, MA: Harvard University Press, 1994.

Gómez Hermosilla, José [Mamerto]. *Arte de hablar en prosa y verso [1826]. Nueva edición, aumentada con muchas é importantes notas*. París: A. Lefevre, 1853. 2 vols.

———. *El jacobinismo, obra útil en todos tiempos y necesaria en las circunstancias presentes*. Madrid: Imprenta de D. León Amarita, 1823. 3 vols.

Gómez Restrepo, Antonio. *Crítica literaria*. Bogotá: Ministerio de Educación Nacional/Editorial Minerva, 1935.

González Stephan, Beatriz. "Cuerpos de la nación: cartografías disciplinarias." *Ciudadanía y nación*. Ed. Roland Anrup and Vicente Oieni. Göteborg: Instituto Iberoamericano-Universidad de Göteborg, 1999. 71–106.

G[ónzalez] Vigil, Francisco de Paula. *Cartas al Papa Pío IX con varios documentos al caso (a la juventud americana)*. Lima: Imprenta de "El Comercio," 1871.

———. *Compendio de la defensa de la autoridad de los obispos contra las pretensiones de la curia romana (dedicado a la juventud americana)*. Lima: Imprenta Libre, 1857.

———. *Importancia de las asociaciones. Importancia de la educación popular*. Camaná: Ediciones Hora del Hombre, 1965.

Gregorius I. *Opera omnia, Tomus secundus*. Paris: Petit-Montrouge, 1841.

Groot, José Manuel. *Historia eclesiástica y civil de Nueva Granada, escrita sobre documentos auténticos*. Bogotá: Imprenta a cargo de F. Mantilla, 1869–1870. 3 vols.

———. *Obras escogidas en prosa y en verso, publicadas é inéditas*. Bogotá: Imprenta y Librería de "El Tradicionista," 1873.

Guerra, François-Xavier. *Modernidad e independencias. Ensayos sobre las revoluciones hispánicas*. Madrid: MAPFRE, 1992.

Guillemin, Henri, ed. "Une prière de Victor Hugo. Extraits inédits des 'Carnets intimes.'" *Figaro Littéraire* (April 21, 1956): 7.

Guillén Martínez, Fernando. *El poder político en Colombia*. Bogotá: Editorial Punta de Lanza, 1979.

———. *La Regeneración. Primer frente nacional*. Bogotá: Carlos Valencia Editores, 1986.

———. *La torre y la plaza. Un ensayo de interpretación de América*. Madrid: Instituto de Cultura Hispánica, 1958.

Gutiérrez, Juan María, ed. *América poética. Colección escojida de composiciones en verso, escritas por americanos en el presente siglo: Parte lírica*. Valparaíso, Chile: Imprenta del Mercurio, 1846. This volume was serialized; pub. concluded in June 1847.

Hardt, Michael. "Jefferson and Democracy." *American Quarterly* 59.1 (March 2007): 41–78.

Hardt, Michael, and Antonio Negri. *Multitude: War and Democracy in the Age of Empire*. New York: The Penguin Press, 2004.

Hastie, W[illiam]. *Outlines of the Science of Jurisprudence: An Introduction to the Systematic Study of Law (Translated and Edited from the Juristic Encyclopaedias of Puchta, Friedländer, Falck, and Ahrens)*. Edinburgh: T. & T. Clark, 1887.

Henao, Jesús María, and Gerardo Arrubla. *Historia de Colombia para la enseñanza secundaria*. Bogotá: Escuela Tipográfica Salesiana, 1911–1912. 2 vols.

Hernández Peñalosa, Guillermo, ed. *Anécdotas y poesías satíricas de Miguel Antonio Caro*. Bogotá: Instituto Caro y Cuervo, 1988.

Hispano, Cornelio. *De París al Amazonas. Las fieras del Putumayo*. París: P[aul] Ollendorf, 1912.

———. *El libro de oro de Bolívar*. París: Casa Editorial Garnier Hermanos, 1926.

Hobbes, Thomas. *Leviathan*. Ed. Richard E. Flathman and David Johnston. A Norton Critical Edition. New York: Norton, 1997.

Holguín Arboleda, Julio. "Religión y poesía (II)." *El Gráfico*, vol. 25, no. 1234 (1935): 264–67.

Hugo, Victor. *Œuvres poétiques, tome I: Avant l'exile, 1802–1851*. Ed. Pierre Albouy. Bibliothèque de la Pléiade. Paris: Gallimard, 1976.

———. *Œuvres poétiques, tome II: Les châtiments. Les contemplations*. Ed. Pierre Albouy. Bibliothèque de la Pléiade. Paris: Gallimard, 1967.

———. *Rayos y sombras. Cantos del crepúsculo. Voces interiores. Hojas de otoño*. Trans. Pedro Pedraza y Páez. Barcelona: Casa Editorial Sopena, n/d.

———. *Selected Poems (from the "Edition Definitive")*. Philadelphia: George Barrie & Son, 1897. 3 vols.

———. *Théâtre complet, tome I*. Intro. Roland Purnal. Ed. J.-J. Thierry et Josette Mélèze. Bibliothèque de la Pléiade. Paris: Gallimard, 1963.

Hugo, Victor. *Works of Victor Hugo: Poems*. Boston: Little, Brown, 1909. 2 vols.

Humboldt, Guillermo de. *Escritos políticos*. German ed., 1901. Trans. Wenceslao Roces. Mexico, D.F.: Fondo de Cultura Económica, 1943.

Isaacs, Jorge. *María*. Bogotá: Editorial Norma, 1989.

Jaksić, Iván A. *Andrés Bello: La pasión por el orden*. Santiago: Editorial Universitaria, 2001.

Jaksić, Iván A. "Introduction" to *Selected Writings of Andrés Bello*. Trans. Frances M. López Morillas. Ed. Iván Jaksić. New York: Oxford University Press, 1997. xxvii–lvi.

Jaramillo Castillo, Carlos Eduardo. "Guerras civiles y vida cotidiana." *Historia de la vida cotidiana en Colombia*. Ed. Beatriz Castro Carvajal. Bogotá: Norma, 1996. 291–309.

Justinian. *The Institutes of Justinian*. Bilingual ed. Trans. and ed. Thomas Collett Sandars. 1853. New York: Longmans, 1900.

Kantorowicz, Ernst H. *The King's Two Bodies: A Study in Mediaeval Political Theology*. Princeton, NJ: Princeton University Press, 1957.

Koselleck, Reinhart. *Futures Past: On the Semantics of Historical Time*. German ed., 1979. Trans. Keith Tribe. Cambridge, MA: MIT Press, 1985.

———. *The Practice of Conceptual History: Timing History, Spacing Concepts*. Trans. Todd Samuel Presner et al. Stanford: Stanford University Press, 2002.

Kristal, Efraín. "Dialogues and Polemics: Sarmiento, Lastarria, and Bello." *Sarmiento and His Argentina*. Ed. Joseph T. Criscenti. Boulder: Lynne Rienner Publishers, 1993. 61–70.

Lafarga, Francisco, ed. *El discurso sobre la traducción en la historia (Antología bilingüe)*. Barcelona: EUB, 1996.

Laín Entralgo, Pedro. *Menéndez Pelayo*. Buenos Aires: Espasa-Calpe Argentina, 1952.

Larrazábal, Felipe. *Correspondencia general del libertador Simón Bolívar, enriquecida con la inserción de los manifiestos, mensa[j]es, exposiciones, proclamas [etc.], publicados por el héroe colombiano desde 1810 hasta 1830. Precede a esta colección interesante la vida de Bolívar*. New York: Imprenta de E.O. Jenkins, 1865–1866. 2 vols.

Lastarria, José Victorino. *Recuerdos literarios*. Santiago: LOM Ediciones, 2001.

Lefort, Claude. *Democracy and Political Theory*. Trans. David Macey. London: Polity, 1988.

———. *The Political Forms of Modern Society: Bureaucracy, Democracy, Totalitarianism*. Trans. and ed. John B. Thompson. Cambridge, MA: MIT Press, 1986.

Liévano Aguirre, Indalecio. "Bolívar y Santander." *Curso superior de historia de Colombia (1781–1830), tomo III*. Ed. Daniel Arias Argáez et al. Bogotá: A.B.C., 1950. 241–79.

Locke, John. *An Essay Concerning Human Understanding*. Ed. Alexander Campbell Fraser. Oxford: Clarendon Press, 1894. 2 vols.

Lorimer, James. *The Institutes of Law: A Treatise of the Principles of Jurisprudence, as Determined by Nature*. Edinburgh: T. & T. Clark, 1872.

Lynch, John. *The Spanish American Revolutions, 1808–1826*. New York: Norton, 1973.

Maistre, Joseph Marie, Comte de. *Considérations sur la France*. 1797. Lyon: J. B. Pélagaud, 1845.

———. *Del Papa y de la Iglesia Galicana (obra impresa en Francia en los años 1819 y 1821, traducida del francés por un eclesiástico)*. Valencia: Oficina de D. Benito Monfort, 1824. 3 vols.

Malavié, Jean. "Victor Hugo et la prière: sa présence dans *Les misérables*." *Travaux de Littérature* 6 (1993): 225–61.

Maravall, José Antonio. *Estado moderno y mentalidad social (siglos XV a XVII)*. 1972. Madrid: Alianza, 1986. 2 vols.

Mariana, Juan de. *The King and the Education of the King (De rege et regis institutione).* Trans. and with an Intro. by George Albert Moore. Washington, D.C.: The Country Dollar Press, 1948.

Marroquín, L[orenzo]. *Pax. Novela de costumbres latinoamericanas.* Bogotá: Imprenta de "La Luz," 1907.

Martí, José. *Obras completas.* Gen. ed. Gonzalo de Quesada y Miranda. La Habana: Trópico, 1936–1953. 74 vols.

Martín Barbero, Jesús. *Pre-textos. Conversaciones sobre la comunicación y sus contextos.* Cali: Ediciones Universidad del Valle, 1995.

Martínez Marina, Francisco. *Discurso sobre el origen de la Monarquía y sobre la naturaleza del gobierno español.* 1813. Ed. José Antonio Maravall. Madrid: Instituto de Estudios Políticos, 1957. 3 vols.

————. *Obras escogidas.* Ed. José Martínez Cardos. Madrid: Atlas, 1966–1969.

Martínez Silva, Carlos. *Capítulos de historia política de Colombia ("revistas políticas" publicadas en "El Repertorio Colombiano").* Bogotá: Biblioteca Banco Popular, 1973. 3 vols.

Marx, Karl. *The Eighteenth Brumaire of Louis Bonaparte.* 1852. Rev. ed., 1869. International Publishers, 1963. Translator's name is not given.

Marx, Karl, and Friedrich Engels. *The German Ideology: Parts I & II.* Trans. and ed. R. Pascal. New York: International Publishers, 1947.

————. *The Holy Family; or, Critique of Critical Critique.* Trans. R. Dixon. Moscow: Foreign Languages Publishing House, 1956.

Melo, Jorge Orlando. "Prólogo." Francisco de Paula Santander, *Escritos políticos.* Bogotá: El Áncora Editores, 2003. 11–23.

Menéndez [y] Pelayo, Marcelino. *Historia de la poesía hispano-americana, tomo II.* Madrid: Librería General de Victoriano Suárez, 1913.

————, ed. *Antología de poetas hispano-americanos, tomo II: Cuba, Santo Domingo, Puerto Rico, Venezuela.* Madrid: Real Academia Española/Est. Tip. "Sucesores de Rivadeneyra," 1893.

Menéndez Pidal, Ramón. *España y su historia.* Madrid: Ediciones Minotauro, 1957. 2 vols.

Minaudier, Jean-Pierre. *Histoire de la Colombie. De la conquête à nos jours.* Paris: L'Harmattan, 1992.

Minio-Paluello, Lorenzo, ed. *Aristoteles Latinus, V.1–3: Topica.* Bruxelles/Paris: Desclée de Brouwer, 1969.

Molina, Gerardo. *Las ideas liberales en Colombia, [vol. 1:] 1849–1914.* Bogotá: Universidad Nacional de Colombia-Dirección de Divulgación Cultural/Tercer Mundo Editores, 1970.

Mollien, G[aspard Théodore]. *Voyage dans la République de Colombia, en 1823.* Paris: Arthus Bertrand, 1824.

Mora, José Joaquín de. *Poesías.* Madrid/Paris: Author's Edition, 1853.

Mosquera, T[omás] C[ipriano] de. *Memoria sobre la vida del general Simón Bolívar, libertador de Colombia, Perú y Bolivia.* Bogotá: Consorcio Editorial, 1940.

Murillo Toro, Manuel. *Obras selectas.* Ed. Jorge Mario Eastman. Bogotá: Imprenta Nacional, 1979.

Nancy, Jean-Luc. "Church, State, Resistance." Trans. Véronique Voruz. De Vries and Sullivan 102–12.

Nariño, Antonio. *Escritos políticos.* Ed. Javier Ocampo López. Bogotá: El Áncora/Panamericana, 2002.

Nietzsche, Friedrich. *Beyond Good and Evil: Prelude to a Philosophy of the Future.* Trans. R. J. Hollingdale. 1963. Rev. ed. Intro. Michael Tanner. London: Penguin, 1990.

Núñez, Rafael. *Diccionario político.* Biblioteca de Autores Colombianos. Bogotá: Ministerio de Educación Nacional-Revista "Bolívar," 1952.

———. *Poesías.* Bogotá: Imprenta de "La Luz," 1887.

———. *Poesías.* Intro. Ramón de Zubiría. Bogotá: Instituto Caro y Cuervo, 1977.

———. *La rebelión. Noticias de la guerra.* Bogotá: Imprenta de "La Luz," 1885.

———. *La reforma política en Colombia. Colección de artículos publicados en "La Luz" de Bogotá y "El Porvenir" de Cartagena, de 1881 a 1884.* Bogotá: Imprenta de "La Luz," 1885. The second edition (1886) incorporates additional articles written since 1878.

———. *La reforma política en Colombia. Colección de artículos publicados en "La Nación" de Bogotá y "El Porvenir" de Cartagena, de 1886 a 1888, y algunos discursos.* Bogotá: Imprenta de "La Luz," 1888.

Ocampo T., José Fernando. "Regeneración y hegemonía política (1880–1902)." *Historia de las ideas políticas en Colombia. De la Independencia hasta nuestros días.* Ed. José Fernando Ocampo T. Bogotá: Taurus, 2008. 145–79.

Ortiz, José Joaquín. *Las Sirenas (Discurso de José Joaquín Ortiz contra la moral sensualista de Jeremías Bentham).* 1868. Paris: Baudry, Librería Europa/Dramard-Baudry Sucesor, n/d [ca. 1873].

———, ed. *El Parnaso granadino. Coleccion escojida de poesias nacionales, tomo I.* Bogotá: Imprenta de Ancízar, 1848.

Padua, Marsiglio of. *Writings on the Empire:* Defensor minor *and* De translatione Imperii. Trans. Cary J. Nederman and Fiona Watson. Ed. Cary J. Nederman. Cambridge: Cambridge University Press, 1993.

Palacios, Marco. *La clase más ruidosa y otros ensayos sobre política e historia.* Bogotá: Norma, 2002.

———. *Estado y clases sociales en Colombia.* Bogotá: Procultura, 1986.

———. *Parábola del liberalismo.* Bogotá: Norma, 1999.

Palti, Elías José. *El tiempo de la política: el siglo XIX reconsiderado.* Buenos Aires: Siglo XXI Editores Argentina, 2007.

Pasquino, Pascale. *Sieyes et l'invention de la Constitution en France.* Paris: Éditions Odile Jacob, 1998.

Paz, Octavio. *Traducción: literatura y literalidad.* Barcelona: Tusquets, 1971.

Pena-Ruiz, Henri, and Jean-Paul Scot. *Un poète en politique. Les combats de Victor Hugo.* Paris: Flammarion, 2002.

Pérez, Felipe et al. *Periodistas liberales del siglo XIX.* Bogotá: Ministerio de Educación Nacional/Editorial Minerva, 1936.

Pérez-Sarmiento, José Manuel, ed. *Proceso de Nariño. Fiel copia del original que existe en el Archivo General de Indias.* Cádiz: Imprenta de M. Álvarez, 1914.

Perú de LaCroix, Luis. *Diario de Bucaramanga; ó, Vida pública y privada del Libertador Simón Bolívar.* Ed. Cornelio Hispano. Paris: Librería Paul Ollendorff, 1912.

Poblete, Juan. "Literary Education and the Making of State Knowledge." *Latin American Literary Culture: Subject to History.* Vol. 3 of *Literary Cultures of Latin America: A Comparative History.* Ed. Mario J. Valdés and Djelal Kadir. New York: Oxford University Press, 2004. 300–309.

Pombo, Manuel Antonio, and José Joaquín Guerra. *Constituciones de Colombia. Recopiladas y precedidas de una breve reseña histórica.* 1892. 2nd ed. Bogotá: Imprenta de "La Luz," 1911. 2 vols.

Pombo, Rafael. *Poesías completas.* Intro. Antonio Gómez Restrepo. Ed. Eduardo Carranza. Madrid: Aguilar, 1957.

Proyecto de Constitución. Bogotá: Imprenta de Rivas, 1886.

Posada Carbó, Eduardo. *La nación soñada. Violencia, liberalismo y democracia en Colombia.* Bogotá: Grupo Editorial Norma, 2006.

Quintana, Manuel José. *Obras completas.* Madrid: M. Rivadeneyra, 1867.

———. *Obras inéditas.* Madrid: Medina y Navarro, 1872.

———. *Poesías completas.* Ed. Albert Dérozier. Madrid: Castalia, 1980.

———. "Proclama del Consejo de Regencia de España e Indias a los americanos españoles (14 de febrero de 1810)." *Gaceta de Buenos Aires* (June 9, 1810): 1–7. http://www.fmmeducacion.com.ar/Historia/Documentoshist/1810aregencia.htm.

Quiñones Pardo, Octavio. *Interpretación de la poesía popular.* Bogotá: Editorial Centro/Publicaciones de la Comisión Nacional de Folklore, 1947.

Rama, Ángel. *La ciudad letrada.* Hanover, NH: Ediciones del Norte, 1984.

Ramos, Julio. *Divergent Modernities: Culture and Politics in Nineteenth-Century Latin America.* Trans. John D. Blanco. Durham, NC: Duke University Press, 2001.

Rancière, Jacques. *Hatred of Democracy.* French ed., 2005. Trans. Steve Corcoran. London: Verso, 2006.

Rausch, Jane M. *La educación durante el federalismo. La reforma escolar de 1870.* Trans. María Restrepo Castro. Bogotá: Instituto Caro y Cuervo/Universidad Pedagógica Nacional, 1993.

Reclus, Élisée. "La poésie et les poètes dans l'Amérique espagnole." *Revue des deux mondes,* vol. 49 (January–February 1864): 902–29.

Reinach, Théodore. *De l'état de siège et des institutions de salut public. Étude historique et juridique.* Paris: Librairie Cotillon/F. Pichon, 1885.

René-Moreno, Gabriel. *Últimos días coloniales en el Alto-Perú.* Santiago: Imprenta Cervantes, 1896–1897. 3 vols. Vol. 3 published in Santiago by Imprenta Barcelona.

Restrepo, José Manuel. *Historia de la revolución de la república de Colombia en la América meridional.* Besanzón [sic]: Imprenta de José Jacquin, 1858. 4 vols.

Restrepo Piedrahita, Carlos. *Las facultades extraordinarias. Pequeña historia de una transfiguración.* Bogotá: Publicaciones Universidad Externado de Colombia, 1973.

———, ed. *Constituciones políticas nacionales de Colombia (compilación).* Bogotá: Universidad Externado de Colombia-Instituto de Estudios Constitucionales, 1995.

Rivas, Medardo. *Obras.* Bogotá: Fernando Pontón, 1883–1885. 2 vols.

Rivas Groot, José M[aría]. *Canto á Bolívar. Laureado en el Concurso Poético del Centenario del Libertador.* Bogotá: Fernando Pontón, 1883.

———. "Estudio preliminar." Soffia and Rivas Groot v–c.

Rivas Sacconi, José Manuel. *El latín en Colombia. Bosquejo histórico del humanismo colombiano.* 1949. 3rd ed. Bogotá: Instituto Caro y Cuervo, 1993.

Rocha Gutiérrez, R[afael]. *La verdadera y la falsa democracia. Doctrina constitucional y proyecto de constitución política para la República de Colombia.* Paris: Garnier Hermanos, 1887.

Rodríguez, Simón. *Obras completas.* Caracas: Universidad Simón Rodríguez, 1975. 2 vols.

Rodríguez Demorizi, Emilio, ed. *Poetas contra Bolívar. El Libertador a través de la calumnia.* Madrid: Gráficas Reunidas, 1966.

Rodríguez García, José María. "The Avoidance of Romanticism in Jovellanos's 'Epístola del Paular.'" *Crítica Hispánica* 24.1–2 (2002): 93–110.

———. "Introduction: Literary into Cultural Translation." *Literary into Cultural Translation*. Guest ed. José María Rodríguez García. Spec. issue of *Diacritics: A Review of Contemporary Criticism* 34.3–4 (2004): 3–30.

———. "Sobre héroes y urnas: Guillermo Valencia, Simón Bolívar y la nación como ruina." *Anales de Literatura Hispanoamericana* 35 (2006): 155–94.

———. "Valencia's Verlaine: The Social History of a Colombian Verse." *MLQ: Modern Language Quarterly* 68.4 (December 2007): 541–73.

Rodríguez Monegal, Emir. *El otro Andrés Bello*. Caracas: Monte Ávila, 1969.

Rojas, Cristina. *Civilization and Violence: Regimes of Representation in Nineteenth-Century Colombia*. Intro. Michael J. Shapiro. Minneapolis: University of Minnesota Press, 2002.

Rojas, José M., ed. *Biblioteca de escritores venezolanos contemporáneos, ordenada con noticias biográficas por José M. Rójas, Ministro plenipotenciario de Venezuela en España*. Caracas/Paris: Rójas Hermanos, Editores/Jouby et Roger, Éditeurs, 1875.

Romero, José Luis, and Luis Alberto Romero, eds. *Pensamiento conservador (1815–1898)*. Caracas: Biblioteca Ayacucho, 1978.

Rotker, Susana. "El evangelio apócrifo de Simón Bolívar." *Estudios. Revista de Investigaciones Literarias y Culturales* 12 (July–December 1998): 29–44.

Rousseau, Jean-Jacques. *Du contrat social*. Ed. with an Intro. by Ronald Grimsley. Oxford: Clarendon Press, 1972.

———. *The Social Contract*. Trans. with an Intro. by Maurice Cranston. Harmondsworth: Penguin, 1968.

Safford, Frank. *The Ideal of the Practical: Colombia's Struggle to Form a Technical Elite*. Austin: University of Texas Press, 1976.

Safford, Frank, and Marco Palacios. *Colombia: Fragmented Land, Divided Society*. New York: Oxford University Press, 2002.

Samper, José María. *Historia de una alma. Memorias íntimas y de historia contemporánea (1834 á 1881)*. Bogotá: Imprenta de Zalamea Hermanos, 1881.

———. *El Libertador Simón Bolívar*. Buenos Aires: C. Casavalle, Editor / Imprenta y Librería de Mayo, 1884.

———. *Los partidos en Colombia. Estudio histórico-político*. Bogotá: Imprenta de Echeverría Hermanos, 1873. Repr. (with the Appendix "La libertad y el Catolicismo") in *Orígenes de los partidos políticos en Colombia*. Ed. Jorge Orlando Melo. Bogotá: Instituto Colombiano de Cultura, 1978. 59–202.

Samper, Miguel. *Selección de escritos*. Ed. Héctor Charry Samper and Santiago Samper Trainer. Bogotá: Instituto Colombiano de Cultura, 1967.

Sánchez Agesta, Luis. *El concepto del Estado en el pensamiento español del siglo XVI*. Madrid: Instituto de Estudios Políticos, 1959.

Sanín Cano, B[aldomero]. *Letras colombianas*. México: Fondo de Cultura Económica, 1944.

La Santa Biblia. Vulgata latina y su traducción al español. Trans. Félix Torres Amat. 1823. Ed. Jaime Catalá y Albosa. Barcelona: Librería Religiosa y Científica de Pablo Riera y Sans, 1885–1886. 12 vols.

Santander, Francisco de Paula. *Cartas y mensajes del General Francisco de Paula Santander, volumen 7: 1827–1828*. Ed. Roberto Cortázar. Bogotá: Talleres Editoriales de Librería Voluntad, 1955.

Santos Molano, Enrique, ed. *Documentos para entender la historia de Colombia*. Bogotá: Planeta, 2000.

Sarmiento, Domingo Faustino. *Facundo. Civilización y barbarie*. Ed. Susana Zanetti. Madrid: Alianza, 1988.

———. *Sarmiento en el destierro: Las polémicas del ostracismo; Contra la gramática; Réplicas a don Andrés Bello; La lengua popular y la literatura; Contra el romanticismo; Mi defensa*. Ed. Armando Donoso. Buenos Aires: M. Gleizer, 1927.

Schivelbusch, Wolfgang. *The Culture of Defeat: On National Trauma, Mourning, and Recovery*. Trans. Jefferson Chase. New York: Metropolitan/Holt, 2003.

Schmitt, Carl. *Constitutional Theory*. German ed., 1928. Trans. and Jeffrey Seitzer. Durham, NC: Duke University Press, 2008.

———. *Die Diktatur. Von den Anfängen des modernen Souveränitätsgedankens bis zum proletarischen Klassenkampf*. München: Duncker & Humblot, 1921.

———. *Donoso Cortés in gesamteuropäischer Interpretation: Vier Aufsätze*. Köln: Greven, 1950.

———. *Legalität und Legitimität*. 1932. Berlin: Duncker & Humblot, 1993.

———. *Legality and Legitimacy*. Trans. Jeffrey Seitzer. Intro. John P. McCormick. Durham, NC: Duke University Press, 2004.

———. *Political Theology: Four Chapters on the Concept of Sovereignty*. Trans. George Schwab. Cambridge, MA: MIT Press, 1985.

———. *Politische Theologie: Vier Kapitel zur Lehre von der Souveränität*. München: Duncker & Humblot, 1922.

Sheehan, Jonathan. *The Enlightenment Bible: Translation, Scholarship, Culture*. Princeton, NJ: Princeton University Press, 2005.

Sieyès, Emmanuel Joseph. *Des manuscrits de Sieyès: 1773–1799*. Ed. Christine Fauré et al. Paris: Honoré Champion Éditeur, 1999.

———. *Opinion de Sieyès, sur plusieurs articles des titres IV et V du projet de constitution, prononcée à la Convention le 9 thermidor de l'an troisième de la République*. Paris: Imprimerie nationale, 1795.

———. *Qu'est-ce que le tiers état?; précédé de L'Essai sur les privilèges*. Ed. Edme Champion. Paris: Au siège de la Société [de l'Histoire de la Révolution Française], 1888.

Silva, José Asunción. *Poesía y prosa (con 44 textos sobre el autor)*. Ed. Santiago Mutis Durán and J. G. Cobo Borda. Bogotá: Instituto Colombiano de Cultura/ Biblioteca Básica Colombiana, 1979.

Silva, Renán. *República Liberal, intelectuales y cultura popular*. Medellín: La Carreta Editores E.U., 2005.

———. *Universidad y sociedad en el Nuevo Reino de Granada. Contribución a un análisis histórico de la formación intelectual de la sociedad colombiana*. Bogotá: Banco de la República, 1992.

Soffia, José A[ntonio], ed. *Romancero colombiano. Homenaje a la memoria del Libertador Simón Bolívar en su primer centenario, 1783–1883*. Bogotá: Imprenta de "La Luz," 1883.

Soffia, José Antonio, and José Rivas Groot, eds. *Víctor Hugo en América (traducciones de ingenios americanos)*. Bogotá: Casa Editorial de M. Rivas, 1889.

Suárez, Francisco. *Defensa de la fe católica y apostólica contra los errores del anglicanismo*. Facsimile of the 1613 Coimbra Latin edition, with Spanish translation by José Ramón Eguillor Muniozguren. Madrid: Instituto de Estudios Políticos, 1970–1971. 4 vols.

Suárez, Marco Fidel. *Obras*. Ed. José Ortega Torres et al. Bogotá: Instituto Caro y Cuervo, 1958–1966. 2 vols.

Tertullianus, Septimus. *Opera omnia, Tomus secundus.* Ed. J.-P. Migne. Paris: Petit-Montrouge, 1844.

Timpanaro, Sebastiano. *La genesi del metodo del Lachmann.* 1963. 3rd ed., rev. Padova: Liviana Editrice, 1985.

———. *Sul materialismo.* Pisa: Nistri-Lischi, 1970.

Tirado Mejía, Álvaro. "El Estado y la política en el siglo XIX." *Manual de historia de Colombia, tomo II.* Dir. Jaime Jaramillo Uribe. Ed. Juan Gustavo Cobo Borda and Santiago Mutis Durán. Bogotá: Procultura/Instituto Colombiano de Cultura, 1979. 325–84.

Tocqueville, Alexis de. *Democracy in America.* French ed., 1835–1840. The Henry Reeve text, rev. by Francis Bowen and further corrected by Phillips Bradley. 1945. New York: Vintage, 1957. 2 vols.

———. *The Old Regime and the Revolution.* French ed., 1856. Trans. Alan S. Kahan. Ed. François Furet and Françoise Mélonio. Chicago: University of Chicago Press, 1998–2001. 2 vols.

Todorov, Tzvetan. *Symbolism and Interpretation.* Trans. Catherine Porter. Ithaca, NY: Cornell University Press, 1982.

Toro, Fermín. *Descripción de los honores fúnebres consagrados a los restos del Libertador Simón Bolívar, en cumplimiento del decreto legislativo de 30 de abril de 1842. Hecha de orden del gobierno.* Caracas: Imprenta de Valentín Espinal, 1843.

Torres Caicedo, J[osé] M[aría]. *Ensayos biográficos y de crítica literaria sobre los principales poetas y literatos hispano-americanos. Primera serie.* Paris: Guillaumin y C^{ia}, Editores, 1863. 2 vols.

Triana Antorveza, Adolfo. "Estado-nación y minorías étnicas." *Grupos étnicos, derecho y cultura.* By Eduardo Umaña Luna et al. Bogotá: Funcol/Cuadernos del Jaguar, 1987. 17–136.

Unamuno, Miguel de. *En torno al casticismo.* 5th ed. Madrid: Espasa-Calpe, 1961.

Uribe Uribe, Rafael. *Obras selectas.* Ed. Jorge Mario Eastman. Bogotá: Imprenta Nacional, 1979. 2 vols.

Uribe White, Enrique. "Don Andrés Bello y Don Fidel Cano, traductores de Victor Hugo." *El Tiempo* (November 14, 1954). Repr. in *Redada, 1934–1976 (Selección de escritos publicados).* Bogotá: Subdirección de Comunicaciones Culturales-Instituto Colombiano de Cultura, 1977. 201–12.

Urueña Cervera, Jaime. *Bolívar republicano. Fundamentos ideológicos e históricos de su pensamiento político.* Bogotá: Ediciones Aurora, 2004.

Uslar Pietri, Arturo. "Bello." *Oraciones para despertar.* Caracas: Ediciones del Cuatricentenario de Caracas-Comité de Ediciones Culturales, 1967. 37–45.

Valderrama Andrade, Carlos. "Estudio preliminar." Miguel Antonio Caro, *Escritos políticos (segunda serie).* Ed. Carlos Valderrama Andrade. Bogotá: Instituto Caro y Cuervo, 1990. xv-lvii.

——— *Miguel Antonio Caro y la Regeneración. Apuntes y documentos para la comprensión de una época.* Bogotá: Publicaciones del Instituto Caro y Cuervo, 1997.

Valencia, Guillermo. *Discursos.* Ed. Guillermo Hernández Peñalosa et al. Intro. J[osé] M[anuel] R[ivas] S[acconi]. Bogotá: Instituto Caro y Cuervo, 1973–1974. 3 vols.

Valera, Juan. *Apuntes sobre el nuevo arte de escribir novelas.* Madrid: Imprenta y Fundición de M. Tello, 1887.

———. *Cartas americanas.* Madrid: Fuentes y Capdeville, 1889.

———. *Obras completas, tomo II.* Madrid: Aguilar, 1961.

Vallenilla Lanz, Laureano. *Cesarismo democrático y otros textos.* Ed. Nikita Harwich Vallenilla. Caracas: Biblioteca Ayacucho, 1991.

Vergara y Vergara, José María. *Historia de la literatura en Nueva Granada desde la Conquista hasta la Independencia (1538–1820).* Ed. Antonio Gómez Restrepo and Gustavo Otero Muñoz. Bogotá: Biblioteca de la Presidencia de Colombia, 1953. 4 vols.

———. "Juicio crítico." Vergara y Vergara et al., *A propósito de Jorge Isaacs y su obra* 9–14.

Vergara y Vergara, José María et al. *A propósito de Jorge Isaacs y su obra.* Bogotá: Editorial Norma, 1989.

Villacañas Berlanga, José Luis. *Res publica. Los fundamentos normativos de la política.* Madrid: Akal, 1999.

Virgil. *Eneida.* Trans. Miguel Antonio Caro. Madrid: Librería Hernando, 1901–1902. 2 vols.

———. *Œuvres de Virgile (texte latin).* Ed. F. Plessis and P. Lejay. Paris: Librairie Hachette, 1918.

Viscardo y Guzmán, Juan Pablo. *Letter to the Spanish Americans (A Facsimile of the Second English Edition [London, 1810]).* Intro. D. A. Brading. Providence, RI: The John Carter Brown Library, 2002.

von der Walde Uribe, Erna. "Limpia, fija y da esplendor: el letrado y la letra en Colombia a fines del siglo XIX." *Revista Iberoamericana* 43.178–179 (1997): 71–83.

von Freising, Otto. *Chronica, sive historia de duabus civitatibus.* Ed. Adolf[us] Hofmeister. Hannover[ae]: Impensis Bibliopolii Hahniani, 1912.

Vossler, Karl. *Algunos caracteres de la cultura española.* Buenos Aires: Espasa-Calpe Argentina, 1942.

Waquet, Françoise. *Latin; or, The Empire of a Sign: From the Sixteenth to the Twentieth Centuries.* French ed., 1998. Trans. John Howe. London: Verso, 2001.

Williams, Raymond. *Marxism and Literature.* Oxford: Oxford University Press, 1977.

Žižek, Slavoj. *The Sublime Object of Ideology.* New York: Verso, 1989.